Teaching Psychology

Registered Office(s)
John Wiley & Sons, Inc., 111 River Street, Hoboken, NJ 07030, USA

Editorial Office
9600 Garsington Road, Oxford, OX4 2DQ, UK

For details of our global editorial offices, customer services, and more information about Wiley products
visit us at www.wiley.com.

Wiley also publishes its books in a variety of electronic formats and by print-on-demand. Some content that
appears in standard print versions of this book may not be available in other formats.

Library of Congress Cataloging-in-Publication Data

Names: Grose-Fifer, Jillian, author. | Brooks, Patricia (Patricia J.), author. |
    O'Connor, Maureen, author.
Title: Teaching psychology : an evidence-based approach / Jillian Grose-Fifer, Patricia J. Brooks,
    Maureen O'Connor.
Description: Hoboken, NJ : John Wiley & Sons, Inc., 2019. | Includes index. |
Identifiers: LCCN 2018032338 (print) | LCCN 2018034860 (ebook) | ISBN 9781118981443 (Adobe PDF) |
    ISBN 9781118981450 (ePub) | ISBN 9781118981436 (hardcover) | ISBN 9781118958056 (pbk.)
Subjects: LCSH: Psychology–Study and teaching.
Classification: LCC BF77 (ebook) | LCC BF77 .G76 2019 (print) | DDC 150.71–dc23
LC record available at https://lccn.loc.gov/2018032338

Cover Design: Wiley
Cover Image: © Jillian Grose-Fifer

Set in 10/12pt Warnock by SPi Global, Pondicherry, India
Printed in Singapore by C.O.S. Printers Pte Ltd

10 9 8 7 6 5 4 3 2 1

Teaching Psychology

An Evidence-Based Approach

Jillian Grose-Fifer
Patricia J. Brooks
Maureen O'Connor

To my students, and to my sons, James and Lucas. Your passion for learning inspires me. J.G.-F.

To past and present members of the Graduate Student Teaching Association, especially Christina Shane-Simpson, Anna Schwartz, Rita Obeid, Teresa Ober, Jeremy Sawyer, Ethlyn Saltzman, Ron Whiteman, Kasey Powers, Emily Dow, Phil Kreniske, Charles Raffaele, Elizabeth Che, Ayşenur Benevento, Peri Yuksel, Ralitza Todorova, Jessica Brodsky, Olga Parshina, and Svetlana Jović. Your enthusiasm and commitment to student-centered pedagogy sustain me. P.J.B.

To my students, and to the best teacher I've ever known, Dennis Murphy, who taught me the meaning of a truly student- (and client-) centered approach, and whose pedagogy of compassion and understanding continues to inspire me each and every day. M.O.C.

Contents

About the Authors

Jill Grose-Fifer, Ph.D., is a cognitive neuroscientist and Associate Professor of Psychology at John Jay College of Criminal Justice and The Graduate Center, City University of New York (CUNY). She earned her bachelors and doctoral degrees from the University of Aston, in Birmingham, U.K. She has been an active participant in several pedagogical initiatives at CUNY, including John Jay College's First-Year Success Program and its Writing Enriched Curriculum Project, the CUNY Pedagogy Taskforce, and the Graduate Center's Futures Initiative. Dr. Grose-Fifer has published on the scholarship of teaching and learning, as well as in the field of cognitive neuroscience. Her current neuroscience research focuses primarily on event-related potential investigations of adolescent brain development. She has received various teaching awards from John Jay College, including the Distinguished Teaching Prize in 2009, the Outstanding Scholarly Mentor award in 2012, and the Faculty Excellence in Research Mentorship Award from the Forensic Psychology Masters Program in 2018.

Patricia J. Brooks, Ph.D., is Professor of Psychology at the College of Staten Island, City University of New York (CUNY), where she directs the Language Learning Laboratory. Her research interests are in three broad areas: (a) individual differences in first- and second-language learning; (b) the impact of digital media on learning and development; and (c) development of effective pedagogy to support diverse learners. Dr. Brooks is an active member of the Doctoral Faculty at the Graduate Center, CUNY, where she currently serves as the Deputy Executive Officer of the Ph.D. Program in Psychology (Area: Pedagogy) and on the Executive Committee of the Ph.D. Program in Educational Psychology. Since 2014, she has served as Faculty Advisor to the Graduate Student Teaching Association of the Society for the Teaching of Psychology (American Psychological Association, Division 2). She was awarded the 2016 Dolphin Award for Outstanding Teaching from the College of Staten Island, CUNY. She is co-author of numerous journal articles, book chapters, and a textbook on language development; she has also co-edited several books, including the 2017 volume *Cognitive Development in Digital Contexts*.

Maureen O'Connor, Ph.D., J.D., is President of Palo Alto University (PAU), an institution dedicated to education and research in psychology. At PAU, she supports an annual evidence-based teaching conference. Prior to that, she was a professor and former Chair of Psychology at John Jay College of Criminal Justice at the City University of New York (CUNY) and Executive Officer of the Doctoral Program in Psychology at CUNY's

Graduate Center, where she initiated the development of a multifaceted pedagogy program for the preparation of graduate student instructors in psychology. Her scholarly and teaching interests are in pedagogy and mentoring, and the intersection of psychology, gender, and law. She is a Fellow of the American Psychological Association (APA), past President of the Society for the Psychological Study of Social Issues, and Chair of the APA's Task Force on Human Rights, and she has received the New York State Psychological Association's Margaret Floy Washburn Women's Mentoring Award.

Foreword

I first stepped foot in the Graduate Center at the City University of New York (CUNY) in 2012 as a keynote speaker for the third annual Pedagogy Day, CUNY's All-Psychology Conference on the Teaching of Psychology. My most vivid memory of this lively, interactive conference is of the Activity Blitz, a series of rapid-fire sessions in which graduate-student instructors presented engaging, evidence-based teaching techniques that they used in their own classrooms. These burgeoning instructors were passionate and smart, up on their scholarship of teaching and learning, and ready to get their students as excited about psychology as they clearly were in their presentations.

My involvement with Pedagogy Day helped me develop a relationship with the personified sparks for the enthusiasm in these graduate students—the professors, and authors of this book, Jill Grose-Fifer, Patricia Brooks, and Maureen O'Connor. Recognizing a need, these three psychological scientists from three different subdisciplines, but sharing a great interest in teaching, joined together to create a program that filled a clear need at CUNY—a program to train graduate students to be instructors. In addition to the annual Pedagogy Day, this dynamic trio created a graduate Seminar and Practicum on the Teaching of Psychology, in which CUNY psychology graduate students could learn how to teach—a skill too rarely taught in psychology doctoral programs in the United States and elsewhere.

Eventually, through their leadership, CUNY became the institutional home of the national Graduate Student Teaching Association (GSTA), the student arm of the Society for the Teaching of Psychology (STP). Thus, the authors' reach extends beyond the more than 500 psychology doctoral students at CUNY to the thousands of others who have benefited from their work on a national level.

Not content with the legacy they have already created, Drs. Grose-Fifer, Brooks, and O'Connor saw a need for a book like this one—an evidence-based, student-centered guide to teaching that can be used as a resource, but also in courses such as their Seminar and Practicum on the Teaching of Psychology. The book has assessment at its core (with, yes, integrated discussions of learning goals and a whole chapter on backward design)—a necessity in an era of accountability at the individual, institutional, and societal levels. It is a game changer.

Student-centered and active-learning focused. First, the book is student-centered, both in terms of its engagement with its audience of emerging instructors and in terms of its guidance as to how to teach most effectively. The student-centered approach veers far from "sage on the stage" lecture-style courses, instead prioritizing active learning. The authors do not use "active learning" as a mere catchphrase. Rather, they explore exactly what types of active learning actually work, outlining the research on why and giving concrete guidance for all of us who are instructors.

This student-centered, active-learning approach mirrors the ways in which the authors developed their program to train new instructors at CUNY—an approach clear to all who have participated in Pedagogy Day or other GSTA events. As an example, several colleagues and I were invited to run a highly interactive workshop at the 2016 Pedagogy Day. The expectations of the student organizers and their faculty advisors were clear—minimal lecture, maximum interaction! The lively response from the graduate student/new instructor audience made it evident that CUNY has indoctrinated its graduate students to expect this type of learning and, in turn, to create such learning experiences for their own students.

Each time I have returned to CUNY, it has been a privilege to engage with the authors and to witness their continual efforts to develop not just skilled future researchers, but also excellent—and prepared—future instructors. I admit that it is also a lot of fun to interact with the many veteran and novice teachers who are excited to be working together in their quest to help their students learn in effective and interactive ways, driven by the scholarship of teaching and learning.

Emphasis on diverse learners and content. Second, the book explicitly engages with the remarkable diversity of the current U.S. undergraduate population. The authors discuss inclusion in the classroom of students from different racial and ethnic groups, from both sexual majority and sexual minority groups, and with disabilities and mental illnesses. They also exhort new and experienced instructors alike to consider other, sometimes more hidden types of diversity in the classroom, including students who are first-generation, who are employed while in school, or who are suffering from housing insecurity. They also explicitly encourage all of us to include cross-cultural and international content examples and research approaches in the classroom. And they champion Universal Design, which helps all students, but especially those who do not disclose disabilities.

The cross-cultural and diversity-oriented approach in their textbook reflects these authors' real-life ethoses. Dr. O'Connor, for example, is current the Chair of the American Psychological Association's Task Force on Human Rights. Dr. Grose-Fifer is currently participating in a seminar series at John Jay College, CUNY, designed to help promote its identity as a Hispanic Serving Institution. The participants in this seminar engage in readings and discussion with outside experts, with the goal of revising John Jay courses to better serve their students. And, in an example that I personally witnessed, Dr. Brooks, along with her graduate students, recently invited a six-person panel to speak to her Teaching of Psychology seminar about International Psychology. The group reflected diversity with respect to age, stage of career, gender, country of origin, and native language. Moreover, it included those working in a wide range of psychology careers, from a clinician whose work focuses on trauma victims in countries with recent pasts of ethnic conflict to instructors teaching statistics and research methods courses at both undergraduate and graduate levels.

The not-so-fluffy-after-all parts of teaching. Third, I am thrilled that this author team embraces the sometimes dismissed, but immensely important aspects of teaching that fall beyond the "nuts and bolts." These include a focus on ethics and instruction on how to incorporate both psychosocial interventions and techniques aimed at developing students' metacognition. The former involves an exhortation for us all to become ethical instructors, in large part by basing our practices on evidence; the latter includes a primer on research into the positive effects of a growth mindset on learning and test-taking. For too long, our field has neglected both an explicit discussion of ethical teaching and an acknowledgment that we may need to bring psychosocial interventions into our classrooms.

Drs. Grose-Fifer, Brooks, and O'Connor make it clear that they value science, and that science includes discussions both of our own ethics and of our students' psychological strengths and limitations with respect to their education. The authors' warmth as instructors, coupled with their firm grounding as scientists, makes them the ideal proselytizers for an ethical, psychosocial, truly student-centered approach to teaching and learning. So, the reader is fully on board when they state, bluntly (and accurately), that "it is no longer ethically acceptable to simply lecture to students," and that "ethical teachers nurture the whole student" by helping them find outside support when necessary. This is wise and welcome advice.

Skills for real life. Fourth, Drs. Grose-Fifer, Brooks, and O'Connor return again and again both to the real-life skills that we need as instructors and the ones that we want to instill in our students. Arguably, the most important life skill is critical thinking, which, in a psychology classroom, encompasses both thinking like a psychological scientist and learning to accurately parse the firehose of information we encounter in our daily lives. Yes, the latter includes sussing out "fake news," which has infiltrated many branches of psychological science almost as thoroughly as it has infected the political arena. Not convinced? For just some of the most clear-cut psychology fake news, think crystals for depression, gay conversion therapy, right-brained versus left-brained skills, and learning styles, the last of which the authors—thankfully—directly address.

So, understandably, critical thinking is a central theme of this book. And I particularly love that they refer to one of my all-time favorite teaching tools, the aptly named CRAAP test, which guides students through the consideration of a source's Currency, Relevance, Authority, Accuracy, and Purpose/Point of View!

Beyond critical thinking, this author team addresses a range of important skills. They outline research on the use (and abuse) of PowerPoint, and how to best incorporate multimedia presentations and student-response systems. They summarize research on how to successfully engage students in collaborative work, how to teach students to write and give oral presentations, and to write excellent quizzes and tests, and on how to instruct students in methods of study. The research they present on these areas—and many others—is thorough and current.

But they also offer instructors tangible guidelines to, well, get things done, based both on their own expertise and on a range of superb resources that have been developed by other experts. Need to pick a textbook, and no idea how to start? The authors outline the process for you. Stumped as to what to put on your syllabus? They offer suggestions and a call-out to the excellent STP resource, Project Syllabus. No idea how to begin your first class? They provide suggestions for time-tested icebreakers. Want to develop rubrics? They offer tips, and links to helpful online resources. Need ideas for formative assessments? They have a handy box for that. And if you want to parlay your graduate teaching experiences into a career, they've got you there, too, with guidance on creating a teaching portfolio and writing a teaching philosophy.

Accessible, engaging, and truly useful. Beyond their expansive coverage of research, combined with practical advice for just about every aspect of teaching in higher education, Drs. Grose-Fifer, Brooks, and O'Connor have written a genuinely accessible book. It's a rare skill to be able to be true to the research without being pedantic, and to write an approachable textbook that does not dilute the science. These authors have succeeded.

I anticipate that this book will be used by instructors who are lucky enough to teach the type of Teaching of Psychology course that these authors have developed at CUNY, by psychology departments seeking to help their graduate students develop as instructors in one-on-one advising contexts, and by instructors—both novice and seasoned—who will treat it as a valued resource, dipping into it semester after semester as they make incremental changes in their teaching practices.

I know that I will.

Susan A. Nolan, Ph.D.
Professor of Psychology, Seton Hall University

About the Companion Website

This book is accompanied by a companion website:

www.wiley.com/go/Grose-Fifer/teaching-psychology

The website includes:

- Pedagogy Course Instructor Resources
- General Teaching Resources

The Pedagogy Course Instructor Resources are for instructors who are using the textbook to teach a Teaching of Psychology course. We provide a syllabus that we have successfully used with our own students, lesson plans for each class in the syllabus, and grading rubrics for the assignments in each class. The lesson plans include learning objectives and descriptions of classroom activities that we have found to be successful with our doctoral students who are preparing to teach a class, or who are making their existing classes more student-centered. One of our most successful class activities occurs on a regular basis: students (usually working in pairs) create and teach a mini-lesson to their peers, who play the role of under-graduates. To help students understand the expectations of student-centered teach-ing, we as instructors model these mini-lessons and show how they fit into a lesson plan for an entire class period. We have provided some examples of these in the Pedagogy Course Instructor Resources, and have duplicated them in the General Teaching Resources.

The General Teaching Resources are useful for students in a Teaching of Psychology class as they plan and teach their own classes. However, we anticipate that these materials will also be useful for other new instructors who are starting their teaching careers, as well as for other, more seasoned faculty who want to make their classes more student-centered. The General Teaching Resources include examples of various interactive mini-lessons, associated lesson plans, templates for games such as Jeopardy, and suggestions for rubrics for various types of assignment.

Introduction

We represent three very different subfields in psychology—Jill Grose-Fifer is a cognitive neuroscientist, Patricia Brooks is a developmental psychologist, and Maureen O'Connor studies the intersection between psychology and the law—but we have a shared passion: teaching! We came up with the idea for this book when all three of us taught at various colleges of the City University of New York (CUNY), arguably one of the most diverse universities in the world. The seeds were sown about 10 years ago, when Maureen O'Connor, as Executive Officer of the Ph.D. program in Psychology at the Graduate Center, was overseeing the training of doctoral students in psychology at CUNY. It became very clear to her that although the majority of the doctoral students had fellowships that required them to teach, most had no training or experience in pedagogy, and they were feeling overwhelmed and unprepared. Together with a group of enthusiastic doctoral students, we formed a Teaching of Psychology Task Force and put together a training program for emerging teachers. This included an annual Pedagogy Day conference and the creation of a graduate Seminar and Practicum on the Teaching of Psychology, which we began running at CUNY in 2012. Over the years, we mostly co-taught (in various combinations) the Teaching of Psychology course, but we consistently struggled to find a manageable set of weekly readings. We wanted to adequately expose our students to the depth and breadth of pedagogical research that would help them hone their developing teaching practices, but it was difficult to achieve this using a small number of primary sources. This book emerged as a result of our trying to summarize the large body of literature on effective pedagogical practices so that students could develop an evidence-based teaching philosophy. We have tried, in particular, to draw on evidence from basic scientific inquiry into learning, memory, and development, in addition to well-designed studies within classrooms. As such, we think that this book is scholarly, but also offers practical advice for the application of evidence from the scholarship of teaching and learning (SoTL) in designing or adapting courses, and maximizing student learning and personal growth.

To orient you to the approach we have taken in writing this book, we want to explain a little more about our teaching philosophies. As undergraduates, all three of us sat through lectures where the professor was the only one talking in the room. This teacher-centered method of instruction is still relatively popular in colleges today. Indeed, many of our doctoral students were taught in this way, but it contrasts strongly with the highly interactive student-centered approach that we have adopted in this book and in our

Teaching Psychology: An Evidence-Based Approach, First Edition. Jillian Grose-Fifer, Patricia J. Brooks, and Maureen O'Connor.
© 2019 John Wiley & Sons, Inc. Published 2019 by John Wiley & Sons, Inc.
Companion website: www.wiley.com/go/Grose-Fifer/teaching-psychology

classes. Like many others in our generation, we were not trained as teachers, but we have improved our teaching by learning from others, and by taking risks and experimenting in our classes. Importantly, we use an evidence-based approach to inform our "experiments." Research has conclusively demonstrated that learning occurs best when students are active participants in the process, rather than just sitting passively in the classroom listening (or mind-wandering) while the instructor talks. Therefore, the focus of our book is on assisting instructors in adopting a student-centered pedagogy. Since psychology is our area of expertise, we have titled this book *Teaching Psychology*, and have provided many suggestions about how to apply best practices for teaching in psychology classes. However, nothing we say about teaching per se applies only to psychology classes. Therefore, we hope that this book will be helpful to instructors in other disciplines too. Similarly, we have couched much of this material in terms of teaching undergraduates, but the general ideas are also applicable when teaching graduate-level classes. Masters and doctoral students also benefit from active learning, and scaffolded support helps to improve their scientific literacy, critical thinking, communication, and collaboration skills.

In Chapter 1, which serves as an extended introduction to the book, we outline the rationale and evidence for using a student-centered approach. Given the emphasis on students (rather than instructors), we also provide demographic information that highlights the diversity of today's undergraduate population and make concrete suggestions about how best to support them in ways that are culturally sensitive. This theme of supporting diverse learners permeates the other chapters of the book too, beginning in Chapter 2, where we introduce the concept of Universal Design for Learning, a framework that acknowledges that building the accommodations that many students need into the curriculum not only supports at-risk students, but benefits all other students, too.

We know from our Teaching of Psychology course that instructors may initially be resistant to adopting a student-centered approach, especially if they have not had personal experience with it. To some, it seems to be a time-consuming and inefficient way of transmitting information—a typical goal of teacher-centered pedagogy. In general, after reading the relevant literature in our Teaching of Psychology class, even reluctant students have gradually become convinced not only that is lecturing a relatively ineffective way of promoting learning, but that teachers of psychology should embrace the tenets of a liberal arts education, a framework that is commensurate with the five broad goals that the American Psychological Association (APA, 2013) endorses for the psychology undergraduate major. APA advocates that, in addition to acquiring a knowledge base in psychology, students are expected to be able to think critically and reason scientifically, communicate well, demonstrate ethical and socially responsible behavior, work effectively with others, and be cognizant of the careers and educational opportunities that they will be qualified for based on the knowledge and skills acquired over the span of their undergraduate studies.

To help achieve these goals, we have devoted chapters to teaching critical thinking, including scientific literacy (Chapter 4), writing (Chapter 6), and learning to collaborate with others (Chapter 5). Critically, throughout the book, we focus on approaches that are likely to help students develop holistically as people. We endorse teaching methods that allow undergraduates to better understand themselves as learners and how they relate to others, as well as those that help them to develop an awareness of the utility of their knowledge and skills in their post-graduation careers, either in the workforce or in graduate school.

Given our evidence-based approach, it is fitting that our book has a heavy emphasis on the importance of assessment. This is also in keeping with the increasing focus on accountability in higher education. In Chapter 2, we describe how to use backward design (Wiggins & McTighe, 2005) for course planning. This begins with envisioning the skills and knowledge (learning objectives) one wants one's students to have gained by the end of the course, then selecting various assessments to evaluate whether one's learning objectives have been met, and finally, planning the curriculum to provide opportunities for students to develop the requisite knowledge and skills. Although many colleges require that syllabi include learning objectives, they can sometimes be added as an afterthought, rather than being the driving force behind course design. Backward design ensures a more intentional approach to instruction and increases the likelihood that a learning objective is both addressed in the curriculum and assessed in appropriate ways. We provide various models to help instructors design learning objectives that emphasize higher-order thinking. Once these and their assessments are formulated, SoTL-established methods can then be used to help students reach these goals. We describe such methods throughout the book. In addition to the chapters already mentioned, Chapter 3 describes how technology can support student learning (this theme is continued in Chapter 8, where we discuss how to move elements of a face-to-face class online in order to promote learning), while Chapter 7 describes how students learn through the use of testing and by developing a metacognitive awareness of their knowledge and skills, and how to improve them. Chapter 7 also provides evidence for psychosocial interventions that can promote student motivation, a key component of effective learning. In Chapter 2, we introduce the importance of ongoing or formative assessment; this is then touched upon in each subsequent chapter. As teacher-scholars, when we adopt evidence-based best practices (such as those described in the various chapters) in our classes, we have to assess how effective they are for our particular students. Frequent formative assessment allows adjustments to be made on the fly and helps us continually learn how to become better teachers.

Although this book does not focus on teaching online, we are mindful that hybrid and fully online courses are increasingly common in higher education. Teaching an online course for the first time is not trivial; fortunately, there are now many excellent resources available to support instructors using this format. Teaching online requires a lot of technological know-how and upfront course preparation, and Chapter 8 provides strong stepping-stones toward making this transition. Finally, in Chapter 9, we discuss ethics in teaching, with the overarching idea that it is our ethical responsibility to teach our students using empirically established methods. We also describe professional development activities, including writing a statement of teaching philosophy, creating a teaching portfolio, and other ways of becoming a life-long learner as a teacher of psychology.

We test-drove various chapters of this book as it was being written, and found that its evidence-based approach helped our doctoral students to embrace a student-centered teaching philosophy. Moreover, we took note of our students' questions in our Teaching of Psychology classes and tried to address them in the text. Our hope is that this book will provide guidance to new teachers of psychology, as well as some inspiration to more seasoned teachers wanting to read about current SoTL research. Learning to teach is a process that evolves with experience, and we urge you to use this book as a resource to gradually expand your teaching practice. We welcome your feedback and suggestions. Finally, we wish to thank our colleagues, Kevin Nadal and Kim Case, for providing helpful comments on introductory portions of this book, and Susan A. Nolan, for her enthusiastic encouragement in the foreword—as well as all of our students, past, present, and future, for teaching us so much.

1

Why a Student-Centered Approach to Teaching?

1.1 A Paradigm Shift?

In this book, we strongly advocate that instructors approach teaching as they would any other discipline in psychology, by using an evidence-based approach. The scholarship of teaching and learning (SoTL) literature is rich with theory-driven empirical studies that determine best practices for maximizing learning and fostering both social and intellectual development in students. These studies conclusively demonstrate that a *student-centered* approach, as opposed to a *teacher-centered* approach such as lecturing, is by far the most effective pedagogical strategy (Freeman et al., 2014; Johnson, Johnson, & Stanne, 2000). Student-centered classes draw on research from cognitive, social, and developmental psychology, and emphasize active learning and collaboration over passive listening. Rather than being the source of all knowledge, student-centered teachers play a critical role as facilitators by providing structure, guidance, feedback, and support for students as they take on various tasks (Alfieri, Brooks, Aldrich, & Tenenbaum, 2011; Barr & Tagg, 1995). Such support has been associated with student gains in perceptions of their own personal social development (Umbach & Wawrzynski, 2005) and academic skills (Alfieri et al., 2011). Thus, approaching teaching from a student-centered perspective is consistent with the mission of a liberal arts education, in that it contributes to the development of the "whole person."

We realize that this focus on active learning may require a considerable paradigm shift for new instructors, who are likely to have been educated by teachers who predominantly used lecture-based teaching in their undergraduate classes. Indeed, when we have asked graduate students in our Teaching of Psychology class to list the qualities of their "best teacher," they have tended to describe those of an excellent public speaker (e.g., knowledgeable, dynamic, entertaining, enthusiastic, funny), as well as caring and supportive attributes (e.g., understanding, caring, warm-hearted, empathetic); for similar results with undergraduates, see Keeley, Furr, and Buskist (2009). Relatedly, when asked to describe the tasks they view as most important when preparing to teach, our graduate students tend to focus on having sufficient content knowledge (e.g., preparing slides and rehearsing lectures, selecting and reviewing textbooks and other readings, making sure that one knows the material), rather than on constructing learning objectives (LOs), designing interactive activities and demonstrations,

Teaching Psychology: An Evidence-Based Approach, First Edition. Jillian Grose-Fifer, Patricia J. Brooks, and Maureen O'Connor.
© 2019 John Wiley & Sons, Inc. Published 2019 by John Wiley & Sons, Inc.
Companion website: www.wiley.com/go/Grose-Fifer/teaching-psychology

and planning how to best assess whether the LOs have been successfully met. Taken together, these data suggest that although novice instructors acknowledge the importance of establishing rapport with their students, they often equate teaching effectiveness with the transmission of as much content knowledge as possible to a class, in an enthusiastic manner.

Teacher-centered instruction not only puts a great deal of pressure on new instructors, who may be worried about their skills as dynamic public speakers or their ability to manage potential "incivilities" in the classroom, but has also been shown to be considerably less effective as compared to a student-centered approach. A meta-analysis of over 200 studies in science, technology, engineering, and mathematics (STEM) classes showed that the grades of students taught using active learning methods were on average half a letter grade higher than among those in lecture classes, with over 50% fewer failing grades (Freeman et al., 2014). Other studies indicate that active learning is associated with lower rates of attrition among college students (Braxton, Milem, & Sullivan, 2000). The overwhelming evidence favoring active learning methods has led Nobel Laureate Carl Wieman to liken lecturing to the archaic practice of "blood-letting in medicine": blood-letting was endorsed as a therapeutic practice for hundreds of years because patients sometimes got better after its application, likely as a result of other factors (Wieman, 2014). Similarly, students who are taught predominantly in lecture classes *do* learn, but this is most likely attributable to their activities outside of class, such as reading and reviewing the materials (Wieman, 2014).

Current trends in higher education emphasize learning skills over memorizing content, which can quickly become outdated in our rapidly changing world. In 2005, the Association of American Colleges and Universities (AAC&U) launched the Liberal Education and America's Promise (LEAP) initiative, which recognized that college graduates need strong intellectual and practical skills in order to enter into and survive in the workforce (http://www.aacu.org/leap). Like the American Psychological Association (APA) Guidelines for the Undergraduate Psychology Major (American Psychological Association, 2013), the AAC&U advocates that undergraduate education should produce improvements in many areas, including critical thinking (CT) and the solving of authentic problems related to real-life situations, oral and written communication, information and technological literacy, scientific inquiry and analysis, and collaborative teamwork. Developing metacognitive skills about what and how best to learn has also been linked to better academic performance in terms of higher test scores and GPA (Coutinho, 2008; Everson & Tobias, 1998; Nietfeld, Cao, & Osborne, 2005; Young & Fry, 2012). Both LEAP and the APA provide well-rounded visions of what constitutes a good education, by requiring that students are engaged as agents in the learning process, with instructors serving as their guides. The Society for the Teaching of Psychology's (STP's) educational taskforce has also suggested that model instructors use methods that actively engage students in the learning process (Richmond et al., 2014).

We argue that using a student-centered perspective puts less pressure on novice instructors, by recognizing that an effective teacher does not need to be extraverted or a stand-up comedian. As Bain (2011) reported in his national study of what the best college teachers do, master teachers challenge their students and help them learn *how* to think, rather than *what* to think. This means that anyone can become a better teacher. Instructors can learn the best ways to facilitate the development of broad-based skills (e.g., CT, information and media literacy, communication, scientific inquiry and analysis, collaboration) in their students. Therefore, with training and experience, instructors should be able to engage students in purposeful problem solving, analysis, and discussion of complex issues, while building respectful communities that value diverse viewpoints.

1.2   Setting the Stage for Transformative Learning

Bain (2011) found that the best college teachers across the United States all helped their students to engage in deep learning by encouraging them to think for themselves. In many cases, transformative learning occurred when instructors gave their students the confidence to take risks and learn from their mistakes. Students were able to alter their long-standing beliefs through knowledge constructed from their own explorations. Although they found classes in which they had to think for themselves challenging, they were motivated to learn because they were able to focus on topics that they found interesting. Echoing the tenets of critical (Freire, 1996), feminist (Brunner, 1992; Robinson-Keilig, Hamill, Gwin-Vinsant, & Dashner, 2014; Scanlon, 1993), and intersectional (Case, 2017) pedagogy, Stetsenko and colleagues have advocated for a transformative activist approach to learning that increases the agency of underserved students and leads the way to social change (Stetsenko, 2017). Within this framework, students identify personal issues that impact their lives and learning, and work collaboratively to research potential solutions to problems of inequality, with the goal of promoting both personal and community agency as they make commitments to social justice (Podluká, 2017; Vianna, Hougaard, & Stetsenko, 2014; Vianna & Stetsenko, 2017).

1.3   Knowing Your Students

Establishing strong rapport in the classroom is of paramount importance if student-centered teaching is to be successful. Positive faculty–student interactions increase feelings of social integration and institutional commitment, which in turn increase student retention (Braxton & McClendon, 2001). For some of you, your own experiences as undergraduates may be quite different from those of your students. Given the diversity of backgrounds of today's student body, regular self-reflection about your world views, implicit biases, and privileges (Case, 2017; Stuart, 2004; Sue & Sue, 2016), as well as taking the time to get to know your students, their particular strengths, and the challenges that they face, will help you to understand how best to support their learning. We begin with a brief review of the general characteristics of today's undergraduates, including some of the challenges they face, and offer concrete suggestions for how to support them in their learning, by building rapport, fostering inclusivity, and teaching in a culturally responsive, student-centered way.

1.3.1   Connecting Identity with Motivation for Learning

In 2014, just under 64% of the 17.3 million undergraduates in the United States (including 88% of undergraduates at 4-year institutions) fell in the "traditional" 18–24-year-old age range (National Center for Education Statistics, 2016a), underscoring the fact that very many other students return to school after years in the workforce, in the military, or at home raising children. Today's students are acutely aware that having a college education significantly increases their likelihood of finding a good job and that most well-paying jobs require a college degree (Chen, 2017; White House Council of Economic Advisors, 2014). Indeed, it has been estimated that attaining a degree from a 4-year institution after graduating high school almost doubles a person's life-time earnings (Carnevale, Smith, & Strohl, 2010). Thus, the majority of today's undergraduates may be pursuing higher education in order to gain or improve their employment credentials, not because they have an intrinsic interest in the sciences and liberal arts. Furthermore, only 20–24% of psychology majors actually enroll in graduate education (American Psychological Association, Center for Workforce Studies, 2014). Therefore, students are more likely to be motivated when their course LOs highlight the development of critical skills or knowledge that will be helpful in the workplace, as well as in graduate school.

1.3.2 Teaching Digital Natives

Today's younger students are members of the Net Generation or Digital Natives (Prensky, 2001), in that they have grown up in a world in which Internet access and personal computers are widely available. Indeed, students born after the mid-1990s have never known a time when the Internet was not available. However, students from low-income families are more likely to come from homes without broadband Internet and computer access (Anderson, 2017), while older college students sometimes experience difficulties using technology (Tyler-Smith, 2006). Moreover, even tech-savvy digital natives are not yet necessarily capable of evaluating the quality of the information that they have at their fingertips (Gross & Latham, 2013; Gross, Latham, & Armstrong, 2012; Head & Eisenberg, 2009; National Survey of Student Engagement, 2015; Wineburg, McGrew, Breakstone, & Ortega, 2016). In a comprehensive study of over 7800 students from a diverse range of middle schools, high schools, and universities, participants consistently exhibited difficulty identifying website sponsors, evaluating evidence and claims, and assessing the authority and motivation behind information posted on the Internet (Wineburg et al., 2016). Therefore, in this book, we suggest various assignments and strategies for helping students to assess the reliability of information that they find online (e.g., see Chapters 3 and 4 for discussion of the use of the CRAAP test and other ways to encourage information literacy and CT).

Despite the widespread use of digital devices in their daily lives, most college students today (regardless of age) lack experience in using instructional technology, such as the course management systems (CMSs) that are essential for online instruction. Furthermore, they may find it tedious and unrewarding to use these systems to learn on their own at home, despite the promise digital technologies hold for delivering content 24/7 at the convenience and pace of the individual student (Powers, Brooks, McCloskey, Sekerina, & Cohen, 2013). This book emphasizes how multimedia instruction can both enhance learning (see Chapter 3) and help students to develop the confidence they need to work with new technologies in the workplace. However, students are best served when they receive scaffolded support while learning how to navigate online learning platforms (e.g., WileyPLUS, MyLab), CMSs (e.g., Canvas, Blackboard), and other new technologies (Powers, Brooks, Galazyn, & Donnelly, 2016).

1.3.3 Our Diverse Student Body

Although many people imagine typical college students as 18–22-year-olds attending a residential 4-year college, the reality is very different. More than 74% of today's under-graduates can be classified as non-traditional; that is, they meet one or more of the following criteria: older than 24 years (adult learner), no high school diploma, financially independent, has dependents, has one or more jobs, attends college part-time, does not live in college residences (Radford, Cominole, & Skomsvold, 2015). In 2014, undergraduates in the United States were characterized as follows: 61% attended 4-year institutions, with the remainder attending 2-year community colleges or technical schools; about 69% attended public colleges or universities, rather than private institutions; and 33% attended 4-year colleges on a part-time basis (National Center for Education Statistics, 2016a). Furthermore, in 2015, 43% of full-time students and 80% of part-time students also had a job (McFarland et al., 2017), and about half of all undergraduates offset the cost of college by living with their immediate family or with more distant relatives (Sallie Mae, 2014). Clearly, "non-traditional" students are now the norm.

In having to juggle a work/school balance, many of today's busy students experience the hassles of commuting and of having to keep up with family responsibilities. For these students, time is particularly precious. Because of the many competing demands they face, adult learners are more likely than their younger counterparts to attend college part-time (National Center for Education Statistics, 2018), and more likely to drop out (Kazis et al., 2007). Commuter students in general are less likely to view attending school social events as an important part of their college life, as compared to those who live on campus (Deil-Amen, 2011). This is particularly worrisome, as student retention is predicted in part by student engagement and by how connected students feel to their schools (Roberts & Styron, 2010). However, student-centered instruction can help to support retention, as it increases faculty–student interaction (Umbach & Wawrzynski, 2005) and provides greater opportunities for students to connect with their peers (see Chapter 5). Both of these factors are likely to lead to increased social integration and, by association, greater feeling of institutional commitment.

The 2010 U.S. Census revealed that 18–34-year-olds in the general population were more diverse than ever before, with about 57% identifying as non-Hispanic White, about 24% speaking a language other than English at home, and 15% being born in a country other than the United States (U.S. Census, 2014). The increased diversity seen in the general population of this generation is also reflected in the current student body (White House Council of Economic Advisors, 2014), especially in broad-access public universities and community colleges, which tend to have wider ranges of students in terms of age, gender, race/ethnicity, and socioeconomic status (SES) as compared to private institutions (Deil-Amen, 2011). Recent estimates also suggest that 2% of under-graduates are undocumented immigrants (Suárez-Orozco, Katsiaficas, et al., 2015), and so face additional challenges. In addition, over one million international students enroll in U.S. colleges and universities each year, with the majority coming from China or India (Institute of International Education, 2017).

Latino/as comprise the largest growing minority group in the United States. Therefore, perhaps not surprisingly, enrollments for Latinx college students have increased significantly in recent years (Krogstad, 2016), especially at community colleges and broad-access public universities (Deil-Amen, 2011). However, graduation rates for Latinx students are disproportionately low compared to other groups (National Conference of State Legislatures, 2011). About 50% of such students are the first in their families to attend college, and they frequently report that they lack access to much-needed information about financial aid or what to expect in college (National Conference of State Legislatures, 2011; see also Section 1.4 on Supporting First-Generation College Students).

Diversity among today's students extends beyond race, ethnicity, and age. Between 2003 and 2007, about 11% of undergraduates reported that they had a disability (Sparks & Malkus, 2013). With changes in legislation, such as the Americans with Disabilities Act (ADA) Amendments Act of 2008 and the 2008 Higher Education Opportunity Act, this number will likely increase in the future, especially at public institutions, where students with disabilities are more likely to enroll (Raue & Lewis, 2011). Although the most commonly registered disability among undergraduates is a specific learning disability (such as dyslexia) or a visual or hearing impairment, increasing numbers of students register with other so-called "invisible" disabilities, such as autism spectrum disorder, attention-deficit hyperactivity disorder, or an anxiety disorder (Raue & Lewis, 2011). Many of these students require accommodations in order to learn effectively; however, they encounter very different support systems in college than they did in high school. In high schools, it is the legal responsibility of the school to identify students who need support and to determine how best to provide it. That is, K–12 students with disabilities receive an Individualized Education Program (IEP), as mandated by the Individuals with Disabilities Education Act (IDEA). However, in accordance with the ADA, once a student enters college, services can only be provided if they have registered their disability status on campus (usually at a Center for Student Accessibility). Students often choose not to register, perhaps due to the stigma associated with their disability or to a lack of skills in self-advocacy (Eckes & Ochoa, 2005; Lynch & Gussel, 1996). In general, instructors should be mindful that many students who are entitled to accommodations under the law may not be receiving them; instructors who are reassuring and sensitive when students disclose information about their disability status are more likely to encourage them to register so that they can receive the support they need.

Keeping an open mind helps us to recognize the potential difficulties students may face as they navigate the college environment. Students who are members of minoritized groups often experience significant discrimination and/or harassment from their peers—and the broader college community—on the basis of their race, ethnicity, gender, sexual orientation, SES, or physical or mental health (Hurtado & Ruiz, 2012; Rankin & Reason, 2005). Although campus climate has most commonly been investigated in terms of race, a growing number of studies have looked at other aspects of diversity, including sexual orientation and gender identity. In 2016, a Gallup Poll reported that the proportion of people in the U.S. population identifying as lesbian, gay, bisexual, or transgender (LGBT) was at an all time high (4.1%), with higher rates of disclosure among Millennials compared to any earlier generation (Gates, 2017). In a survey of over 33 000 college students in the same year, even higher proportions (9.9%) self-identified as non-heterosexual, with the majority identifying as bisexual or asexual[1] (American College Health Association, 2016). There is an increasing awareness of the rights of

---

1 Some students in the survey identified as pansexual, a term increasingly used to describe sexual identity (Belous & Bauman, 2017).

LGBT and queer (Q) people at U.S. colleges and universities (Beemyn & Rankin, 2011). Many more students are disclosing their sexual identities in high school, and a growing number of campuses have LGBTQ centers and mission statements that affirm policies of tolerance and appreciation of diversity. A 2010 Campus Pride survey of more than 5000 LGBT students and faculty in different institutions reported that 50–76% of LGBT individuals indicated that they felt comfortable on campus; however, LGBT students were still twice as likely to experience harassment on campus as were heterosexual cis-gendered students (Rankin, Weber, Blumenfeld, & Frazer, 2010). Transgender and gen-der-nonconforming students experience particularly high rates of discrimination, in addition to often being denied access to appropriate housing and bathroom/locker room facilities on campus (Grant et al., 2011). Thus, despite some improvements, the campus climate at many colleges (or in many college classrooms) may still not be one of inclusivity toward sexual minorities.

Although overt racism and other forms of discrimination have generally reduced over the years, members of minoritized groups are often the recipients of other more subtle forms of discrimination, commonly known as "microaggressions" (Nadal, Wong, Griffin, Davidoff, & Sriken, 2014; Sue, Lin, Torino, Capodilupo, & Rivera, 2009). Microaggressions include stereotyping, making derogatory remarks related to anoth-er's minoritized status, making racial jokes, and invalidating another's lived experience (e.g., by using verbal or non-verbal behaviors to suggest they are overly sensitive to their minoritized status and are misinterpreting the behavior of others) (Sue, 2010; Sue et al., 2007). Students belonging to various underrepresented groups have been shown to experience high levels of microaggressions in U.S. colleges (McCabe, 2009; Nadal et al., 2014; Suárez-Orozco, Casanova, et al., 2015; Sue et al., 2009). As Nadal et al. (2014) point out, experiencing microaggressions is stressful, and this can negatively impact a student's self-esteem and mental health.

The student body is different at every institution. Some demographic information can be found on an institution's website, and institutional centers for research, planning, and assessment are typically happy to share the data they collect about the student body with college instructors. Some of their statistics may be very surprising. For example, Broton and Goldrick-Rab (2016) reported that an increasing number of students expe-rience housing and food insecurity, meaning that they are at risk of losing their home or do not have enough money to buy adequate amounts of healthy food on a regular basis. Our institution, the City University of New York (CUNY), reported that during 2011, 1% of its undergraduates lived in a shelter, 42% had an insecure housing situation, and 39% had food security issues (Freudenberg et al., 2013). Having an awareness of this kind of information may affect your decisions about accepting late work, allowing make-up tests, or making sure that students who are waiting for financial aid are not penalized or handicapped if they cannot yet purchase textbooks or other materials for the class.

In sum, many of today's students face multiple challenges in their lives. According to the American College Health Association (ACHA), increasing numbers of students feel stressed and suffer from stress-related mental health issues. Indeed, stress is the leading impediment to academic performance (http://www.acha-ncha.org/data/IMPEDIMENTSF06.html). Therefore, trying to help students manage the stress in their lives may be an important goal in many psychology classes. In terms of course planning, it is also helpful to know the range of SAT scores at your institution, the percentage of first-generation students (i.e., students whose parents did not attend college), and how many hours a week the typical student is likely to work. Such information will help you to design instruction that better meets your students' needs. However, we also want to emphasize that even with prior awareness of the characteristics of the students at your institution, every student—and therefore every class—is unique. Discovering information about the individual students in your classes is the only way to really get to know them.

1.4   Supporting First-Generation College Students

The diversity of college students today brings both rewards and challenges. Having a college population that reflects the diversity within the United States bodes well for social mobility and for increased equity for minoritized groups. It enriches our classrooms by providing students with exposure to a greater range of experiences and perspectives. However, it also brings about variability in the barriers to success that students encounter during their college years. About 29% of all college students are first-generation students, and so do not have a person at home they can ask about navigating the college environment. This may explain why first-generation college students are less likely to seek help (Deil-Amen, 2011; Stephens, Fryberg, Markus, Johnson, & Covarrubias, 2012), or to engage in activities that increase the likelihood of academic success, such as interacting with faculty, studying with peers, and making use of support services (Engle & Tinto, 2008), as compared to their continuing-generation peers. Barriers to first-generation student success are particularly prevalent in institutions where large lecture-based classes are the norm and instructors take the role of the "sage on the stage" (Kim, 2009), which again underscores the deficiency of this model of teaching. Low-income and working class first-generation college students in particular face many more challenges that their continuing-generation peers; not only are they more likely to have attended lower-quality schools, but they often struggle financially and have to work to support themselves (and sometimes their families) during college (Covarrubias & Fryberg, 2015). Not surprisingly, first-generation students have lower retention rates than their continuing-generation peers, and they may find it particularly difficult to thrive in college environments that value independence (Stephens et al., 2012), or fail to acknowledge that many students need help adjusting to college life. Student-centered classrooms may help counteract some of these problems by providing more opportunities for dialogic interactions with both instructors and peers, encouraging collaboration, and placing increased emphasis on scaffolding the development of academic skills.

First-generation college students are also at risk of experiencing the "imposter syndrome," where they feel they do not belong in higher education (Jehangir, 2010; Rendon, 1992; Stebleton & Soria, 2013), and they may contend with "family achievement guilt," as they surpass the educational achievements of their close family members (Covarrubias & Fryberg, 2015). These feelings can lead to depression and loneliness (Stebleton & Soria, 2013) and increase the risk of dropping out (Pathways to College Success Network, 2004). Members of underrepresented groups in general are likely to experience stress related to feelings of exclusion in the college environment. Creating an inclusive classroom environment that is welcoming to all students is critical in addressing such issues (see Section 1.5.1).

In 2007–08, 20% of first-year students required at least one remedial class (Sparks & Malkus, 2013) due to lack of proficiency in academic reading, writing, or mathematics. In Chapter 2, we will describe Universal Design (UD) as an approach to supporting students with varying levels of skills, abilities, and preparedness for college. UD promotes the view that pedagogical tools designed to support at-risk students are often beneficial for the student body in general (Silver, Bourke, & Strehorn, 1998). In recognition of the developmental needs of incoming students, many institutions now offer first-year seminars or summer bridge programs aimed at helping them make the transition from high school to college. These courses focus on the development of academic skills, such as time management, test taking, note taking, use of campus support services, and strategies for dealing with stress. Such initiatives have been shown to increase GPAs (Covarrubias, Gallimore, & Okagaki, 2016; Kuh, Cruce, Shoup, Kinzie, & Gonyea, 2008; Lotkowski, Robbins, & Noeth, 2004) and graduation rates (Kuh et al., 2008; Lotkowski et al., 2004; Schnell & Doetkott, 2003). Teaching broad-based skills and providing opportunities for students to practice such skills makes it possible for all students, regardless of their level of preparedness, to gain the essential foundation upon which to build their future educational experiences.

1.5   Culturally Responsive Instruction

Given the diversity within today's student body, in order for teaching to be truly student-centered, it also needs to be culturally responsive, so that every student regardless of their background feels empowered and valued. The growing need for culturally responsive instruction is highlighted by the fact that diversity within the student body has outpaced that among college faculty. In fall 2013, profiles of full-time faculty at degree-granting institutions were reported as 78% White, 10% Asian/Pacific Islander, 6% Black, and 4% Hispanic, with less than 1% Native American or of two or more races (National Center for Education Statistics, 2016b). In contrast, profiles of college students were reported as 58% White, 17% Hispanic, 15% Black, 6% Asian/Pacific Islander, and 1% Native American (Kena et al., 2016).

Ginsberg and Wlodkowski (2009) suggest that there are four key elements to culturally responsive teaching. First, an environment of inclusivity needs to be established, by building a culture of mutual respect in which different opinions, values, and beliefs are validated, so that students develop an appreciation of the fact that we are all shaped by our experiences. Second, learning activities need to be structured to provide students with choices and assignments that are personally relevant and that foster positive attitudes toward the learning process. Third, instructors need to use active collaborative methods shown to enhance student learning (we provide many suggestions of such methods throughout this book). Finally, instructors need to foster a sense of competence by using a variety of assessments that encourage students to reflect on their learning and how it might be helpful to them. In the following sections, we expand on the first three of these elements. To avoid excessive duplication, with the exception of assessment of student participation, we have not covered the fourth (fostering a sense of competence with varied assessments) in this chapter, as assessment is addressed throughout the book.

1.5.1 Fostering an Environment of Inclusivity

Cultivating an atmosphere of respect in which students feel that the instructor is invested in their personal success, and in which cultural differences are discussed and valued, helps them to feel more included and builds self-confidence (Rendon, 1992). When students feel safe and respected, they are more likely to be motivated to take the kinds of academic risks that can lead to deep learning (Ginsberg & Wlodkowski, 2009). The APA has three sets of guidelines for psychologists spanning the domains of practice, research, consultation, and education, focusing on multiculturalism (American Psychological Association, 2017b), working with LGB individuals (American Psychological Association, 2012), and working with transgender/gender-nonconforming individuals (American Psychological Association, 2015). All three sets highlight the need for psychologists to educate themselves about the complexities of the lives of minoritized groups and the struggles they face, and to develop a greater self-awareness regarding their own personal views and implicit biases.

Regular self-reflection is a helpful exercise toward becoming more mindful of one's world views, biases, and privileges, and may reduce the likelihood that these will impose on one's professional life (Case, 2017; Stuart, 2004; Sue & Sue, 2016; see also Chapter 4 for a discussion of Beverly Daniel Tatum's work on racial identity development in college students and Kim Case's work on intersectional pedagogy). For example, many of us have been influenced by mainstream U.S. culture, in that we tend to value independence, single-mindedness, and rational decision-making over interdependence, a desire to get on well with others, and a willingness to acquiesce, but our students (especially those from collectivistic cultures) may not share these values. Culturally responsive teachers try to counteract their biases by broadening the range of assignments and assessments that they use in classes, so that they can draw on the diverse strengths and talents of their students. As described in Chapter 7, self-affirmation psychosocial interventions have also been shown to be effective in validating minoritized students' lived experiences and boosting their self-esteem, problem solving, academic performance, and graduation rate (e.g., Covarrubias, Herrmann, & Fryberg, 2016; Yeager & Dweck, 2012). Student-centered classes help to break down barriers between faculty and students and to lessen the power differential, because the instructor acts as the "guide on the side" rather than the "sage on the stage." Greater instructor immediacy—actions that communicate openness, warmth, interest, and availability—has also been linked to increased rapport and greater motivation for learning (Frisby & Martin, 2010). Immediacy behaviors can be verbal, such as using encouraging language, affirming students' points of view, addressing students by their names, and being receptive to students' ideas and contributions, or non-verbal, which includes smiling, making eye contact, nodding, using other expressive gestures, adopting a pleasant tone of voice, having a relaxed posture, and moving easily around the classroom (Georgakopoulos & Guerrero, 2010; Wilson & Ryan, 2013). Both types of immediacy have been linked to positive perceptions of professors (Georgakopoulos & Guerrero, 2010; Wilson & Ryan, 2013), increased motivation in students (Frymier & Shulman, 1995), and greater class participation (Rocca, 2008). Even in cultures[2] where

---

2 To get a better feel of how these values vary by country, Geert Hofstede provides a useful Web resource with statistics for a wide range of cultural values in many different countries (https://www.hofstede-insights.com/product/compare-countries/).

there is a high power differential between students and professors, or a greater focus on verbal than on non-verbal behaviors, non-verbal behavior still plays an important role in students' perceptions of instructor friendliness, approachability, openness, and respectfulness (Georgakopoulos & Guerrero, 2010). In a six-country study (the United States, Australia, Japan, Korea, Taiwan, and Sweden), Georgakopoulos and Guerrero (2010) found that across all countries, students reported that the best professors used more non-verbal expressions of immediacy than did the worst.

Students also report feeling greater rapport with professors who are compassionate and who encourage their questions (Wilson & Ryan, 2013). Similarly, using multicultural images and names in examples and on exams can help foster an environment of inclusivity and demonstrates that the instructor values diversity (Simon & Nolan, 2017). Positive student perceptions of instructor rapport have been associated with better instructor evaluations (Richmond, Berglund, Epelbaum, & Klein, 2015; Wilson & Ryan, 2013), as well as increased attendance and higher final grades (Wilson & Ryan, 2013).

Taking students on field trips and meeting with them outside of class deepens an instructor's understanding of them and increases the likelihood that the students feel that their identity is valued (Rendon, 1992). In their international study, Georgakopoulos and Guerrero (2010) found that the best professors met with students outside the classroom more frequently (and had more in-class discussions) than did the worst. Similarly, in a large multi-institutional study of over 4000 U.S. students, Lundberg and Schreiner (2004) found that the frequency of faculty–student out-of-class interactions correlated with students' perceptions of learning gains in both academic and personal development. During such meetings, faculty encouragement to work harder was particularly influential in promoting student growth. This relationship held across racial groups. African American and Native American students were most likely to interact with faculty, but were less likely to find the quality of the interactions as satisfying as White students. Even so, faculty–student interactions had a greater effect on learning for students of color than for White students. The results of this study were extended by Einarson and Clarkberg (2010), who surveyed over 30 000 students at research universities. In addition to replicating the general finding that increased interactions with faculty were associated with increased intellectual and personal development, they also reported that Asian Americans had least contact with faculty. They suggested that this may be because in many Asian cultures, there is a high power differential between faculty and students, and so students may feel that it is disrespectful to ask questions or to say that they don't understand (Chu & Walters, 2013).

Inclusivity can also be fostered by building a sense of community among students, through cooperative learning activities (Ginsberg & Wlodkowski, 2009; see Chapter 5 on Group Work). In cooperative learning, students mutually support one another, rather than competing against one another. This enhances both their academic and their social development (Johnson, Johnson, & Stanne, 2000), and provides them with strategies for effectively working with others—skills that are likely to help them succeed in the workplace as well as in college.

Diverse groups of students gain the most when they work together for extended periods of time (Watson, Kumar, & Michaelsen, 1993), and so it is wise to begin collaborative work at the very outset of the course (see Chapter 5). Having students establish ground rules for class discussions as an introductory activity on the first or second day fosters respect and inclusivity, helps instill a sense of community, and diminishes negative behaviors (Case, 2011; DiClementi & Handelsman, 2005). Modeling immediacy behaviors, such as taking the time to get to know one's students and using interactive teaching strategies to help the students get to know one another, helps increase student connectedness and participation (Sidelinger & Booth-Butterfield, 2010).

Classroom dynamics evolve over time both within small groups and at the whole-class level (see Chapter 5). In class, and in small groups, students initially may lack trust and fail to identify with their classmates; as such, their interactions may be driven by their own interests, and they may have difficulty working together (Birmingham & McCord, 2004). But, in the supportive environment of a student-centered classroom, students' anxiety levels will decrease over time as they acquire collaborative skills that allow them to respect and trust one another while working synergistically to tackle academically demanding tasks (Birmingham & McCord, 2004). When students work cooperatively, they feel more socially integrated with and supported by their peers (Johnson, Johnson, & Stanne, 2000). Social integration has been shown to be particularly important in building academic confidence and motivation (Pathways to College Success Network, 2004). In fact, Kennedy, Sheckley, and Kehrhahn (2000) found that even students with low GPAs were likely to persist at an institution if they felt strongly socially connected. In the same vein, Tinto (2000) found that students who developed close peer relationships were more likely to experience a sense of belonging within an institution and had better GPAs and graduation rates compared to those who did not.

Providing opportunities for peer mentoring and the formation of study groups in classes also instills a sense of inclusivity and has been linked to increased student engagement (Mangold, Bean, Adams, Schwab, & Lynch, 2002; Padgett & Reid, 2002). Community building through peer mentorship can extend outside the classroom. For example, as described in Chapter 7, at-risk students have been shown to benefit from hearing more senior students describe the difficulties they experienced during their first year of college and how they overcame them (for review, see Yeager & Walton, 2011). A final tip for helping establish connectedness from the outset is to mirror what outstanding professors do on the first day of class (Iannarelli, Bardsley, & Foote, 2010): they establish community by gathering information about their students (both orally and in writing), display immediacy by giving information about themselves and their willingness to assist students, go over the syllabus in detail, and attempt to stimulate interest in the course. It has been shown that students particularly value having their professors review the syllabus in detail and provide an overview of the class (Henslee, Burgess, & Buskist, 2006; Perlman & McCann, 2001).

Outstanding professors also use icebreakers, especially with more junior students (Iannarelli et al., 2010), to help them get to know their students better and to give the students a chance to get to know one another in an informal setting. However, some studies have shown that not all students appreciate icebreaker activities (Henslee et al., 2006), so it is probably best to use ones that are related to the content of the course itself (Iannarelli et al., 2010) or that help establish guidelines for the discussion of sensitive issues that are likely to arise in class (Case, 2011; DiClementi & Handelsman, 2005; Tatum, 1992). One such activity is the reciprocal interview technique, whereby students answer questions posed by the instructor in terms of their goals, concerns, relevant experience/expertise, and willingness to contribute to discussions of sensitive topics, as well as their suggestions for how the instructor can best support their learning

(Case, 2011; Hermann, Foster, & Hardin, 2010). Students answer the questions individually and then discuss their answers in small groups and later with the whole class. They then collaboratively formulate questions to ask the instructor in turn (Case, 2011; Hermann et al., 2010). This method has been shown to be effective in making the class atmosphere more comfortable for students, as well as in clarifying their expectations for the course (Case, 2011; Hermann et al., 2010). Hermann et al. (2010) found that the benefits persisted beyond the first day of the course, and that end-of-semester ratings were higher for courses that used the reciprocal interview technique on the first day. For icebreaker activities like these, it is very helpful for students to wear nametags. We also like to ask each student to write their name very clearly in thick, black marker on a folded index card, and to place it on the table in front of them at the start of each class. This practice helps the instructor (and their classmates) to learn their name and makes it easier to call on them. The cards can be collected at the end of each class period and used for taking attendance. Giving them out at the beginning of class helps the instructor to memorize the students' names more quickly and provides an opportunity to interact with them. If your class is too large for you to efficiently collect and distribute these name tents yourself each session, you could instead ask a representative from each row to pick up a bag containing that row's names from the front of the class and pass them out. If students are absent, then their name tents can be bundled together with an elastic band and left in the bag, making it easy to record attendance. Alternatively, consider taking photos of your jumbo-sized class (row by row) and creating a seating map to use as you call on different students. Box 1.1 provides some resources for icebreakers and other first-day-of-class activities that work well in student-centered classes.

Box 1.1 Suggestions for Icebreakers and Other First-Day-of-Class Activities

Use our class website link, http://futuresinitiative.org/teachingpsychology/2017/05/24/ice-breakers/, to find a game of Human Bingo. This game requires students (and the instructor) to go around the class looking for people who fit the boxes on their card. Once one or two people complete a line the game stops, but it is then fun to go through the items on a card and ask students to stand up if they match each one.

Also consider a syllabus scavenger hunt or a college or library scavenger hunt, with students working together in small groups!

Introduce students to the concept of CT in psychological science by using a myth-busting demonstration. For suggestions, see Chapter 4, and this book by Scott Lilienfeld and colleagues:
Lilienfeld, S. O., Lynn, S. J., Ruscio, J., & Beyerstein, B. L. (2011). *50 great myths of popular psychology: Shattering widespread misconceptions about human behavior.* Chichester, U.K.: John Wiley and Sons.

Here are some other resources you might find useful:
http://topix.teachpsych.org/w/page/55139707/First%20Day%20Activities
http://teachpsych.org/resources/Documents/otrp/resources/eggleston04.pdf

This site makes specific suggestions for a first-day lesson plan:
https://www.cmu.edu/teaching/designteach/teach/firstday.html

Colleges that have made concerted efforts to make learning experiences more relevant to underserved students have made great strides in increasing student graduation rates. For example, graduation rates were substantially increased when Tribal Colleges and Universities connected the curricula of STEM disciplines to local culture (Ambler, 1998), and when other minority-serving institutions introduced authentic assignments, in which students grapple with real-life problems (National Science Foundation, 2017). Knowles, Holton, and Swanson (2012) suggest that adult learners also learn better when engaged in authentic problem solving.

Relatedly, Simon and Nolan (2017) suggest "internationalizing" psychology courses as a way to validate students' diverse cultural backgrounds and enhance their preparedness for employment in an increasingly global workforce. Learning about people whose experiences, culture, and language background are different from one's own increases perspective-taking skills (Kurtiş & Adams, 2017) and can promote insights into one's own identity development (Tatum, 1992). Examining the linguistic landscape of various communities by analyzing the signage in different neighborhoods is another technique that can be used to explore immigration, bilingualism, cultural diversity, and social use of language (Sayer, 2009).

Simon and colleagues offer helpful resources for finding relevant news stories that provide insights into how psychological science is similar or varies across different countries and cultures (Simon, Galazyn, & Nolan, 2012; Simon & Nolan, 2017). For example, the U.N. monthly video newsmagazine (http://www.unmultimedia.org/tv/21stcentury/) hosts short documentaries that deal with a variety of social issues of relevance to psychology. To illustrate our point, in a quick search of this resource, we found a host of stories that would be suitable to incorporate into undergraduate psychology courses. One was about the high incidence of teenage pregnancies in the Dominican Republic, which could fit well in a developmental psychology course. Another was about the caste system in India, which is of relevance to the issues of prejudice and discrimination typically covered in a social psychology course. A third linked the diabetes epidemic in the wealthy Gulf state of Qatar to the sharp increase in sedentary lifestyles and obesity, which would be relevant in a physiological psychology or health psychology course.

1.5.2 Fostering Positive Attitudes toward Learning

Ginsberg and Wlodkowski (2009) emphasize the importance of fostering positive attitudes toward learning in culturally responsive classrooms by making classes relevant, affording students choices and variety in learning activities and assignments, and providing clear goals and guidance. Being explicit about why and how various assignments are relevant to students' lives and future careers has been associated with increased motivation (Frymier & Shulman, 1995). Therefore, even though the initial motives for taking a course may be extrinsically driven, if a class is sufficiently interesting to students, they should develop intrinsic motivation that will give them the affective push typically needed in order to learn effectively (Ginsberg & Wlodkowski, 2009).

Student motivation can be improved by using a range of instructional methods and assessments—a principle that is also at the heart of UD (see Chapter 2). Every student has strengths, weaknesses, and preferences for different types of assignment, and so adding variety helps to make learning and assessment more equitable. UD is more flexible than traditional teaching methods, and, as emphasized by Ginsberg and Wlodkowski (2009), greater flexibility in instruction increases students' intrinsic motivation and may also decrease stress. Students feel empowered when they are invited to give their input to the course. This can be achieved in a number of different ways; for example, you might ask students for their feedback on the efficacy of a particular activity or teaching method (this provides a formative assessment of your teaching efficacy), you might allow students to make collaborative decisions about due dates for assignments or grading structures (Ginsberg & Wlodkowski, 2009), or you might even have your students help to design your course (Case, Miller, & Jackson, 2012; Davidson, 2017).

Expanding students' choices within a class (such as letting them choose their own topic for a research study) has been shown to increase motivation, self-efficacy, and self-regulated learning (Ames, 1992; Pintrich & Schunk, 1996). However, it also has its downsides, especially in large classes. First, if every student chooses a different topic, then the time required to give effective feedback to each is likely to be unmanageable. Second, if students work individually on different topics, then they are constrained in terms of what information and/or data it is feasible to collect and assimilate over the course of a single semester, which may in turn limit their learning gains. Third, students often need guidance in picking suitable topics for further exploration. Thus, we highly recommend that assignments are designed so that students can work with peers with similar interests on literature reviews, research studies, and other projects. Ideally, instructors should first solicit ideas from students about topics of interest and then assign a limited number of choices, so that the time and effort required for grading and feedback are manageable (see Chapter 5 on Group Work and Chapter 6 on Writing).

1.5.3   Enhancing Meaning for Students through Active Learning

Ginsberg and Wlodkowski (2009) advocate using a variety of student-centered active learning activities, especially within cooperative structures, to help students learn in a culturally responsive classroom. Working cooperatively with others from diverse groups on real-world problems encourages students from different backgrounds to share their experiences in order to find solutions. Diverse groups typically offer a wider range of perspectives and generate more potential solutions than do homogeneous ones (Watson et al., 1993). Having students tackle real-life problems makes it easier for them to recall strategies and solutions in the future, and so provides practice for life after college (Lattuca, Voigt, & Fath, 2004). Questions that are relatively open-ended and have multiple solutions are likely to promote students' epistemic development in terms of their flexibility and acceptance of multiple viewpoints (Lattuca et al., 2004). Solving challenging authentic problems with peers has been found to be effective in increasing graduation rates among underserved students (National Science Foundation, 2017). Moreover, assigning challenging problems helps to convey that one has high expectations of and confidence in one's students, which helps to build self-esteem. Simon and Nolan (2017) also champion the need for instructors to broaden their students' experiences with research methodologies by making sure that considerations are given to cultural differences and by exposing students to a form of community-based research called participatory action research. Participatory action research is a practice in which researchers work with community members to identify their most pressing needs; subsequently, both groups participate in designing and implementing research projects aimed at identifying how best to bring about social change (Reardon, 1998; see also Section 4.7 on Service Learning and Community-Based Research).

In active learning classes, every student needs to participate in order to benefit. The phrase "total participation" was popularized by Himmele and Himmele (2011) in their book on techniques for K–12 classes; it conveys the expectation that every student in the class will be engaged in active learning. Similarly, Doug Lemov, in his book *Teach Like a Champion*, describes 62 techniques that elicit total participation and enhance learning in K–12 classes (Lemov, 2015). We encourage instructors to review these techniques, as many of them are applicable in college settings. Examples include using the Think–Write–Pair–Share (T-W-P-S) technique to prepare students to engage in discussions; gathering data on a daily basis in order to gauge students' understanding, and acting upon this; asking students for an exit ticket, on which they write the most important thing (or the muddiest point) from the day's class; and cold-calling. We particularly like using the T-W-P-S method to help level the playing field when asking students to respond to discussion questions (see Box 4.2). It is not unusual for students to be reluctant to speak in class, perhaps due to a lack of assertiveness, non-native fluency in English, or a cultural background in which thinking is valued over speaking (Chu & Walters, 2013). Using a technique like T-W-P-S allows everyone to participate in the thinking process, as they write down their answers to the questions. If called upon, students are likely to feel more confident because they can read their answers and have already shared them with a peer. In Chapters 4 and 5, we describe a wide range of methods by which to engage every student in the classroom.

Fostering a classroom climate of respect, encouragement, and collaboration also encourages greater participation, as does self-disclosing information that makes students feel more connected to their instructor (Rocca, 2010). Affirmation of student participation also helps in this regard (Rocca, 2010). In large classes, the use of clickers or other audience response systems is invaluable in ensuring that all students are engaged (see Chapter 3 on Effective Multimedia Instruction for more ideas). In the absence of such technology, response cards marked with True/False or A, B, C, D (or different colors) can be held up by students; this too has been shown to increase participation (Marmolejo, Wilder, & Bradley, 2004).

At some but not all institutions, student attendance is mandatory; however, if you have designed a course in which important learning occurs in every class, you want students to attend regardless of your institution's attendance policy. One way to increase student attendance is to have classroom participation factor into the final course grade. This practice is also consistent with the principles of UD and culturally responsive instruction, which call for student learning to be assessed using a variety of methods. However, as Petress (2006) points out, participation can be difficult to operationalize and grade, and students and instructors have been shown to have different ideas about what constitutes participation (Fritschner, 2000). Fritschner (2000) found that in traditional classes, students tended to consider being very interested in the course and exhibiting non-verbal behaviors associated with paying attention as important indicators of participation, whereas instructors focused on verbal contributions to class discussions. Clearly, it is important to be transparent about grading policies in this regard.

Participation in a student-centered classroom may encompass a multitude of behaviors. Keeping track of each student's verbal contribution to a class discussion can be challenging, especially in large classes. However, students are often required to produce multiple pieces of low-stakes writing during each class period (see Chapter 6 on Learning to Write and Writing to Learn). These can be collected and graded as complete/incomplete, and thus collectively can make up a participation grade that is not solely dependent on verbal exchanges in the classroom. Using short in-class formative assessments that count toward the final grade has been shown to increase attendance (Butler, Phillmann, & Smart, 2001; Drabick, Weisberg, Paul, & Bubier, 2007). Dancer and Kamvounias (2005) found that student participation improved when students first defined and then self-evaluated their participation at various points across the semester, while receiving formative written feedback along the way. Although Dancer and Kamvounias found that students' self-assessments were somewhat higher than those given by teaching assistants (TAs) within the class, they found consistency between TA ratings and peer assessments given by other group members. Thus, self- and peer assessment could potentially be used to grade participation. This strategy lifts the burden of assessment from the instructor and empowers students in a way that is consistent with culturally responsive teaching (Ginsberg & Wlodkowski, 2009).

1.6   Starting Off with a Student-Centered Philosophy

Throughout this book, we provide evidence for the efficacy of student-centered teaching practices. We realize that embarking on a whole new way of teaching may feel like a daunting task, and we very much encourage new instructors to seek mentorship from more experienced teachers and peers who are already using a student-centered approach. Box 1.2 provides some suggestions for locating helpful resources. We have found that collaborative course preparation, in which resources are shared among instructors teaching the same or related courses, is a great way to both jump-start and grow your teaching practice; see Schwartz, Powers, Galazyn, and Brooks (2017) for ideas on how to organize a teaching collective. We hope that this book will provide you with lots of specific suggestions to help enrich your teaching.

Box 1.2 Locating Resources for Student-Centered Teaching

Society for the Teaching of Psychology
teachpsych.org

Graduate Student Teaching Association
http://teachpsych.org/gsta/index.php
http://teachpsych.org/ebooks/howweteachnow

Campus-Based Centers for Teaching and Learning
Most campuses have a Teaching and Learning Center (often referred to as TLCs). We have provided a few here:
https://tlc.commons.gc.cuny.edu/
https://tlc.commons.gc.cuny.edu/college-of-staten-island/
http://www.jjay.cuny.edu/tlc-teaching-and-learning-center
https://www.cmu.edu/teaching/
http://wacenter.evergreen.edu/

1.7   Summary

1) Student-centered teaching utilizes active learning methods that develop the whole student, emphasizing personal growth and academic and professional skills, in addition to content knowledge.
2) Student-centered teaching is culturally responsive, through recognizing and valuing students' diverse experiences and talents. Drawing on principles of Universal Design, student-centered teaching provides multiple ways for students to learn.
3) Abundant research indicates that traditional lecture-based teaching is ineffective and should be abandoned in favor of active learning approaches.

2

Designing a Course Based on Learning Objectives

2.1 Backward Course Design

Teaching is often and appropriately compared to lighting a fire for student learning, rather than filling an empty pail (Pychyl, 2008). Successful "pedagogical pyromania" (Pychyl, 2008, p. 1) requires thoughtful, evidence-based course design. However, we don't want instructors to spend all night and day tending their fires; rather, we are firm believers in collaborative course design and preparation. New instructors in particular are encouraged to work with those who have taught a given course before, and to adapt courses that others have designed. This makes pragmatic sense, and can often lead to productive collaborations. Over time, improvements in course design will come from enacting a student-centered philosophy that meets the particular needs of the students in your classes.

In this chapter, we provide an orientation to strategic course design by introducing the critical concept of *backward design*, which involves starting with the end in mind and building back from there (Wiggins & McTighe, 2005). Backward design entails identifying broad learning goals (or adopting those already in place in the department) and using them to develop course-specific learning objectives (LOs) (also often referred to as "learning outcomes"). LOs in turn guide the choice of assessment strategies and pedagogical decisions about how to teach the course. Each of these steps is meaningfully informed by an appreciation of the needs and backgrounds of the particular students within a class. Backward design helps instructors to make the paradigm shift from using the course textbook as the central point of the curriculum to using it as a resource within that curriculum (McTighe & Wiggins, 2012). Furthermore, backward design increases the likelihood that instructors will assess the effectiveness of their teaching and make improvements to enhance student learning. Backward design also facilitates assessment at the institutional level. A culture of assessment has developed in many colleges, in response to evolving demands from accrediting bodies and the need to attract and retain students (Fuller, Skidmore, Bustamante, & Holzweiss, 2016). Most institutions and departments want to be able to demonstrate that they provide high-quality education, and so need to consider how this is defined and assessed (Dwyer, Millett, & Payne, 2006). Using backward design facilitates curriculum development by focusing on what skills and knowledge students are expected to gain. Graff (2011) showed that the majority of student teachers who were instructed in backward design

Teaching Psychology: An Evidence-Based Approach, First Edition. Jillian Grose-Fifer, Patricia J. Brooks, and Maureen O'Connor.
Companion website: www.wiley.com/go/Grose-Fifer/teaching-psychology

found it useful in planning their curricula. Kelting-Gibson (2005) also showed that student elementary school teachers who were instructed in backward design produced better lesson plans than those who were instructed in traditional (topic-based) course development. Perhaps not surprisingly, many of the best college teachers in the United States use backward design in their courses; their syllabi reveal that they explain to students what they will get out of the course (the LOs), how they will achieve this, and what methods of assessment will be used to evaluate whether they have done so (Bain, 2011).

2.2   Step 1: Developing Learning Goals and Objectives

Because backward course design begins with the "destination," the first step is deciding which skills/knowledge you want your students to have acquired by the end of the course, and how they will be different as a result of taking it. Fortunately, for psychology instructors, the American Psychological Association (APA) has five overarching learning goals for the psychology undergraduate major (Box 2.1) that should be used in the creation of specific course LOs. In line with the paradigm shift in higher education toward developing students' academic skills, the APA goals are broad, with only one of them addressing content; this underscores that it is no longer acceptable to create a curriculum based on the textbook alone. Individual departments may have specific LOs for particular courses in the major, and it is always advisable to clarify this with your department chair before you create your own. Furthermore, asking for a course syllabus may save you the effort of reinventing the wheel; it is likely that someone else in your department has already created excellent LOs for the course you are planning to teach. The APA guidelines for the undergraduate psychology major (American Psychological Association, 2013) provide suggestions for LOs that can easily be adapted for specific courses (foundational and upper-level), along with ideas for assessment.

   When creating LOs, it is particularly important to consider long-term goals: what lasting effects do you want the course to have on your students? As noted in the *APS Observer* (Association for Psychological Science, 2013; Myers et al., 2010), psychological science is

---

Box 2.1 APA Undergraduate Learning Goals (2013)

1) **Knowledge Base in Psychology** (key ideas; working knowledge of breadth of psychology; application to daily life)
2) **Scientific Inquiry and Critical Thinking** (use scientific reasoning to interpret psychological phenomena; information literacy; innovative and integrative thinking; interpret, design and conduct psychological research; sociocultural factors)
3) **Ethical and Social Responsibility in a Diverse World** (apply and evaluate ethics of psychological studies and practice; build and improve relationships; community building)
4) **Communication** (writing and oral presentation skills; communicating with others)
5) **Professional Development** (preparation for the workforce; teamwork skills; self-efficacy/regulation; project skills; lifelong learning)

Source: Based on information from the American Psychological Association (2013).

a constantly evolving field, in which there have been significant changes over the past 25 years. The strong likelihood that the knowledge base students acquire in their psychology classes today will become outdated adds impetus for creating LOs that go beyond merely learning content. Instruction focusing on academic skills, such as effective methods for remembering and understanding topics covered in class (see Chapter 7), is highly transferrable and likely to be useful in students' future lives. Thinking scientifically, critically, and ethically, engaging in effective problem solving (see Chapter 4), collaborating well with others (see Chapter 5), and communicating effectively when speaking and writing (see Chapter 6) are all enduring skills that are likely to be beneficial in life beyond the college experience. Clearly, APA wants psychology majors to graduate as well-rounded individuals who are aware of cultural and individual differences in how people think, feel, and behave, and who understand the ethical implications of psychological science and practice. Therefore, these priorities should be reflected in course LOs.

When deciding upon LOs that pertain to the development of a knowledge base in psychology, it is helpful to use taxonomies of learning that extend beyond rote memorization of basic concepts. Perhaps the most well known of these is Bloom's cognitive taxonomy, updated by Anderson et al. (2001) (see Figure 2.1). Forehand (2005) and others (Boysen, 2012; Noyd & The Staff of The Center for Educational Excellence, 2010) have provided verbs for each level of the pyramid that are particularly useful in constructing actionable LOs. When choosing which verbs to use for LOs, it is best to avoid those that are open-ended; for example, "list" and "summarize" are preferable to "demonstrate an understanding of a concept," and more clearly dictate what kind of assessments will be appropriate in evaluating whether the LO has been met. Along similar lines, Fink's taxonomy (see Figure 2.2) uses elements from Bloom's cognitive and affective taxonomies to ensure the provision of what he terms "significant learning experiences" for students across six intersecting domains, including personal development (Fink, 2007; 2013).

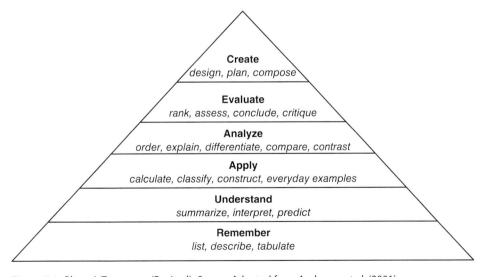

Figure 2.1 Bloom's Taxonomy (Revised). *Source:* Adapted from Anderson et al. (2001).

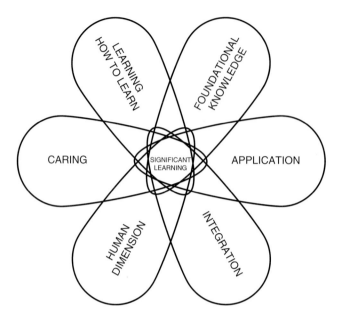

LEARNING
HOW TO LEARN

FOUNDATIONAL
KNOWLEDGE

CARING

SIGNIFICANT
LEARNING

APPLICATION

HUMAN
DIMENSION

INTEGRATION

Figure 2.2 Fink's Taxonomy of Significant Learning Experiences. *Source:* Reproduced from Fink (2007).

Boysen (2012) and Noyd et al. (2010) provide some excellent tips for writing LOs. They are typically phrased in terms of what a student should be able to do by the end of the course. For example, in a Brain and Behavior course, one might use the following: *By the end of this course, you should be able to label the basic parts of the human nervous system and describe how these parts affect behavior.* Note that the learning is described in specific, simple, but actionable terms, which make the expectations transparent and allow the behavior to be readily measured. Students are more likely to feel motivated about learning if a course's LOs seem important or are relevant to their lives or future work. In the Brain and Behavior example, the LO describes a big-picture issue and translates it to daily life. It is imperative that LOs are developmentally appropriate; for example, the use of the word *basic* in this example suggests that it might be an appropriate objective for an introductory rather than an advanced-level course. Also, as advocated by Boysen (2012), this LO describes the condition under which the behavior will be demonstrated: *when* students are provided with a diagram of the human nervous system, they should be able to generate appropriate labels.

2.3   Step 2: Developing Assessment Strategies

Having decided on the LOs for a course, the next step is to determine how you will assess whether or not students have achieved them. Sometimes, instructors lament that students are only interested in learning enough to get a good grade in the class (Whetten, 2007). However, as Whetten (2007) points out, grade orientation can actually be beneficial when assessments authentically measure course LOs, because students will prioritize learning what is most important for that course. So, clearly, assessments should align with the LOs. High-stakes (worth a significant percentage of the final grade) assessments are typically used to decide whether students have achieved a course's LOs (Angelo & Cross, 1993; Wiggins & McTighe, 2005). These types of assessment are usually summative; that is, they are evaluations of a final product, typically papers, presentations, and/or exams. In a culturally responsive and student-centered classroom, however, assessments should also include assignments that may have more currency for today's students (see Chapter 4), such as podcasts (Grose-Fifer, Helmer, & Zottoli, 2014), pamphlets, posters (Beins & Beins, 2011; Moule, Judd, & Girot, 1998), websites or wikis (Slotter, 2010), children's books or toys (e.g., for a Developmental Psychology course), newspapers, and newsletters. Another, perhaps more integrative way of assessing whether students have met the LOs is to use physical or electronic portfolios. Portfolios can be assembled to showcase your students' best work (Birkett, Neff, & Pieper, 2012). They can also provide a record of learning over time. The latter may be particularly useful in allowing students to evaluate their own academic and personal growth across the semester; indeed, reflection is a typical element in any portfolio (Buzzetto-More, 2010). Students can annotate their portfolios to indicate how various pieces of work show evidence for how they have developed during the course. For more suggestions on how to design different types of assessments, consult the Assessment Cyberguide for Learning Goals and Outcomes, produced by the APA Board of Education Affairs' Task Force on Psychology Major Competencies (Pusateri, Halonen, Hill, & McCarthy, 2009) and available at https://www.apa.org/ed/governance/bea/assessment-cyberguide-v2.pdf, as well as APA's Project Assessment at http://pass.apa.org/. Another helpful resource is the National Institute for Learning Outcomes Assessment (NILOA)'s library of assignments, which was designed to assess specific proficiencies at various levels of higher education and is available at www.assignmentlibrary.org.

Regardless of the format chosen for assessment, students typically perform best when they understand what is expected of them and know what success looks like (Hattie, 2015). Distributing grading rubrics with assignments is an effective way to make the instructor's expectations explicit by providing clear descriptions of work completed at various levels of mastery (e.g., ranging from "does not meet expectations" to "exceeds expectations") (Andrade, 1997; Jonsson & Svingby, 2007). In Box 2.2, we provide an example of a rubric for grading a summary of a primary source article (Grose-Fifer & Davis-Ferreira, 2018). For complex assignments or projects, rubrics provide guidelines for each component part of the assignment, which can serve as an organizational tool. By making expectations explicit, rubrics help to increase reliability when evaluating whether students have met a given LO (Jonsson & Svingby, 2007). The Association of American Colleges and Universities (AAC&U) has formulated a set of Valid Assessment of Learning in Undergraduate Education (VALUE) rubrics that can be used to assess performance in multiple areas, including written communication, oral communication, creative thinking, teamwork, and ethical reasoning (see http://www.aacu.org/value-rubrics). The APA Assessment Cyberguide references articles and websites containing helpful rubrics (Pusateri et al., 2009), and we provide several examples in this book of rubrics for grading specific assignments, such as for peer evaluation of group work (Chapter 5).

Student-centered course design is more process- than product-oriented; in other words, the focus is on building skills, rather than on the grades attained for a single test, paper, or project. In student-centered classes, students typically practice by working on

Box 2.2 Rubric for Summary of a Primary Source Article

Criteria and qualities	Weak	Adequate	Good	Excellent	Points
Article marked as instructed	Not marked as instructed	Some markings present but some missing	Minor corrections needed	Article marked as instructed	5
Goal of the study	Not clearly stated OR phrases are copied from the article	The general idea of the goal is presented but need more details	Goal well described—minor corrections needed	Excellent description of study goals	5
Hypotheses	Not clearly stated OR phrases are copied from the article	More detail needed	Hypotheses well described—minor corrections needed	Excellent description of hypotheses	10
Participants	Not enough detail is given to understand who participated in the studies OR phrases are copied from the articles	Some of the important information about participants is present but need more details	Participants well described—minor corrections needed	Excellent description of participants in terms of age, gender, n, and other relevant info	10
Techniques	Not enough detail is given to understand how the study was conducted OR phrases are copied from the articles	Some of the important information about techniques is present but need more details	Techniques well described—minor corrections needed	Excellent description of techniques written in own words	20
Demonstrates understanding of findings	The main findings of the studies are not well described OR there are many errors in the interpretation or copying from articles	Some of the findings are described but some important information is missing	Findings described clearly—minor omissions	Excellent description of findings written in own words	15
Demonstrates understanding of conclusions	There are no conclusions OR conclusions are incorrect	Some of the conclusions are described but some important conclusions are missing No reference to hypotheses	Conclusions described clearly, with reference to whether or not hypotheses were met—minor omissions	Excellent description of conclusions written in own words, with reference to hypotheses Relevance to goal of study is clearly stated	10
Clarity of writing and writing technique	In places, it is hard to know what the writer is trying to express Writing is convoluted Misspelled words, incorrect grammar, and improper punctuation are evident	Writing is generally clear, but contains many grammatical errors and typos Active voice and past tense not consistently used Organization could be better	Writing is generally clear, but unnecessary words are occasionally used Paragraph or sentence structure is too repetitive Active voice and past tense not consistently used	Writing is crisp, clear, and succinct The writer incorporates the active voice and past tense The use of pronouns, modifiers, parallel construction, and non-sexist language are appropriate	20
Citations/ References	Citation not included OR wrong article cited	Citation included but not APA style	Citation present and minor APA formatting issues	Reference correctly formatted in APA style	5
				Total	100

Source: Adapted from Grose-Fifer and Davis-Ferreira (2018).

low-stakes assignments and then use feedback (provided by peers and/or the instructor) to either improve the existing product or do better on similar future assignments. For example, in Chapters 4 and 6, we emphasize the need to deconstruct or scaffold complex assignments by breaking them down into more manageable parts, so that students produce a more polished final product. Again, rubrics can be used to provide targeted feedback in stages. This formative (ongoing) assessment is an important part of the learning process, because it highlights where students should focus their efforts and helps them to reflect on their academic habits (see also Chapter 7). Such feedback given over the duration of a course has been shown to improve students' skills and the quality of their work (Hattie & Timperley, 2007). Formative assessment helps students to develop mastery by encouraging them to learn from their mistakes without fear of penalty. Students may be more likely to engage with and work harder on these skill-building, low-stakes assignments (which can be graded on a pass/fail basis) if, collectively, they count toward the final grade. This grading practice also acknowledges that the instructor recognizes the importance of rewarding the process as well as the product. Angelo and Cross (1993) provide a large number of useful suggestions for formative assessments in the classroom (see Box 2.3); note that index cards are often very helpful for collecting and reading student responses to these items (e.g., muddiest point, one-sentence summary). We also provide additional ideas for formative assessment in Chapter 6, in the context of writing.

Box 2.3 Suggestions for Formative Assessment

I) **Knowing Your Students**
  - **Interest/skills/knowledge checklist:** Provide a list of course-relevant topics and use Likert scales to gauge level of student interest/skills/knowledge base in relation to each topic.

II) **Content and Skills**
  - **Minute paper** at end of class/activity: *What is the most important thing that you learned today? What don't you understand?* Can also be used to assess what students gained from watching a video/demonstration or doing a homework assignment or exam.
  - **Muddiest point:** *What are you still not clear about?* Could be administered after a class, assignment, reading a peer's paper, watching a demonstration or video.
  - **One-sentence summary:** Response to a how/why prompt about a procedure or concept.
  - **Directed paraphrasing:** Explain a concept/procedure to a specific audience (e.g., a child or grandmother).
  - **Applications cards:** *How do concepts apply to real life?*
  - **Defining features matrix:** Students organize/categorize information in a matrix based on key features. Helpful for differentiating between theories, techniques, and study results.
  - **Problem/principle recognition tasks:** *What kind of problem is this? What kind of principles do I need to use to solve this?* Helpful for differentiating between psychopathologies or problems in statistics/research methods.
  - **Background knowledge probe:** Mini-quiz to assess students' knowledge at start of class, topic, or course.

- **Focused listing:** *What are the most important points related to a topic?* Helps students to develop psychology-related vocabulary and to differentiate it from everyday use (e.g., negative correlation).
- **Misconception check:** Probe to see whether students endorse myths (e.g., *We only use 10% of our brain*).
- **Empty outline:** Provide students with headings/subheadings and ask them to fill in the blanks.
- **Two sides of the argument grid:** Students list a few main points for each side of an ambiguous question.
- **Student-generated test questions and answers:** Select the best questions and use them on the test.
- **Role-plays:** Act out how a neuron works; Tuskegee tribunal (see Chapter 4).

III) **Personal Growth and Metacognition**
- **Everyday ethical dilemmas:** Students describe and justify their position in relation to a prompt about an everyday ethical dilemma.
- **Course-related self-confidence survey:** Use the Likert scale to probe how confident students are about various skills targeted in the course.
- **Group-work evaluations:** Students assess the performance of their group and of individual group members; see Chapter 5 for more suggestions.

IV) **Efficacy of Teaching**
- **Teacher-designed feedback forms:** *What aspect of today's class was most effective in enhancing your understanding of [specific concept] and why? What would have improved today's class? What was the most interesting part of the class?*
- **Chain notes:** A large envelope is passed around the class, and each student writes for 1 minute in response to the question: *What were you paying attention to just before this envelope reached you?* Helps to evaluate whether students are engaged and on-task.
- **Assignment assessment:** *How valuable was this assignment in enhancing your learning?*

Source: Summarized and adapted from Angelo and Cross (1993)

Formative assessments may sound very time-consuming, but we want to stress that most are very quick to administer and evaluate. For example, the minute paper, which is perhaps the most widely used method of formative assessment (Angelo & Cross, 1993), literally only takes a minute (or two) of class time. Also, because formative assessments are designed to help students learn without penalty, they are often ungraded, or are graded on a complete/incomplete or pass/fail basis. As such, it only takes about a minute to read each student's paper and tabulate the responses. Using short in-class formative assessments that count toward the final grade has been shown to increase attendance (Butler, Phillmann, & Smart, 2001; Drabick, Weisberg, Paul, & Bubier, 2007). Formative assessments also allow the instructor to evaluate the efficacy of their instructional strategies and to make adjustments when necessary, as will be discussed further in Chapters 7 and 9.

2.4   Step 3: Creating Meaningful Learning Experiences in the Classroom

The final step in backward design is figuring out the best way to help your students achieve the course's LOs. In various chapters of this book, we offer practical advice about how best to help students learn to think critically, to work effectively with others, and to improve their writing, quantitative reasoning, information and scientific literacy, and study habits. The learning experiences described throughout follow the American Association of Higher Education (AAHE)'s Principles for Effective Undergraduate Education (see Box 2.4).

The creators of backward design (McTighe & Wiggins, 2012; Wiggins & McTighe, 2005) advocate dividing a course into smaller units, each with a cohesive theme and measurable learning outcomes. Backward design is then used to create these units, as well as the individual lesson plans within them. Ask yourself, "What do I want my students to be able to do by the end of the unit/class, and how will I know if they can?" Using this approach will increase the likelihood that you will meet your course LOs by deciding what to prioritize in any given class. This strategy helps to provide a convincing rationale for the class activities on a given day, which in turn is likely to increase student motivation; see Box 2.5 for the general framework of a student-centered lesson plan. It also makes overall course planning more manageable, by breaking it into concise steps that build toward the whole.

Surveying students' interests and skill levels at the start of a course (see Box 2.3, point I) is a culturally responsive strategy that fosters inclusivity and motivation (Ginsberg & Wlodkowski, 2009) and allows instructors to assess whether planned class activities are pitched at the appropriate level. Adjustments in instructional design can be made accordingly.

2.4.1   Pre-Class Preparation and Using Readings

In order for a student-centered classroom to work effectively, students need to prepare adequately before coming to class. This usually entails completing pre-assigned

---

Box 2.4 American Association of Higher Education (AAHE)'s Principles for Effective Undergraduate Education

"Good practice in undergraduate education:

1) Encourages contacts between students and faculty.
2) Develops reciprocity and cooperation among students.
3) Uses active learning techniques.
4) Gives prompt feedback.
5) Emphasizes time on task.
6) Communicates high expectations.
7) Respects diverse talents and ways of learning."

Source: Chickering and Gamson (1987, p. 2)

Box 2.5 General Framework for a Student-Centered Lesson Plan

Start–end times	Activity	Function
0 min	Welcome Relevant announcements	Establish rapport
3–5 min	Introduce the big picture Introduce LOs for class Describe how pre-class activities are relevant to today's class	Create interest
5–15 min	Background knowledge assessment	Reactivate prior knowledge needed for today's class Clear up any misunderstandings
15–55 min	Concept/skill exploration	Students work together and learn more deeply
55–70 min	Wrap-up Assessment of LOs	Formative assessment of LOs allows for modifications of next lesson

Source: Adapted from Sagendorf, Noyd, & Morris (2009).

---

homework, which might include watching a video, listening to a podcast, completing worksheets, or answering discussion questions, in addition to reading. Required written homework may serve as a formative assessment, allowing you to assess how effectively your students are engaging with course materials between classes. To the extent that students review course materials before coming to class, more of the class period can be spent deepening understanding rather than introducing basic materials for the first time (Mazur, 1997).

Despite this logic, data suggest that anywhere from 70 to 80% of students come to class without having done the assigned reading (Clump, Bauer, & Breadley, 2004; Hobson, 2004; Sikorski et al., 2002). There are several reasons for this. As many have pointed out, textbooks are expensive, and students often decide not to buy them, especially if they think they can do well enough in the course without them (Sikorski et al., 2002). Instructors who spend class time summarizing textbook information for their students help to foster this attitude (Hobson, 2004). Indeed, Sikorski and colleagues found that many students thought that taking and studying their notes (without reading the textbook) was the best predictor of whether they would do well in a class (Sikorski et al., 2002). However, even though students often *think* they can get by without reading the textbook, Landrum, Gurung, and Spann (2012) found that test scores were correlated with the amount of assigned reading students had actually completed.

Berry, Cook, Hill, and Stevens (2010) reported that even when students believed that reading would improve their performance in class, they often failed to do it. Others have suggested ways of increasing the likelihood that students will complete their out-of-class reading. Hobson (2004) suggested that students are more likely to read if instructors provide guiding questions that require written answers prior to coming to class. In-class quizzing has also generally been shown to increase reading compliance (Connor-Greene, 2000a; Marchant, 2002; Ruscio, 2001). Spending class time helping students to develop reading strategies (e.g., by introducing techniques such as SQ3R— survey, question, read, recite, review) also increases the likelihood that when students actually read their textbook, they will process the information at a deeper level (Johnson & Carton, 2006).

2.4.2 Selecting a Textbook

You should check with your department to see if there is a required textbook for the course you are going to teach; some departments have a committee of instructors who decide whether a particular book should be used by all sections of a specific course. This is usually done in an attempt to standardize content coverage, and in some cases might defray costs to students if a special deal has been negotiated with the publisher. If you are free to choose the textbook by yourself, the choices may seem overwhelming. Your decision can be guided by consulting with more experienced colleagues about books they particularly like or dislike (and why). Most publisher websites have a portal for each of their books that allows you to electronically request a free review copy. Alternatively, with the assistance of your department, you could contact the publisher representative for your campus directly. Many textbooks come packaged with a host of instructor resources, such as banks of test questions and associated software for creating tests, video clips, PowerPoint slides containing text and figures from the book, suggestions for active learning activities, and lesson plans. Be mindful that publisher-provided materials often are not student-centered. We would caution against wholesale adoption of publisher-created content, as it may not match with your LOs. When requesting review copies of textbooks, be sure to explore what resources are available for student and instructor use, and use what works for your course.

When choosing a textbook, research has shown that students are more likely to use one if it is easy to read, contains study aids and chapter reviews, and, perhaps most importantly, is actually used by the instructor (Gurung & Martin, 2011). Students have been shown to prefer books that show the applicability of theories to real life, are accessible, contain graphs and tables (Gurung & Martin, 2011), and use a narrative format (Fernald, 1989). However, as Hobson (2004) has pointed out, students are often too over-scheduled to read lengthy textbook chapters, especially when the content is difficult, and so are more likely to comply if readings are concise. For this reason, some instructors, such as Johnson and Carton (2006), have argued against using large comprehensive textbooks in Introductory Psychology in favor of shorter texts, such as Hock's *Forty Studies that Changed Psychology* (Hock, 2012). In recognition of this problem, several textbooks now have editions in which chapters are broken down into smaller, more manageable modules.

Increasingly, textbooks are bundled with access to a publisher's learning platform (e.g., WileyPlus, Connect, Launchpad, MindTap, MyLab Psychology, PsychInquiry); these platforms are somewhat similar to an institutional course management system (CMS) in that they provide an online portal for course materials. The intention is for the instructor to assign the various multimedia elements embedded within the platform (e.g., e-book chapters, video clips, mini-experiments, multiple-choice quizzes, short-answer questions) as online homework. Such platforms are especially useful for online and hybrid teaching (see Chapter 8) because they keep track of student progress, often with minimal grading effort on the part of the instructor. In many (but not all) cases, the platforms can be integrated with the institution's CMS, making their use more seamless. Publishers may offer training on how to use their specific platform or have personnel who can troubleshoot with instructors who are learning the ropes.

One caveat is that requiring students to use these non-institutional platforms means that everyone needs to purchase access at the beginning of the semester and must have access to a computer with reliable and fast Internet service. In Chapter 1, we emphasize the diversity among today's undergraduates; some may find it a hardship to meet these requirements, or may not have access to financial aid at the start of the semester. If this is likely to be the case at your institution, it is possible that the publisher may grant special access for a limited amount of time for some students, but this needs to be arranged in advance.

As recognized by the Higher Education Opportunity Act (HEOA), signed into law in 2008, the cost of a textbook (and other course materials) is an important consideration for many students. To help increase transparency and to reduce the cost of textbooks, it is a legal requirement that students have access to information about which textbooks (and other materials, such as clickers) are required or recommended before they enroll in a course. This information is typically made available through the college bookstore, and so it is important to meet college deadlines for book orders in order to comply with this law. Students do not have to buy their textbooks from college bookstores, but they can use them to access information about ISBNs and pricing options. Providing this information well in advance gives them time to hunt down the cheapest option or to find a format that is accessible (e.g., for students with visual impairments). It also increases the likelihood that students will have the book on the first day of class.

To cut costs even further, you might also consider using open educational resources (OERs), which can be downloaded from the Internet free of charge. The NOBA project (nobaproject.com) provides a growing number of free online textbook chapters, often written by prominent psychologists, along with instructor resources. NOBA chapters can be compiled into custom e-books and printed very inexpensively. Alternatively, if you find a textbook that you really like, then consider whether an earlier edition could be used, as these are likely to be much cheaper and more readily available in the second-hand market. As a result of the HEOA, if you enquire about a book, publishers are legally obliged to provide information about the past three editions, including prices and information about any substantive changes. Also, new textbooks are typically available in multiple different types of binding and at different prices, including e-books, loose-leaf binder versions, and rentals. It is helpful to provide information in your syllabus about the various options students have for buying the textbook (e.g., renting versus buying, ISBNs, and approximate costs). Post this information prior to the start of the course to give students enough time to shop around before the first week of classes.

Finally, although textbooks are commonly assigned in psychology courses, it is sometimes difficult to find a good fit, and often much of the book is underused (Landrum, 2012). One way to increase the utility of the textbook is to create writing assignments in which students must support claims using evidence (for examples, see Nevid, Pastva, & McClelland, 2012; Soysa, Dunn, Dottolo, Burns-Glover, & Gurung, 2013) from sections that might otherwise go unread. If much of the book is still likely to be unused, then assigning individual readings is probably a better option. Pitching the readings at the appropriate developmental level will increase compliance; for instance, most undergraduates struggle to read primary source articles without considerable guided instruction (see Section 6.2 on Strategies for Teaching Reading and Writing), and so it may be better initially to assign articles from other sources, such as *Scientific American*. Articles in *Current Directions in Psychological Science* are also pitched at an appropriate level for undergraduates (Zehr, 1998), and the journal *Teaching Current Directions in Psychological Science* provides suggestions for learning activities for some of these (https://www.psychologicalscience.org/publications/teaching-current-directions), which may be helpful for lesson planning. As you help students to develop the skills they need to read academic articles, you can introduce other sources.

2.5   Universal Design

Chickering and Gamson (1987) stress that effective educational practices respect diversity among students. This principle is increasingly important in today's classroom. In Chapter 1, we provided compelling evidence that today's college students reflect unprecedented diversity. Of particular note are the increasing numbers of "at-risk" students now enrolling in college. Some of these students have disabilities that impact their learning, and others may be underprepared for college by virtue of their previous educational experiences. As we pointed out in Chapter 1, at-risk students are especially challenged when it comes to succeeding in traditional teacher-centered classes. Whereas in K–12 settings it is the responsibility of the staff and faculty to identify and support students with disabilities, college students have to self-advocate for accommodations, which are usually granted by a campus Center for Student Accessibility. Requesting accommodations is daunting for many students, especially if they feel stigmatized (Ketterlin-Geller & Johnstone, 2006) or lack self-efficacy skills (Scott, Mcguire, & Shaw, 2003). Perhaps not surprisingly, several studies have shown that the vast majority of college students choose not to disclose their disabilities (Schelly, Davies, & Spooner, 2011; Wagner, Newman, Cameto, Garza, & Levine, 2005). Furthermore, when students with hard-to-diagnose cognitive difficulties do seek accommodations for learning disabilities (LDs), they are often not granted any accommodations (Ketterlin-Geller & Johnstone, 2006). An alternative way of improving the learning environment to better support at-risk students is to use Universal Design (UD).

UD principles were initially developed in the fields of architecture and design, in order to create widely accessible physical environments and products (Connell et al., 1997). They have since been adapted to create various models of UD for educational contexts (Burgstahler, 2001, 2015; Higbee, 2003; Rose, Harbour, Johnston, Daley, & Abarbanell, 2006; Rose & Meyer, 2002; Scott et al., 2003). UD models encourage instructors to build the accommodations that students typically seek directly into the curriculum. This particularly ensures that at-risk students are supported in their learning, but all students benefit from these pedagogical enhancements (Silver, Bourke, & Strehorn, 1998).

The HEOA specifically mentions the need for training and implementation of one specific UD model, Universal Design for Learning (UDL) (Rose et al., 2006; Rose & Meyer, 2002), to help remove barriers to learning for all students, including those with disabilities or limited English proficiency. UDL is based on three broad guiding principles: providing multiple means of representation, action and expression, and student engagement. Box 2.6 lays out the basic framework. The Center for Applied Special Technology (CAST) website provides many helpful resources for applying the UDL framework to college courses (http://udloncampus.cast.org/).

Box 2.6 Basic Framework of Universal Design for Learning (UDL)

I) **Representation:**
- Present information in a variety of perceptual modalities.
- Provide or teach in advance any required information/skills (e.g., vocabulary, how to read a graph, meaning of symbols).
- Enhance comprehension in multiple ways, by reactivating background knowledge, highlighting the big picture, summarizing the main ideas, encouraging metacognitive strategies through use of scaffolding, and providing best practices for learning.

II) **Action and expression:**
- Ensure that the physical environment in which students learn can be adapted to accommodate students with motor difficulties (e.g., with mouse or keyboard use).
- Use multimedia assignments to allow students to communicate their ideas.
- Provide tools to enhance student communication, such as spell and grammar checks.
- Use a variety of examples to model products or skills.
- Use scaffolding, rubrics, and checklists to ensure that students develop good planning skills.
- Promote self-regulation and reflection about learning.

III) **Student engagement:**
- Help students to set personal goals.
- Allow choice and autonomy, when possible.
- Create a supportive, non-threatening environment.
- Make clear connections between content and goals.
- Use authentic assignments that resonate with students' interests/real life.
- Use scaffolding to help students sustain effort.
- Foster collaboration and community.

Source: Adapted from the Universal Design for Learning Guidelines (CAST, 2018)

UDL is similar to other UD models in that it advocates for flexibility (including the use of technology) to enhance accessibility and reduce obstacles to learning, and emphasizes that there should be variety in the types of learning experience offered, as well as in the kinds of assessment used to evaluate what students have learned. In a similar manner to backward design (McTighe & Wiggins, 2012; Wiggins & McTighe, 2005), UD models stress the need for clearly articulated goals that align with assessment and curricular activities, and for students to have opportunities to learn from their mistakes by allowing them to revise their work or to practice without penalty. UD also requires instructors to create inclusive, supportive environments in the classroom and to foster the development of interpersonal relationships among students and between students and teachers. The CAST team has suggested that it is better for instructors to examine and fix the "disabilities in the curriculum" than to focus on and try to "fix" the disabilities of their students. For example, one common accommodation for students with LDs is to provide extra time on exams, but designing exams that allow ample time for students to demonstrate what they know, rather than how quickly they can remember it or write it down, is advantageous to everyone in the class.

Providing course materials electronically via a CMS (e.g., syllabus, readings, notes, assignments) makes it easier for students who struggle with print-based formats to customize the materials for their individual perceptual needs (e.g., by increasing text size, reversing the contrast of the text, or interfacing with an assistive device). However, all digital materials and technologies should follow the Web Content Accessibility Guidelines (WCAG) 2.0, developed by the World Wide Web Consortium (W3C) Level AA, to ensure that they are truly accessible.

Research on using UD in college courses is somewhat limited, but preliminary studies suggest that it is associated with higher student ratings (Davies, Schelly, & Spooner, 2013; Schelly et al., 2011) and improved grades, and with fewer course withdrawals among students with LDs (Scott & Edwards, 2012). In addition, the UDL website, http://www.udlcenter.org/research/researchevidence/, cites multiple studies (mostly in K–12 settings) demonstrating that using various principles from within the UDL framework enhances learning. For additional resources on implementing UD in your classes, see http://udloncampus.cast.org/page/media_oer_creating#.V2mI9hIkmVo and http://www.washington.edu/accessibility/checklist/.

We want to stress again that using UDL in your classes benefits all students, not only those who struggle in college. The provision of scaffolded instruction is designed to level the playing field, but this does not mean that the curriculum is "dumbed down." Rather, it simply ensures that students have the skills they need to engage in challenging authentic assignments that resonate with their interests (see Haggis, 2006 for a similar viewpoint). When instructors from multiple sections of Introductory Psychology were given UDL training partway through the semester, survey data showed that their students felt more challenged by meaningful assignments after the training had taken place (Schelly et al., 2011). Similarly, in a follow-up study across several different psychology courses, students who were taught by instructors trained in UDL reported engaging in more active learning (Davies et al., 2013).

2.5.1 Should Instruction Be Tailored to Students' Preferred Learning Styles?

We have emphasized that individual students vary in terms of their strengths and in the challenges that they face, and that it is important to use a variety of teaching methods, assignments, and assessments to support your students. However, we wish to be clear that we are not advocating that different people have different learning styles and that each student requires an individualized learning plan. Although the belief that people have a preferred modality for learning (e.g., visual, auditory, or kinesthetic) is widespread even among teachers, there is little scientific evidence to support learning-style theories (for reviews, see Newton, 2015; Willingham, Hughes, & Dobolyi, 2015). Despite a great deal of research on the subject of learning styles, there is a lack of empirical support for the "meshing hypothesis": that tailoring instruction to individual students' preferred modalities enhances their learning. Specifically, research has failed to demonstrate aptitude × treatment interactions, where students with one learning style (e.g., visual) exhibit better learning outcomes with one type of instruction while students with a different learning style (e.g., auditory) fare better with a different type (Pashler, McDaniel, Rohrer, & Bjork, 2008).

Gardner's research on multiple intelligences has often been misinterpreted as evidence that different learning styles exist, but having an ability in one domain (e.g., being good at math) does not mean that working in that domain ("thinking mathematically") will benefit learning in others (Gardner, 2013; Willingham et al., 2015). Instead, different types of information call for different learning strategies and skill sets, such as visual-spatial processing for neuroanatomy, logical reasoning for research methods, and interpersonal skills for learning how to interview someone. In general, pluralistic approaches that emphasize multimodal learning increase the likelihood of greater understanding and learning for all students (Gardner, 2013).

2.6   Creating a Syllabus

When using backward design to create a student-centered course, it is important to communicate your goals, assessment strategies, and course structure to students, so that they understand what is expected of them and why. This information should be clearly conveyed through the course syllabus, which serves as an important reference document for students to use when you are unavailable to answer questions, when they are seeking to transfer credits, or when they are disputing a grade.

The course syllabus also provides an initial opportunity for instructors to generate excitement and motivation for the course and to build rapport with their students (Bain, 2011). Telling students what they will get out of the course and being explicit about how this will occur is likely to increase their motivation (Bain, 2011). We highly encourage you to go over the syllabus during class time, to allow your students opportunities to ask questions; indeed, a review of outstanding instructors found that this was a common activity on the first day of class (Iannarelli, Bardsley, & Foote, 2010; see Chapter 1 for more about first-day-of-class tactics). Syllabi that are well organized and worded in a positive way tend to create a favorable first impression. Tone is particularly important to students; Ishiyama and Hartlaub (2002) found that first- and second-year students were more likely to perceive the instructor as approachable if encouraging language was present in the syllabus. So, in general, try to use rewarding rather than punitive language (e.g., "Attendance will enhance your learning in this course and will boost your attendance grade," rather than "You will be penalized if you do not attend; points will be deducted from your participation grade"). Also, explicitly state what students can expect of you—alongside what you expect of them—and emphasize that you understand that the course will be demanding but that "you are willing and available to meet and assist students outside of class." This increases the likelihood that students will actually seek help (Perrine, Lisle, & Tucker, 1995; Richmond, Boysen, & Gurung, 2016).

Many colleges have templates for model syllabi that outline the standard information that should be present on the syllabus (see Appendix 2.A for the checklist we have assembled based on the requirements of various colleges within our institution, City University of New York [CUNY]). Colleges usually require that syllabi include the official course description from the college bulletin, but this may be very brief, formal, and/or non-comprehensive, so consider adding a short description of your "take" on the class that highlights the content you will cover and which reflects your student-centered approach to teaching. Ask your faculty colleagues to share their successful syllabi with you—but bear in mind that studies reviewing large numbers of syllabi have typically found the majority lack many essential elements (Habanek, 2005; Newton, Eberly, & Wiggins, 2001; Parkes, Fix, & Harris, 2003).

Project Syllabus, available at http://teachpsych.org/otrp/syllabi/index.php, provides a repository of syllabi that are considered exemplary by the Society for the Teaching of Psychology (STP). Of particular help when constructing a syllabus is the rubric used by the Project Syllabus committee for syllabus evaluation. We have modified this rubric for students in our Teaching of Psychology class (see Box 2.7), placing greater emphasis on student-centered instruction, which is consistent with the philosophy that we espouse in this book.

Box 2.7 Rubric for Syllabus Design

Grading rubric for course syllabus	Absent	Present	Strong	Very Strong	Score	Possible points
1) Backward design						
Unambiguous and measurable learning objectives (LOs)						6
LOs go beyond content knowledge, i.e., span APA Big 5						8
LOs are connected to assignments/assessments, etc.						6
Backward design total score						**20**
2) Evidence of student-centered approach						
Shows how discussion is used in class or online						6
Shows use of interactive activities to promote critical thinking (CT)						8
Indicates students have opportunities to collaborate						6
Incorporates writing and public speaking						8
Shows that students are required to apply course content to real-world issues						6
Provides creative learning opportunities and teaching methods						6
Student-centered approach total score						**40**
3) Student support						
Uses positive language and encouragement						6
Provides strategies for success						6
Clearly communicates attainable, developmentally appropriate expectations						6
Supports learning through varied assignments and teaching approaches						6
Provides evidence of scaffolding complex assignments/projects in course calendar						6
Student support total score						**30**
4) Organization and basic information						
Basic syllabus info present (checklist)						2
Clear course policies, e.g., lateness, absences						2
Explicit grading systems						2
Easy-to-read course calendar						2
All information attractive and readable						2
Organization total score						**10**
				GRADE		**100**

O'Brien, Millis, and Cohen (2008) provide many excellent examples of various elements of a student-centered syllabus. They emphasize that the syllabus should set up the expectation that students will be responsible for their own learning, while at the same time conveying an understanding of students' needs by providing strategies and resources to increase the likelihood of success. To this end, the syllabus should include information about resources such as tutoring services, the library, the writing center, and the counseling center. Although we strongly recommend the use of UD in course design, the syllabus should, at a minimum, provide information about seeking accommodations to facilitate learning by providing information about the Center for Student Accessibility on your campus. Furthermore, because students have to actively seek accommodations for themselves, the syllabus should use a supportive and respectful tone in advising them to advocate for their rights. From a UD perspective, it is important to provide electronic copies (usually via a CMS). This practice benefits those who may need to access the information in a different format, and provides all students with quick and easy access to the document for the duration of the course.

When planning out the course calendar, it is vital to make sure that sufficient classroom time is devoted to practicing and building important skills that will be needed to complete complex assignments. Also, formative assessment will only enhance learning if enough time is left between assignments for instructors to provide feedback and for students to incorporate this in their revision or next assignment. You should not feel compelled to introduce topics in the same order as they appear in your textbook. The textbook is a resource, not the foundational structure of your course. For example, when teaching Introductory Psychology, it may be more helpful to your students to begin the course by teaching them how to learn than to start with the more abstract and difficult topics, such as the history and systems of psychology, the biological basis of psychology, or research methods.

Studies have shown that faculty and students frequently have different perceptions about the most important elements of a syllabus. Garavalia, Hummel, Wiley, and Huitt (2000) found that both faculty and students agreed that a syllabus should be comprehensive and clear in describing the expectations for a course. Indeed, Serafin (1990) found students did better on final exams if the LOs were comprehensive. From an administrative point of view, a detailed syllabus is useful in allowing departments to assess whether or not a course is transferrable from one institution to another (Garavalia et al., 2000), as well as for assessment and accreditation purposes (Parkes & Harris, 2002). Although the syllabus is often considered to be a form of quasi-contract (Parkes & Harris, 2002), Garavalia and colleagues found that both students and faculty felt that it should be flexible in nature so that changes could be made to it over the course of the semester. Therefore, it is important to include a statement that acknowledges the syllabus is subject to change (Garavalia et al., 2000). Two more recent studies have shown that students pay particular attention to dates and details of exams, quizzes, and assignments (Calhoon & Becker, 2008; Marcis & Carr, 2004). The provision of explicit grading policies and expectations allows students to understand what is expected of them and is important in the event that a student disputes a grade.

We have found that students in our Teaching of Psychology class often struggle with creating student-centered grading schemes that both assess course LOs and motivate their students to engage in the *process* of effective learning by rewarding them for their low-stakes work. There is no "one-size-fits-all" grading scheme; they will vary from course to course, depending on the LOs and assignments, and on the level of the students. However, to try and help instructors with this process, we have provided some examples in Box 2.8, all of which have multiple elements that contribute to the final grade.

Finally, syllabi provide a permanent record of teaching. With experience, you should expect your syllabus to change as you figure out how best to teach your courses. The evolution of a course syllabus can then provide excellent documentation of the ways in which you have used student feedback and assessment data to improve your course (Richmond et al., 2014, see also Section 9.7 on Developing a Teaching Portfolio).

Box 2.8 Examples of Course Grading Schemes at Various Course Levels

Introductory Psychology (entry-level course)
1. In-class assignments	15%
2. Posts to online discussion and study guides	15%
3. Tests ×3 (15% each)	45%
4. Group presentation	10%

Breakdown: Instructor grade (5%); Peer grade (5%)
5. Wikipedia editing	15%

Breakdown: Training (5%); Initial edits (5%); Revision/upload (5%)

Brain and Behavior (intermediate-level course)
1. In-class assignments	10%
2. Weekly online quiz homework (can redo for max points)	10%
3. Tests ×4 (10% each)	40%
4. Writing assignments	40%

Using primary sources to understand research methods
Breakdown: Note-taking assignments (8%); Database search (6%); Summary (10%)
Using secondary sources to create a webpage (wiki)
Breakdown: Evaluating websites (4%); Wiki (12%)

Psychology of Race (upper-level course)
1. In-class discussion and written reflections	15%
2. Journal (10 entries × 1.5%)	15%
3. Tests ×2 (15% each)	30%
4. Compare and contrast controversial issue paper	15%

Breakdown: First draft (5%); Final draft (10%)
5. Applying theories—interview or media analysis	25%

Breakdown: First draft (5%); Final draft (20%)

Research Methods (upper-level course)
1. Tests ×2 (10% each)	20%
2. Human subject's certification	5%
3. APA format assignment	5%
4. Website article evaluation	5%
5. Database search	5%
6. Journal article evaluation	5%
7. Annotated bibliography	5%
8. Introduction	10%
9. Method and results	10%
10. Discussion	10%
11. Research presentation	10%
12. Final research paper	10%

2.7 Interim and Post-Course Reflection and Student Evaluation: How Is it Going?

Although much of this chapter has focused on assessment of students, inevitably most instructors want to assess the effectiveness of their own teaching; after all, good teaching is evidence-based. Research has shown that when instructors self-assess, they are just as prone to the "better-than-average effect" (Alicke, Klotz, Breitenbecher, Yurak, & Vredenburg, 1995) as anyone else. In fact, Cross (1977) found that 94% of faculty surveyed rated themselves as better than their peers. So, what are more objective ways of ascertaining whether we are effective teachers? When the STP charged a task force to identify multiple characteristics of model teachers, the task force concluded that model teachers use varied instructional methods that encourage active learning and provide opportunities for students to practice and develop foundational skills, including information literacy, communication, and critical thinking (CT) (Richmond et al., 2014, 2016). In addition, model teachers establish rapport, respect, and positive regard toward their students and build the students' appreciation for values of good citizenship, including respect for ethics and diversity (Richmond et al., 2016); they use clear and measurable LOs; and they collect data to evaluate whether students attain the LOs and use these to make adjustments in their course planning in order to improve their effectiveness as teachers (Richmond et al., 2014). Model teachers use feedback from student evaluations of teaching (SETs) and peer classroom observations to improve their lesson plans and document evidence of changes in their syllabi and curriculum in response to prior experiences/assessments (Richmond et al., 2014). They also engage in professional development to maintain current knowledge about effective pedagogy and share the results of their own assessments with peers (see also Chapter 9).

Fortunately, in many institutions, senior colleagues are willing and able to provide constructive criticism based on a review of the course syllabus and/or classroom observation. But perhaps the most ubiquitous type of teaching assessment comes from formal SETs that are administered near or at the end of the course. There is a considerable amount of controversy as to whether these assessments are valid measures of teaching effectiveness; some have suggested that they encourage instructors to focus on student entertainment as opposed to learning, and contribute to grade inflation (Stroebe, 2016). Indeed, analyses of data from ratemyprofessors.com have shown that ratings for overall quality, helpfulness, and clarity are higher for instructors who are rated as "hot" compared to those who do not receive the "hot" rating (Silva et al., 2008). However, because these data reflect the opinions of only a small proportion of students in any one class, institutional surveys are more likely to be more reliable. In general, one might expect instructors with better SET ratings to be more effective instructors, as student–faculty rapport is a key predictor of learning outcomes (Wilson & Ryan, 2013). Although some meta-analyses have reported positive correlations between student learning gains and SET ratings (e.g., Clayson, 2009; Cohen, 1981), a re-analysis by Uttl, White, and Gonzalez (2017) revealed this to be an artifact of small sample studies. In their more carefully controlled meta-analysis of over 90 studies, Uttl, White, and Gonzalez (2017) found no relationship between SET and student learning. Thus, SETs are likely to reflect *perceptions* of student learning rather than learning per se, and should be used accordingly.

Unfortunately, formal end-of-course SETs are often treated as summative assessments and used to make high-stakes administrative decisions about reappointment, tenure, and promotion. But SETs can also be considered formative assessments if an instructor makes changes in their pedagogy or curriculum in response to the feedback. However, there are some further disadvantages to using SETs as the sole source for instructional change. Because they are costly when administered in paper format, instructors often have to wait long periods before receiving the feedback, and so it may not be possible to make adjustments in a timely fashion (Adams & Umbach, 2012). To address this concern, online administration of SETs is becoming increasingly popular (Adams & Umbach, 2012). However, response rates are typically much lower when SETs are administered online. Studies have reported that although overall instructor ratings seem to be comparable (Stowell, Addison, & Smith, 2012), there is about a 20% decrease in response rates with Web-based systems (Adams & Umbach, 2012; Avery, Bryant, Mathios, Kang, & Bell, 2006; Stowell et al., 2012). Furthermore, these online SETs may be less representative than those in paper format; students with lower grades are the least likely to complete online SETs (Adams & Umbach, 2012; Avery et al., 2006). Finally, SETs may have limited value as a formative assessment if the questions fail to keep up with recent changes in best practices for learning. Often, students are asked to evaluate behaviors that are typical of a teacher-centered classroom, as assessed through items such as "The instructor provides clear lectures," as opposed to behaviors reflective of a student-centered approach, such as "The instructor creates assignments that help me to learn."

In view of all these limitations, administering your own formative assessments (see Box 2.3) at regular intervals during the course will assist you in evaluating how your teaching is going. These will impact your current class of students if you make adjustments that are responsive to their comments. An advantage of formative feedback is that you are not limited to the questions that are on the formal student evaluation form. One of the simplest ways of having students give feedback on your teaching is to ask them to describe one thing that you could do differently that would improve their learning in your class (Angelo & Cross, 1993). To make sure you also receive reinforcement for good pedagogical practices, also ask your students to tell you what you do that helps them to learn. To encourage honesty, this information should be collected anonymously, such as by having students write their responses on an index card without giving their name. Formative assessments are often administered at the mid-point of a course (frequently referred to as mid-semester evaluations [MSEs]), but they are also particularly helpful when you try a new activity, technique, or demonstration and you want to know whether the students thought that it influenced their learning in a positive way. Performing formative assessment of the course helps students to appreciate that you are invested in their learning (Brown, 2008), especially if you share your analyses with them and explain how and why you are changing some aspect of the course or your method of teaching (Keutzer, 1993b; Lewis, 2001). Consulting with other, more experienced instructors or with the Teaching and Learning Center (TLC) at your college may help you to use this feedback to your best advantage. Formative assessment therefore allows you to improve as a teacher (Diamond, 2004; Keutzer, 1993b; Lewis, 2001); as such, it should also lead to better summative formal course evaluations at the end of the term. If, despite your best attempts, your final course evaluations suggest that there is room for improvement, using this feedback to improve future courses is likely to be viewed in a favorable light by personnel committees and others who are assessing the quality of your teaching (Halonen, Dunn, McCarthy, & Baker, 2012; Richmond et al., 2014; see also Section 9.7 on Developing a Teaching Portfolio).

2.8   Summary

1) Well-designed courses are based on backward design. First, decide what you want your students to be able to do, what you want them to know, and how you want them to be different by the end of the course. Next, decide how you will assess whether they have reached these objectives. Finally, plan your course of instruction to help students attain these goals.

2) Effective learning occurs when students are actively engaged in meaningful experiences.

3) Students should be challenged but supported in their learning, using Universal Design principles.

4) Frequent formative assessment allows you to evaluate your students' progress and the efficacy of your instruction.

2.A   Syllabus Checklist

Information	Did you include it?
1) Instructor's name and contact information (include college email address)	
2) Instructor's office location and regular office hours	
3) Title of course, course and section numbers	
4) Semester, year, day, time, and classroom location of course	
5) College name and address	
6) Course description *exactly* as listed in the Undergraduate College Bulletin/Catalog, and Course Prerequisites	
7) Measurable course learning objectives (LOs), spanning the APA "BIG FIVE"	
8) Description of assignments/assessments and how they link to the LOs	
9) Grading and evaluation criteria, spelled out clearly, including the number of tests, other graded assignments, and weights to calculate final grade	
10) Required texts (in APA format) and other instructional materials (e.g., clickers)	
11) ISBNs and prices (new) of textbooks	
12) Attendance and lateness policy, and its relation to grades	
13) Reference to College Academic Integrity Policies. Note: If you plan to use anti-plagiarism software (e.g., Turnitin, SafeAssign), this should be stated on the syllabus	
14) Reference to College Accessibility Policies and information about the Center of Student Accessibility	
15) Week/class course calendar, with a general description of what will happen in class every week and when assignments are due	
16) Exact date and time of final exam (always during finals week); leave a place marker if this is to be announced by the college or department	

3

Effective Multimedia Instruction

In this chapter, we describe how multimedia can be used to foster student-centered learning. Technological changes are occurring rapidly, so we have tried to focus on the pedagogical basis of using technology rather than the use of specific systems, which are likely to change. In the following sections, we provide evidence for best practices in multimedia instruction. As you incorporate technology into your teaching, we strongly recommend that you test it out in advance of class to make sure that it works and to troubleshoot any problems. Also, it is prudent to have a back-up plan for the rare occasion when classroom technology fails and you are waiting for help or the problem cannot be resolved quickly.

3.1   Use (and Abuse) of PowerPoint (PPT) in Higher Education

The widespread availability of computer-linked LCD projection systems in college classrooms has led to the ubiquitous use of Microsoft PowerPoint (PPT) or other similar slideware to deliver lectures (Hill, Arford, Lubitow, & Smollin, 2012). This practice may be promoted in part by the almost universal availability of publishers' textbook-related slideshows (Jordan & Papp, 2013). Students have reported preferring slideware-supported lectures to more traditional lecture formats (for review, see Berk, 2011), although there is some evidence that the tides are turning. Recently, there have been complaints of "death by PowerPoint" at many colleges; students increasingly associate heavy reliance on PPT with reduced student–instructor interaction and less discussion (Hill et al., 2012)— two vital elements of student-centered instruction. Throughout this book, we provide evidence that active participation is more effective for learning than passive listening (Freeman et al., 2014), and we seek to promote the idea that teaching is not presenting. Therefore, we urge you to carefully consider *how* you use slideware in your classes.

As Daniel (2011) points out, PPT was originally designed for *presenting* information to peers, not for teaching. Publisher-produced slideshows are typically packed with slides; when considering whether to adopt these materials (see also Section 2.4.2 on Selecting a Textbook), it is crucial to be mindful of students' limited capacity to pay attention for extended periods of time. Difficulties in maintaining attention may be exacerbated when information is unfamiliar and complex (Risko, Anderson, Sarwal,

Teaching Psychology: An Evidence-Based Approach, First Edition. Jillian Grose-Fifer, Patricia J. Brooks, and Maureen O'Connor.
© 2019 John Wiley & Sons, Inc. Published 2019 by John Wiley & Sons, Inc.
Companion website: www.wiley.com/go/Grose-Fifer/teaching-psychology

Engelhardt, & Kingstone, 2012; Van Merrienboer & Sweller, 2005) or when instructors do not follow best practices for multimedia presentations (see Section 3.1.1). For example, instructors may read from the slides instead of explaining concepts using diagrams and graphics, or there may be too many words packed on to each slide—making it nearly impossible for students to simultaneously read them *and* pay attention to what the instructor is saying. Perhaps, then, it is not surprising that studies have shown that slide use in lectures does not enhance learning (Jordan & Papp, 2013; Levasseur & Kanan Sawyer, 2006; Worthington & Levasseur, 2015); learning gains have only been shown when students have access to the slides before or after class, presumably because it helps them engage more actively with course materials outside of class (Jordan & Papp, 2013; Levasseur & Kanan Sawyer, 2006; Worthington & Levasseur, 2015).

In general, students report liking PPT presentations because they feel that they help to highlight the key points in a lecture (Hill et al., 2012; Levasseur & Kanan Sawyer, 2006). This perception could be misleading, however. Critics of PPT lectures have suggested that using traditional bulleted slides with general headings (such as those provided by textbook publishers) tends to oversimplify information, and because it is difficult to show interconnections between concepts, instructors tend to approach topics in a linear rather than an integrative fashion (Adams, 2006; Alley, Schreiber, Ramsdell, & Muffo, 2006; Levasseur & Kanan Sawyer, 2006; Tufte, 2006). Indeed, this simplification may be why students perceive PPT lectures to be better organized than traditional lectures (Hill et al., 2012; Levasseur & Kanan Sawyer, 2006). A possible solution to the linearity issue is to use Prezi instead of PPT. Prezi is a free Web-based presentation program in which items are placed on a large canvas in a similar way to a concept map (Novak & Gowin, 1984; Strasser, 2014); the user can then zoom in to highlight individual items at different time points (Conboy, Fletcher, Russell, & Wilson, 2012). This allows the audience to see how concepts are interconnected and facilitates the conceptualization of hierarchical or other organizational relationships.

Prezi has only been available since 2009, and its efficacy has not yet been widely assessed in educational settings. Preliminary research suggests that students view Prezi favorably and perceive Prezi presentations to be more attention-grabbing and interactive than those using PPT (Conboy et al., 2012; Virtanen, Myllärniemi, & Wallander, 2012). It is not clear whether this preference is driven by differences in presentation format, Prezi's relative novelty, or the likelihood that instructors who use Prezi are generally more innovative in their teaching methods than those who do not (Conboy et al., 2012). The pan and zoom features of the Prezi software help to focus attention on what is important at a given moment. Additionally, Prezi has more of a graphics-focus than PPT, and so reduces the tendency to produce poorly designed text-heavy presentations. On the downside, excessive zooming can make students feel nauseous or dizzy (Conboy et al., 2012), so this feature should be used with care. Also, Prezi tends to crash more frequently than PPT, perhaps in part because it is reliant on the quality of the Internet connection (Conboy et al., 2012).

3.1.1 Best Practices for Slideware and Other Multimedia Presentations in the Classroom

Giving lengthy lectures is not an effective teaching method, but using a handful of slides *is* useful for presenting pictorial representations of organizational charts or anatomical diagrams, graphical representations of datasets and research findings, or animations that help clarify complex psychological processes. Under these circumstances, student learning is maximized if research-based principles for multimedia instruction are followed (for review, see Mayer, 2014a, 2014b). Research (conducted mostly on college students in laboratory settings using brief presentations) shows that people learn better from a combination of spoken words and pictures than from spoken words or pictures alone (Mayer, 2014a). This phenomenon is explained by dual-coding theory, which posits that the brain processes verbal and visual information in separate channels, each of which has limited capacity (Paivio, 1991). Hence, it is easy to overload the verbal channel if poorly designed slides are loaded with text, especially if you are trying to explain something out loud at the same time. Moreover, information overload is even more likely when students have little prior knowledge of the subject area, because their working memories are already taxed by the novelty of the material (Kosslyn, 2007; Sweller, 1988). Mental representations of concepts are more easily generated when verbal and visual channels provide complementary information, such as when explaining a concept verbally using a figure or a diagram (with minimal text) that helps to illustrate the point.

Mayer's cognitive theory of multimedia learning acknowledges the limits of working memory and emphasizes simplicity when using multimedia (Mayer & Moreno, 2003; see also Brunken, Plass, & Leutner, 2003). Box 3.1 provides evidence-based best-practice principles for multimedia design (for review, see Mayer, 2014b), while Box 3.2 provides complementary suggestions for slide design based on empirical research in sensation and perception (Kosslyn, 2007) and slideware use in classroom settings (Berk, 2011; Holzl, 1997).

Box 3.1 Best Practices for Multimedia Design

A) **To reduce interference from extraneous information and reduce cognitive load:**
   1) *Increase coherence* by removing irrelevant images (logos, etc.) and text.
   2) *Decrease redundancy* by minimizing text and not reading it aloud; instead, elaborate upon it.
   3) *Increase contiguity* by organizing any text so that it appears both next to, and at the same time as any related graphic.
   4) *Signal important information* using a different color, font, or text style.

B) **To help focus on relevant information:**
   1) *Segment* concepts into manageable chunks.
   2) *Pre-train* by exposing students to key terms and explaining how to interpret tables and graphs.
   3) Spread cognitive load across modalities by explaining graphics/animations instead of using text (some text can be helpful for technical terms or for students for whom English is a second language).

C) **To motivate students to process information generatively (at a deep level):**
   1) *Use informal conversational style and personalize* information—e.g., "The cornea is the transparent curved surface at the front of *your* eye."
   2) *Make eye contact* with your audience as you explain materials on slides.

Source: Adapted from Mayer (2014b).

Box 3.2 Further Suggestions for Effective Slideware Presentations

- Minimize text: pictures are more effective than words
- Use high contrast to prevent having to use reduced lighting and the possibility of inducing sleep
- Make sure slides contain no more than four items
- Consider adding illustrative (but not decorative) animation to visuals to enhance understanding
- If you must use text:
  - Use simple, easy-to-read fonts
  - Don't use all CAPITAL LETTERS
- Check that the text is legible from the back of the room (a minimum of 20–28 point font), depending on the size of the class

Source: Adapted from Berk (2011) and Holzl (1997).

When creating a slideshow, first remember to keep it brief. Also, learning is optimized by engaging students with conversational language and simple slides that focus their attention on the important information (Mayer, 2014a). Alley et al. (2006) found that using summary headlines (e.g., "Anxiety and Depression are More Prevalent in Females") rather than general headers (e.g., "Gender Differences in Mental Illnesses"), along with supporting graphics (e.g., graphs of data), boosted students' recall of slide-presented material. The use of graphics offers added benefits by providing opportunities for students to develop their quantitative reasoning skills as they interpret research findings. As discussed in Chapter 2, developing students' critical thinking (CT) around data is a common learning objective (LO) in psychology classes (see also Section 4.6.2 on Quantitative Reasoning). Students often have difficulties comprehending information in graphs (cf. Shah & Hoeffner, 2002), and so will gain more from having to interpret graphical displays of data themselves than by listening to an instructor's explanation. As a complement to slideware, Excel and other spreadsheet programs can readily be adapted for in-class simulations of psychological phenomena (Gordon & Gordon, 2009; Renner, 2004). For example, Gordon and Gordon (2009) created a variety of simulations to illustrate probability and other statistical concepts, while Renner (2004) used interactive simulations of Pavlovian conditioning to increase students' understanding of the Rescorla–Wagner model of associative learning. Spreadsheet programs provide useful tools for teaching students how to visualize datasets, evaluate the quality of graphs (e.g., distinguishing between informative and misleading graphs), and to think more critically about observed patterns of results.

3.1.2   More Innovative Use of Slideware

Slideware can be used in more ways than simply to present information to students. For example, it can be used to create simulations of psychological experiments, such as measuring the duration and capacity of working memory (e.g., Muir & Cleary, 2011). Simulations allow students to learn experientially about experimental design and data analysis, and to develop a better understanding of psychological theories (see Chapter 4, particularly Box 4.5, for additional suggestions and resources for simulations). Slideware can also be used to construct games, such as Jeopardy and Bingo, which are both enjoyable for students and enhance their learning (Gibson, 1991; Keutzer, 1993a; Massey, Brown, & Johnston, 2005; Revere, 2004; Ritzko & Robinson, 2011; see Section 5.5 on Cooperative Learning Games). Another option is to invite students to use PPT or Prezi slideware to create their own in-class presentations, which provides them opportunities to learn about effective multimedia use and to practice public speaking (for more suggestions on this and other student-produced multimedia projects, see Section 3.5).

3.2 Student Response Systems

The use of a student response system (SRS), also known as classroom or audience response systems or clickers, can foster student engagement and promote active learning, especially in large classes (Mayer et al., 2009; Morling, McAuliffe, Cohen, & DiLorenzo, 2008; Poirier & Feldman, 2007). SRSs are typically used in conjunction with slideware, such as PPT. After the instructor asks a question, students use electronic devices (which vary depending on the software used) to indicate their responses. Within seconds, the responses are transmitted wirelessly to the classroom computer and displayed graphically on a projector screen. Using an SRS encourages total class participation by allowing students to register their attitudes, opinions, and answers to questions related to course content in real time. Traditionally, students had to use purpose-built devices (clickers), and responses were received via an electronic receiver inserted in the USB port of the classroom computer. However, technological advances have led to the development of Web-based software that can process responses from laptops, cell phones, and other electronic devices (see Box 3.3). Before you decide on a specific SRS, you should check with the Department of Information Technology at your college to inquire about software installation/availability on the classroom computer; alternatively, you could download software to your own laptop and connect it to the classroom projector. As with all technology, it is likely that new systems will continue to be developed, so we list just a few in Box 3.3, and focus primarily on reviewing the evidence that shows how learning can be enhanced with an SRS.

Box 3.3 Popular Student Response Systems (SRSs)

Clickers and smart devices
- Turning Technologies
- iClicker

Open-source software
- Poll Everywhere (students can text or access a webpage via phone or laptop)
- Socrative

Web-based (need license)
- Qualtrics

SRSs have been used predominantly as quizzing tools, allowing instructors to perform formative assessment of student learning with relative ease (for review, see Muir & Cleary, 2011). Quizzing at the start of a class is useful for evaluating whether students have understood material in assigned readings and may help motivate students to read before class, especially if the quiz scores count toward their final grade (Zhu, 2007). Quizzing during and at the end of the class, on the other hand, allows the instructor to evaluate whether their teaching is effective; if many students are failing to understand, this indicates the need for a different approach.

Two recent meta-analyses summarize research showing that students do better on tests in classes that use SRSs compared to standard lecture sections (Chien, Chang, & Chang, 2016; Hunsu, Adesope, & Bayly, 2016). This advantage has been attributed to the *testing effect* (Roediger & Karpicke, 2006; Tran, Rohrer, & Pashler, 2014) rather than to the use of SRS technology per se. That is, having students generate answers to (clicker) questions boosts their memory for the course material; see Chapter 7 for further discussion of the benefits of retrieval practice through testing. This view is supported by research (including a meta-analysis of 86 studies by Hunsu et al., 2016) showing that exam performance is comparable for students in classes where they are tested frequently, regardless of whether they respond using clickers, by raising their hand, or via a response card (Anthis, 2011; Hunsu et al., 2016; Stowell & Nelson, 2007). However, another meta-analysis of 72 studies found that students who used clickers had an academic edge over students who did not use them but were still frequently tested (Chien et al., 2016).

Students have reported liking the anonymity afforded them by SRSs (Draper & Brown, 2004; Freeman, Blayney, & Ginns, 2006; Jones, Connolly, Gear, & Read, 2001), which Chien and colleagues suggested might help explain why they found that SRS use enhanced learning. They hypothesized that because SRS responses are not made public at the individual level, students will tend to focus on the feedback— which promotes learning (Kang, McDermott, & Roediger, 2007)—instead of on their embarrassment at getting an answer wrong. This anonymity may help students to feel more comfortable in taking intellectual risks, which is often a foundational step in deep learning when mastery is emphasized over performance. On a related note, Stowell and Nelson (2007) found that students tend to conform when they see or hear other students' answers, which makes it difficult to know how many students in a class actually have the correct answer. When students respond anonymously, clickers may provide more accurate formative assessment data regarding individual learning.

SRS use has also been shown to increase attention, engagement, and attendance (Bunce, Flens, & Neiles, 2010): even though students using SRSs had lapses of attention about every 5 minutes during a lecture, their inattention decreased during times when they were responding to a clicker question or were involved in demonstrations. SRS use is probably less prevalent in small than in large classes, because instructors may feel that with fewer students, they are able to encourage total participation without the hassles of using technology. However, it may be worth rethinking this, because research has shown that the benefits of clicker technology are largest in classes with 21–49 students (Hunsu et al., 2016).

3.2.1   Student Collaboration and SRSs

Engaging in discussions with peers has been shown to enhance learning (Crouch & Mazur, 2001; Smith et al., 2009). It is thus not surprising to find that learning benefits are largest in SRS classes when students engage in peer discussion, as shown in the results of a recent meta-analysis (Chien et al., 2016). The large effect size observed for discussion-enhanced learning ($g = 1.19$) in this meta-analysis may reflect a greater level of student preparation for class in terms of reading, watching videos, or listening to podcasts for homework, as well as the use of conceptual rather than basic questions in classes that utilized peer discussions (Beatty, Gerace, Leonard, & Dufresne, 2006; Crouch & Mazur, 2001). Conceptual questions—such as applying theories to solve a problem—foster higher order-thinking that extends beyond the basic "remembering" level of Bloom's taxonomy (see Figure 2.1), and so are likely to result in deeper learning. Indeed, fostering CT is a common LO in psychology classes; see also Chapter 2. Collaborative discussion around conceptual questions has become a highly advocated mode of instruction in science undergraduate classes (Beatty & Gerace, 2009; Caldwell, 2007; Crouch & Mazur, 2001; Mazur, 2009; Wieman et al., 2009). Students often begin by answering a conceptual SRS question by themselves. They then explain their answer to a peer (preferably someone with a different answer), and the instructor facilitates the discussion while moving around the classroom. The instructor then poses the same SRS question again, which gives students a chance to change their answer based on their conversations (Mazur, 2009).

Beatty et al. (2006) describe a slightly different approach. Students answer an SRS question only after discussing their ideas in small groups. Once the data are visible, representative students are asked to explain the rationale and supporting evidence for their answers. The process is repeated three to four times in a 50-minute class, using carefully chosen questions to encourage reflection and to challenge students. Beatty and Gerace (2009) suggest asking questions that target a common misconception, and following up with a question that helps students to realize their mistake. This approach could work well in psychology classes. For example, in a Brain and Behavior class, students could first be asked, "How much of our brain do we use?", with the assumption that they will tend to grossly underestimate the answer. This could then be followed up with a question such as, "Why do we need to use baseline conditions for fMRI or PET scans to make inferences about what types of behavior are dependent on a particular area of the brain?" In figuring out the answer to the second question, students will likely come to the realization that much of the brain is active even at rest, and so we have to subtract this baseline activity out to be able to elucidate the behavior-specific brain activity. Generating their own explanations is more likely to effect a change in this particular pseudoscientific belief (i.e., that people use only 10% of their brains; Boyd, 2008) than just being told the answers. Many of the problem-based learning tasks described in Section 5.4.3 would work well with the discussion techniques used by Beatty, Mazur, and their colleagues. Discussion enhances students' understanding of the class materials by requiring that they construct knowledge with their peers, but it also contributes to personal development, as students have to learn how to successfully collaborate with others and reach a consensus (Smith et al., 2009). Wieman and colleagues suggest that instructors who are new to using SRSs may want to gradually ease into the use of conceptual clicker questions in their classes (Wieman et al., 2009). As a prelude to more conceptual quizzing, you might also consider adapting Jeopardy and other slideware games for use with an SRS, and having students work in pairs or teams to answer relatively straightforward questions.

3.2.2 Scientific Literacy and SRSs

Muir and Cleary (2011) describe how SRSs can be used to improve students' quantitative reasoning and scientific literacy. In their classes, they collected SRS data using a wide variety of psychological study simulations, including the Deese–Roediger–McDermott (DRM) false-memory paradigm (Roediger & McDermott, 1995), how depth of processing affects memory recall (Craik & Tulving, 1975), and the serial position effect (Murdock, 1962). Students learned to interpret the SRS display of the central tendencies of their data and to assess whether the replication was successful. These exercises are not only engaging for students, but help them develop a deeper understanding of experimental design. Discussions about why results are not always replicated are likely to promote a greater appreciation of the factors that can affect reproducibility in psychological science. Muir and Cleary (2011) also describe the use of an SRS to help students better understand frequency distributions, by analyzing class data on the students' height. Students viewed these exercises very positively, and the vast majority reported that they felt that they had increased their learning.

3.3 Use of Videos and Video Clips in Classes

Although using films or film segments (clips) in educational settings is not a new idea, there is now a tremendous range of free videos that are readily available on websites like YouTube. See Box 3.4 for resources for videos and video clips for psychology classes (note that not all of these are free, but some may be available through your college library).

In addition to using existing media, it is also relatively easy for instructors to create their own educational digital presentations (podcasts or videos), which can be uploaded to websites like YouTube; see Box 3.5 for tips on using YouTube videos for teaching purposes. Watching video clips or podcasts before coming to class is a common feature of the flipped classroom (described in more detail in Chapter 8 on Gearing Up to Teach Online), because it allows students to spend class time working on problem solving and the application of basic ideas. We describe various methods of creating narrated slideshows and other instructional videos in Chapter 8, along with the associated research that shows the benefits of having students watch videos or listen to podcasts for homework, which can lay the groundwork for discussions and other classroom activities.

A number of articles have described the use of documentaries, feature films, educational videos, TV shows, and video clips in psychology courses with the goal of deepening understanding of psychological concepts and engaging students in higher-order thinking. These include courses in Social Psychology (Christopher, Walter, Marek, & Koenig, 2004; Dorris & Ducey, 1978; Eaton & Uskul, 2004; Roskos-Ewoldsen & Roskos-Ewoldsen, 2001; Simpson, 2008), Developmental Psychology

---

Box 3.4 Resources for Video Suggestions

- Documentary films and clips (12 minutes to more than 2 hours) available on DVD and via streaming, with comprehensive descriptions, lengths, and ratings that make them suitable for psychology classes, e.g., Developmental Psychology, Psychology and the Law, Clinical and Counseling Psychology, Health Psychology, and Social Psychology (Taylor, 2011)
- Diversity videos (Lim, Diamond, Chang, Primm, & Lu, 2008; Tejeda, 2008)
- Films about memory (Kelley & Calkins, 2006)
- Video clips for Social Psychology (Roskos-Ewoldsen & Roskos-Ewoldsen, 2001)
- Psychology of the Holocaust (Simpson, 2012).
- Psychology of Persuasion clips (Simpson, 2008)
- Scaffolded assignments for writing integrative essay in Introductory Psychology based on identifying examples from the movie *Twelve Angry Men* (http://utweb.ut.edu/sblessing; Blessing & Blessing, 2015)
- Videos for debunking pseudoscience (Lilienfeld, Lohr, & Morier, 2001)
- teachwithmovies.com: videos with ready-constructed lesson plans
- TED.com
- Ed-TED.com: short video clips with associated quizzes and ideas for how to embed the clips into a larger lesson plan
- BigThink.com
- psychmovies.com
- clipsforclass.com
- http://interteachpsy.org/Resources/IntroductoryPsychologyTeachingResources
- Films on demand: digital educational videos

Box 3.5 Tips for Using YouTube

1) Make sure the classroom computer is able to play YouTube videos (needs Flash Player).
2) Download videos to a flashdrive before class to avoid issues with Internet connectivity; this also prevents you from losing your favorite clips if they are removed from YouTube. There are several different ways you can download a YouTube video (mp4 format), including using RealPlayer or one of any number of free Internet-based programs. Some of these work just by inserting a few letters within the YouTube part of the URL:
   a) www.ssyoutube.com/—SaveFrom.net
   b) www.youmagictube.com/—SaveTheVideo.com
   c) www.youtubemonkey.com—YoutubeMonkey Video Downloader
3) If you are providing URLs to students, make sure that they are current.
4) You can get the URL for a specific point in a video by pausing it and right-clicking on the video, which gives the option to "copy URL at current time."

(Boyatzis, 1994; Kirsh, 1998), Abnormal Psychology (Badura, 2002; Fleming, Piedmont, & Hiam, 1990; Nissim-Sabat, 1979), Introductory Psychology (Blessing & Blessing, 2015; Hemenover, Caster, & Mizumoto, 1999), Cognitive Psychology (Conner, 1996), Personality Psychology (Logan, 1988; Paddock, Terranova, & Giles, 2001), and Psychology and the Law (Anderson, 1992). In many of these courses, videos were used to provide illustrations of concepts or behaviors; students then analyzed what they viewed in a class discussion or written assignment.

Taylor (2011) suggested that documentaries may enhance learning by exposing students to real-life examples of concepts or behaviors that are complex or for which they have little personal experience, such as infant/child behavior, homelessness, marginalization, and psychological disorders. Research suggests that the use of non-fictional videos can increase perspective taking and empathy. For instance, Lowman, Judge, & Wiss (2010) found that students in an Abnormal Psychology course developed a better understanding of how psychopathology affects different people in different ways after watching YouTube clips and reading blogs and discussion board postings that people suffering from a particular disorder had uploaded to the Internet. After watching the videos, students researched the disorder further and wrote a paper on it (Lowman, Judge, & Wiss, 2010). Others have suggested that analyzing fictional depictions of behavior can also be used to strengthen learning (Eaton & Uskul, 2004; Melchiori & Mallett, 2015; Simpson, 2008). In general, students find fictional videos enjoyable; furthermore, videos can also offer opportunities for students to critique whether or not a psychological concept has been accurately portrayed (Anderson, 1992). For instance, amnesia is notoriously poorly depicted in feature films (Kelley & Calkins, 2006).

Research shows that students get more out of watching videos if they are given some background information and some guidance as to what to look for (Berk, 2009). Answering a set of guiding questions while watching a video enhances learning more than passive viewing (Kreiner, 1997; Lawson, Bodle, Houlette, & Haubner, 2006; Lawson, Bodle, & McDonough, 2007). Kreiner (1997) found that students who took brief notes in response to guiding questions while they watched an educational video about language development were able to interpret the video content better than those who watched the video passively. However, stopping the video at intervals and having students discuss the film produced similar learning gains as writing notes. Lawson et al. (2006) also found that students who wrote short answers to broad questions related to an educational video on social psychology had better test scores on factual knowledge related to the video compared to students who just watched the video (Lawson et al., 2006). In a follow-up study, they found that writing answers to guiding questions improved test scores more than just thinking about (and not discussing) the answers or taking unguided notes (Lawson et al., 2007). If the goal of the assignment is to have students analyze a video independently, Dorris and Ducey (1978) found that modeling the process in class, providing worksheets that guided students as to what to look for, and engaging students in small-group discussions increased students' abilities to complete the assignment effectively.

In general, studies have shown students believe that videos make concepts clearer and more memorable (Cherney, 2008; Cleveland, 2011; Connor-Greene, 2007; VanderStoep, Fagerlin, & Feenstra, 2000), that they can facilitate discussion (Cleveland, 2011; Lyons, Bradley, & White, 1984), and that they increase student participation (Roskos-Ewoldsen & Roskos-Ewoldsen, 2001). Also, when asked to analyze and critique films by applying what they know about psychological theories, students feel that they are better able to view information more objectively (Anderson, 1992). Video-related assignments have also been shown to boost test scores in Social Psychology classes (Eaton & Uskul, 2004; Melchiori & Mallett, 2015; Simpson, 2008). For example, Eaton and Uskul (2004) showed that students who viewed clips from the *Simpsons* television show and discussed how they illustrated various social psychology principles had better test scores on video-related items than on other items. Melchiori and Mallett (2015) found that students who used worksheets to identify instances of stereotyping and stigma in the movie *Shrek* had better exam scores relating to those concepts compared to students who did not do this exercise. Similarly, Simpson (2008) reported that a class that saw video clips and discussed various examples of persuasive techniques had higher scores on test items related to the psychology of persuasion than a class in which clips were not shown. Sawyer et al. (2017) found that students in a Developmental Psychology class who watched and analyzed video clips illustrating development concepts such as *joint attention*, *object permanence*, and *egocentrism* performed better on test items that probed the underlying concepts than did students who had the behaviors of children verbally described to them using text projected in standard PPT slides.

Video clips that depict classical psychological studies are frequently used in psychology classes to enhance student understanding of related psychological theories, experimental design, and ethics in relation to research practices. In a national survey of over 100 Introductory Psychology instructors, Bartels, Milovich, and Moussier (2016) found that over 75% showed students a video of the Stanford prison experiment. A number of studies have shown that other types of video assignments can be used to enhance CT and scientific inquiry skills (Adam & Manson, 2014; Connor-Greene, 2007; Hatch et al., 2014; Thompson & Fisher-Thompson, 2013). Connor-Greene (2007) used a video assignment to help students better understand the difficulties associated with objectivity when making scientific observations. Students watched a 3-minute clip from the movie *Baraka* (a documentary film without narrative or voice-over, depicting various natural events and human activities). After students wrote down what they had observed in the clip, they then wrote their interpretation of what they had seen. After comparing their two answers, 96% of students identified that they had included at least one interpretive comment in their observation. Students felt that the exercise allowed them to gain insights into the tendency for subjectivity even when making "objective" observations.

Adam and Manson (2014) found that students who worked together in small groups to identify and evaluate claims made in a short pseudoscientific infomercial improved their ability to recognize flawed arguments; for additional resources for pseudoscience demonstrations, see Chapter 4, particularly Box 4.6. In a similar vein, students exhibited improvements in research and statistical skills after participating in a series of activities using clips from the *Scientific American Frontiers* series (Thompson & Fisher-Thompson, 2013). In one assignment, students watched people administering therapeutic touch, and then discussed how they might design a study to test the efficacy of the technique. Next, they watched a depiction of a published scientific study that tested whether practitioners could detect the energy field of their patients. The instructors generated simulated data based on the statistical findings of the actual study, after figuring out which statistical tests would be appropriate; students then ran the analyses and wrote up the results and conclusions. Students' abilities to use appropriate statistical tests improved after the activity. On a related theme, Hatch and colleagues found that students who made behavioral observations while watching a video of animal behavior (i.e., laboratory demonstrations involving mice who were exposed to methamphetamines) performed comparably on tests to students who actually observed the animal behavior in the lab (Hatch et al., 2014). This finding is particularly reassuring for instructors who want to engage their students in empirical research but do not have access to physical labs.

3.3.1 Guidance on Using Potentially Distressing Video Materials

Whether videos are fictional or not, some may produce an emotional response in students. In certain cases, this might serve to better engage students, and may even promote clearer insights about why people behave the way that they do. For example, some persuasive techniques work because they are emotionally arousing; experiencing this first-hand may be a particularly powerful method to gain understanding (Simpson, 2008). However, as Anderson (1992) found, some video materials may elicit an undesirably strong emotional response in some students that may actually inhibit their learning. Recently, there has been considerable media publicity and academic debate around the issuing of warnings before exposing students to materials that could potentially trigger symptoms of post-traumatic stress disorder (PTSD) (Carter, 2015). This concern is particularly salient given the relatively high numbers of students who suffer from symptoms of PTSD or who have a history of trauma. In 2011, a study of over 3000 students from two large universities found that 9% of first-year students had PTSD symptoms (Read, Ouimette, White, Colder, & Farrow, 2011). Similar proportions have been reported among a smaller sample of Introductory Psychology students, where an additional 11% had subclinical symptoms (Smyth, Hockemeyer, Heron, Wonderlich, & Pennebaker, 2008). Disproportionately large numbers of graduate students in clinical training programs have trauma histories, and so are in danger of experiencing re-traumatization in their course work (for review, see Butler, Carello, & Maguin, 2017). Furthermore, in 2016, a study of over 750 students from 11 different community colleges found that twice as many of those who were veterans (25.7%) screened positive for PTSD compared to those who were non-veterans (12.6%) (Fortney et al., 2016). Given that increasing numbers of veterans are enrolling in college, these figures are likely to rise further. Carter (2015) has argued that it is appropriate to warn students about potentially disturbing materials so that they can prepare themselves for how best to deal with any PTSD symptoms or extreme distress that they might potentially cause.

In sharp contrast, the American Association of University Professors (AAUP, 2014) has argued that trigger warnings threaten academic freedom by potentially allowing students to avoid difficult conversations. They advocate instead that students with PTSD should apply for accommodations so they may be exempted from exposure to materials/situations/assignments that could elicit symptoms. We find this approach difficult to reconcile with the principles of Universal Design (UD), especially with the knowledge that many students do not seek the accommodations to which they are entitled. Similarly, we find fundamental flaws with the argument (e.g., McNally, 2016) that trigger warnings are "countertherapeutic" because they tend to exacerbate symptoms of PTSD by encouraging avoidance. As Boysen (2017) points out, although exposure therapy is often used to treat PTSD, this occurs in a therapeutic context, not a class setting. Giving trigger warnings allows students with PTSD to avoid contact with materials if they deem that it is necessary (Carter, 2015). Carter suggests that using trigger warnings acknowledges the diversity in the classroom, which may help to reduce the stigma of mental illness. However, Carter also emphasizes that trauma is not the same as discomfort, and advises that instructors should not steer away from "difficult" topics that make students feel uncomfortable; indeed this could prevent transformative learning—instead, they should strive to create a safe environment where students can discuss their feelings and know how (and where) to seek support if distressed. Trigger warnings are particularly relevant in classes that teach about trauma, including Abnormal (Clinical) Psychology and more specific special topics courses in which trauma is the primary focus. Indeed, some specialists who teach these special topics courses call for a trauma-informed pedagogical approach (Carello & Butler, 2015), by providing information about self-care and resources for seeking help alongside trigger warnings. Boysen and Prieto (2018) reported that about 39% of the psychology instructors that they surveyed issued warnings to students before covering/showing sensitive materials, especially trauma-related topics. Respondents reported that materials relating to sexual assault elicited both more visible signs of distress and more requests from students for trigger warnings than any other topic. Finally, loud sudden noises are perhaps the most common trigger of distressing symptoms among people who have experienced trauma (Glad, Hafstad, Jensen, & Dyb, 2017), and so students (especially veterans) may appreciate receiving advance notice if these are likely to occur in a video (Sinski, 2012).

3.4 Information Literacy and the Effective Use of the Internet

College students are frequently tasked with seeking, evaluating, and utilizing information to help answer a research question. However, in large national surveys of undergraduates, 80% reported having difficulties knowing where to start with a research assignment, and although 50% were uncertain about the quality of their search, the vast majority did not seek help from a librarian (Head & Eisenberg, 2009, 2010). In general, when students use the Internet to seek information, they are most likely to take the path of least resistance, by initially searching using familiar tools, such as Google and Wikipedia (Head & Eisenberg, 2009). Undergraduate students place high value on Google as an academic resource (Traphagan, Traphagan, Neavel Dickens, & Resta, 2014), and they often do not know the difference between searching for information on Google and searching on Google Scholar. In the 2015 National Survey of Student Engagement (NSSE), 52% of first-year students and 64% of seniors said that they frequently used their college library's electronic sources to complete an assignment, but far fewer thought critically about the quality of source materials. Only 37% of first-year students and 36% of seniors indicated that they were likely to *not* use a source if they thought it was of poor quality (National Survey of Student Engagement, 2015). First-year students, in particular, have been found to have low levels of information literacy, and less skilled students have been shown to overestimate their abilities, which reduces the likelihood that they will seek help (Gross & Latham, 2012; Gross, Latham, & Armstrong, 2012). Issues with information literacy have also been shown to extend to graduate students. Lampert (2005) found that on the whole, students in a masters-level counseling course did not feel comfortable with using electronic databases such as PsycINFO.

It is evident that the majority of college students today need information literacy instruction, as well as practice with formulating effective research questions, searching for information using discipline-specific databases, evaluating the credibility of the information they find, and using this information to support their arguments (Wineburg et al., 2016). The American Psychological Association (APA) has endorsed the importance of these skills in the psychology major—a sentiment echoed by the Association of College and Research Libraries (ACRL). In 2016, the ACRL adopted an information literacy framework that highlights the complex nature of information literacy in a world with increasing diversity in the formats of available information (see Box 3.6).

It is often difficult for instructors to imagine why the process of seeking and using reliable information is so difficult for students when it is relatively automatic for them (Bodi, 2002). However, for students to develop competencies in this area, this process

Box 3.6 Information Literacy Framework for Higher Education

- **Authority is Constructed and Contextual**
  Students learn how to recognize who has credibility or authority in an area, but that this may vary depending on context. Different situations may call for information from different sources.
- **Information Creation as a Process**
  Students learn how different types of information are created, e.g., the difference between a peer-reviewed journal article and a magazine blog, and how this affects how and when different kinds of information are used.
- **Information Has Value**
  Students learn about how to use information in a responsible way by avoiding plagiarism and being mindful about what personal information they make public. They develop an understanding of how and why marginalized groups are less likely to be represented.
- **Research as Inquiry**
  Students learn how to formulate research questions and conduct appropriately constrained searches for information, which they synthesize and use to draw conclusions. This process is iterative, as simple questions lead to the development of more sophisticated ones, which may require integrating information from different fields or perspectives.
- **Scholarship as Conversation**
  Students learn that information is generated in an iterative way and evolves as it encompasses a greater range of perspectives over time; for many issues, there is no one single answer.
- **Searching as Strategic Exploration**
  Students learn the best ways to conduct a search to answer a given question, recognizing that different information sources may be useful in different contexts. Searching is iterative and often not linear.

Source: Summarized and adapted from the Association of College and Research Libraries (2015).

needs to be deconstructed. Two models may be particularly helpful for thinking about this: Kuhlthau's Information Search Process, which focuses on the affective responses that students are likely to feel during the process (Kuhlthau, 1999, 2004), and the Big6 Skills Model, which was primarily developed for K–12 instruction (Eisenberg, 2008; Eisenberg & Berkowitz, 1990) but is also relevant for college students in thinking about how to break the process down (see Box 3.7).

Collaborations between librarians and psychology faculty have been found to be particularly successful in improving students' information literacy (Birkett & Hughes, 2013; Lampert, 2005; Paglia & Donahue, 2003; Thaxton, Faccioli, & Mosby, 2004), and so we encourage you to reach out to the librarians at your college. Not surprisingly, having a short one-shot (often generic) lecture from a librarian about how to use library databases does little to improve students' information-seeking competencies and confidence (Paglia & Donahue, 2003; Rosman, Mayer, & Krampen, 2016). Embedded instruction that uses a series of scaffolded *active* learning exercises that are authentic in nature (i.e., they help students to answer a research question of interest), on the other hand, is very effective (Birkett & Hughes, 2013; Lampert, 2005; Paglia & Donahue, 2003; Thaxton et al., 2004). Ideally, information literacy instruction should occur in multiple classes at all levels of education. Wong and Cmor (2011) found that students' GPAs correlated with the amount of information literacy instruction they had received across their classes. Bowles-Terry (2012) also found that seniors who had received information

---

Box 3.7 The Big6 Skills Model

Task Definition
  Define the problem
  Identify information needed

Information-Seeking Strategies
  Determine all possible sources
  Select the best sources

Location and Access
  Locate sources
  Find information within sources

Use of Information
  Engage (e.g., read, hear, view)
  Extract relevant information

Synthesis
  Organize information from multiple sources
  Present information

Evaluation
  Judge the result (effectiveness)
  Judge the process (efficiency)

Source: The Big6™© (1987) Michael B. Eisenberg and Robert E. Berkowitz. Presented with permission of the authors.

literacy instruction in their upper-level classes had higher GPAs than those who had not, which underscores the need for developmentally appropriate instruction for students at all levels.

Gross and colleagues found that an hour-long Analyze, Search, and Evaluate workshop improved community college students' information literacy skills and so felt this might be helpful in preparing them for more sophisticated searches later in their college careers (Gross & Latham, 2013). Students practiced using Google to seek answers to research questions in which they were inherently interested, such as finding information that would help them to make a decision about a purchase (Gross, Armstrong, & Latham, 2012; Gross, Latham, et al., 2012). In the *analysis* phase, they practiced defining what it was that they wanted to know, making sure that their questions were focused and not too broad. In the *search* phase, they generated keywords and looked for information. In the *evaluation* stage, they evaluated the credibility and currency of the information, as well as its relevance for answering the search question. In Chapter 4, we discuss ways to foster students' information literacy around pseudoscience activities and suggest teaching students how to engage in fact checking so that they can assess the credibility of information found on the Internet (Carmichael & MacMillan, 2011; McGrew, Ortega, Breakstone, & Wineburg, 2017; Meriam Library, 2010). For example, the CRAAP test helps students to evaluate the Currency, Relevance, Authority, Accuracy, and Purpose of information (Meriam Library, 2010), and its use has been found to improve students' abilities to critically evaluate information found on websites (Myhre, 2012; Seely, Fry, & Ruppel, 2011; Wichowski & Kohl, 2012).

More advanced workshops in psychology classes have been shown to be effective in helping students improve their skills at various levels of the Big6 model (Lampert, 2005; Larkin & Pines, 2005; Radhakrishnan, Lam, & Tamura, 2010; Rosman et al., 2016; Shane-Simpson, Che, & Brooks, 2016; Thaxton et al., 2004). As described in more detail in the next section, showing students in introductory-level Human Development classes how to use library databases to find information in order to edit Wikipedia entries increased their ability to describe what a peer-reviewed article was, and to differentiate between scholarly and non-scholarly articles, and between empirical and non-empirical articles (Shane-Simpson et al., 2016). Similarly, guided in-class practice in formulating research questions, generating descriptors and key words, using a database thesaurus to find synonyms for key terms, focusing a search using Boolean operators, wild cards, and truncation, identifying ways in which to evaluate the credibility of an author or source, and understanding the peer-review process has been shown to increase students' comfort and ability around using electronic databases (Lampert, 2005; Larkin & Pines, 2005; Rosman et al., 2016; Thaxton et al., 2004). Radhakrishnan et al. (2010) also found that this type of practice improved students' ability to use arguments in their research papers.

3.4.1 Benefits of Wikipedia Editing Assignments

College students, especially first-years, frequently use the open-access encyclopedia, Wikipedia, as a resource in their assignments (Head & Eisenberg, 2010; Jones, Johnson-Yale, Millermaier, & Perez, 2009; Lim, 2009; Rainie & Tancer, 2007; Traphagan et al., 2014). Unlike traditional encyclopedia entries, which are presumably written by experts, anyone can contribute to Wikipedia. As a consequence, some Wikipedia entries are accurate and comprehensive, but others are not (e.g., Chesney, 2006; Giles, 2005). This leaves plenty of room for instructors to utilize Wikipedia editing assignments as a means of "giving psychology away"; that is, making it more accessible to the general public (Shane-Simpson et al., 2016). Wikipedia assignments, where students edit existing entries or post new articles after doing appropriate research, are a powerful tool for teaching information literacy and research skills, such as how to locate and cite reputable source materials, paraphrase ideas, and write from a neutral point of view (Burdo, 2012; Chandler & Gregory, 2010; Chiang et al., 2012; Miller, 2014; Shane-Simpson et al., 2016; Traphagan et al., 2014). Teaching with Wikipedia provides ample opportunities for discussing gender bias in media coverage, as gaps are apparent in both Wikipedia's coverage of women and the involvement of women as contributors of Wikipedia content (Hargittai & Shaw, 2015; Hill & Shaw, 2013). Engaging students in writing Wikipedia articles about prominent women can serve to promote agency and activism while at the same time enhancing their research and writing skills (Brooks, Che, Walters, & Shane-Simpson, 2017; Edwards, 2015; Evans, Mabey, & Mandiberg, 2015).

In 2011, the Association for Psychological Science (APS) launched its Wikipedia Initiative, encouraging instructors of psychology courses to engage their students in editing Wikipedia, with the goal of making information about psychology as complete and accurate as possible (http://www.psychologicalscience.org/members/aps-wikipedia-initiative). The APS views Wikipedia editing assignments as an effective tool for teaching students how to communicate effectively to a general audience, support statements with citations, and organize writing for clarity and logical flow. Wikipedia editing often requires students to respond to external feedback, as their contributions are vetted by "Wikipedians" (i.e., members of the public who are editing Wikipedia) and by automatized "bots" that check for plagiarism and formatting errors. Quite often, student contributions are flagged as needing further work, and they may be removed if deemed inappropriate. This feedback creates critical learning opportunities for students to discover how content is negotiated and standards are upheld in the Wikipedia community.

To demonstrate the feasibility of introducing Wikipedia editing in an introductory-level course, Shane-Simpson et al. (2016) assigned teams of students in a large Human Development class (~100 students) to edit psychology-related articles on Wikipedia that had been flagged as in need of further work. Some of the articles were "stubs" that were too short to be considered comprehensive; others contained statements that were not adequately supported with citations. Over a 2-month period, the students added over 50 000 words to 24 articles. They demonstrated gains in information literacy (e.g., how to distinguish primary and secondary sources, how to locate primary sources through the library) and knowledge about Wikipedia (e.g., how contributions are tracked, how editors communicate with one another).

The Wiki Education Foundation provides resources and online training modules to help instructors and students learn editing basics (wikiedu.org) and a course management system (CMS) (Wiki Education Dashboard) to help instructors monitor their students' editing work (https://dashboard.wikiedu.org/). The Wiki Education Dashboard serves as a portal for accessing student accounts, thus simplifying the logistics of organizing assignments and peer review. Exploring the Dashboard allows users to view articles edited by students from various colleges and universities across the United States and beyond—current estimates indicate that over 40 000 registered students in over 2000 classes have contributed to over 60 000 Wikipedia articles since 2010 (https://dashboard.wikiedu.org/).

In addition to using the Wiki Education Foundation resources, Shane-Simpson and Brooks (2016) strongly encourage instructors to collaborate with campus-based experts (such as librarians) in assisting students with the technical aspects of Wikipedia editing, as well as with finding and citing appropriate sources. As with other complex assignments, Shane-Simpson and Brooks (2016) stress the importance of using class time to teach students how to find and cite appropriate secondary sources (preferred by Wikipedia), which might include reputable newspapers, and to develop important writing skills, like effective paraphrasing and avoiding jargon. They also stress that Wikipedia assignments need to be developmentally appropriate. For example, editing a biography stub may be an appropriate activity for introductory students, but students in a capstone class are better served creating new entries that meet Wikipedia's "good article" criteria (http://en.wikipedia.org/wiki/Wikipedia:Good_article_criteria). Brooks et al. (2017) recommend creating a template to structure new articles (theirs is available at https://en.wikipedia.org/wiki/User:Celizas/BioTemplate), as it is much easier for students to insert information into a pre-existing format than to structure an article from scratch (Brooks et al., 2017). Use of a template ensures that new articles will be formatted appropriately for Wikipedia, reducing the likelihood that students' work will be flagged as needing further revision; see also https://en.wikipedia.org/wiki/Wikipedia:Writing_better_articles.

Contributing to Wikipedia can elevate students' sensibilities around identifying potential inaccuracies within its entries (Chandler & Gregory, 2010; Miller, 2014; Traphagan et al., 2014). Moreover, research across various disciplines has shown that well-designed Wikipedia assignments can improve student writing (Burdo, 2012; Chiang et al., 2012; Miller, 2014; Nix, 2010), information literacy (Chiang et al., 2012; Miller, 2014; Shane-Simpson et al., 2016), and engagement with—or understanding of—course materials (Burdo, 2012; Shane-Simpson et al., 2016). Miller (2014) argued that Wikipedia assignments improve students' writing because numerous Wikipedians in the general public enforce the stipulation that articles must be well-written and neutrally worded in a formal but jargon-free manner, and so encourage students to write to the best of their abilities. Many students find these external editorial comments to be generally helpful (Shane-Simpson et al., 2016), and Nix (2010) reported that students were more attentive to comments made by Wikipedians than to her own comments on more traditional assignments. Furthermore, students' exposure to Wiki-etiquette may help their professional development, as they become aware of the need for suitable user names, correct spelling and grammar, paraphrasing of content, citations for source materials, and prohibitions against posting copyright-protected materials (Chandler & Gregory, 2010). Unsuitable entries are quickly flagged for removal by the Wikipedians, who also have the capacity to temporarily ban rule-breakers from posting new entries (Chandler & Gregory, 2010; Shane-Simpson et al., 2016).

3.5   Other Multimedia Projects

Multimedia projects, such as the Wikipedia assignments just described, as well as contributions to wikis, webpages, and blogs (see Chapter 8 on Gearing Up to Teach Online), give students the opportunity to develop their technological literacy, and may be perceived by students as having more relevance in today's world than more traditional assignments. In this section, we describe a selection of other multimedia assignments that can be used to foster student learning.

Consistent with the APA's recent emphasis on the development of liberal arts skills, such as effective communication, in the psychology major, many instructors include student oral presentations as a component of their assessment of student research projects. Increasingly, students elect to use PPT or Prezi in their presentations (Beyer, 2011). Therefore, learning about,and enacting the research-informed best principles of multimedia learning (see Section 3.1.1) will serve them well, not only in their other college classes, but also in their future professional lives, especially if they choose to pursue business or academic careers. Projects need to be scaffolded to ensure adequate time for background research (and appropriate information literacy instruction), preparation and editing of the presentation, public speaking practice, and incorporation of feedback before the final presentation is due. Students often use too many slides, and so it is advisable to give instruction on how to give an effective presentation with just a few (e.g., five slides in 6 minutes) (Dow, Kukucka, Galazyn, Powers, & Brooks, 2013; Schwartz, Powers, Galazyn, & Brooks, 2017). We recommend that you provide students with a template, a good example that they can use as a model, and a grading rubric for their presentation; see Schwartz et al. (2017) for a sample template and grading rubric for five-slide presentations on psychological disorders. As noted by Oliver and Kowalczyk (2013), students are frequently underprepared for presentations and rely on reading from text-heavy slides, often turning their back on their audience. In an attempt to address these issues, some instructors have moved to using a novel (but more rigid) style format, Pecha Kucha, to improve the delivery quality of student presentations (Beyer, 2011; Oliver & Kowalczyk, 2013). Pecha Kucha (Japanese for "chitchat") in its traditional format uses 20 slides (images only), each automatically presented for 20 seconds (Beyer, 2011), although Oliver and Kowalczyk (2013) modified this slightly by allowing students to advance the slides themselves as long as they did not exceed the total allowed time of just over 6.5 minutes. Pecha Kucha's use of complementary verbal and visual information adheres to Mayer's best principles for multimedia design (Mayer, 2014b). Students are also typically better prepared for this style of presentation, because they have to rehearse to make sure that their narration fits to the timing of the slides, and there is no text for them to read (Beyer, 2011; Oliver & Kowalczyk, 2013).

3.5.1   Student-Created Videos and Podcasts

Widespread access to cell phones, laptops, and other mobile devices that have video recording capabilities (either owned by the students themselves or borrowed from the college) has made it increasingly feasible to ask students to create videos (Benedict & Pence, 2012; Lyons et al., 1984; Malouff & Emmerton, 2014; Pettijohn & Perelli, 2005; Zacchilli, 2014) or video podcasts (vodcasts) (Grose-Fifer, Helmer, & Zottoli, 2014) in their psychology classes, especially if they work in small groups. There are several advantages to having students create videos or vodcasts. Student-created media files can be hosted on the Web to be viewed by classmates or a wider audience, which may increase motivation to produce a high-quality product (Lyons et al., 1984; Malouff & Emmerton, 2014; Malouff & Shearer, 2016). It has also been suggested that video presentations are of a higher quality than "live presentations" because students are less anxious and can edit or re-record files as needed (Lyons et al., 1984; Malouff & Emmerton, 2014). Grading video presentations may also be easier than grading in-person presentations, because they can be replayed, allowing more time to reflect on the students' work (Malouff & Emmerton, 2014).

When assigning students to create their own videos or vodcasts it is important that you allow them sufficient time to explore and research what they want to convey and to learn about production techniques and the relevant technology (e.g., how to record video, how to edit it, how to upload it to a host website, and how to submit it for grading). Thus, this type of assignment is likely to require a fairly long lead-time before the final product is due. For example, over the course of an entire semester, Grose-Fifer, Helmer, and Zottoli (2014) created a series of linked assignments for students in their first-year Psychology-English learning community that culminated in their producing 5-minute image-enhanced podcasts (audio recordings with still images). Each podcast, created by a group of students, portrayed a major theme from a selected book through a psychological lens. For example, after reading *Tweak: Growing Up on Methamphetamines* (Sheff, 2008), one group wanted to know whether it was possible to truly kick an addiction; their podcast focused on portraying a relapse scene from the book and included a mock interview with an "expert" on drug addiction (played by a group member). Students worked on their group project during multiple class periods; they first analyzed model podcasts from *This American Life* and then brainstormed to generate the research question from their book. Once this question was honed by incorporating instructor feedback, they were given instruction and practice in searching PsycINFO and Google Scholar to find relevant source material. They planned their productions by writing a script and creating a storyboard, and they received some acting instruction. Additionally, they participated in a workshop from an IT professional in a computer lab, where they learned how to use GarageBand software to record and edit their work.

There are various programs students can use to edit their multimedia projects. Audio files can also be edited using free software such as Audacity, and vodcasts and videos can be created and edited using GarageBand, iMovie, or Windows Movie Maker, most of which are preinstalled on computers, especially those available to students either in a college computer lab or via a loan program. To help students use the technology effectively, IT departments are often willing to give in-class tutorials; alternatively, students could watch a video and then practice in class.

Video assignments appear to have multiple benefits, and students seem to view them positively (Lyons et al., 1984; Malouff & Emmerton, 2014; Zacchilli, 2014). Malouff and Emmerton (2014) found that making and critiquing videos (which were uploaded to YouTube) on using behavioral modification principles to change a particular behavior, such as nail biting, helped students build confidence about their public speaking skills and their perceived knowledge of psychological theories. Lyons et al. (1984) also found that creating videos of clinical interviews with a partner in an Abnormal Psychology class helped students develop better interpersonal relationships with their classmates. In the videos, one student played the part of a client who had a psychological disorder, and had to display as many signs and symptoms as possible, while the other played the interviewer (Lyons et al., 1984). Students felt that the videos were successful in promoting class discussion. Each video was played at the start of a class, and all the other students had to identify the disorder and explain the rationale for their decisions (see also Section 4.3.3 on how role-play can be used to develop CT skills).

Other studies have demonstrated that creating videos improved students' test scores for video-related materials. Pettijohn and Perelli (2005) assigned small groups of Introductory Psychology students to first create a webpage about a broad course-related topic (e.g., Biopsychology, Personality, Social Psychology), and then make a 3-minute video demonstrating the application of a concept within the topic to real life. They found that students scored significantly higher on test items relating to their webpage/video topic compared to other topics. Zacchilli (2014) assigned small groups of students in a Research Methods and Statistics class to create a music video about course-related materials, such as t-tests, ANOVA, steps involved in hypothesis testing, and validity. They were graded on their participation, creativity, and ability to convey information correctly. Students found the project to be enjoyable and helpful for understanding their chosen topic, and recommended the use of similar video-based projects in other courses.

3.5.2 Digital Stories

Digital stories use many of the same technologies as podcasts (see previous section), but have the additional advantage that stories are powerful vehicles for invoking emotions. Cognitive psychology research has convincingly demonstrated that presenting information in a narrative format makes it more memorable (Bower & Clark, 1969; Gamst & Freund, 1978; Graesser, Hauft-Smith, Cohen, & Pyles, 1980; Murray, 1974; Wolfe, 2005). This may explain students' preferences for narrative-style textbooks (Fernald, 1989) and their enhanced recall of materials when told in a story format over simple descriptions in a lecture (Grobman, 2015). Bruner (1990) posited that creating stories is crucial for making meaning of experiences; given that student-produced digital stories tend to be autobiographical in nature (Rossiter & Garcia, 2010), such stories allow students to self-reflect about their learning and accomplishments, their identity and personal development, the application of theories to their everyday lives, ethical issues in the context of internships, perspective-taking and issues of diversity, and their preparation for the future.

Making an effective digital story requires students to be able to distill the essential elements of their narrative into a short (2–10-minute) video that has a beginning, a middle, and an end and that evokes interest in the audience through the use of pictures (moving or still), narration, music, and sound effects. Stories are designed to be shared. Hence, such projects have a public performance element that may serve to motivate students to produce their best work. StoryCenter (formerly the Center for Digital Storytelling; www.storycenter.org) has partnered with various organizations (including some in higher education) to help individuals develop digital story projects to promote and advocate for various health, justice, and other community issues. Their website hosts digital stories that can serve as helpful models for students. Joe Lambert, one of the founders of the digital storytelling movement, has also produced a "cookbook" containing valuable recipes for creating effective digital stories (Lambert, 2010). He describes several basic principles for digital story production, which we have adapted and condensed (see Box 3.8). Barrett (2006) has used these elements (along with some additional ones) to create comprehensive rubrics that are useful for evaluating students' digital stories.

Box 3.8 Principles for Digital Story Production

1) **Point of view:** Who is telling the story and what is it about?
2) **Dramatic question:** What is the key attention-grabbing question that the story poses and answers in its conclusion?
3) **Emotional content:** How will you help your audience feel connected to the story?
4) **Using your voice:** How will you tell your story?
5) **Soundtrack:** What sound effects/music will you use to enhance your story?
6) **Economy:** Digital stories are short and sweet!
7) **Pacing:** How quickly (or slowly) does your story develop?

Source: Adapted from Lambert (2010).

A number of authors have described digital story assignments in various disciplines in higher education, including the humanities (Leon, 2008; Oppermann, 2008), anthropology (Fletcher & Cambre, 2009), teacher training (Heo, 2009; Kocaman-Karoglu, 2016), and health-related fields (Gazarian, 2010; Robin, 2008; Sandars & Murray, 2009; Stacey & Hardy, 2011). Watching other students' digital stories can be a way of beginning class discussions and opening students' minds to different cultures and experiences. Although relatively few studies have investigated the effects of digital stories on student learning, there is emerging evidence that these assignments tend to increase student engagement (Rowinsky-Geurts, 2013), motivation (Kocaman-Karoglu, 2016), and self-efficacy (Spicer & Miller, 2014); use of digital stories can effect attitudinal changes about stereotypes (Anderson, Kinnair, Hardy, & Sumner, 2012) and may increase patient advocacy among students in health-related fields (Gazarian, 2010).

To our knowledge, there are as yet no published studies on the efficacy of digital stories in psychology classes, although research suggests that other forms of stories can enhance student learning (Dunn, 1997; Fields, Thompson, & Huisma, 2015; Nordstrom, 2014). Dunn (1997) found that when students were asked to write about a personal life-myth in a Personality class, they not only enjoyed the exercise but reported learning a lot about themselves. Similarly, Fields et al. (2015) found that when students in a Human Development class wrote a cultural autobiography in which they reflected on how their development was shaped by their experiences, they felt that writing stories increased their self-knowledge and knowledge about others. Nordstrom (2014) explored the impact of participation in the Voices Project in reducing racism among White students in an Introductory Psychology course: students identified a minority group that they had negative feelings toward and then interviewed a member of that group about their cultural experiences; they also attended an event representative of that culture, and then wrote a first-person memoir from the perspective of their interviewee. Student interviews were woven together to create a staged reading event, which was presented to the class and to campus. Students who participated in the Voices Project exhibited less prejudice, greater empathy, and increased acknowledgment of White privilege than students in a control class, with some of the gains still evident one year later.

3.6   Summary

1) Multimedia can be used in student-centered ways to foster active learning, enhance quantitative reasoning and scientific literacy, and develop students' technological skills, while promoting agency and mastery motivation.
2) Classroom technology should be well tested before "going live."
3) Student response systems (SRSs) are an effective and flexible tool for achieving total class participation and formative assessment in classes of various sizes.
4) Multimedia projects must be scaffolded so that students are supported in their learning. We recommend using templates, examples of completed work, and grading rubrics to convey project expectations.

4

Advancing Critical Thinking Through Active Learning

4.1   What is Critical Thinking?

Most college instructors endorse critical thinking (CT) as an essential learning outcome for undergraduates, although they may disagree about how it should be defined and operationalized. CT is often defined as deliberative thinking, in which evidence from multiple viewpoints is weighed in order to reach a considered conclusion about what to think or do (Halpern, 1998). It has been closely linked to proficiency in the use of the scientific method (Staib, 2003). Not surprisingly, the American Psychological Association (APA) charges psychology departments to promote scientific inquiry and CT skills within the major (American Psychological Association, 2013). More specifi- cally, it suggests that by graduation, psychology majors should be able to interpret behavior, use scientific reasoning to interpret psychological phenomena, be literate with regards to psychology-related information, and be able to engage in innovative, integrative thinking and problem solving (American Psychological Association, 2013). The breadth of these learning outcomes—especially the last three—underscores the fact that CT is a multifaceted construct. This raises instructional challenges about which CT skills to focus on within a class and how best to assess whether they have improved (Bensley & Murtagh, 2012; see also Section 4.8). There is a continuing debate about whether CT skills are domain-general or discipline-specific, and whether they are best taught from a multidisciplinary perspective (Bensley & Murtagh, 2012). Halpern (1999) has pointed out that many CT skills are transferrable across disciplines and situ- ations, *if* students are taught in such a way that they become disposed to think reflec- tively and with open-minded skepticism. Therefore, helping students to develop appropriate metacognitive skills—wherein they learn to reflect on their beliefs, how they make sense of things, and how their beliefs might change over time—is clearly an important feature of CT instruction (see also Section 7.3 on Students' Metacognitive Biases). CT skills are also more likely to be transferrable to the world outside the class- room when instruction focuses on real-world problems (Halpern, 1999).

As many authors have noted, asking students to change the kind of thinking that they do in their classes is no small task (e.g., Benassi & Goldstein, 2006; Halonen, 2008; Halpern, 1998, 1999; King & Kitchener, 2004). CT requires students to expend a great deal more effort than simply learning facts and regurgitating them for exams; thus,

Teaching Psychology: An Evidence-Based Approach, First Edition. Jillian Grose-Fifer, Patricia J. Brooks, and Maureen O'Connor.
© 2019 John Wiley & Sons, Inc. Published 2019 by John Wiley & Sons, Inc.
Companion website: www.wiley.com/go/Grose-Fifer/teaching-psychology

students will be best served if psychology departments institute a developmental program of student-centered CT instruction that supports them as they progress through the major. Such a curriculum would provide the frequent practice needed to make engaging in higher-order thinking more reflexive.

When considering how best to help students improve their CT abilities, it is useful to reflect on some common hierarchical taxonomies of higher-order thinking skills, two of which we introduced in Chapter 2: Bloom's taxonomy (Anderson et al., 2001), with six levels of increasingly complex cognitive skills (Remember, Understand, Apply, Analyze, Evaluate, Create), and Fink's taxonomy (Fink, 2007; 2013), which defines "significant learning experiences" for students across six intersecting domains, including personal development (see Figures 2.1 and 2.2). In addition, King and Kitchener's (2004) reflective judgment model, which builds on previous models by Perry (1970) and Dewey (1933), shows how CT skills develop over time (see Figure 4.1).

King and Kitchener (2004) reviewed several studies that tracked epistemological development of CT in U.S. high-school and college students. In general, participants were evaluated on their ability to respond to "ill-defined problems" for which there are no definitive answers, such as, "Why does alcoholism occur?" They found that most first-year college students had progressed from using absolutist, pre-reflective thinking (commonly seen in high-school students), which is based largely on personal opinion and dichotomous thinking that answers as either right or wrong, to the quasi-reflective stage, wherein they were able to recognize that many issues can be debated from multiple different perspectives. However, first-year students were often confused about how to evaluate the credibility or validity of evidence supporting a particular viewpoint (see also Wineburg, McGrew, Breakstone, & Ortega, 2016). Perhaps more tellingly, after 4 years of college, although seniors were more likely to use evidence in making claims than first-year students, only graduate students reached the next epistemological milestone (the reflective stage). On the whole, graduate students were able to evaluate

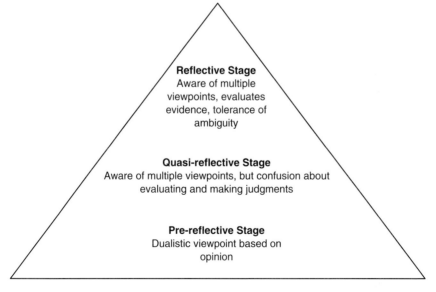

Figure 4.1 Reflective Judgment Model. *Source:* Adapted from King and Kitchener (2004).

Box 4.1 Assessment of Epistemic Level and Critical Thinking Disposition

Note these could be assigned as homework. For review, see also Duell and Schommer-Aikins (2001).

- Although King and Kitchener used interviews to collect their data, Kitchener (1994) also developed a pen-and-paper instrument to assess **Reflective Judgment**. The instrument consists of two questions: *How were the pyramids built?* and *Is it safe to consume artificial sweeteners?* It then has a multiple-choice portion that teases apart how students reached their answers. It takes 40–60 minutes to administer.
- Similarly, the **Epistemological Understanding by Judgment Domain Belief(s)** was developed by Kuhn, Cheney, and Weinstock (2000). It takes about 10–20 minutes to administer and consists of 15 statements, each one followed by two forced-choice answers that allows students' epistemic beliefs across different domains to be categorized as absolutist, multiplist, or evaluativist (which are similar to King and Kitchener's three stages; see Figure 4.1).
- Based on earlier work by Schommer (1990) that assessed epistemic development across multiple domains, including orientation toward learning (after Dweck & Leggett, 1988), the **Epistemic Beliefs Inventory** (Schraw, Bendixen, & Dunkle, 2002) can be used to assess epistemic development. It takes about 15–20 minutes to administer and consists of 28 statements (five of which are reverse scored). Students answer on a 1–5 Likert scale (1 = strongly disagree and 5 = strongly agree), and scores are summed for five different areas: **certain knowledge** (willingness to believe that truth means different things to different people); **simple knowledge** (e.g., things are simpler than most professors would have you believe); **quick learning** (belief that learning something should be quick); **omniscient authority** (belief that professors or other experts know all the answers); and **innate ability** (belief that intelligence is fixed from birth).

---

evidence in order to formulate an argument and were tolerant of ambiguity (King & Kitchener, 2004). It is possible that the relatively modest gains that King and Kitchener (2004) found in CT over the course of the baccalaureate may be attributable in part to a lack of formal instruction in CT skills (see discussion of CT instruction in Section 4.2). Students vary considerably in their epistemic levels, and the speed with which they shift their beliefs may be linked to their dispositional tendency to be open-minded and curious (Cross & Steadman, 1996). Therefore, it may be very helpful for an instructor to assess both epistemic developmental level and CT disposition at the beginning and the end of the course in order to evaluate the efficacy and appropriateness of the CT instruction (Box 4.1).

4.2 Critical Thinking Instruction

Various models have been used to teach CT to undergraduates, but the immersion approach (Ennis, 1989) is probably the most common (Bensley, Crowe, Bernhardt, Buckner, & Allman, 2010). The immersion model promotes the idea that CT will improve "naturalistically" if students are provided with "thought-provoking materials" in their classes but no formal CT instruction or assessment is provided (Ennis, 1989). Furthermore, these classes are often taught from a teacher-centered approach, wherein students focus on what the teacher is doing rather than on their own activities as learners. Bensley et al. (2010) found some support for the immersion model by showing that CT skills (defined as better argument analysis skills on a psychology CT test) were correlated with the number of psychology classes that students had taken. Nevertheless, the immersion method in general does *not* seem to be the most effective way to improve CT. A meta-analysis of 117 studies with a wide age span of participants (including undergraduates) concluded that although immersion significantly improved CT, gains were considerably greater if a student had received explicit CT instruction within the context of a content-specific course, especially if the instructor had received appropriate teacher training to hone these skills (Abrami et al., 2008). Therefore, we strongly recommend that instructors explicitly identify the CT skills that they want their students to acquire, and provide targeted instruction for the development of these skills. This will also lead to a deeper understanding of the material.

4.2.1   Activity-Based Instruction

CT instruction is inherently student-centered, and so draws on the principles of activity-based learning championed by pioneers such as Dewey, Piaget, Vygotsky, and Bruner (as cited by Kolb, 2014), who suggested that learners need to explore materials (especially with peers) and construct their own knowledge in order to learn effectively. In higher-education contexts, CT instruction may be grounded in purposeful action aimed at meaningful goals—addressing, for example, issues of citizenship, participatory democracy, and social justice (Stetsenko, 2017). Engaging students in collaborative problem-solving activities imbued with ethics and values offers opportunities for *being-through-doing*, with the activities creating contexts for personal development and transformation (Podlucká, 2017; Vianna, Hougaard, & Stetsenko, 2014; Vianna & Stetsenko, 2017).

In 1987, the American Association of Higher Education (AAHE) formulated seven evidence-based principles for effective undergraduate education (Chickering & Gamson, 1987), three of which underscore the need for active learning, practice, and collaboration—all essential elements of discovery-based learning. In a meta-analytical study that assessed the efficacy of various pedagogical techniques, Alfieri, Brooks, Aldrich, and Tenenbaum (2011) determined that *scaffolded* or *guided discovery* was a particularly effective learning practice in terms of fostering retention of information, whereas *pure discovery* (i.e., without feedback, worked examples, or other forms of support) was ineffective (relative to explicit teaching), presumably because it is too cognitively taxing, especially when students lack awareness of what a successful outcome looks like (see also Hattie & Yates, 2014; Kirschner, Sweller, & Clark, 2006). Richmond and Hagan (2011) demonstrated that structured active learning promotes higher-order thinking to a greater extent than traditional lecturing. In a study comparing the effectiveness of different methods of active learning, Sawyer et al. (2017) observed better learning of critical concepts in Developmental Psychology (e.g., *object permanence*, *joint attention*) when students were given a worked example of how another "student" had answered a set of minute-paper questions (note that the example was generated by the instructor, rather than by an actual student), compared to when they simply discussed their answer with a partner. Students who were instructed to critique the responses could use them to model the level of analysis that was expected, and may thus have delved more deeply in thinking about the concepts than did students engaged in a traditional verbal Think–Pair–Share with a peer (Sawyer et al., 2017).

In guided discovery, the instructor breaks a complex task into smaller subtasks and provides feedback to steer students toward their goal. Students still have some freedom in how they go about the task, but because it is semi-structured, the cognitive demands are manageable, and so students are more efficient than when they engage in totally unstructured activities in which they are given free rein to go in any direction that they please (Alfieri et al., 2011). Such scaffolding seems to be necessary for preventing frustration, especially in novice learners, who may lack the necessary expertise to organize their exploration of a topic (Moreno, 2004). Allowing students to construct knowledge for themselves is valuable because it makes them more likely not only to understand concepts and remember them for longer periods of time, but also to transfer their knowledge and skills to other situations, such as other classes, the workplace, and community life (Kolb, 2014).

4.3   Oral Communication: Talking to Learn (and Learning to Talk)

To explicitly demonstrate to students that improving CT is an important course learning outcome, Buskist and Irons (2008) suggest that instructors should set the stage in the very first class of the semester. They propose that instructors begin by eliciting student opinions about common psychological myths that relate directly to the course. For example, in a Brain and Behavior class, instructors might ask whether students believe that humans use only 10% of their brains; for lists of other common misconceptions, see Lilienfeld, Lynn, Ruscio, and Beyerstein (2010), Standing and Huber (2003), or Vaughan (1977). An effective strategy to ensure total class participation during this exercise is to use the Think–Pair–Share technique (Lyman, 1981), or one of its variants, such as Think–Write–Pair–Share (T-W-P-S) (Lyman, 1987; see Box 4.2). T-W-P-S exercises have been shown to increase student performance on psychology exams (Butler, Phillmann, & Smart, 2001) and on discipline-related CT assessments in nursing students (Kaddoura, 2013).

4.3.1   Fostering Inclusive Discussion

Classroom discussion, either in small groups or as an entire class, is an effective way to increase students' CT skills, as they draw connections between course material, societal issues, and their lived experiences (Garside, 1996; Tsui, 2002). Talking in class helps students to develop a greater awareness of their own ideas, and allows them to modify their knowledge after listening to the opinions and explanations of others (Garside, 1996). Classroom discussion yields greater learning gains if students are prepared ahead of time and understand the purpose of the activity (Zinn & Saville, 2008). Pre-discussion assignments such as asking students to summarize the main points of a reading or having them generate discussion points ensure they will have some familiarity with the concepts before they come to class. However, the goal of most discussions is for students to engage in the kinds of CT where they have to analyze, interpret, or critique

---

Box 4.2 How to Use the Think–Write–Pair–Share Technique

1) **The instructor asks a question of the whole class.**
2) **Students decide on their answer and write down a justification of it.** Having students justify their answers helps to set them on the road to understanding the difference between personal opinion and evidence-supported arguments (Benassi & Goldstein, 2006). This low-stakes writing assignment can help students to organize their thoughts.
3) **Students then pair up for a short (5-minute) discussion.** This extends the amount of time students are typically given to come up with an answer (Tanner, 2013), normalizing the idea that CT is effortful.
4) **After a few minutes, the instructor calls on students to share the results of their discussion with the rest of the class.** Because every student has written down an answer, the instructor can call on them randomly without anyone feeling that they are put on the spot—they can simply read their answer. This process of "cold calling" helps to avoid classroom discussions being dominated by students who always raise their hands, and is an effective strategy for establishing a participatory culture where all students contribute.

   Placing folded index cards with students' names on their desks personalizes and facilitates this cold-calling practice, while greatly aiding instructors in learning the names of their students. Another technique that fosters good listening skills is to ask students to explain what their partner told them in the preceding discussion.

---

concepts (McKeachie & Svinicki, 2013). Therefore, it is imperative that students be given guidance about what to look for in the reading (Zinn & Saville, 2008). For example, instructors can ask students to make note of similarities or differences between the viewpoints of the authors and those expressed by students in a previous class.

It is important to ensure at the outset that students understand that class discussions are designed to promote greater tolerance for other people's opinions, and time should be spent establishing rules to create a safe and respectful discussion environment (Case, 2011; DiClementi & Handelsman, 2005). Faculty (and students) frequently avoid talking about sensitive issues (e.g., race, sexual orientation) in classroom settings because they are unsure of how to handle the tension such subjects can create (Sue, Lin, Torino, Capodilupo, &, Rivera, 2009). However, students can benefit immensely from discussions that increase their understanding of both their own and other people's identities and behaviors. Talking about race and the intersectionality of social identities (e.g., gender, race, class) in class helps students gain a greater awareness of privilege and what underlies oppression (Case, 2007; Lawrence & Tatum, 1999; Tatum, 1992). Discussions of race have also been shown to be effective in increasing student support for affirmative action (Case, 2007). In their Psychology of Race classes, Beverly Daniel Tatum and her colleagues successfully used the following rules to encourage students to engage openly in difficult conversations about discrimination and prejudice: students were asked to (a) address one another by name; (b) refrain from identifying what a particular student may have said outside of the classroom environment; (c) avoid using put-downs; and (d) use phrases such as "In my experience, I have found..." when referring to a personal situation, to differentiate personal opinion from arguments formed using wider, more generally accepted evidence (Lawrence & Tatum, 1999; Tatum, 1992). In a similar vein, Johnson and Johnson (2009a) advocate that in class discussions, discussants should treat one another as they themselves would like to be treated. This requires students to be open and willing to change, to listen carefully, and to try and understand diverse viewpoints, even if they do not agree with them. Students are asked to focus their criticism on ideas and not on other people; likewise, they should not take criticism personally (Johnson & Johnson, 2009a). These seem like important ground rules if students are to feel that their opinions are valued and can be safely voiced in class discussions. Another tack, mentioned in Chapter 1, is to use the reciprocal interview technique on the first day of class to set the scene for open communication and establish a sense of community (Case, 2011; Hermann, Foster, & Hardin, 2010).

Case and others also highlight the need for instructors to regularly self-reflect on their own privileges, biases, and assumptions, and how these could affect the learning environment (Case, 2017; Case, Miller, & Jackson, 2012; Stuart, 2004; Sue & Sue, 2016). In addition, instructors can promote metacognitive development in their students by asking them to journal about how their personal experiences are relevant to the sensitive discussions in the classroom; for example, by writing about their own racial identity development (Lawrence & Tatum, 1999; Tatum, 1992) or the contexts in which they are privileged (Case et al., 2012).

To foster constructive dialogues about controversial topics, one should try to link questions directly to psychological theories, thereby asking students to consider how psychological science might inform the controversy. As an example, when teaching Introductory Psychology to New York City college students following the exoneration of police in the Eric Garner case (Baker, Goodman, & Mueller, 2015), Cumiskey (2015) posed the following problem: "We have discussed the theories of conformity, deindividuation, and obedience to authority. Use one of these theories to explain how this may lead police to use excessive force against civilians, like in the Eric Garner case. Explain one way that might help to break this cycle." Given that students were likely to view the topic of policing as potentially polarizing, they were instructed to write their answers anonymously. Cumiskey collated their responses by grouping them to form themes. She then showed them to the class, thus providing a "social mirror" that allowed the students to see the breadth of personal opinions within the class. Because the viewpoints were displayed anonymously, students felt that they could express themselves within a safe environment. Also, to prevent students from feeling marginalized in the case that only a few others seemed to share their perspective, Cumiskey also asked them to raise their hands if they had heard something that they agreed with but hadn't written down in their initial response. This type of exercise, where students link social psychological concepts to current events and offer their own suggestions of how best to counteract human tendencies to conform and yield to obedience, aims to build a learning community where students can talk about contentious issues in a climate of respect.

For less controversial topics, asking a leading question is often an effective way to launch a discussion (Zinn & Saville, 2008). If the topic you wish to discuss is complex, be sure to scaffold it by asking one question at a time, thus building the dialogue incrementally so as not to overwhelm or confuse your students. It is also vitally important to allow sufficient time for students to respond. Thinking on their feet is often difficult for students, and their silence can often feel uncomfortably long, especially to new instructors. We recommend using methods like the T-W-P-S technique to give students time to organize their thinking while letting you see that they are actively engaged in the process. Ultimately, every student should be ready to participate when called on, so that you can use "cold calling" to foster a climate of equal participation in discussions. Writing the key points that students raise on the board will make it easier for the class to follow the thread of the discussion. This practice validates students' contributions and helps them to recognize that there is a perspective broader than their own. Similarly, asking students to organize the information on the board by (a) ranking their top three responses to a prompt and (b) providing a justification for their ranking (Himmele & Himmele, 2011) can help them to synthesize the main points of the discussion. Finally, it is important to provide students with time at the end of the discussion period to reflect on what they have learned (Zinn & Saville, 2008). Assigning a minute paper or a related homework assignment may be another effective way to do this.

In mid to large classes with flexible seating, you might try the fishbowl technique as a method for increasing participation and active listening in class discussions. This involves arranging seats in concentric circles, with members of the inner circle fielding questions and members of the outer circle(s) taking notes, generating questions, and formulating comments (Kramer & Korn, 1999). In an open fishbowl, one chair in the inner circle is left open so that students in the outer circles can come forward to express their viewpoints throughout the discussion. Typically, each time a student moves forward to take the empty seat, a member of the inner circle who has already contributed will move to the outer circle to free up their seat for the next participant.

4.3.2 Debates

Debates provide another way for students to practice their oral communication skills and improve their CT (Allen, Berkowitz, Hunt, & Louden, 1999; Colbert, 1987). Additionally, submitting an annotated outline of their argument prior to the debate helps students to strengthen their written communication skills. Engaging in debates is especially effective for enhancing students' critical analysis abilities (D'Souza, 2013). To prevent students from gathering data that support only their own personal viewpoint (biased assimilation), it is important sometimes to assign them to argue in opposition to their personal views (Budesheim & Lundquist, 1999). Although traditionally only a very small number of students can participate in a debate, there have been various suggestions for achieving total class participation (for review, see Kennedy, 2007). For example, you can assign students to participate in panels rather than as individuals, and have them decide collectively what points they will make and who will put forward each one. Another way to increase participation is to have students work in groups of six, consisting of two debaters and four audience members (Dundes, 2001). Audience members can ask questions, which helps to deepen the level of thinking that the debaters need to engage in, or they can act as conciliators, who at the end of the debate adopt a position that takes into account both viewpoints or proposes an alternative (Musselman, 2004).

In the 1970s, Johnson and Johnson pioneered an alternative type of debate-related learning practice that they called "constructive controversy" (Johnson & Johnson, 2009b). They found that this method was highly effective in helping students learn how to construct rational evidence-based arguments and develop the ability to listen to diverse viewpoints with an open mind (Johnson & Johnson, 2009b). In this

---

Box 4.3 Helpful Resources for Debate Topics

Halgin, R. P. (Ed.). (2002). *Taking sides: Clashing views on controversial issues in abnormal psychology*. Guilford, CT: McGraw-Hill/Dushkin.

Slife, B. (2013). *Taking sides: Clashing views on psychological issues*, 18th edition. Guilford, CT: Duskin/McGraw-Hill.

---

technique, students are organized into groups of four to work collaboratively toward reaching a consensus about a controversial issue that has two well-documented sides to it. Initially, the instructor assigns one pair in the group to argue for one side and the other pair for the other side. Each pair adds to evidence provided by the instructor by doing its own research, and uses this information to construct a cohesive argument for the debate. The two pairs then present their arguments to each other during class. This may sound like a standard debate, but once the pairs have presented both sides, they switch sides and argue for the opposite position. Finally, the group members collectively review all the evidence, reach a consensus about their group's position, and collaboratively write a report that documents their decision and the evidence that they used to reach it. This multifaceted assignment targets many important skills for undergraduates, such as public speaking, listening, researching, flexibility in thinking, ability to weigh evidence, and writing. Perhaps not surprisingly, a meta-analysis showed that constructive criticism debates were even more effective than traditional debates in increasing student achievement and the tendency to use higher-order reasoning (Johnson, Johnson, & Smith, 2000). Box 4.3 provides additional resources for enhancing CT skills through class debates.

4.3.3 Role-Playing

Role-playing has been shown to enhance comprehension of basic knowledge better than listening to a lecture (McCarthy & Anderson, 2000; Poling & Hupp, 2009), while also honing communication (Stroessner, Beckerman, & Whittaker, 2009) and CT skills (Poling & Hupp, 2009). It has been used extensively in clinical environments, where medical students, counselors, or clinical psychologists either play the role of a patient/client with a particular disorder or practice their assessment skills by acting the part of a clinician (for review, see Stroessner et al., 2009). Role-playing exercises have been shown to be highly effective, not only in helping students to recognize signs and symptoms associated with particular disorders, but also in developing the communication skills and sensibilities needed to work with patient populations (for review, see Stroessner et al., 2009). Moving beyond clinical settings, role-plays can be used in any psychology class to foster perspective-taking skills (Pusateri, Halonen, Hill, & McCarthy, 2009), an important factor in CT development. In classroom role-plays, students typically take on the parts of central characters from a reading and then act out a scenario. Clearly, these types of activities tap into multiple levels of Bloom's taxonomy (see Figure 2.1). For example, students must be able to *remember* and *understand* the details from the reading, *apply* psychological concepts to the scenario, and *analyze* different perspectives as they *create* dramatic representations of their assigned characters. Finally, students are often asked to collaborate with other students in these exercises, and so they need to learn how to work with others who may have viewpoints different from their own.

Extensive use of role-playing within a single course is exemplified in the nationally acclaimed first-year seminar, Reacting to the Past, first introduced at Barnard College (Stroessner et al., 2009). Students typically play three "games" over the course of a semester, in which they act out a specific role from a classic text that portrays an important historical event. They must conduct research in groups and use persuasive argument to address a particular objective. In comparison to controls, students who took the seminar in various institutions across the country not only had better rhetorical skills, but also had higher levels of self-esteem and empathy, and were less likely to believe that people's intellectual abilities are fixed (Stroessner et al., 2009). These findings underscore the power of role-playing in fostering a growth mindset (Yeager & Dweck, 2012) and eliciting other changes in beliefs and attitudes that are critical for epistemic development (see also Section 7.5 on Mindsets around Testing and Learning). Most role-play activities are not as lengthy as the Reacting to the Past seminar, and data suggest that even short role-plays are beneficial for student learning. McCarthy and Anderson (2000) found that although each student in a history class played only one role during a particular exercise, they demonstrated a deep understanding of the other perspectives that their peers represented during the activity.

One of our favorite role-play exercises centers around the Tuskegee syphilis study (Reverby, 2000). To prepare them for the role-play, students read an overview article as homework (Thomas & Quinn, 1991), which may be supplemented by additional articles or websites on specific people and organizations involved in the study. In class, students work in small groups to play the part of one of the people or organizations mentioned in the readings; such roles typically include representatives of the U.S. Public Health Service, Nurse Eunice Rivers who was associated with the project, study participants, and Peter Buxton, the whistle-blower. Groups are given time in class to come up with a script that explains their role and provides a justification for their behavior in the study. Students then come to a tribunal, where the characters explain their different perspectives. Every person in each group speaks for at least 1 minute, and while they are speaking, other members of the group mimic their body language to convey the impression that they are in fact part of the same person. People are encouraged to air their grievances and question others about their role in the study. Finally, students answer questions about the study and research ethics in a homework assignment—although others have suggested that summarization of role-play conclusions can also be done in the form of a class-wide discussion (Hertel & Millis, 2002). Such class discussion may be particularly effective when, after the role-play, students write minute papers that summarize what they have learned and what remains puzzling or confusing, or that ask them to relate the role-play exercise to a broader issue, such as the need for protections of human subjects in research (for more on this exercise, see Grose-Fifer, 2017).

Role-play activities such as these have been found to be more effective in deepening students' understanding about ethical issues in psychology than simply discussing the matter in class (Grose-Fifer, 2017; Strohmetz, 1992). Furthermore, the particular form of role-play that we describe here requires students to collaborate in a structured way and so is useful for scaffolding the kinds of skills that are needed in more extensive teamwork projects. We provide other suggestions for role-play exercises in Box 4.4; note that some of these activities have been modified from the originals. One word of

Box 4.4 Suggestions for Role-Play Scenarios

Class/topic	Scenario	Roles	Related references
Developmental Psychology	Students play a well-known psychologist debating with another psychologist(s) about the best way to teach a young child how to tie a shoe.	Vygotsky Skinner	
Ethics/Social Psychology	Students play either the author of a study that is considered to be ethically controversial (in which case they have to defend your study) or a member of the institutional review board (IRB) that has received complaints about the study.	Milgram Zimbardo	Rosnow (1990) Strohmetz (1992)
Social Psychology	Students must design a study that taps into a situation where obedience, conformity, or social roles are investigated. They then act out the study for the class and describe the variables they will measure.	Researcher	Bleske-Rechek (2001)
Abnormal Psychology	Students practice clinical interview skills for suicide prevention. Pairs of students role-play the client and the counselor, switching roles periodically to allow equal practice with both.	Person with suicidal ideation Counselor	
History of Psychology	Students explain how their character influenced the field of psychology, using a speed-dating type forum in which they briefly interview one another.	Binet Cattell Galton Yerkes Witner	Zehr (2004)
Ethics/Research Methods	Students make up skits that portray ethical dilemmas related to: confidentiality, voluntary participation, anonymity, deception, analysis and reporting, debriefing, participant harm, competence, respect for rights, dignity, and diversity.		Kraus (2008)
Child Psychology	Groups of students act as co-parents to a virtual baby who has one of the following issues: attention deficit hyperactivity disorder, fetal alcohol syndrome, Down's syndrome, and autistic spectrum disorder. They explain the problems their child has and how their development is affected.	Parent of a child with a developmental disorder	Poling and Hupp (2009)

caution: some role-plays may touch on sensitive issues, so it is important to establish ground rules ahead of time. For example, some students may be hurt if they feel that their classmates are portraying people with mental illnesses in an insensitive way. This can be guarded against in part by having students research and receive feedback on such illnesses (or their scripts) prior to the exercise. As already mentioned, it is also important for students to discuss the role-play before leaving the class, which allows them to voice any concerns and to talk about issues such as stereotyping and stigma.

4.4   In-Class Demonstrations and Simulations

In-class demonstrations and simulations of classic psychological experiments allow for experiential learning about experimental design and theoretically based content. These experiences often spark interest (and sometimes disequilibrium) in students, such that they feel motivated to think more critically about issues in psychology (Lawrence, Serdikoff, Zinn, & Baker, 2009). For example, when learning about Milgram's (1963) classic experiment on obedience to authority, many students do not believe that they would be as easily manipulated as Milgram's participants. However, if the class starts with a demonstration in which students are asked to do something out of their comfort zone, such as giving personal information to a confederate posing as an instructor (LoSchiavo, Buckingham, & Yurak, 2002) or taking off their shoe and placing it in the middle of the room (Bolt, 2013), they are likely to have a greater appreciation for the validity of Milgram's results. In a related exercise, Beins (1993) found that after students had been deceived in a demonstration, they had greater empathy for participants in classical psychology studies involving deception.

Most areas of psychology readily lend themselves to the use of demonstrations and simulations, and many excellent resources (some are given in Box 4.5) are available as guides. In-class demonstrations also provide opportunities for even introductory-level students to acquire first-hand experience of data collection and central tendencies. In classes using student response systems (SRSs) or clickers, data can be rapidly collected and displayed (Cleary, 2008; see also Chapter 3 on Effective Multimedia Instruction). Alternatively, data collected via other means (e.g., pen-and-paper) can be entered into a spreadsheet program like Excel, either in class or between classes depending on the amount of data and the class size; later, the class can use the program to calculate statistics (e.g., basic descriptive statistics and correlations) and graph the data, providing students with additional opportunities to learn basic statistical concepts and strengthen their quantitative reasoning skills (Nash, 2008; Warner & Meehan, 2001; see also Section 4.6.2). Reviewing the class data can facilitate discussions in which students compare the data from the class to the published data (e.g., creating tables and graphs to summarize key findings) and consider reasons why their results might differ. Such activities promote discussion of issues pertaining to replication (including the "replicability crisis" in psychology), indicators of research quality, and what it means to do good science (Pashler & Harris, 2012; Simons, 2014).

Some activities require considerable preparation on the part of the students and instructor, whereas others can be inserted into a lesson plan as a brief demonstration paired with a discussion of key concepts. To illustrate, we describe here one of our favorite in-class activities, called "Smarties and Dum Dums," which we adapted from

---

Box 4.5 Resources for Simulations and Demonstrations

- Hanover College psychological tutorials and demonstrations: http://psych.hanover. edu/Krantz/tutor.html
- Go Cognitive: http://gocognitive.net/demos
- Dr. Timothy Bender Missouri State Memory and Cognition: http://courses.missouristate. edu/timothybender/mem/mydemos.html
- Jennifer McCabe Learning and Memory demos (links embedded in document): http:// teachpsych.org/Resources/Documents/otrp/resources/mccabe14.pdf
- Forensic Psychology Gary Wells (eye-witness memory demonstrations): www.psychology. iastate.edu/~glwells/
- Implicit Association Test: https://implicit.harvard.edu/implicit/demo/
- Promoting Student Engagement: http://teachpsych.org/ebooks/pse2011/vol2/ index.php
- Noba Project: http://nobaproject.com/resources/instructor-manual

Benjamin, L. T., Jr. (Ed.). (2010). *Favorite activities for the teaching of psychology*, 2nd edition. Washington, DC: American Psychological Association.

Ware, M. E., & Johnson, D. E. (Eds.). (2000). *Handbook of demonstrations and activities in the teaching of psychology*, 2nd edition. Vol. I: *Introductory, statistics, research methods, and history*. Mahwah, NJ: Erlbaum.

Ware, M. E., & Johnson, D. E. (Eds.). (2000). *Handbook of demonstrations and activities in the teaching of psychology*, 2nd edition. Vol. II: *Physiological-comparative, perception, learning, cognitive, and developmental*. Mahwah, NJ: Erlbaum.

Ware, M. E., & Johnson, D. E. (Eds.). (2000). *Handbook of demonstrations and activities in the teaching of psychology*, 2nd edition. Vol. III: *Personality, abnormal, clinical, counseling, and social*. Mahwah, NJ: Erlbaum.

Lewandowski (2003). The main point of this activity is to provide students with an example of a flawed experiment that can be used to hone their skills in operationalizing variables and recognizing threats to experimental validity. Here is our set-up. First, we distribute a bag of candy containing Smarties and Dum Dums and ask each student to select a piece. Based on their selections, they are instructed to write on a piece of paper *I am one of the Smarties* or *I am a Dum Dum*. Next, we give them a 10-item "intelligence test" administered via a PowerPoint slideshow; each pair of slides presents a question followed by the answer (e.g., "Is there a Fourth of July in England?", "Yes, it follows the 3rd of July"; "Is it legal for a man in California to marry his widow's sister?", "No, he's dead"). As they complete the test, the students tally up how many questions they answered correctly. Then, using an Excel spreadsheet, the class quickly computes the average for the Smarties and Dum Dums groups, makes a graph, and computes a t-test.

Following the activity, we engage students in a structured discussion that starts off with the research question: *Are students who self-identify as Smarties more intelligent than students who self-identify as Dum Dums?* Through discussion, we tease apart the experimental design by asking students to identify the independent and dependent variables, whether random assignment was used, how intelligence was operationalized, and what we can conclude based on the findings. We then introduce issues of validity, such as construct validity (e.g., "Do you think that the test adequately measured your intelligence?"), predictive validity (e.g., "Do you think that the results of the intelligence test will predict your grade in this class?"), and external validity (e.g., "Do you think that the experiment is a realistic simulation of what happens in the real world with respect to students labeling themselves as smart or dumb?"). This can lead to a critical discussion of how, as a society, we define and measure human intelligence and the validity of standardized tests. Alternatively, as suggested by Hattie and Yates (2014), you might use the "intelligence test" to help students contrast System 1 (fast, automatic) and System 2 (slow, effortful) modes of thinking (cf. Kahneman, 2011; Stanovich & West, 2000). Initially, students are likely to engage in System 1 thinking, as the answers seem obvious. After a few questions, they usually realize they need to consider the phrasing more carefully. Talking about different modes of thinking may help students to better understand that effective learning is effortful (Hattie & Yates, 2014).

4.5 Distinguishing Science from Pseudoscience in Psychology Classes

Another popular approach to improving CT involves designing lessons to help students debunk pseudoscientific phenomena (for examples, see Adam & Manson, 2014; Beins, 1993; Benassi & Goldstein, 2006; Lawson & Crane, 2014; Lilienfeld, Lohr, & Morier, 2001; McLean & Miller, 2010; Wesp & Montgomery, 1998). Beliefs in pseudoscience are widespread, with a 2005 Gallup Poll reporting that 73% of Americans believed in some kind of paranormal phenomenon and 25% believed in astrology (McLean & Miller, 2010). Students in Introductory Psychology classes typically endorse similarly high levels of pseudoscientific beliefs, and many read their horoscopes regularly or take stock in "personality" surveys in magazines (McLean & Miller, 2010). Although some instructors have designed entire courses around pseudoscientific claims (Benassi & Goldstein, 2006; Burke, Sears, Kraus, & Roberts-Cady, 2014; Lilienfeld et al., 2001; McLean & Miller, 2010; Wesp & Montgomery, 1998), many others have simply used activities within their courses to jog students into thinking more deeply about these ideas (see Box 4.6 for resources for pseudoscience demonstrations and classroom activities).

One way to incentivize students to think skeptically about horoscopes and other personality surveys is by using a demonstration based on a classic study by Forer (1949). Forer asked students in his class to take a "personality" test and then generated a personality profile for each. Students rated their personality assessments as quite accurate, but Forer later revealed that they had all received the same assessment, based on random phrases from an astrology textbook. In classroom replications of Forer's study, students are typically very surprised and often a little mad or embarrassed at being duped (Beins, 1993). However, in a supportive learning environment, this state of disequilibrium can be used as an important catalyst for deeper thinking (Lawrence et al., 2009). Ultimately, these types of exercises may help to shift students' epistemological beliefs toward more scientific thinking about pseudoscientific phenomena (King & Kitchener, 2004). Without being judgmental about their beliefs, instructors can ask students why it is that their personality assessment seemed so accurate (Bolt, 2013). When students scrutinize the text more carefully, they are usually able to conclude that many of the statements are very general and could apply to anyone (Barnum effect), or that they were quite

Box 4.6 Pseudoscientific Activity Resources

Exercise	Claim(s)	Source
After watching the video https://www.youtube.com/watch?v=ZV5IIlNWDVk, students work in small groups to identify the claims made in the video and evaluate the evidence for those claims. After working for 10 minutes in this way, they engage in a class-wide discussion. Students describe issues related to order effects, the placebo effect, anecdotal evidence, use of small samples, and experimenter bias—for which instructors can provide the correct psychological terms.	I-renew bracelets improve strength and balance	Adam and Manson (2014)
The instructor explains the dowsing effect: some people can find water using dowsing rods; when the rods are held one in each hand over water, they automatically cross over each other. The instructor then pretends to demonstrate the technique by crossing the rods when holding them over an open cup of water and keeping them parallel over an empty cup. Student volunteers take turns and likely replicate this, believing that they also have the gift for dowsing. After *covering* the cups, other students try to dowse for the water, but the instructor has secretly switched the positions of the cups first. Students will likely cross the rods over the cup that they believe to contain water, but is actually empty. After revealing the deception, the instructor explains that this is called the ideomotor effect, where one's movements can be biased by one's beliefs. This can be linked with other ideomotor explanations of other pseudoscientific phenomena like Ouija boards, pendulum swinging to determine the sex of an unborn child, and facilitated communication.	Some people are able to dowse for water	Lawson and Crane (2014)
Students locate magazine or newspaper articles making pseudoscientific claims and identify misleading statements about research design and conclusions in these articles.	Cell phones cause cancer; vaccinations cause autism	Stark (2012)
The instructor demonstrates "telepathic powers" with the help of a colleague or student who is a confederate. The instructor asks a student volunteer to deal three rows of five cards; another student picks a card unseen by the instructor (but seen by the confederate). The confederate points to various cards and asks the instructor, "Is it this card?" or "Is it that card?" The clue is in the questioning— the top and bottom rows are "this" rows" and the middle row is a "that" row. If the question is a mismatch for the row then the instructor knows that it is the correct card. Students are asked to generate a testable hypothesis for how the trick worked.	People can communicate telepathically	Bates (1991)
Students work in small groups to research a pre-assigned claim (some of which are true) and then give a 4–5-minute presentation to the class.	Various claims (some true)	Blessing and Blessing (2010)
1) Describe a media portrayal of a claim; 2) Describe scientific evidence related to that claim, e.g., use of deception and contrast with media portrayal; 3) Write a critical analysis of the scientific evidence.	Various pseudoscientific claims, like ESP, clairvoyance, and fire-walking	Benassi and Goldstein (2006)

flattering (confirmation bias). With a little more careful questioning, they will probably acknowledge that they had in fact ignored statements that were not very accurate in the context of other seemingly accurate statements (fallacy of positive instances) (Bolt, 2013). Beins (1993) also showed that such demonstrations were effective in increasing students' understanding about the experiences of participants who had been deceived within the context of a psychology study. Students realized both how relatively easy it was to be deceived and that this experience was somewhat uncomfortable; this then prompted a class discussion on institutional review board (IRB) responsibilities and the importance of debriefing.

Various authors have shown that activities like these, which focus on pseudoscientific phenomena, tend to reduce students' beliefs in the paranormal (Burke et al., 2014; Lawson & Crane, 2014) and improve CT abilities, such as the ability to identify flawed arguments (Adam & Manson, 2014). However, instructors should not be lulled into a false sense of security: often, the changes produced are relatively small and do not occur for all students or across all testing conditions (i.e., they have limited transferability). Benassi and Goldstein (2006) have stressed that because beliefs in paranormal phenomena are very resistant to change, the ability to recognize similarities across different scenarios only comes with ample practice. Therefore, it is desirable to assign activities and discussions that relate to pseudoscience across all levels of courses in the Psychology major, in addition to asking students to reflect on why some beliefs are particularly resistant to change.

4.5.1   Developing Digital Literacy Skills

Pseudoscience activities can provide excellent opportunities to introduce information literacy instruction that focuses on evaluating the credibility of information retrieved from the Internet. The digital age has led to a drastic increase in the sheer volume of information that is quickly and easily available. Given concerns about the proliferation of fake news from newsfeeds, social media, and other online sources, and evidence that students lack skills in evaluating information credibility, students benefit from media literacy training that is embedded into the curriculum (Wineburg et al., 2016). Recent estimates suggest that two out of every three Americans get some of their news from social media (Shearer & Gottfried, 2017) and may have difficulty recognizing sources of bias in their newsfeeds. Given the nearly constant bombardment of alerts, updates, and other messages appearing on their mobile devices, students are likely to experience cognitive overload in their efforts to distinguish the veracity of information (Metzger & Flanagin, 2013). Concern about digital information literacy in college students has led to a proliferation of frameworks, assessments, and recommendations (for review, see Sparks, Katz, & Beile, 2016).

Carmichael and McMillan (2011) produced a useful rubric for students to use as a framework when evaluating online information, which was shown to be effective for improving information literacy. They suggest that students should take note of the author(s), date, intended audience, and purpose of an article (Carmichael & MacMillan, 2011). Similarly, the Meriam Library at the University of California, Chico created the CRAAP test to aid students in their evaluation of websites (Meriam Library, 2010); CRAAP stands for Currency, Relevance, Authority, Accuracy, and Purpose (see Box 4.7 for links to worksheets to be used with the CRAAP test and other resources for teaching

Box 4.7 Links to CRAAP Test Worksheets and Other Resources for Teaching Digital
Information Literacy

http://ctjlibrary.pbworks.com/w/file/fetch/72590366/CRAAP%20Test%20Worksheet.pdf
http://library.lsco.edu/help/web-page-rubric.pdf
https://docs.google.com/document/d/1seVfZVO_4V75heNRUsQe6CzTHh8rmYkEH2PIk
  Mdk988/edit
https://webliteracy.pressbooks.com/

digital information literacy). The CRAAP test provides a checklist to help students
determine the reliability of information they find on the Internet. It has been shown to
be effective in improving students' information literacy (Myhre, 2012; Wichowski &
Kohl, 2013). Small-group discussion has also been shown to help students to identify
"red flags" concerning the credibility of news articles or websites (Connor-Greene &
Greene, 2002).

  A complementary approach developed by the Stanford History Education Group
(SHEG) involves teaching students the behaviors and skills that expert fact-checkers use
to evaluate websites and online content (McGrew, Ortega, Breakstone, & Wineburg,
2017). Fact-checkers first leave the website they are evaluating and engage in "lateral"
reading of related content on other websites, including Wikipedia, in order to vet its
creators and content (McGrew et al., 2017). Building on this work, Caulfield (2017) suggests that students use the following four "moves" when evaluating evidence: (a) check
trusted sources for previous work on the disputed topic or claim; (b) go to another source
to find the original claim; (c) read what others say about the source; and (d) start over
with different search terms if the original search is not fruitful. Lessons and assessments
for developing students' online civic reasoning and information literacy can be downloaded free of charge from SHEG's website: https://sheg.stanford.edu/civic-online-
reasoning. These lessons are particularly valuable in helping students to differentiate
between bona fide news sites and native advertisements, which at first blush look very
credible, but are in fact promoting a non-neutral viewpoint. Additional materials for
teaching students how to vet online content are available at https://fourmoves.blog/.

4.6 Developing Qualitative and Quantitative Reasoning Skills

4.6.1 Qualitative Reasoning

A key skill for any college graduate is the ability to write persuasively using well-
constructed arguments. To do so, students must learn how to objectively gather and
evaluate credible evidence that argues both for and against a particular position. As we
outline in Chapter 6 on Learning to Write and Writing to Learn, writing persuasively is
a complex, multifaceted task; as such, students benefit from explicit guided instruction
at each step of the process. Ultimately, with sufficient practice, students may develop
appropriate pre-writing planning strategies that they can transfer to other situations.
As mentioned previously, we suggest using the CRAAP test (Meriam Library, 2010),

Carmichael and McMillan's (2011) framework, and SHEG's approach (McGrew et al., 2017; Wineburg et al., 2016) to help educate students about the credibility of information on the Internet. In addition, it is helpful to provide students with instruction on how to use search engines and academic databases to search for relevant information efficiently and effectively (Debowski, Wood, & Bandura, 2001). McGrew et al. (2017) commented that students often mistakenly believe that the first website located by Google or any other search engine is the most reliable, whereas expert fact-checkers scroll through multiple pages of search results, reading the available descriptive "snippets" of information, before making a selection; therefore, training students in this technique is likely to be very valuable.

Guided instruction in database searching can also improve students' written argumentation skills (Radhakrishnan, Lam, & Tamura, 2010). Students who practiced with an instructor on breaking down a research question, identifying synonyms for key concepts, and linking the concepts together using Boolean operators wrote better argumentative papers than those who merely received the instruction without the practice. Such guided practice provides students with opportunities to make logical inferences, which later helps them in organizing their papers (Radhakrishnan et al., 2010). Several authors have shown that modeling and practice can help students to develop a range of CT skills, including the ability to identify a well-reasoned argument (Bensley et al., 2010; Halpern, 1998; Nieto & Saiz, 2008; Penningroth, Despain, & Gray, 2007), and can subsequently improve the quality of their argumentative papers (Bensley & Haynes, 1995).

In general, CT skills improve more when students are explicitly shown the rules (e.g., how to recognize an argument) and are given frequent opportunities to practice them using a range of real-life examples. When implementing CT exercises in your classes, be sure to give your students timely feedback so that they can reflect on their work and correct their mistakes before turning in their next assignment. There are a number of books that provide exercises for students to use in practicing argumentation and more general CT skills (see Box 4.8).

Box 4.8 Useful Books for Critical Thinking Instruction

Bell, J. (2004). *Evaluating psychological information*. Boston, MA: Allyn & Bacon.

Browne, M. N., & Keeley, S. M. (2011). *Asking the right questions: A guide to critical thinking*, 10th edition. Englewood Cliffs, NJ: Pearson Prentice Hall.

Forshaw, M. (2012). *Critical thinking in psychology: A student guide*. Chichester, U.K.: John Wiley and Sons.

Halpern, D. F. (2013). *Thought and knowledge: An introduction to critical thinking*, 5th edition. Abingdon, U.K.: Routledge. (Note that the workbook that accompanies this text has exercises within it.)

Levy, D. A. (2009). *Tools of critical thinking: Metathoughts for psychology*, 2nd edition. Long Grove, IL: Waveland Press.

McBurney, D. H. (2001). *How to think like a psychologist*. Englewood Cliffs, NJ: Pearson Prentice Hall.

Ruscio, J. (2005). *Critical thinking in psychology*, 2nd edition. Belmont, CA: Wadsworth.

Smith, R. A. (2001). *Challenging your preconceptions*, 2nd edition. Belmont, CA: Wadsworth.

Stanovich, K. E. (2012). *How to think straight about psychology*, 10th edition. Boston, MA: Pearson.

4.6.2 Quantitative Reasoning

Students often approach quantitative psychology classes, such as Statistics and Research Methods, with both low confidence and high anxiety. These problems may be exacerbated by traditional pedagogical practices that emphasize a chiefly theoretical approach to statistics (Harlow, 2013) and in which coursework in research design (Research Methods) is often not integrated with training in data analysis (Statistics) (Wilson, 2017). In 2005, the American Statistical Association (ASA) published guidelines for teaching statistics in college that advocated the use of active learning techniques, in which students apply concepts rather than simply memorizing theories and formulae (Aliaga et al., 2005). The guidelines also emphasized the need for students to use real-world data and appropriate technology, such as statistical software. Real-world problems are more likely to motivate students to expend the time and energy needed to think critically about a topic (Halpern, 1999)—which may be an increasingly relevant issue for today's busy college students! Active learning exercises in Statistics classes, especially when conducted in small groups, have been shown to be effective in reducing anxiety, particularly among students with low confidence (Harlow, 2013).

In alignment with the ASA guidelines, Garfield & Ben-Zvi (2009) developed the Statistical Reasoning Learning Environment model for statistics instruction, which stresses the social construction of knowledge as students work with data collaboratively in small groups. A typical class begins with a research question, such as, "Do women use cell phones more than men?" After discussing their predictions within the groups, the students are given a relevant dataset, which they graph and analyze. Each dataset is generated prior to class by asking the students to respond to a series of online questions. Analyzing their own data may enhance interest in the findings, as students discover information about themselves and their peers. This model of instruction provides students with ample opportunities to practice skills, while requiring them to think critically about which tests are appropriate to use in various situations. In a similar vein, Kolar and McBride (2003) found that students were better able to know which statistical test to apply in a particular situation when they took a class in which they collaboratively generated problems for other students to solve, practiced solving the problems, and then received feedback from both their peers and the instructor in a class discussion. Such hands-on experiences have been shown to be effective in enhancing students' understanding of concepts in research methods and statistics, such as hypothesis testing and operationalization of variables (Lipsitz, 2000), multiple regression (Timmerman, 2000), and factorial design (Stansbury & Munro, 2013) (see Box 4.9 for a brief description of these and other active learning exercises for research methods and statistics).

Although designing, executing, and writing up empirical research is considered best practice in Research Methods courses, a national survey demonstrated that this only occurs in about 50% of courses, with students conducting research on an individual basis in about 20% and collaboratively in about 30% (Landrum & Smith, 2007). While considered a best practice, encouraging students to design their own studies is not without its challenges. Smith (2007) found that students have a propensity for non-causal designs even when the assignment requires them to design a study that involves an experimental manipulation. Furthermore, carrying out an entire research project within a single semester can be very challenging when students are still learning about research design.

Box 4.9 Resources for Active Learning Exercises for Research Methods and Statistics

Concept	Activity	Reference
Hypothesis testing and operationalization	Students are asked to make predictions about whether or not males smile more than females. They discuss how to identify a smile in a photo and then bring in yearbooks and use the criteria they have generated to study the photos.	Lipsitz (2000)
Multiple regression	Students are asked to generate a small number of survey items that, when considered together, might explain a student's performance on a prior test. These items are then used in a multiple-regression model to predict test grades.	Timmerman (2000)
Factorial design	Students are asked to design a 2×2 study, using scores from the Wii game Dance Dance Revolution as the dependent variable. They then participate in the study and collect and analyze class data.	Stansbury and Munro (2013)
Sampling	Each student is given a fun-sized pack of M&M's and makes a frequency distribution for color. They then make hypotheses about the distribution of M&M colors in the population. Student results are pooled to generate an overall hypothesis. Students can write to Mars to find out the distribution that they use in their packaging.	Smith (2010)
Between-subjects design (independent t-test)	Hypothesis: Feeling cold increases feelings of loneliness (embodied cognition). Before learning about the hypothesis, one group of students looks at a photo of a cold scene and a second group looks at a photo of a hot scene. Both groups then complete a loneliness questionnaire. Students compare the responses of the two groups.	Rounding and Adelheid (2015)
Using real-world problems to enhance quantitative reasoning	The Chance project (http://www.dartmouth.edu/~chance/index.html) provides suggestions for courses and assignments using real-world problems. A common theme is the use of current news items that may impact students' lives. For example, students might be required to think deeply about current medical research on the consequences of drug use, as they grapple with figuring out which statistical tests to use and how.	Halpern (1999)

See also:

Gelman, A., & Nolan, D. (2002). *Teaching statistics: A bag of tricks*. Oxford, U.K.: Oxford University Press.

Selden, M. P. (2014). *Increasing graphing literacy and graphing ability in undergraduate psychology majors through active learning based exercises* Retrieved from the Teaching of Psychology website: http://teachpsych.org/Resources/Documents/otrp/resources/selden14.pdf.

http://www.teachpsychscience.org

One suggestion for dealing with these challenges is to assign students to work on research projects in mid-size groups or as an entire class, which makes giving feedback much more manageable and ensures that students receive a more uniform level of instruction and support (see Chapter 5 on Group Work). Once the research design has been established, individual students can be assigned to collect small amounts of data, which collectively can yield an adequately large dataset for analysis. Another suggestion is to involve your students in replication studies—as organized, for example, through the Collaborative Replications and Education Project (CREP) (Grahe, 2017).

4.6.3 Problem-Based Learning

Problem-based learning (PBL) is a way to engage students in qualitative or quantitative reasoning in a more naturalistic way than through the use of worked examples from a textbook. It also has all the benefits of collaborative learning. PBL was first developed in the 1960s at McMaster University as a way to create a student-centered educational approach that would allow medical students to see the practical relevance of the mountains of information that they needed to know for their clinical practice, improve their skills in clinical diagnosis, and become self-directed learners (Barrows, 1996). Given its popularity and perceived advantages in motivating students to learn, retain, and apply information when compared with traditional lecture-based teaching, PBL has been used in a variety of disciplines (Hmelo-Silver, 2004), including undergraduate psychology classes. Although definitions vary quite substantially, PBL requires that students work in groups to collaboratively solve an "ill-defined problem"; that is, one with more than one possible solution. Students are required to decide together what it is that they need to know in order to reach a solution, locate the relevant information, and share the information among themselves (Hmelo-Silver, 2004). Although instructors can provide resources (e.g., readings or pre-recorded slide shows), students have to decide what information is relevant to solving their problem (Neville & Norman, 2007; see also Chapter 5 for more details about PBL).

4.7 Service Learning and Community-Based Research

Experiential learning in real-world settings is a powerful educational experience that results in multiple learning gains. Service learning situates community service within the academic curriculum and is common in both K–12 and college settings (Celio, Durlak, & Dymnicki, 2011). Given its focus on human interactions, psychology courses (especially those that focus on social, developmental, abnormal, or cognitive psychology) seem particularly suited to incorporating service learning (Bringle, Ruiz, Brown, & Reeb, 2016; Connor-Greene, 2002; Fleck, Hussey, & Rutledge-Ellison, 2017; Hammer, 2009). In service learning courses, psychology students might provide administrative and research support to organizations, or social support, education, tutoring, and other services to community members. Such courses might involve fieldwork at various worksites, such as homeless centers, domestic violence shelters, mental health centers, centers for the elderly, preschools, K–12 schools, college campus helplines, afterschool programs, boys' and girls' clubs, and prisons (Bringle et al., 2016; Dunlap, 1998; Hammer,

2009; Katz, DuBois, & Wigderson, 2014; Kretchmar, 2001; Lundy, 2007; Meyer et al., 2016). Bringle et al. (2016) have argued that service learning is a particularly effective pedagogical practice because it can target all five of the APA's broad goals for the undergraduate psychology major (American Psychological Association, 2013).

In service learning courses, classes are designed to develop the knowledge and skill sets that students need to better serve the community with which they are working. At the same time, community work deepens a student's understanding of the course content (Weiss & Seplowitz, 2017; Yorio & Ye, 2012). Having course learning objectives (LOs) that emphasize service (in addition to academic elements) helps to ensure that students will devote sufficient time and effort to their community placement. For example, in a Developmental Psychology service learning course, Dunlap (1998) required that her students "contributed to the healthy development of children/families." CT in service learning courses is fostered by having students write *structured* reflections at frequent intervals, in which they document their personal growth and reflect on how their learning experiences in the field have deepened their understanding of the course content, and vice versa (Ash & Clayton, 2009; Bringle et al., 2016). For example, Ash and Clayton's DEAL model instructs students to "**D**escribe experience, **E**xamine experience from academic, social and/or civic perspective, **A**rticulate **L**earning include future actions" (Ash & Clayton, 2009, p. 41). The structured nature of the assignments is designed to move students beyond making superficial observations and engage them in deeper, more analytical thinking (Ash & Clayton, 2009; Bringle et al., 2016; Hammer, 2009). For example, Hammer (2009) encouraged students to apply psychological theories to their service learning experiences and then analyze how this knowledge altered their behavior or their interpretation of an interaction in the field. A meta-analysis showed that discussing their reflections increased students' understanding of social issues more than just writing them down (Yorio & Ye, 2012). Eyler's (2002) reflection map model also underscores that such discussions should occur within the community organization as well as in the classroom, and that students should be encouraged not only to analyze their experiences, but also to consider how they will affect their future thinking and behaviors.

Several meta-analyses have documented that service learning promotes gains across multiple domains (Celio et al., 2011; Conway, Amel, & Gerwien, 2009; Novak, Markey, & Allen, 2007; Yorio & Ye, 2012). Although increasing civic responsibility is a primary LO for service learning courses (for suggestions on how to assess this outcome, see Simons, 2015), meta-analyses consistently show that the greatest gains associated with service learning are related to academics (better GPAs, grades, and exam scores, increased understanding of social issues). A meta-analysis of nine studies that focused on specific aspects of CT found that service learning increased students' understanding of course content, as well as their ability to apply that knowledge and reframe social issues (Novak et al., 2007). That said, meta-analyses have also shown that service learning produces small effect size gains in social or personal growth, including increased civic responsibility (Conway et al., 2009; Yorio & Ye, 2012). However, Bowman, Brandenberger, Lapsley, Hill, and Quaranto (2010) found that 13 years after graduation, taking a service learning course was associated with higher rates of volunteer work and increased prosocial attitudes.

So, where to start? First, check in with your department to ensure that you have the support you will need. Other instructors may already have adopted this approach, in which case they will be able to share their experiences and resources with you. Also, many campuses have a service learning office that can support you and suggest suitable fieldwork sites for your course. Student motivation is likely to be enhanced when students are strongly invested in the community in which they work; as such, Hammer (2009) suggests establishing relationships with four or five organizations that students can choose between. Relatedly, Yorio and Ye (2012) found that students who engaged in voluntary service learning had greater cognitive gains than those for whom the experience was mandatory.

One concern about service learning is that students may benefit more than the community that they are serving (Blouin & Perry, 2009; Stoecker, Tryon, & Hilgendorf, 2009; Worrall, 2007). To maximize benefits, it is important to meet in advance with community partners to discuss their needs and expectations and ensure that students can make a meaningful contribution over a relatively short period of time. When students feel that their efforts make a difference, they are more likely to put forth effort, even when the task itself is less than glamorous (Eyler, 2002). It is important that students, faculty, and members of the community work together to establish ground rules. In particular, students should be aware that failing to turn up for community service is particularly damaging to positive community relationships, especially if members of a vulnerable population form strong emotional bonds with a student and are hurt by their nonappearance (Blouin & Perry, 2009).

Although many service learning courses focus on providing services *for* a community, others have reported on the benefits (and challenges) of involving undergraduates in research project partnerships *with* a community, in what is referred to as "community-based research" (CBR) (Chapdelaine & Chapman, 1999; Elwood, 2009; McConnell, Albert, & Marton, 2008; McConnell & Marton, 2011; McNicoll, 1999; Reardon, 1998; Stocking & Cutforth, 2006; Strand, 2000). CBR (including participatory research and participatory action research) is designed to bring about social change for members of marginalized groups. It emphasizes shared power and collaboration, as community members work together with researchers to first define a problem and then design and carry out a program of research that results in action that helps ameliorate that problem (McNicoll, 1999). CBR is heavily dependent on the ability of team members to negotiate and collaborate with one another. Among a number of specially designed CBR courses, undergraduates have been involved in projects including creating summer literacy programs, lobbying for the rights of day laborers after documenting narratives of their struggles, identifying issues underlying the digital divide to provide better technology education to children in underserved communities, and fostering better relationships between the police and victims of domestic violence (Chapdelaine & Chapman, 1999; Giles, 2014; McConnell et al., 2008; Stocking & Cutforth, 2006).

Students report multiple academic and personal benefits to participating in CBR, including an improved understanding of research methods, greater knowledge about local and social issues, and increased civic engagement (Chapdelaine & Chapman, 1999; Giles, 2014; McConnell et al., 2008; McConnell & Marton, 2011; Willis, 2002). In some cases, students experience dramatic changes in their worldview as a result of their CBR experiences (Giles, 2014; Willis, 2002). This transformative learning is often catalyzed by initial feelings of dissonance, which occur when one's worldview is challenged by exposure to the lived experiences of members of other communities or when one witnesses others in distress (Giles, 2014; Willis, 2002). On the other hand, Giles (2014) cautions that if students have very different political views from those of the community members with whom they are working, then such feelings of dissonance may inhibit the learning process and cause them to become more entrenched in their personal viewpoints. This can be circumvented by having students work on projects in which they have a vested interest (Giles, 2014).

The time constraints imposed by a college course are challenging for CBR. Projects are likely to progress faster if students already have ties within a community; CBR involving campus-based groups (McNicoll, 1999) or external organizations at which students have already interned (Chapdelaine & Chapman, 1999) may be more easily established and completed within the timeframe of the class. Traditional course-related research projects are often designed, carried out, and written up over the span of a 15-week semester, whereas CBR projects typically last much longer, especially since the proposed action also needs to be carried out. Further, CBR needs IRB approval, whereas more traditional course-related projects often do not, if there is no intent to publish or disseminate the findings at scientific meetings. Instructors have dealt with the time challenge in various ways. In some cases, students become involved in existing projects, and so are exposed only to those processes that coincide with the timeframe of their course (McConnell et al., 2008; McConnell & Marton, 2011; Reardon, 1998). This approach has allowed students in introductory-level courses to get involved in CBR at an early stage in their academic careers (McConnell & Marton, 2011). Alternatively, students can continue working on a project after their course has ended by taking an independent study or capstone course, completing an honors thesis, or participating as a volunteer (Stocking & Cutforth, 2006; Strand, 2000; Willis, 2002).

When students participate in CBR as part of their course work, instructors often need to be more creative in their assessment of student learning. Often, it is not feasible for a student to write a traditional research report, especially if they have only participated in one part of the process. As in service learning, some have suggested using observations and reports from other members of the research team, as well as journaling, as important elements of the assessment process (Elwood, 2009; Giles, 2014). Journaling allows students to think metacognitively about how their CBR involvement has influenced their personal and academic development.

4.8   Challenges of Assessing Improvements in Critical Thinking

As we alluded to earlier in this chapter, instructors need to carefully consider how they will measure the efficacy of the CT instruction in their classes. As always, assessment has to align with course LOs; CT is a multifaceted construct, and so it is particularly important to use an appropriate assessment tool. Different types of CT instruction improve different CT skills. For example, a longitudinal study of college students showed that seniors who were psychology majors made greater gains in statistical-methodological reasoning compared to those who were natural science or humanities majors (Lehman & Nisbett, 1990). However, unlike science and humanities majors, psychology majors showed little improvement in conditional reasoning over the course of their college careers, presumably because of differences in targeted instruction across disciplines. Therefore, it makes little sense to assess conditional reasoning skills if the LOs of a course focus on reasoning about the scientific method. Similarly, Burke et al. (2014) found that a semester-long psychology course that focused on evaluating pseudoscientific claims helped to reduce students' beliefs in paranormal phenomena but did not improve their scores on the Watson Glaser Critical Thinking Appraisal (WGCTA), a measure commonly used to evaluate general CT skills. In contrast, students in a semester-long philosophy course showed significant improvements in their WGCTA scores (Burke et al., 2014). As Burke et al. (2014) point out, the WGCTA focuses primarily on assessing deductive reasoning—a major focus of philosophy but not of psychology classes— and so is probably not the best tool for assessing CT in your classes, unless you have a course LO that specifically focuses on honing these abilities.

The APA Guidelines for the Undergraduate Psychology Major (American Psychological Association, 2013) provide descriptions of various nationally normed tests of CT, all of which assess general CT skills—with the exception of one, the Psychological Critical Thinking Exam (PCTE) (Lawson, 1999), which was specifically developed to assess students' ability to evaluate claims using psychological science principles. The PCTE, which was revised relatively recently (Lawson, Jordan-Fleming, & Bodle, 2015), has been used to show gains in CT in relation to instruction in psychology classes (see, for example, Penningroth et al., 2007; Stark, 2012; Williams, Oliver, Allin, Winn, & Booher, 2003). It has strong psychometric properties, but you can create your own CT assessments based on your LOs. Note that under Goal 2: Scientific Inquiry and Critical Thinking, the APA lists indicators for CT at both introductory and upper levels, which you might want to adopt (American Psychological Association, 2013). You might also consider using the Critical Thinking Value Rubric provided by the Association of American Colleges and Universities (AAC&U), available at https://www.aacu.org/sites/default/files/files/VALUE/CriticalThinking.pdf. CT assessments are varied; for example, you might ask students to apply psychological theories to real-life settings, argue both sides of a controversial issue, think of possible solutions to an ill-structured problem, take the perspectives of different parties involved in a workplace or legal dispute, design a study to test a hypothesis, or evaluate evidence in support of a claim. Instructors may also be interested in measuring dispositional changes over the course of a semester, using tests such as the California Critical Thinking Disposition Inventory (Facione, Facione, & Giancarlo, 2001).

4.9   Summary

1) Engaging in CT is effortful and benefits from explicit CT instruction directed toward specific learning outcomes.
2) Active learning promotes CT. In activity-based learning contexts, students need guidance and scaffolding through feedback, worked examples, and other forms of support.
3) CT is multifaceted; hence, CT assessment must be carefully aligned with learning outcomes and instruction.

5

Group Work

5.1 Benefits of Group Work

The concept of students learning together in groups is not new. Small-group learning gained popularity in the 1930s and '40s, spurred by John Dewey, one of the founders of progressive education (Sharan, 2010). Dewey emphasized the need for educators to focus on teaching skills that would be useful in society in general, and advocated that students should learn to work together to solve the kinds of problems that are encountered in real life. Social psychologists Kurt Lewin and Morton Deutsch further advanced the field of group learning by establishing the field of group dynamics and social interdependence theory, respectively (Sharan, 2010). Collaborative learning practices have been widely used for decades in K–12 settings, and have been shown to be highly effective (for review, see Johnson & Johnson, 1989, 2005; Johnson, Johnson, & Smith, 1998; Slavin, 2011). More recently, research showing how college students learn best has led to an increased frequency in the use of small-group work in higher education (Johnson, Johnson, & Smith, 2014). Professional bodies such as the American Psychological Association (APA, 2013) and National Survey of Student Engagement (NSSE, 2013) believe that group work is essential for educating undergraduates because it requires a myriad of skills, including the ability to work effectively with others from diverse backgrounds. Meanwhile, employers place high value on new graduates who can demonstrate that they have an aptitude for team work (National Association of Colleges and Employers, 2014), again because it is increasingly common for employees to interact with others from a variety of countries and cultural backgrounds (Dede, 2010). On a different note, understanding how people work in groups can also help to improve relationships, not only at the workplace, but also in college, at home, and in other social settings (Johnson & Johnson, 2009c).

Small-group pedagogical approaches range from relatively brief and informal peer collaborations, such as Think–Pair–Share exercises (Lyman, 1981), to more formal semester-long project-based work with the same group members (e.g., Millis, 2001). We have described some informal group techniques (e.g., discussion, think-pair-share, debates, and role-play) in Chapter 4 on Advancing Critical Thinking Through Active Learning, as well as several longer-term projects suitable for more formal groups (e.g., podcasts, webpage design, digital stories, Wikipedia editing) in Chapter 3. In this

Teaching Psychology: An Evidence-Based Approach, First Edition. Jillian Grose-Fifer, Patricia J. Brooks, and Maureen O'Connor.
© 2019 John Wiley & Sons, Inc. Published 2019 by John Wiley & Sons, Inc.
Companion website: www.wiley.com/go/Grose-Fifer/teaching-psychology

chapter, we focus on how to ensure that group work is successful, and make further suggestions for ways in which students can work together in their classes.

Most research on group work has focused on assessing the efficacy of *cooperative* learning. Cooperative instructional strategies may vary considerably in their specific design, but they are most effective when the success of a student is highly dependent on the success of the other members in their group (positive interdependence) and when the performance of each student is assessed in some way that ensures the individual accountability of all group members (Aronson, Blaney, Stephin, Sikes, & Snapp, 1978; Hmelo-Silver, 2004; Johnson et al., 2014; Michaelsen & Sweet, 2008; Slavin, 1995, 2011). In contrast, fewer studies have assessed the efficacy of unstructured group learning—sometimes referred to as *collaborative* learning (Springer, Stanne, & Donovan, 1999)—although not all researchers distinguish between these two learning practices in their assessments (Tomcho & Foels, 2012). Bruffee (1995) suggested that structured cooperative learning is more appropriate for school-aged children than for college students, and argued that undergraduates should be sufficiently experienced that they will benefit more from working autonomously within an unstructured framework. However, in many ways, unstructured group work can be likened to *unguided* discovery learning. As discussed in Chapter 4, this practice has been shown to be less effective than *scaffolded* or *guided* discovery in producing learning gains, even in undergraduates (Alfieri, Brooks, Aldrich, & Tenenbaum, 2011). Critics of discovery learning have argued that unstructured tasks can be frustrating for students if they lack the necessary skills to explore effectively by themselves (Kirschner, Sweller, & Clark, 2006; Moreno, 2004). Indeed, many college students appear to lack collaboration skills (Grose-Fifer & Helmer, unpublished data) and struggle to manage dysfunctional group members (Colbeck, Campbell, & Bjorklund, 2000), while a meta-analysis showed that college students do not appear to benefit very much from unstructured group work (Lou, Abrami, & Spence, 2000). Furthermore, many of the issues associated with group work that students tend to complain about, such as unfair grading and inequitable workload (Colbeck et al., 2000), can be addressed by implementing cooperative structures (i.e., positive interdependence coupled with individual accountability); see Section 5.3 for how cooperative structures help to lessen the effects of dysfunctional group members. For these reasons, we focus in this chapter primarily on describing structured cooperative group work, with the rationale that if students gain sufficient practice with these types of learning practices, they will be able to employ them in other settings, such as the workplace.

According to various meta-analyses summarized by Johnson et al. (2014), cooperative learning leads to greater learning gains in terms of knowledge acquisition, retention of information, creativity, productivity, and higher-order reasoning skills (such as problem-solving and planning) than when students work alone or in competition with one another. The effect sizes for these results were moderate to large, even in college students. Working with others has been shown to promote the development of time-management, conflict-resolution, and active-listening skills, and helps students to become better communicators (Johnson & Johnson, 2005; Johnson et al., 1998). Furthermore, by fostering the development of interpersonal relationships, cooperative learning has been associated with reduced attrition rates in college students (Johnson et al., 2014). A meta-analysis of 24 studies (consisting predominantly of undergraduate samples working in pairs) also showed that small-group work resulted in better transfer of knowledge/skills to novel situations, likely because it fostered deeper learning

(Pai, Sears, & Maeda, 2014). Springer et al. (1999) found that small-group work improved achievement, course persistence, and self-esteem in college students enrolled in science, technology, engineering, and mathematics (STEM) courses. These benefits were greatest for African-American and Latinx students, and were found to occur whether the activity was structured or not. These findings contrast with those of Lou et al. (2000), who showed that learning gains associated with structured group work greatly surpassed those for unstructured work in college students. In a meta-analysis of 37 publications from the *Teaching of Psychology* journal, Tomcho and Foels (2012) provided further support for the use of structured group activities. They found that small-group work increased achievement, particularly when activities required group members to be highly interdependent (i.e., the success of the group required that everyone contributed), which is a key feature of structured cooperative learning practices (Johnson et al., 2014).

Another advantage of having students work together is that they can tackle larger, more complex tasks than if they worked alone. This is facilitated in part by the division of labor, but also by the synergistic relationships among group members; consequently, in terms of the final product, the whole is greater than the sum of its parts. In small-group work, peers serve as teachers, and so students benefit from receiving a greater volume of feedback than could be provided by a single instructor (Nicol, 2010). Furthermore, because instructors can respond to the group rather than to individual students, they have the time to give more detailed, and therefore more effective feedback. In sum, requiring students to collaborate can make it feasible for them to work on more interesting projects that tap higher-order thinking skills. These considerations are particularly relevant in large classes, where it would be very difficult to give frequent, high-quality feedback to every individual in a timely manner. Including group work in large classes is particularly important for student success. In many institutions, it is common to have very large sections of introductory courses, often taught in a traditional lecture format (Deslauriers, Schelew, & Wieman, 2011; Twigg, 2003). Not only do students typically rate large classes less favorably than small ones (Barefoot, 1993; Bedard & Kuhn, 2008; Marsh, 1987), but failure rates are often high in such settings (Twigg, 2003). Including small-group work helps to mitigate some of these problems by making large classes seem smaller (Cooper & Robinson, 2000) through increased student interactivity (Deslauriers et al., 2011; Twigg, 2003) and by engaging students in active learning (Cooper, MacGregor, Smith, & Robinson, 2000; Smith, 2000). Using this approach has been shown to help improve student learning outcomes (Deslauriers et al., 2011; Twigg, 2003) and retention (Twigg, 2003).

5.1.1 Theoretical Underpinnings of Why Small-Group Work Works

Slavin (2011) reviewed four inter-related theoretical perspectives that have been put forward by researchers to explain why structured, cooperative learning practices result in greater learning gains than when students work independently. From a *motivational* standpoint, students in cooperative learning structures are driven to help one another because their success depends on their fellow group members' success. Students are also motivated to put forward more effort if a task is intrinsically interesting. One advantage of group work is that it allows more interesting complex projects to be assigned, which would likely be unmanageable if students worked individually.

For instance, it is more feasible for a group of students to design a study and collect pilot data within a single semester than it would be for individual students working alone. Second, *social cohesion/social interdependence* theories (for summary, see Johnson & Johnson, 2009a) suggest that because group members feel socially connected, they are motivated to help one another. Greater cohesion leads to an increased sense of responsibility, which motivates students to work together because they do not want to negatively affect their peers' grades or learning and they want to be liked by them. From a *cognitive developmental* viewpoint, building on work by Piaget and Vygotsky, learning from peers is more effective than learning from an expert instructor, in part because students feel more comfortable discussing and arguing with one another than they do with an instructor. Peers also are likely to have similar life experiences and vocabularies, which makes it easier for them to communicate using easily relatable examples. Finally, from a *cognitive elaboration* perspective, when explaining concepts to other group members, students need to reorganize their thoughts, which helps them to elaborate on their ideas; this leads to greater understanding and better retention of information (Pressley et al., 1992).

5.2 Effective Strategies for Participation

5.2.1 Setting the Scene for Group Work

Many of today's younger students have worked in small groups in high school and enter college with the expectation that they will continue to have group assignments (Elam, Stratton, & Gibson, 2007). Similarly, adult learners have often had experience with teams in the workplace. Unfortunately, some students may have had negative group-work experiences and so may be reticent to collaborate with their peers (Colbeck et al., 2000). Merely asking students to work together is not sufficient to foster cooperation and is likely to result in groups being dominated by individual members, with others slacking off (Johnson et al., 2014). To create a positive group learning experience, it is essential that assignments are carefully planned and scaffolded by the instructor. Another potential roadblock when assigning group work is that some students believe that learning in college consists of listening to an expert (the instructor), taking notes, and repeating back what they have been told in examinations. This belief may make students skeptical about what they can learn from one another (Nuhfer, 2010). To help counteract any reluctance from students toward engaging in group work, it is important that instructors are highly transparent about the rationale and benefits of peer learning from the very beginning of the course. The learning objectives (LOs) and assessments on your syllabus should also reflect that you, as an instructor, value group work (see also Section 2.1 on Backward Course Design). In support of this approach, Chapman and Van Auken (2001) found that when instructors made the benefits of group learning explicit, students had better attitudes toward group work.

An effective strategy for increasing student motivation for collaboration is to establish a class culture of working with peers from the outset of the course (Shadle, 2010; see also Section 1.5.1 on Fostering an Environment of Inclusivity for ideas about how to begin to foster positive attitudes toward working collaboratively on the first day of class). Although this may seem daunting, it can be limited to the use of brief informal group exercises to help students get used to working together (Johnson & Johnson, 2009c). In fact, delaying the formation of more permanent groups until later in the semester allows instructors to develop a better sense of their students' relative strengths, and makes it easier to deal with any changes in enrollment during the first few weeks of class (Oakley, Felder, Brent, & Elhajj, 2004). Informal groups can be formed quickly by asking students to discuss with their neighbor(s) or with the person/people sitting behind them (e.g., Think–Pair–Share). Alternatively, you can divide the number of students in the class by the number of students per group (e.g., 36 students divided into groups of 4 = 9 groups) and then count off (in this case, 1 through 9) from student to student to form the nine groups (all students with the number 1 sit together, etc.). Changing informal groupings in this way across class periods allows students to get to know more of their classmates.

Kagan (2014) suggests that Think–Pair–Share exercises should be timed, with a reminder to switch who is talking, so that each student has an equal opportunity to contribute to the discussion (Timed Pair Share) or students take turns in generating answers (also called Round Robin or Rally Robin). These kinds of practices help students to develop the active-listening and communication skills that are essential for more long-term group work. Another informal cooperative group structure advocated by Kagan (2014) to promote total class participation is a technique known as Numbered Heads Together. Each student within a group of four is assigned a number from 1 to 4. Students must collaboratively decide on their answer to a particular problem/question, ensuring that everyone in the group agrees and understands the rationale for this answer. The instructor then randomly calls on a particular number, and the corresponding person within a particular group has to explain the answer to the rest of the class.

Collecting information about your students in the first class is an effective way to begin to establish rapport at the outset of group work (see also Chapter 1, particularly Box 1.1, for other suggestions for what to do on the first day of class). This information can be used later in the course to ensure that group members are relatively heterogeneous (Shadle, 2010). To set the scene for group work, Panitz (2010) suggests that on the first day of class, students should get to know one another by working in small groups (four to six students). They should first split into pairs to interview one another on their likes and dislikes about group work, and then share this information with the rest of the group. This exercise helps to open the conversation about why group work is important. To increase motivation further, it is helpful for students to construct for themselves why they think group work might be beneficial to them. Students are likely to think about the value of collaboration in the work place if they brainstorm in their small groups about the kinds of skills that they think that employers might be looking for in college graduates (Miller, Groccia, & Wilkes, 1996). This can be further reinforced by providing National Association of Colleges and Employers (NACE) data (http://www.naceweb.org/about-us/press/class-2015-skills-qualities-employers-want.aspx), which shows that employers rate being able to work in a team and being able to lead others as the two most important skills for a new graduate entering the workforce. This exercise can be followed up with another brainstorming question about other possible advantages of working with peers. Making sure that students take turns in their groups in coming up with an answer (Round Robin; Kagan, 2014) helps to establish that it is important for everyone to contribute to the conversation. Students are likely to acknowledge that there are several reasons why working with others might be helpful (Cabrera et al., 2002), and these ideas can be backed up by familiarizing the students with the evidence-based research outlined earlier.

Finally, students can work together in their small groups to ask or answer questions about the course syllabus and voice any concerns that they might have. Instructors who plan to use group work as an essential feature of their pedagogy are advised to include improving teamwork skills in their learning outcomes so that students can see that these abilities are valued as much as learning about the content of the course (Shadle, 2010). When students see that they will be collaborating on a group project, they often worry that they will be left to do more than their fair share of the work. This is a good opportunity for instructors to address such concerns by pointing out how individual accountability will be assessed in the course (see more under Section 5.2.3). Furthermore, students should be informed that when they eventually work in formal groups, they will consensually formulate their own rules, with the understanding that a student who does not pull their weight can be penalized by the group (Oakley et al., 2004). Depending on your philosophy, this penalty could result in the exclusion of the noncompliant student's name from a group project, in their receiving a poor peer evaluation (affecting their final grade), or even in their being fired from the group (Oakley et al., 2004). The prospect of potentially being expelled from a group and having to work alone to complete a complex project is typically enough to ensure students cooperate fairly with their fellow group members. Nuhfer (2010) found that using brainstorming activities on the first day of class and asking students to reflect on whether they had gained insights from their peers helped them appreciate the value of working collaboratively with their classmates.

5.2.2   Gearing Up for Formal Group Work

Assuming that formal group work will begin a little way into the semester, it may be helpful to revisit the reasons for doing group projects and to address any lingering anxieties during or just prior to the first formal group session. Group work typically gets off to a better start when students engage in team-building activities. Team-building exercises build trust and allow group members to feel more connected with one another (Johnson & Johnson, 2009a; Slavin, 2011). According to social-identity theories, increasing feelings of social cohesion should also increase motivation for cooperative learning (Johnson et al., 2014; Slavin, 2011). A positive psychology exercise (Seligman, 2012) that seems to work well for alleviating anxiety and motivating students for the first session is to ask them each to write down one strength that they will bring to group work. Within their formal groups, the students can pair up and ask their partner about their strengths, and then share this information with the rest of the group. Students should exchange contact information and establish how best to communicate with one another outside of class. Group members should be encouraged to take on specific roles (e.g., timekeeper, recorder, summarizer, encourager, checker, reporter) before deciding on the group's rules, because this helps to establish interdependence (Johnson & Johnson, 2009c; Oakley et al., 2004). Everyone has to do their job for the group to be successful.

Cox and Bobrowski (2000) found that establishing a group "charter," in which members agreed about basic rules and came up with a team name and logo, was helpful for clarifying the group's objectives and improving its performance. The charter included items such as whether it was permissible to miss a meeting and what kinds of interruptions were acceptable, and required students to operationalize what good participation within the group would look like. Page and Donelan (2003) provide Group Development and Group Decision-Making scales based on Tuckman's model of sequential group development (Tuckman & Jensen, 1977); these describe typical behaviors and feelings that arise at various stages of the group process. Administering such instruments at the first meeting may reassure students that feelings of confusion, and having one person dominate, are normal when a group first begins to form. These scales are also useful for reflection over the course of group projects.

5.2.3 Structuring a Cooperative Learning Task

Assigning students to work together on a particular project will not necessarily result in better learning outcomes unless the task itself is complex enough to warrant collaboration (Pai et al., 2014), sufficient time (especially in-class) is allocated for such collaboration (Oakley et al., 2004; Pfaff & Huddleston, 2003), and the group work itself is structured in such a way that cooperation among students is necessary (for review, see Johnson et al., 2014). As already noted, cooperative learning structures stress the importance of positive interdependence and individual accountability. Creating positive interdependence among group members, so that each student's success is contingent on the success of all the others, increases the likelihood that they will help one another to learn. This can be achieved in a number of different ways. For example, students may have to pool information and resources with others in order to complete a research project (such as in the jigsaw classroom described in Section 5.4.5). Alternatively, interdependent grading structures can motivate students to create a community of learners who help one another (e.g., inter-teaching and team-based learning [TBL], described in Sections 5.4.2 and 5.4.4, respectively). In these structures, students benefit if their team members also do well on tests and assignments. Even in informal group work, such as Numbered Heads Together (see Section 5.2.1), students are interdependent because they need to ensure that every member can explain the group's answer or decision. In a meta-analysis, Slavin (2011) found that student performance increased only if there were group rewards for individual contributions to a project, rather than a single group project grade.

Several authors have suggested that interdependence is promoted if students within a group have specific but complementary roles and so the success of the group hinges on everyone doing their job effectively (for review, see Johnson & Johnson, 2009a). As suggested in Section 5.2.2, in informal groups and at initial formal group meetings, these roles can be relatively simple, such as timekeeper, recorder (takes notes), summarizer (summarizes what has been said/decided), encourager (makes sure everyone participates), checker (double checks the written product and turns in assignment), and reporter (orally presents the group's findings and/or opinions in a larger class discussion) (Johnson & Johnson, 2009c; Oakley et al., 2004). Rotating roles ensures an equal division of labor and helps to broaden students' skills. Erez, Lepine, and Elms (2002) found that rotating the leadership role among students led to better cooperation, participation, and performance.

The second crucial feature of cooperative learning is that there must be individual accountability (Johnson et al., 2014; Kagan, 2014; Slavin, 2011). For example, in Numbered Heads Together (Kagan, 2014; see also Section 5.2.1), students work together on a product or a question, but any student can be randomly selected to represent their group's ideas or answers. Alternatively, groups can provide a breakdown of each student's contribution to the product, or the group project grade can be modified by peer evaluations of effort, quality of work, and productivity (Sweet & Michaelsen, 2012).

Cooperative learning practices vary in their emphasis on the group process. However, we, like others (e.g., Johnson & Johnson, 2002), believe that for students to be able to interact with one another effectively, instruction should include social skills development and should foster students' awareness of how groups form (e.g., Tuckman & Jensen, 1977) and the typical dynamics that occur within them (Johnson & Johnson, 2009c). In support of this view, Chapman and Van Auken (2001) found that students had more positive attitudes toward group work when instruction included work on group dynamics.

Finally, it takes time to work out the bumps when students start to work in groups for more extended periods, but it is helpful for them to know that this is normal. Reflecting about their own participation and that of group members allows students to develop a better understanding of the group process and how to become a better group member. It can also allow them to provide constructive feedback to their peers (Johnson & Johnson, 2009c). Formative peer evaluation of group members has been shown to improve interpersonal skills over the course of a semester (Cestone, Levine, & Lane, 2008; Michaelsen, Fink, & Knight, 1997). To aid with the reflection process, instructors may want to provide students with a variety of instruments to assess typical behaviors and dynamics within their group; see Page and Donelan's (2003) Group Development and Group Decision-Making scales, as well as various peer-evaluation rubrics available from the Eberly Center at Carnegie Mellon University (https://www.cmu.edu/teaching/designteach/teach/instructionalstrategies/groupprojects/tools/index.html). Other instruments are useful in helping students to evaluate their own performance and growth as a group member, such as the Collaboration Self-Assessment Tool from the Academy for Co-Teaching and Collaboration at St. Cloud State University (2012).

5.2.4 Group Composition

Most cooperative learning practices recommend that instructors should set up the groups rather than let students choose their teammates (Oakley et al., 2004). Although students may balk at this initially, self-selected groups have less ecological validity in terms of the types of situations that students will encounter in the workforce (Oakley et al., 2004). Furthermore, research suggests that in the long run, group-work experiences are more positive when instructors select the groups (Feichtner & Davis, 1984). Instructor-selected groups reduce the likelihood of cliques, and if groups are sufficiently diverse, students benefit from being exposed to a wider range of perspectives (Aronson et al., 1978)—although it is often challenging to create diverse groups within classes with small enrollments. Some authors suggest forming student groups around mutual project-based interests (e.g., Sharan, 2010), whereas others strongly recommend that groups should be heterogeneous in terms of academic strengths (e.g., Johnson & Johnson, 2009c). Heterogeneous groups have been shown to be particularly beneficial for boosting academic performance in lower-performing students, without being detrimental to high-performing students (Kuhn, Pease, & Wirkala, 2009). However, we acknowledge that lower-performing students may be excluded if their peers believe that they are not up to the task (see Section 5.3 for strategies for dealing with uneven participation within groups).

There are various opinions with respect to the optimum group size. Within larger groups, group dynamics are more complex and take longer to develop, because there are more interpersonal relationships to deal with (Johnson & Johnson, 2009c). For this reason, Johnson and Johnson (2009c) suggest that informal group work should only use very small groups (e.g., pairs or trios), as there is not enough time to establish effective group relationships. Also, from a very practical point of view, if formal group work requires out-of-class meetings, coordination is easier with a smaller number of people (Barkley, Cross, & Major, 2014). However, very small groups may suffer from a lack of diversity in perspectives (Oakley et al., 2004). A meta-analysis of 103 findings from 51 studies (including elementary- to college-level students) showed that groups of three or four students attained better academic performance than groups of five to seven students (Lou et al., 1996).

5.2.5   Helping Students Develop Collaborative, Leadership, and Planning Skills

Seating arrangements can affect the quality of student interactions during group work, so where possible students should sit in a circle or in such a way that no one is physically located outside the group. If this is not feasible, then asking students to physically shift their seats every 10–15 minutes (e.g., move two seats to the right; www. teambasedlearning.org) should ensure that no one student has to sit in a non-optimal spot for the entirety of the class session. Group work is enhanced when students communicate clearly with one another about their ideas, feelings, and questions. Students may have to be reminded about how to use their active-listening skills, and that part of working cooperatively is encouraging everyone within the group to participate. It might be helpful to model some of these behaviors in class, for example by calling on a student who has not raised their hand and encouraging them to speak, or paraphrasing what a student has said in a nonjudgmental way and checking whether this is an accurate reflection of what they meant or felt. Studies in K–12 education have shown that having students identify desirable (e.g., looking at the person who is speaking) and undesirable (e.g., interrupting, texting while someone is talking) verbal and non-verbal behaviors in group settings can facilitate the development of collaborative skills (Johnson & Johnson, 2002).

Discussing, disagreeing, and elaborating on different views typically leads to better group decisions (Johnson & Johnson, 2009c), but students need the skills to resolve conflicts in order to learn from them (Johnson & Johnson, 2002). Conflicts are very common during the early "storming" stage of group formation (Tuckman & Jensen, 1977), when students are first learning how to communicate with one another. In this stage, it is important for students to understand that they should critique ideas rather than people. Johnson and Johnson (2009c) suggest that in order for students to be able to resolve conflict effectively, they should be cognizant of five strategies that people often use to deal with conflicts, depending on how strongly they feel about their own goals versus their relationships with other group members. In conflicts, people may try to dominate others with their opinions (sometimes resorting to making threats); they may withdraw from the situation and avoid the conflict; they may try and smooth things over by apologizing, or by giving in if they feel that the other person has a greater stake;

they may engage in problem-solving (i.e., explaining what they want, while remaining open to opposing ideas and negotiation); or they may compromise and meet the other person halfway. These five strategies can be demonstrated through role-play before beginning a long-term group activity.

Cooperative learning structures emphasize equal leadership, power, and participation among students (Johnson & Johnson, 2009c). Yet, students may not be familiar with what it takes to be an effective leader. Shertzer and Schuh (2004) found that students frequently perceive leaders to be extroverted and charismatic, which implies that leaders are born and not made. Furthermore, they may believe that it is the leader's job to do the lion's share of the work (Colbeck et al., 2000). In cooperative learning structures, leaders are facilitators. Effective facilitators need to be able to keep track of who has spoken and how often to encourage equal participation, check understanding, summarize group decisions, and make plans for future directions (Johnson & Johnson, 2009c).

We highly recommend scheduling the majority of group work during class time. This not only ensures that students have enough time to work on projects, which is a common concern (Colbeck et al., 2000), but it also allows instructors to observe the interactions between group members so that they can intervene where necessary (McKendall, 2000). When the learning outcomes of the course emphasize the development of social skills, students and/or the instructor can take turns observing the dynamics within the group and giving feedback to other group members. Individual group members can then reflect on this feedback so that they can modify their future behavior (Johnson & Johnson, 2009c).

Finally, another goal of group work is often to improve students' planning skills. In long-term projects, effective planning is crucial. We have found it helpful for students to learn how to create action plans that have "SMART" goals: they are Specific, Measurable, Achievable, Realistic, and Timely. This scaffolding seems especially important for first-year students, who frequently express concerns about their planning abilities (Grose-Fifer, unpublished data). SMART goals are used in many different settings, including counseling and rehabilitation (Wade, 2009), education (Conzemius & O'Neill, 2005), and business (Bowles, Cunningham, De La Rosa, & Picano, 2007). Once a SMART plan (see Box 5.1) has been made and carried out, students assess whether they have successfully attained their goals. Frequently, however, even the best-laid plans go

---

Box 5.1 SMART Action Plans

Goals must be:

- **Specific**—What exactly will you do? ("Find some articles in the library" is too vague—how many, and on which topic?)
- **Measurable**—How will you assess whether you have met your goal? (e.g., "Find three papers and print them out" is a measurable criterion)
- **Achievable**—How motivated are you to do this? What will you get out of doing it?
- **Realistic**—Can you really do what you are planning, given your skills/schedule/resources etc.? What are the obstacles you might face? How can you overcome them?
- **Timely**—When will you complete the goal? Be very specific.

Source: Adapted from Conzemius and O'Neill (2005).

awry. Therefore, as students revise their planning, they should try to identify what derailed them, as well as any potential obstacles that could prevent them from succeeding in the future. In further support of the benefits of working with peers, students often set unrealistic goals or lack the motivation to carry out their plans when they work individually. When they make themselves more accountable by working with others (or telling others about their plan), they have better success (Grose-Fifer, unpublished data). Similarly, motivation (and action-plan success) can be increased if students decide that they will reward themselves in some way if they complete their task. Sometimes, students choose tangible rewards, like ice cream or candy, but they also frequently recognize that the approval of their peer group is enough to motivate them to complete their task.

5.3   How to Minimize Undesirable Group Behaviors

Social psychology research clearly demonstrates that people behave differently when they are in groups than when they are alone. Positive behaviors, such as excitement and feelings of trust and connectedness, are likely to increase social cohesion between group members, which contributes to successful group interactions (Johnson & Johnson, 2009c). However, negative behaviors, like social loafing, free-riding, group think, and willingness to be dominated by others, usually lead to dysfunctional groups (Johnson & Johnson, 2009c). Similarly, some groups may have "lone-wolf" students who refuse to allow other students to contribute to a final product, because they feel that they can do the task better and faster alone. We offer some evidence-based advice about how best to deal with some of these problems. One proactive strategy for dealing with these issues is to talk about them before group work begins in earnest. This can be done by creating profiles of people with interpersonal styles that are problematic for group work, and then troubleshooting with students (in small groups, of course!) about how best to deal with them (Barr, Dixon, & Gassenheimer, 2005; Lerner, 1995). Students should be reminded that open communication is particularly important when they perceive that one of their group members is not pulling their weight. It is easy to make the fundamental attribution error and assume that the student who fails to participate or respond promptly to email or text communications from other group members is not engaged, when in actuality they might have a job outside of school or may not have reliable phone or Internet access.

5.3.1   Social Loafing and Free-Riding

Social loafing is said to occur when individuals put forward reduced effort when working collaboratively compared to working alone (Latané, Williams, & Harkins, 1979). Social loafing tends to increase with group size, and may be particularly prevalent in situations where a task can be completed without individuals needing to exert maximum effort or where individuals feel an increased sense of anonymity (Latané et al., 1979). Based on meta-analytical data, Karau and Williams (1993) found that students were more likely to engage in social loafing when a group assignment was perceived to be easy and therefore not to warrant group effort, or if it was uninteresting. Typically, students like to work on projects that are authentic (i.e., have real-world applications) and that tap their personal interests. It is important to find out about students' interests at the outset of a course in order to hone project-based assignments (Halonen, 2008). Karau and Williams (1993) also found that the reward for working with others must be sufficiently high (e.g., a large percentage of the final grade) to motivate students to cooperate and work hard. Making sure that students are held accountable for their individual contributions also reduces feelings of deindividuation and makes diffusion of responsibility less likely to occur. As mentioned in Section 5.2.3, it must be clear what or how each student has contributed to a group product.

One of the most common reasons that students give for disliking group work in college is that they have had one or more free-riders in previous groups (Aggarwal & O'Brien, 2008; Hall & Buzwell, 2012). In project-based work, students consider it to be unfair when some group members do more of the work but all students receive the same grade (Aggarwal & O'Brien, 2008; Hall & Buzwell, 2012). Free-riders who do little work themselves benefit from the efforts of others (Hall & Buzwell, 2012), who may then feel they were suckered into doing more than their fair share (Dommeyer, 2007). Like social loafing, free-riding is more likely to happen in large than in small groups (Aggarwal & O'Brien, 2008). To discourage intentional free-riding, it is important that grading structures assess individual performance in some way (Johnson & Johnson, 2009c). This could be done through individual exams or assignments, or through peer evaluation. Aggarwal and O'Brien (2008) found that multiple peer evaluations over the course of the semester were associated with reduced free-riding and increased grade satisfaction. If students engage in this kind of formative assessment then problems can be identified and potentially solved before it is too late. However, it seems that too much reflection on the group process might be a bad thing! Dommeyer (2007) found that when students were asked to keep a diary reflecting on group process, which was read by the instructor every 2 weeks, there was no reduction in social loafing. Students who kept diaries were more likely to fire free-riders from their group and gave lower peer evaluations than those who did not keep one. In that situation, aside from advising group members to email a warning to the free-riding students, little advice on how to improve their problem-solving or conflict-resolution skills was provided.

5.3.2 Supporting "Involuntary" Free-Riders

Hall and Buzwell (2012) point out that free-riding may not necessarily be a conscious choice, although most students think it reflects deliberate laziness on the part of the free-rider. Sometimes free-riders struggle because they feel that they lack sufficient competency to complete a task, perhaps because of language-proficiency issues or a lack of understanding of what their group requires of them. Weaker students may even be purposefully excluded from contributing to the group product, if their group members do not feel that they are up to the task (Hall & Buzwell, 2012). Sometimes, if a group feels that a particular student lacks necessary skills, they may allot them tasks that are so uninteresting it is hard for them to stay motivated enough to complete them. One possible solution is for low-performing students to work together so that they can be given more support and are less likely to be ostracized by their peers (Aggarwal & O'Brien, 2008). However, if this tack is taken, then these students cannot benefit from working with students with greater aptitude, which has been shown to produce greater learning gains (Kuhn et al., 2009). Vernon (2008) addressed the challenge of involuntary free-riders by asking groups to reflect on the fairness of the task/role assignments midway through the group project. As a result, roles were reassigned, dominant students who had taken over the project acquiesced, and the lower-performing students took on roles that were more substantial.

5.3.3   Lone Wolves

Another type of dysfunctional group member is the lone wolf (Barr et al., 2005). Lone wolves refuse to work cooperatively with others because they do not trust other group members to have the same level of strengths or skills as they do. These students may be very driven, and so feel frustrated when others work at a slower pace. Barr et al. (2005) suggested that because lone wolves are extremely task-driven, it is necessary to assess both the group product *and* the group process in order to reduce their tendency to shut out other group members. In other words, if a lone wolf knows that they will be assessed on their interpersonal skills as well as the project content, this may provide the necessary motivation for them to become a better team player.

5.4   Cooperative Learning Structures

In this section, we outline some formal cooperative group structures that have been used in higher education environments and shown to produce greater learning gains than when students work individually or within a lecture format.

5.4.1   Learning Together and Alone

The Johnson brothers developed a cooperative learning approach, which they called Learning Together and Alone (for a summary, see Johnson & Johnson, 2002). Their approach is based on five contingencies. Two (positive interdependence and individual accountability) are common to all cooperative learning approaches, but they also heavily emphasize group process. Thus, the other three contingencies are social-skills development, "promotive" interaction (learning how to encourage others and share resources), and reflection. A major advantage of this approach is that it is inherently flexible. For example, students could be charged with writing a report, solving a problem (see also Section 4.6.3 and Section 5.4.3 on Problem-Based Learning [PBL]), coming to a decision about a controversial issue (see Section 4.3.2 on Debates), designing and conducting a study (see Section 4.6.2 on Quantitative Reasoning), or even producing a presentation or podcast (see Section 3.5.1 on Student-Created Videos and Podcasts).

5.4.2   Inter-Teaching

The idea of inter-teaching was first put forward by Boyce and Hineline (2002), who suggested that the most effective way to learn something is to teach it to someone else. Therefore, during inter-teaching classes, students work together in pairs to explain and discuss concepts from a pre-assigned reading. Inter-teaching discussions are facilitated by the use of a reading guide, typically completed prior to class (Saville, Lawrence, & Jakobsen, 2012), which asks questions about key concepts that are likely to be covered in forthcoming quizzes and exams. Therefore, inter-teaching increases the likelihood that students will come prepared to class, especially if points are awarded for completing the guide (Filipiak, Rehfeldt, Heal, & Baker, 2010). Student inter-teaching discussions constitute a large proportion of a class period (as much as 75% of total time); during this time, the instructor and teaching assistants (TAs) (if available) circulate among the students to answer questions and guide the conversations; this helps ensure that students are on task and are not misleading one another. Finally, students fill out an inter-teaching record, in which they identify which items from the reading guide they found difficult to understand, and what they would like to review in the upcoming class. They also assess the quality of the discussion (e.g., rated on a scale of 1–10 and then justified in writing), which increases individual accountability and emphasizes the need for all students to come prepared for class (Boyce & Hineline, 2002). Students switch partners frequently during the semester, so if one student in the class is chronically underprepared then no one student has to deal with them on a regular basis. Another tack to help students cope with underprepared peers is to introduce research showing that students who teach or give feedback learn better than those who merely listen (Cho & Cho, 2011; White & Kirby, 2005). Preparing to explain a topic to someone else requires clarifying and organizing one's thoughts on the topic so that they can be communicated effectively, leading to deeper learning (Nestojko, Bui, Kornell, & Bjork, 2014).

When engaged in inter-teaching, the instructor typically spends the first 15 minutes of the class clarifying the points that students had difficulty understanding in the previous one, which helps to clear up any muddy issues or misconceptions. Instructors using inter-teaching typically give frequent tests throughout the semester (see Chapter 7 on the benefits of testing). Several studies have shown that inter-teaching not only leads to substantial (~12%) improvement in exam performance when compared to lecturing (e.g., Filipiak et al., 2010; Saville et al., 2012) but is also more likely to increase critical thinking (CT). Students have been shown to prefer inter-teaching to lectures and to feel that they learn more when they have to teach their peers (Goto & Schneider, 2009; Saville, Zinn, Neef, Norman, & Ferreri, 2006). Motivation to complete the discussion guides and teach peers during class periods can be increased by assigning a substantial part (e.g., ~10%) of the final grade for inter-teaching participation (Boyce & Hineline, 2002). Furthermore, positive interdependence, which is a key feature of cooperative learning, is established by the use of quality points. Quality points are rewards that are based on the individual performance of students within an inter-teaching pair. They may be awarded if a student dyad is observed by the instructional staff to be engaging in focused discussion during the inter-teaching period, or if both students attain above a certain grade on an exam or assignment related to a specific inter-teaching session (Saville et al., 2006).

5.4.3 Problem-Based Learning

As introduced in Section 4.6.3, in PBL students work in groups to solve a problem that has more than one possible solution. They collaboratively decide on the information they need, how best to find it, and how best to share it with one another

(Hmelo-Silver, 2004). In some cases, instructors provide some of the resources, but students still need to figure out what is most relevant for the problem in hand (Neville & Norman, 2007). PBL instructors use modeling to help direct students in solving the problem and to guide their interactions with one another (Hmelo-Silver, 2004). To maximize efficiency, individual students typically work on individual parts of the problem first and then pool their knowledge through discussion with their group (Faidley, Evensen, Salisbury-Glennon, Glenn, & Hmelo, 2000). This division of labor is similar to that seen in jigsaw design (see Section 5.4.5), and helps to establish positive interdependency (everyone needs to contribute in order to know how best to solve the problem). During class sessions, the instructor must refrain from providing the critical information needed to solve the problem, and instead ask metacognitive questions that help students to recognize what it is they need to know and how to get to the next level in solving the problem (Hmelo-Silver, 2004). Developing students' metacognitive awareness is facilitated by having them chart their problem-solving process using a four-column matrix, consisting of Facts (what they know already, either from the original problem or through subsequent research), Ideas (a record of their thinking about possible solutions), Learning Issues (what they need to know in order to test their hypotheses), and an Action Plan (what they need to do in order to gather the information required for the next step). At the end of the class, students reflect on the group process, with the instructor modeling observations of how individual students contributed (e.g., "You seemed to want to take over the discussion," or "Your resources didn't help to move the problem-solving forward") so that the students feel more comfortable critiquing other people's collaborative skills. This essential part of PBL has sometimes been neglected, which can lead to dysfunctional group behavior (Faidley et al., 2000). To this end, Faidley and colleagues developed two measures (a survey and a checklist) to better help students assess how their group was functioning. The scores on these measures were found to be closely aligned with behaviors observed in videotapes of the groups (Faidley et al., 2000). Finally, for PBL to be truly cooperative, peer assessment needs to factor into any grading.

Some critics of PBL have emphasized the results of meta-analyses showing that students in PBL classes do less well on exams compared to those in traditional classes (Kirschner et al., 2006). In a meta-synthesis of several meta-analyses, Strobel and Van Barneveld (2009) confirmed that PBL students did not perform as well as traditional students on multiple-choice examinations of content-based knowledge taken at the end of semester. However, students in PBL classes performed *better* on similar tests that used free recall and were able to remember information longer than students in traditional classes, suggesting that they engaged in deeper learning. Moreover, PBL students also outperformed their peers in traditional classes on tests of the application of skills and in oral examinations (Strobel & van Barneveld, 2009). Although PBL is not used as widely in psychology as in other disciplines, it has gained popularity in Counseling Psychology (Norton, 2004, 2009) and Abnormal Psychology courses (Connor-Greene, 2002), where the need for students to develop clinical diagnostic abilities matches PBL's original aim of helping medical students learn how to apply their knowledge in order to diagnose and manage hypothetical clinical cases. For further suggestions on how to develop PBL assignments in a variety of psychology classes, see Box 5.2.

Box 5.2 Resources for Problem-Based Learning Assignments

Discipline	Abbreviated Sample Problem	Reference
Counseling Psychology	Unmotivated student seeks help from college counseling center. What advice do you give?	Norton (2004)
Abnormal Psychology	Put together a resource guide that would be useful for someone with a family member with a psychological disorder.	Connor-Greene (2002)
Statistics	Are certain groups discriminated against in mortgage lending?	Karpiak (2011)
Sensation and Perception	Make recommendations on lighting for nighttime road construction.	Kreiner (2009)
Introductory Psychology	A student has been found to be abusing prescription drugs. Should she be suspended?	Muehlenkamp, Weiss, & Hansen (2015)
Introductory Psychology	Parents complain to the college president that they are concerned that their children are viewing violent films in one of their classes and could be adversely affected. Is there any ground to their argument? What should the college president do?	Yandell & Giordano (2008)

5.4.4 Team-Based Learning

TBL was originally developed in the late 1970s for business students in large classes, but has been adapted for courses in a range of disciplines (see www.teambasedlearning. org). Like inter-teaching, TBL motivates students to do the assigned reading before they come to class and to help their teammates understand the material at a deeper level (for a review, see Sweet & Michaelsen, 2012). At the beginning of each new topic, students are given a reading guide with 5–20 questions that cover the main concepts of the assigned readings, which they must complete before class. To ensure that they understand the materials well enough that they can apply them to solve problems related to real-world issues in later classes, they take a "readiness-assurance" test in class, first individually and then in a small group. These tests are relatively challenging, so it is difficult for individual students to get an A (a typical range of scores would be 65–80%). When re-taking the test in the small-group setting, the students are required to reach a consensus for each answer. In this stage of the process, Michaelsen and Sweet (2008) underscore the importance of immediate feedback for each group, and suggest the use of scratch-off multiple-choice answer sheets to achieve this (Immediate Feedback Assessment Technique [IF-AT] cards; www.epsteineducation.com). If students scratch off their first answer and find that they are incorrect, they can decide on a second choice (which could receive partial credit), and continue until they find the right answer. An alternative strategy could be to use clickers or other student response systems (SRSs) (see Chapter 3 on Effective Multimedia Instruction). If a group of students disagrees with an answer, they may make an appeal by submitting a collaborative document that explains and provides evidence for why they think an alternative is correct. Although TBL has a second application stage (described later), the benefits of this kind of two-stage testing (individual and then cooperative) has also been shown by others (for review, see Zipp, 2007) even when immediate feedback is not provided. Therefore, group testing can be another form of cooperative learning even outside TBL structures.

After the testing stage, the instructor clarifies any remaining issues (identified from test scores) before moving to the application stage. Students then work in groups to apply their knowledge and come to a decision about a real-world issue. In this regard, TBL is similar to PBL (see Section 5.4.3). However, unlike PBL, the TBL application activity question has to meet four requirements: (a) to motivate students and increase the likelihood of transfer, it must be a *significant* real-world problem; (b) students must take a *specific* position on what to do; (c) the whole class must work on the *same* problem, which allows groups to learn from one another and promotes active listening across groups; and (d) to avoid being influenced by others, groups must report their decisions *simultaneously*. The last of these "4-S" requirements may sound challenging, but it can be achieved by having students write out their answers on poster paper in different parts of the classroom, or on different parts of a white/chalk board, or on index cards showing a letter indicating their choice. Students may also be asked to provide a group document summarizing the rationale for their decision.

Unlike in inter-teaching, where groups change frequently, TBL students usually stay in the same small groups (five to seven students, with heterogeneity in terms of experience and skills) for the duration of the semester. Sweet and Michaelsen's (2007) rationale for this is that the quality of decision-making within a group changes over time; the initial problems that often occur during the group-forming stage need to be ironed out, and in later classes students focus more on problem-solving and so are more likely to reach a consensus than a compromise. This is supported by Tuckman's theory of sequential group formation (Tuckman & Jensen, 1977). Although others suggest that smaller groups (two to four members) increase interdependence and reduce the incidence of social loafing (Johnson, Johnson, & Smith, 1991), larger groups are recommended in TBL to compensate for potential class absences over the course of the semester. An important element of TBL is the use of peer evaluation: Sweet and Michaelsen (2012) suggest that students should provide a numerical rating along with comments detailing what they felt each team-mate did well and how they think they could improve. Peer feedback, which factors into the grading system, helps to prevent free-riding. Furthermore, if administered more than once over the course of the semester, peer feedback can provide formative assessment of students' interpersonal skills, which can be used to modify future behavior. With one method of grading, a peer evaluation score is calculated by dividing a set number of points across the team members (e.g., 50 points between five members) and making sure that there is some distribution in the scores (e.g., 7–13) (Sweet & Michaelsen, 2012). Although this method seemed to work well for business majors, Thompson et al. (2007) found that students in the health sciences balked at the need to discriminate among members; they resolved this by allowing the students to divide the points equally if they wanted. Sweet and Michaelsen (2012) suggest that grading in a TBL class should be based on three components: individual scores (includes individual readiness test scores and other tests, such as a final exam), group scores (includes group test scores and application activity scores), and peer evaluations. However, the relative weights of these elements can vary, and could be decided on by the class at the beginning of the semester. Group scores should not harm individual scores, and so could be assigned as extra credit (rather like the quality points in inter-teaching). One potential system is to divide the total points for a semester between each of the three elements, making sure that peer evaluations count for at least 5% of the final grade. Alternatively, you could use a multiplier system, where the group score is calculated by multiplying the raw group score by the peer evaluation score (with students within a group allowed to distribute points equally).

Kubitz and Lightner (2012) found that TBL was effective for reducing misconceptions about psychology (e.g., pseudoscientific beliefs) and increased students' ability to transfer such knowledge to novel situations. Many of the resources for PBL (see Box 5.2) might be adapted for the application phase of TBL, as could case studies, bearing in mind that the final answer has to be a specific choice. For example, in a Personality class, Kubitz and Lightner (2012) asked groups to consider who would win if Sigmund Freud, Carl Rogers, George Kelly, and B. F. Skinner were to play a game of poker. Students were given worksheets that required them to think about the various strengths and weaknesses of each of the theorists, and after all the groups had presented their answer and rationale, the entire class voted on the best. Asking groups to construct concept maps on posters is another effective way to use TBL in psychology classes (Kubitz & Lightner, 2012). Concept maps employ a graphical/pictorial format to show how ideas or concepts are inter-related; a meta-analysis shows that they are particularly effective in deepening learning in group settings in higher education (Nesbit & Adesope, 2006). Novak provides a step-by-step guide to helping students learn how to create concept maps (Novak & Cañas, 2006), and we have found the suggestions on the Eberly Center on Carnegie Mellon's website to also be very helpful (https://www.cmu.edu/teaching/assessment/assesslearning/conceptmaps.html).

5.4.5 Jigsaw Classroom Design

The jigsaw classroom was first developed as a cooperative learning practice by Aronson et al. (1978) in the 1970s, in an attempt to improve relationships among students after public schools were desegregated. In its original format, students were divided into heterogeneous (in terms of race and ability) jigsaw groups, wherein each member was assigned to become an expert on a unique piece of a larger puzzle or project. For example, for a group project on schizophrenia, one group member might have to become an expert on symptoms, another on biological explanations of the illness, a third on psychosocial explanations, and a fourth on treatment options. In the original jigsaw format, each student read only the assigned materials that were pertinent to their designated area of expertise (e.g., if they were assigned symptoms, they only read the materials that related to symptoms), then they met with students from other groups with the same assignment (e.g., symptoms) to discuss what they had learned, to ask questions of one another, and to practice how and what they should report back to their groups. The students then went back to their original groups and taught one another what they had learned, so that they could piece together the entire jigsaw puzzle. Students were then quizzed about the general question or project, and graded based on their individual quiz scores. In the jigsaw classroom, it is clear that the instructor is no longer the only expert in the room.

Jigsaw techniques have been shown to be effective in improving interpersonal relationships and self-esteem among students (Aronson et al., 1978). However, Slavin (2011) suggested that the original technique could be improved if all students read the same materials at the outset and then each took responsibility for an individual chunk, thereby increasing each student's exposure to the materials. Furthermore, he found that increasing reward interdependence (e.g., improvements in students' quiz scores contributed extra points to their groups) increased learning gains (for review, see Slavin, 2011).

Jigsaw activities, or modified versions thereof, have also been used in higher education, including psychology classes. Jigsaw design has been shown to be successful in improving academic performance in a Statistics class (Perkins & Saris, 2001), reducing student failure and withdrawals from a Research Methods class (Carroll, 1986), and increasing confidence in the ability to teach others in a Cognitive Psychology class (Crone & Portillo, 2013). Clump (2012) also found that students in a Sensation and Perception class reported that they read the textbook more thoroughly when they were taught using the jigsaw technique.

5.5 Cooperative Learning Games

Although the idea of cooperative learning is for students to work together noncompetitively, under some circumstances it might be advantageous to have a competitive element to some assignments. Inter-group competition within cooperative learning structures has been shown to enhance motivation and performance in some cases (Slavin, 1980). One way in which inter-group competition has been exploited successfully in psychology and other college classes has been in the playing of games as a way of reviewing course material, either at the beginning of the semester (Weisskirch, 2009) or before an exam (Vanags, George, Grace, & Brown, 2012). According to game development theory (Robison, 2014), classroom games increase learning if they hold students' attention, have an emotional or challenging element to them, and require that every student participates. PowerPoint® (PPT) can be used to create various different versions of popular games, such as Bingo, Jeopardy®, and Who Wants to Be a Millionaire®? (multiple different templates and instructions can be found at http://people.uncw.edu/ertzbergerj/ppt_games.html). In general, college students appear to enjoy playing games as a way of reviewing for exams (Gibson, 1991; Keutzer, 1993a) and to perceive games like Jeopardy® as helpful in learning course material (Massey, Brown, & Johnston, 2005; Ritzko & Robinson, 2011). In the spirit of universal design (i.e., allowing students of all abilities to contribute fully to a game), Rotter (2004) suggests that students be allowed to bring notes (or their textbook) to the review session and, within each team, to take turns in answering questions.

From a purely logistical point of view, in large classes it is not optimal to play a game like Jeopardy exactly as it is played on TV. As an instructor, you will need to create a set of rules for team competition and to explain them to your students at the outset of the game (including, e.g., specific rules for Double Jeopardy and Final Jeopardy). Having teams take turns in answering questions and rolling a die or taking turns to determine which team can "steal" a question is easier than trying to determine whose hand went up first (Ritzko & Robinson, 2011). Setting strict limits on the amount of time a team has to answer a question (e.g., 2 or 3 minutes) before it is offered to another team improves the pacing of the game and prevents students from searching their notes until they find the correct answer.

Alternatively, you could use SRSs to allow total class participation on every question, with points awarded to the team with the greatest number of correct answers. We have used this method to play a game of Jeopardy in a Brain and Behavior class with a large student enrollment. Students were asked to pair with their neighbor, and the pairs were assigned to teams by counting off around the class; this allowed for some collaboration between students on the same team without a lot of movement around the class. Revere (2004) used a PPT Jeopardy format in a Statistics class to administer a group-based exam (students took turns within their groups, to ensure everyone was accountable) and found that students taking the test in this way outperformed those taking the test individually.

5.6   Summary

1) The ability to work effectively in a group is a crucial skill for today's students, both in college and within the workforce.
2) Cooperative learning structures that require positive interdependence and individual accountability can be used to motivate students to help one another and have been shown to produce gains across many domains, including academic performance. Students benefit directly from teaching one another.
3) Social skills development, knowledge of group dynamics, and conflict resolution are highly useful and transferrable skills that can be fostered through reflection.
4) When students work cooperatively on interesting complex problems, the whole should be greater than the sum of the parts.

6

Learning to Write and Writing to Learn

6.1 The Value of Writing in Learning

It may come as a bit of a shock to psychology instructors when they realize that *they* will have to teach their students how to become better writers. Instructors often assume that the students in their classes have already learned how to write proficiently by taking courses such as English Composition in high school and college. However, as Arum and Roska (2011) concluded, many U.S. colleges (and high schools, for that matter) lack the necessary curricular emphasis and rigor for students to learn how to write well. Indeed, most students in large public universities take only two English Composition classes during their undergraduate careers; this bare minimum does not provide a sufficient amount of practice to allow them to develop proficiency in writing, editing, and revising their work (Arum & Roksa, 2011). Not surprisingly, students' writing in psychology classes may not live up to an instructor's expectations. Kuh (2003) suggests that the poor quality of student writing has led to a reduction in writing assignments in college, which stems from an "I won't bother you if you won't bother me" philosophy. This approach simply exacerbates the problem. We know that deliberate practice and experience are necessary if we want our students to develop expertise (Ericsson, Krampe, & Tesch-Römer, 1993). Assigning less writing because it is hard to understand what students are trying to communicate is self-defeating. We encourage you to design coursework that provides your students with developmentally appropriate writing instruction *and* ample opportunities to practice writing in every class you teach.

Concerns about the quality of student writing have energized the Writing Across the Curriculum (WAC) movement in higher education (for a review, see Zawacki & Rogers, 2012). WAC emphasizes that writing is an integral part of a liberal arts education, and that writing facilitates thinking. Indeed, the National Survey of Student Engagement (NSSE) has shown that higher-order thinking skills are correlated with the amount of writing that a student does in college (National Survey of Student Engagement, 2013). The WAC philosophy is somewhat akin to the African proverb, "It takes a village to raise a child," because it recognizes that instructors from all disciplines need to help students learn how to write effectively. It acknowledges that each discipline stresses different kinds of thinking and writing, and that students will benefit from exposure to a wide variety of disciplinary genres and styles. Writing assignments in classes such as

Teaching Psychology: An Evidence-Based Approach, First Edition. Jillian Grose-Fifer, Patricia J. Brooks, and Maureen O'Connor.
© 2019 John Wiley & Sons, Inc. Published 2019 by John Wiley & Sons, Inc.
Companion website: www.wiley.com/go/Grose-Fifer/teaching-psychology

psychology serve two main purposes: students not only learn to write better, but also write in order to learn better (Butler, Phillmann, & Smart, 2001; Connor-Greene, 2000b; Conrad, 2013; Drabick, Weisberg, Paul, & Bubier, 2007; Nevid, Pastva, & McClelland, 2012; Stewart, Myers, & Culley, 2010). In this chapter, we will provide evidence-based guidelines for developing both high- and low-stakes writing assignments. As we have emphasized in Chapter 2, using backward design is key to creating effective assignments. That is, once you have decided what kinds of skills you want your students to develop in the course, it is easier to identify and assign developmentally appropriate writing assignments to meet your instructional goals (Bean, 2011).

6.2   Strategies for Teaching Reading and Writing

Like WAC, a parallel movement called Writing in the Disciplines (WID) stresses that it is crucial for instructors to deconstruct for students how to structure their writing for a given discipline or audience, at all levels of training. The American Psychological Association (APA) Guidelines for the Undergraduate Psychology Major state that effective writing skills are a crucial student learning outcome for undergraduate programs in psychology (American Psychological Association, 2013). APA expects students graduating with a psychology major to be able clearly express their ideas and present a well-reasoned scientific argument. In the past, it was frequently assumed that students would "pick up these skills along the way" (Coffin et al., 2005). As emphasized by the WAC and WID movements, however, if students are to produce quality written work, then it is critical for instructors to show them how to do so, and to provide numerous opportunities for them to practice their writing skills (Kellogg & Raulerson, 2007). The more writing exercises we assign, the sooner our students will become proficient with the surface elements of the writing process, such as spelling and grammar. This will help free up working memory to deal with more global issues, such as how to organize ideas and present a cogent argument (Hayes, 2006).

Some instructors believe that the best way to help students to write effectively within the discipline of psychology is to offer writing courses devoted specifically to this purpose (e.g., see Goddard, 2003; Johnson, Tuskenis, Howell, & Jaroszewski, 2011). Cook and Murowchick (2014) showed that the quality and sophistication of students' writing improved after taking an intermediate-level writing course that provided them with detailed instructions on how to write a critical literature review paper, and that the skills they obtained were transferrable to other upper-level courses. However, not all departments have the necessary resources or infrastructure to mount such a course. Furthermore, there is evidence that embedding writing instruction in other courses also improves student writing (Fallahi, Wood, Austad, & Fallahi, 2006; Grose-Fifer & Davis-Ferreira, 2018; Jorgensen & Marek, 2013). Therefore, in this chapter, we have focused on designing writing assignments within content-based classes, with an emphasis on organizing assignments in steps that are manageable for students to complete, while building skills that allow them to gradually take on more complicated and difficult work.

Deconstructing the writing process is often challenging for experienced writers, such as graduate students and faculty, because we put relatively little conscious thought into the mechanics of our own writing. As Nodine (2002) points out, it is important to remember that writing is complex and challenging for novice undergraduate writers;

although others have shown that these difficulties often persist among graduate students (Alter & Adkins, 2006; Nelson, Range, & Ross, 2012). Nodine suggests that one major problem with long, multifaceted assignments, such as writing an empirical research paper, is that students often do not know where to start. Although expert writers have well-rehearsed strategies for breaking down writing assignments into more manageable chunks, most undergraduates do not. Therefore, it is imperative for instructors to help their students develop the appropriate strategies by scaffolding assignments appropriately—for example, by using class time to practice writing an outline, or breaking a longer research report into sections that are due at different time points. In a related vein, Bean (2011) has cited a number of studies indicating that very challenging writing tasks often lead to increases in surface-level spelling and grammatical errors. This is an important point, because if your students' writing is full of sentence-level mistakes, this may indicate that an assignment is too complex. Scaffolding the assignment appropriately lessens the cognitive demands of retrieving unfamiliar content and assembling it to construct a coherent argument.

One of the key elements in designing developmentally appropriate writing assignments is to assess where your students are in terms of their writing skills and discipline-specific knowledge, which will allow you to create and scaffold assignments in ways that build on their existing skills. A common high-stakes writing assignment in undergraduate psychology classes is to ask students to write a literature review using primary sources. In a survey of faculty at 84 U.S. colleges, over 70% reported that they had asked students to read and summarize primary source articles at least once in their courses (Oldenburg, 2005). Moreover, 46% reported that they had assigned primary source readings in Introductory Psychology classes, although many acknowledged that these types of assignment were more beneficial in upper-level courses and classes with small enrollments (Oldenburg, 2005). We suggest that although instructors may feel that writing a literature review is straightforward, this is only because they have acquired a considerable amount of expertise in completing this task. In general, writing a literature review is a very challenging assignment for undergraduates, even in intermediate-level classes (Soysa, Dunn, Dottolo, Burns-Glover, & Gurung, 2013). In Section 6.2.2, we discuss how to help students to write a literature review by scaffolding the assignment, but first we encourage you to think more broadly about adopting a more developmental approach to writing in your psychology classes. To this end, a few publications offer pragmatic guidance for designing writing assignments that are pitched appropriately across various levels of the psychology major (for review, see Soysa et al., 2013), some of which is summarized in the following sections.

6.2.1 Strategies for Designing Introductory Psychology Writing Assignments

Beins, Smith, and Dunn (2010) recommend that writing assignments for introductory-level classes focus on basic skills, such as summarizing psychological concepts from textbook readings and applying these to everyday life. Similarly, Soysa et al. (2013) suggest that in introductory classes, instructors should emphasize the use of evidence-based statements rather than opinion in written assignments, using concrete prompts to help focus students' thinking. For example, you might ask students to read a textbook chapter about sleep and consciousness and then summarize how being sleep-deprived might cause problems for them as a college student. However, you should not assume that you are teaching students how to use evidence to support an argument simply by giving them a writing prompt or a written homework assignment. In a national survey of psychology faculty, Landrum (2013) found that the most commonly reported problem in undergraduate writing was that students made claims without empirical support. This suggests that class time would be well spent explaining the difference between opinion and evidence-based claims, and then giving students time to practice citing evidence to support an argument (see also Chapter 4 on Advancing Critical Thinking Through Active Learning).

Class time should also be used to teach students how to paraphrase effectively. Students in introductory classes are often surprised to learn that they should avoid quoting passages of text from their sources when writing papers in psychology, as this type of writing practice is expected and actively encouraged in other academic disciplines (Madigan, Johnson, & Linton, 1995). Often, the most effective piece of advice for teaching paraphrasing is to ask students to first read a paragraph that has the information needed to back up their claim and then write from memory without looking at the material (Howard, 1999). This helps to prevent "patchwriting," where students rely heavily on paraphrasing individual sentences from their sources. Instructors can assign paraphrasing exercises for homework, which can help students to "warm up" to paraphrasing before submitting a longer literature review paper. Using the SafeAssign or Turnitin feature of Blackboard (or any other anti-plagiarism software available through an online course management system [CMS]) is a quick and easy way for students (and instructors) to check whether they are paraphrasing effectively. In addition to teaching students to paraphrase, rather than quoting from their sources, instructors will also need to show them how to use in-text citations and how to reference their sources in APA format.

As a new instructor, you may feel anxious about spending class time teaching *writing* as opposed to *content*, but the benefits of providing writing instruction have been empirically demonstrated (Fallahi et al., 2006; Grose-Fifer & Davis-Ferreira, 2018; Grose-Fifer, Davis, & Pryiomka, 2014; Jorgensen & Marek, 2013). Furthermore, instruction is often necessary to ensure that students develop the writing proficiencies that the APA expects of psychology majors (American Psychological Association, 2013) and which will better prepare students for success in their chosen careers and/or graduate school. The amount of time dedicated to in-class writing instruction need not be lengthy. For example, Jorgensen and Marek (2013) found that attendance at a brief 30-minute workshop on APA style improved editing skills in Introductory Psychology students, especially when the students took notes during the workshop. Similarly, Fallahi et al. (2006) found that five brief (15-minute) instructional periods on the mechanics of writing and the use of APA format led to improved referencing and grammar in students in a General Psychology class. Importantly, in terms of instructional efficacy, Zimmerman and Kitsantas (2002) found that watching someone write and self-correct was more beneficial for students than watching someone produce a perfect model. Such instruction highlights the value of re-reading one's work and editing it to improve writing style and organization.

6.2.2   Next Steps in Designing Psychology Writing Assignments

Once students have gained some basic writing skills in introductory-level courses, Soysa et al. (2013) suggest that they should be ready to write an analytical essay, provided that the prompt is appropriately pitched. Soysa et al. (2013) asked students in a mid-level Psychology of Women course to describe and then analyze two printed advertisements, using a series of structured questions regarding gender stereotypes. Students also had to use course-related materials (such as textbook readings) to connect their claims to psychological theories about gender roles in society. The instructor spent class time modeling the difference between description and analysis, and provided opportunities for students to practice writing and to discuss their work with peers. The exercises were successful because they gave students opportunities to learn from their mistakes, which made it more likely that they would use the correct strategies when writing their papers. Students reported that they found the exercises extremely valuable (ratings of 4.3/5 for helpfulness) when writing a paper.

Once students have gained some proficiency in analytical writing, they are probably ready to move on to summarizing and critiquing psychological research articles; accordingly, Soysa et al. (2013) have suggested that intermediate courses (200 or 300 level, depending on the course numbering system) are appropriate for teaching students how to write brief literature reviews using a small selection of primary source articles. Reading primary sources familiarizes students with the format of psychological articles and APA-style language, and provides a basis on which to model their own future writing (Kellogg, 1994). Nevertheless, a considerable amount of class time is needed to support students completing these kinds of assignments (Grose-Fifer & Davis-Ferreira, 2018; Grose-Fifer, Davis, & Pryiomka, 2014; Poe, 1990; Soysa et al., 2013), and even then, students may still find it difficult to write a truly integrative essay (Soysa et al., 2013).

Students will likely need instruction on how to use online databases to find primary sources; such training often can be arranged by consulting with a college librarian. It is important to be mindful that students may have no prior experience using Google Scholar, PsycInfo, or any other database—despite their familiarity with the Internet and with Google—and they may not know how to select appropriate keywords and search criteria to use databases effectively (see also Section 4.5.1 for advice about helping students to search for and evaluate information). It is helpful if training in using databases takes place in a classroom or computer lab where students can access the databases themselves, as this ensures they will be more actively involved in the learning process and will have opportunities to practice the search techniques they are shown.

Another important consideration when incorporating primary source articles in writing assignments is that students' reading skills are strongly linked to their writing skills (Hayes, 2006; Kellogg, 1994). Unfortunately, instructors often fail to recognize that undergraduates may need instruction on how to *read* as well as *write* academic texts—it is easy for instructors to take reading skills for granted after years of practice in extracting key information from complex primary source materials. Instruction in how to closely read a primary source article is particularly important in classes where the material is very technical or novel (such as in a Neuroscience or Cognitive Psychology course). There is clear evidence that instructing students on how to read and interpret primary sources improves their understanding of the content, as well as the quality of their writing (Christopher & Walter, 2006; Grose-Fifer & Davis-Ferreira, 2018; Grose-Fifer, Davis, & Pryiomka, 2014). Christopher and Walter (2006) compared test scores in a Research Methods course in which one class received a reading/writing assignment where they were required to answer specific questions related to the methodology of a primary source article and another class (the control) did not. Students who were guided in reading a primary source article outperformed their peers in the control group for test items that required them to interpret statistics and research design. Similarly, Grose-Fifer and colleagues (Grose-Fifer & Davis-Ferreira, 2018; Grose-Fifer, Davis, & Pryiomka, 2014) found that teaching students how to read primary source articles in a Biological Psychology course improved their writing assignment grades and promoted persistence in the class. Students were given worksheets with specific instructions about where to find information in a primary source article and how to take notes; they were specifically instructed that reading the assigned primary source article would take them a considerable amount of time (about 6 hours), which helped them to recognize the difficulty of the task and to plan accordingly. Class time was spent practicing analyzing a representative article from the field of neuroscience and paraphrasing the main points using the past tense and the active voice. Such in-class exercises help students gain a better understanding of how to structure their own papers and how to use APA-style sentence structure and vocabulary (Coffin et al., 2005).

If a literature review assignment is properly scaffolded, then much of a student's time over the course of the semester will be spent preparing to write the final product. Therefore, you should consider allotting a considerable amount of the writing assignment grade to the various steps in the process: finding relevant primary sources, providing detailed information from a PsycInfo record (or other database), taking notes on primary source articles, and revising work in response to feedback from you, their peers or from the college writing center, for example (Soysa et al., 2013). The importance of considering students' work in completing each step of a complex assignment is highlighted in the findings of Soysa et al. (2013), who showed that the vast majority of students fared well in their overall writing assignment, with over 90% earning a C– or better, when the grade was inclusive of the various steps in the writing process, but that fewer than 50% received a grade of C– or better for their final literature review paper. This underscores that many college students need a considerable amount of scaffolding and practice to become proficient at writing literature review papers, and that they should be graded for their efforts in completing steps that are developmentally appropriate.

Soysa et al. (2013) suggested that empirical research papers and longer traditional literature reviews may be appropriate writing assignments for seniors taking capstone psychology classes. However, in light of their findings about students' limited proficiency in writing literature review papers in intermediate-level courses, it is still important in upper-level courses for writing assignments to be appropriately scaffolded. For example, an initial assignment might require students to brainstorm ideas for the topic that they will write about, while subsequent ones might require them to produce an outline of the paper, to draw up a plan for how to accomplish other parts of the assignment (such as data collection and analysis, in the case of an empirical research paper), to submit one or more drafts of key sections of the paper, and to edit and revise their work (Nodine, 2002). Even in upper-level courses, students often need help in formulating a research question, and they may need assistance in using databases to gather appropriate sources. Upper-level students continue to benefit from exercises that ensure that they have engaged in careful reading of their primary sources and can paraphrase key points (Cook & Murowchick, 2014). It is also helpful to show them how to write an annotated bibliography. Requiring students to select key concepts from their sources and link them to the thesis of their review paper in an annotated bibliography taps skills in the lower levels of Bloom's taxonomy (i.e., remember, understand, and apply). As the next step, students can be given exercises in which they are shown how to synthesize and integrate information to draw conclusions that go beyond what was stated in the source articles. Clearly, this last step is the most challenging part of writing a literature review (and reflects upper levels of Bloom's taxonomy, i.e., analyze, evaluate, create), and so will require even more instructor support. At each step of the process, students benefit from timely feedback from their peers, the instructor, or both.

Essays or literature reviews that require students to compare and contrast concepts or studies are probably the most challenging assignments for college students (Spivey, 1991). They require them to understand the content and express their knowledge effectively, but they also demand high levels of cognitive effort in order to organize information in an integrative fashion (Hammann & Stevens, 2003; Spivey, 1991). Like Cook and Murowchick (2014), Spivey (1991) found that teaching students how to write summaries was an important part of the scaffolding process, as it helped them remember materials better, which in turn helped them to organize their ideas. Spivey also required students to analyze models in which differences and similarities were summarized from texts; this helped them gain a better understanding of the strategies that they would need to use in their own essays. Completing a planner in which similarities and differences are tabulated (Spivey, 1991) or represented in graphical format (Robinson & Kiewra, 1995) has been shown to help students perceive conceptual relationships more effectively, and to improve the quality of the final product. Finally, it is helpful to analyze and discuss various text exemplars that show different ways of integrating materials in an essay, so that students can appreciate that more than one type of approach may be effective (e.g., a text might be organized by topic or by clusters of similarities and differences; Spivey, 1991).

6.3   Helping Students to Improve Writing Drafts

If instructors want to help students to improve their writing skills, they should encourage them to think carefully about the process of writing. To be effective writers, students need to see the value of their assignments in order to be motivated to write to the best of their ability. It is also important that students have opportunities to learn from their mistakes, so that they can make improvements over the duration of the course.

6.3.1   Encouraging Students to Think Metacognitively about Writing

Of course, one way to improve student writing is to give effective feedback. However, instructors often struggle with deciding how much feedback to give and on what kinds of issues to focus. Dedicating large amounts of time to giving feedback may be unfeasible for many instructors, which could serve as a deterrent to the inclusion of writing assignments in the curriculum. Moreover, detailed feedback is likely to be perceived as unhelpful if it is given at the end of the semester, when students no longer have the opportunity to improve on their work (Carless, 2006; Hattie & Yates, 2014). One suggestion for making giving feedback more manageable is to encourage students to think carefully about the assignment, even before they start to write. Carless (2006) found that students are often puzzled about the assessment criteria at the outset of an assignment, and benefit from having clear instructions and rubrics that detail how grades will be assigned. Coffin et al. (2005) suggest that students should have a clear understanding of who their audience is, and that they may be more motivated if the pedagogical value of the assignment is made explicit. However, explaining the assignment may not be enough. Students often misinterpret what they need to do simply because they do not share the same level of expertise as their instructor. Class discussion and having the students rewrite the assignment criteria in their own words can help overcome this issue (Nicol, 2010). Another approach that has been shown to improve students' understanding of grading metrics is to spend time analyzing the strengths and weakness of exemplars of student work on similar assignments (Price & O'Donovan, 2006).

Similarly, increasing students' metacognitive awareness about their own writing errors may lead to more assiduous editing. To this end, you could ask students to revise their own drafts during a class period, after sharing research findings that demonstrate best practices for correcting one's own writing. Many students think that they can edit as they write, but as Chenoweth and Hayes (2001) have reported, writing quality improves more when students edit after they have finished writing than when they edit "online." Training students to more thoroughly check their work is effective in reducing sentence-level errors (grammar and spelling), as these commonly result from a lack of proof-reading (for review, see Bean, 2011). Indeed, Stellmack, Keenan, Sandidge, Sippl, and Konheim-Kalkstein (2012) found that engaging students in a Research Methods class in self-assessment improved the first drafts of their papers as much as having another student provide feedback. Reading drafts aloud has also been shown to aid self-correction (Bartholomae, 1980). Taking it a few steps further, when students completed a checklist stating that they had read their paper aloud and had used a spell check or grammar check, they produced more carefully written first drafts (Norton, Clifford, Hopkins, Toner, & Norton, 2002).

6.3.2 Using Peer Review to Give Feedback

Another popular strategy to help improve the quality of student writing is to implement peer review of drafts of papers, prior to their submission to the instructor for grading (see Box 6.1 for resources on the peer-review process). Nicol (2010) has argued that most college classes are too large for instructors to provide feedback on all writing drafts, and that peer review can substantially increase the amount of feedback that students receive. Peer review is common in college-level writing courses (Haswell, 2005), and research suggests that it improves the quality of student writing, especially if students receive more than one review (Cho & MacArthur, 2010; Cho, Schunn, & Wilson, 2006; Stellmack et al., 2012; Topping, 1998). In support of this, Cho et al., (2006) demonstrated that when students (N = 708) from a large variety of courses received feedback from four peer-reviewers, their papers improved more than when they

---

Box 6.1 Resources for Peer Review

Templates for peer editing can be found at http://writingproject.fas.harvard.edu/files/hwp/files/psychology_teaching_08.30.pdf.

received feedback from the instructor (or a single peer). Furthermore, Cho and Cho (2011) found that students were more likely to make more conceptual or large-scale changes in response to peer feedback, whereas they were more likely to make more surface-level changes in response to instructor feedback. Peer review was clearly effective in bringing about substantive changes in their papers; 80% of the participants felt that the quality of their writing improved as a result of the peer-review process, but approximately 50% also felt concerned that their peers lacked the expertise to evaluate their work effectively. Instructors may also be concerned that students who have less developed writing skills or poorer understanding of the topic material may be less helpful in the peer-review process. However, Strijbos, Narciss, and Dünnebier (2010) showed that, at least among graduate students, feedback from less competent students was just as (or even more) effective in improving the quality of a person's writing than feedback from a highly competent student.

Nicol (2010) has suggested that performing peer review particularly enhances the reviewer's critical thinking (CT) and writing. Cho and Cho (2011) found that students improved the quality of their writing more by giving comments than by receiving them; this was especially true for students who provided high-quality comments. Similarly, in a Research Methods course, White and Kirby (2005) found that students felt that they benefitted more from giving peer feedback than from receiving it. These results suggest that engaging in peer review enhances students' abilities to think deeply about their own writing.

Several authors have suggested that peer feedback is most effective when students are prompted to look for particular elements in the papers that they are reviewing—elements that will vary according to the learning outcomes of the writing assignment. Cho et al., (2006) asked peer-reviewers to evaluate written work in terms of its flow, logic, and insights using 1–7-point Likert scales, and provided them with rubrics to guide their grading criteria. Similarly, Mayo (2006) asked students to use 1–10-point Likert scales to evaluate their peers' writing style (fluency, clarity), logical organization, mechanics (punctuation, spelling, grammar), content (relevance, accuracy), and references (in-text citations, completeness). To increase the validity of the peer-review process, it is helpful to model the steps students should take by going over the process in class. Although peer-reviewers have been shown to make more positive comments than instructors (Beason, 1993), they should be explicitly instructed to comment on the strongest parts of the paper as well as the weakest, as this helps the recipient understand when they have been successful (Cho & Cho, 2011), and may also increase their self-esteem and motivation to make further improvements (Beason, 1993). For example, you could ask students to mark a place in the paper where the writer has effectively used a citation to provide evidence to support a statement. You might also ask them to mark an area that they found particularly difficult to understand.

6.3.3 Giving Effective Feedback and Helping Students Respond to Feedback

If you are feeling alarmed about the amount of time you might spend giving feedback on writing, you should bear in mind that not all feedback needs to be written. Fallahi assigned five four- or five-page papers in her General Psychology classes and spent class time going over common mistakes when she handed each back. This approach, coupled with brief instruction on grammar, mechanics, and APA style, led to a significant improvement in the quality of her students' writing over the course of the semester and took less time than writing individual comments on papers (Fallahi et al., 2006).

Somewhat worryingly, instructors and students often differ considerably in their perceptions of the value of written feedback on writing assignments (Carless, 2006). Instructors may write extensive commentary on the final draft of a paper, believing that their students will examine the feedback carefully in order to learn from their mistakes. However, Carless (2006) showed that students pay much more attention to comments on drafts than on the final version, so instructors should proportion the time spent on each accordingly. Students can be motivated to revise their work in successive drafts by using an appropriate grading structure. Mastery is encouraged if initial drafts are graded on a pass/fail basis. Although they are crucial for honing the final product, the quality of drafts should count relatively little toward the final grade. In contrast, the final (and hopefully more polished) product should carry a higher proportion of the grade (Bean, 2011).

Carless (2006) and Weaver (2006) both found that students often reacted very emotionally to feedback, and felt unmotivated to make revisions. Therefore, it is a good idea to balance critical feedback with positive comments, in combination with suggestions for improvement (Nicol, 2010). It is also important to note that students often report that feedback can be difficult to interpret (Carless, 2006; Weaver, 2006). Handwriting issues aside, simply writing the word "unclear" is usually insufficient for students to understand what they need to do to improve. Students learn more when they correct their own errors (Dragga, 2010; Willingham, 1990), so asking leading questions is preferable to providing answers.

Nicol (2010) emphasized that dialoging about feedback is an effective way to improve student writing. For example, asking students to summarize the main points of the instructor's feedback and to write questions about any comments that they feel are unclear may assist them in using feedback more effectively (Elbow & Sorcinelli, 2011). This technique can also aid instructors in refining the type of feedback that they give. However, as Bloxham and Campbell (2010) have pointed out, it is not always practical to engage in a conversation with every student on every paper, especially for instructors with large classes or heavy teaching loads. Instead, they encouraged students to evaluate their own writing by having them submit a cover letter with their assignments, in which they described where they needed the most guidance (Bloxham & Campbell, 2010). Daniel, Gaze, and Braasch (2015) used a similar approach in a Research Methods class, and found that requiring students to write cover letters summarizing the changes they had made in response to feedback improved the quality of their final papers.

In general, Bean (2011) has advised against the time-consuming practice of correcting all the surface-level errors in a paper, as this may inadvertently signal that this is all that the student needs to do to improve their writing. Instead, he suggests simply telling the student to "fix the spelling and grammar errors," and focusing your feedback on the content of the essay. In support of this, Beason (1993) found that although instructors commonly line-edited *and* offered advice for revisions (e.g., requests for better support for claims and argument development), students were likely to address only the mechanical issues in their revised work. If you really feel that you cannot let sentence-level errors go without comment, consider using a technique suggested by

Haswell (1983), who demonstrated that marking a line of text that contained an error with a check in the margin was sufficient for students to find and correct 61% of sentence-level errors themselves. Alternatively, and perhaps preferably, when students make mechanical errors they tend to be relatively systematic, so you can provide one or two global comments to address them. However, it is important that students understand these comments: you cannot simply say "avoid comma splices" without marking an example to show what you mean. Finally, correcting the first paragraph and adding a comment suggesting that the student should fix the rest of the paper accordingly helps students recognize the frequency of errors in their grammar and spelling (Bean, 2011).

Relatedly, many institutions have writing centers, which when used regularly have been shown to improve students' writing, grades, and retention (Bell, 2000; Henson & Stephenson, 2009; Casey Jones, 2001; Karp, O'Gara, & Hughes, 2008; Williams & Takaku, 2011). In most centers, peer tutors provide individualized assistance, although they may also offer group sessions, online tutorials, and/or workshops on more general topics (e.g., how to format references in APA style, write a thesis statement, or avoid patch writing), which can extend and reinforce the concepts that you teach in class. Unfortunately, students and instructors often have misperceptions about the functions of a writing center, believing that it provides proof-reading or other editing services, or only serves students who are in need of remedial help (Garner, 2005; Leahy, 1990). In actuality, writing centers strive to develop writers rather than to improve one specific piece of writing; thus, all students are likely to benefit from their services, regardless of their writing proficiency (Leahy, 1990; Williams & Takaku, 2011). Students may be unaware of the existence of the writing center or that the services it offers are free and available to all, especially if they are first-generation college students (Karp et al., 2008). Additionally, students often feel that they are too busy to visit the writing center, and so only go if an instructor has required them to do so as part of an assignment or if they have been told it could substantially improve their grade (Bishop, 1990; Clark, 1985). Historically (and anecdotally), it was suggested that students should seek help from writing centers on a purely voluntary basis, because mandatory visits were likely to induce negative feelings that would hamper the efficacy of the tutoring (North, 1984). However, survey data suggest that requiring students to go to a writing center helps them to develop positive perceptions about such centers (Bishop, 1990; Clark, 1985; Wells, 2016) and increases their intention to revisit, even if initially they are reluctant or annoyed by the requirement (Gordon, 2008). Once they have visited a writing center, students are likely to recommend them to their friends and to suggest that visits should be mandated by instructors (Bishop, 1990; Gordon, 2008; Wells, 2016). Therefore, requiring all students to visit a writing center at least once for your course may encourage them to continue to seek assistance with their writing, which is likely to impact their future academic success. We suggest that you consult with your writing center to ensure that it has the capacity to accommodate all of the students in your class, as resources vary across institutions. Also, ask how you can make visits most productive for your students; at a minimum, you should counsel them to bring their assignment instructions, along with any instructor or peer feedback that they want help addressing.

As we move deeper into the twenty-first century, it is increasingly common for instructors to grade papers electronically using the commenting feature in word-processing programs. One advantage of this method is that the written comments are legible; illegible handwriting has frequently been cited as a cause of student frustration over feedback (Weaver, 2006). Another advantage is that any commonly used phrases can be copied and duplicated across student papers. Gleaves and Walker (2013) showed that students who received feedback in the form of short mp3 audio clips found it to be clearer and more directive than those who received written feedback, although this did not significantly improve the quality of their writing. Some instructors may find this approach to be less time-consuming than writing comments.

In summarizing guidelines from evidence-based research on the most effective types of feedback, Nicol (2010) recommended that feedback should be given in a timely manner so that it can be used to improve future drafts, that it should be written in a form that students can easily understand, and that it should focus on two or three substantive issues that need to be addressed. Substantive feedback that addresses global issues, such as conceptualization of ideas, is more powerful in stimulating deep transferrable learning than very detailed feedback, where it might be difficult to "see the woods for the trees" (Carless, 2006). Ideally, comments should be general enough to be applicable to other assignments. To try and avoid evoking strong emotions, feedback should be neutral in tone, and should simply describe the issues without judgment. It is helpful to comment on the strengths of a paper as well as giving advice for improvement, as this provides positive reinforcement for good writing.

6.3.4 Using Rubrics to Provide Feedback

Rubrics are particularly helpful in assessing whether students are meeting specific learning outcomes (either within a specific course or more widely within the context of a department, or even an institution). Rubrics can be holistic or analytical: the former provide guidelines for an overall evaluation, while the latter typically describe performance criteria at different levels (excellent to weak) for a number of different evaluation criteria (Reddy & Andrade, 2010). As mentioned previously, giving students grading rubrics at the outset can help them to understand requirements more clearly. Similarly, using rubrics to grade increases the transparency of feedback, and if an analytical rubric is used to provide feedback on different aspects of a paper, it may be easier for students to understand where they need to marshal their efforts (Jonsson & Svingby, 2007). Students generally have positive attitudes toward rubrics for this very reason (Reddy & Andrade, 2010). Rubrics also help to standardize the grading process (Jonsson & Svingby, 2007), and can reduce the time spent writing generic comments on every student's paper (see Box 6.2 for a link to a developmental rubric for a research report).

Box 6.2 Developmental Rubric for Empirical Research Reports

http://teachpsych.org/resources/Documents/otrp/resources/gottfried09.pdf

Note that this particular rubric was designed to be used over the entire duration of a major, and takes a developmental approach such that a paper that earns an A in an introductory class would not meet the highest criteria in later classes.

6.4   Plagiarism

Unfortunately, plagiarism is very common in undergraduate writing (McCabe, 2005). We have already mentioned that various online CMSs, such as Blackboard, Canvas, and Moodle, give access to various plagiarism detection tools, such as SafeAssign and Turnitin. Alternatively, you can "Google" phrases that look suspiciously out of place in a student's essay to identify instances of plagiarism (McCullough & Holmberg, 2005). As an instructor, it is important to understand when and why students plagiarize, and to use this information to develop strategies to help prevent it. Students often plagiarize because they have a poor understanding of what plagiarism is (Belter & du Pré, 2009); this seems to be true even in intermediate or upper-level psychology classes (Estow, Lawrence, & Adams, 2011). Teaching students about plagiarism has been shown to be effective in reducing its incidence. Obeid and Hill (2017) found that a 2-hour intervention was effective in reducing plagiarism across multiple sections of a Research Methods course. In the intervention condition, students took a plagiarism course, distributed free of charge through the Society for the Teaching of Psychology (STP) (Lamoreaux, Darnell, Sheehan, & Tusher, 2012), whereas in the control condition, instructors taught the course as usual (i.e., with a statement about academic integrity and plagiarism in the syllabus). At the end of the semester, the authors used SafeAssign to calculate the amount of plagiarism in students' final research papers, and found significantly lower rates of plagiarized content (14 vs. 21%) in classes that received the intervention compared to those that did not. Estow et al. (2011) took an immersive approach and designed a Research Methods class around issues of plagiarism: students analyzed a primary source about plagiarism and designed a study that manipulated it. Students in the class were better able to identify plagiarism than students in a regular section, who simply received a typical lecture about what constitutes plagiarism. In a Developmental Psychology class, Schuetze (2004) used a training technique that required relatively little effort on the part of the instructor and would be feasible to implement in a variety of settings. After giving a brief in-class lecture about plagiarism, Schuetze assigned two related homework exercises (each worth 5% of the final grade). For each assignment, students read a passage from the introduction of an article, but with the references removed; they had to identify the sentences that needed citations. After the first assignment, Shuetze went over common misperceptions about plagiarism in class. When students repeated the exercise, they did substantially better the second time around. Furthermore, students who did the homework assignments not only reported feeling more confident about correctly citing source materials than those who had merely heard the lecture, but also made fewer citation errors in their final papers. Landau, Druen, and Arcuri (2002) also found that showing students examples of plagiarism and giving them feedback about their ability to recognize it improved their ability to recognize it effectively.

Another strategy to educate students about plagiarism is for them to take (and pass) an online course on the subject (see Box 6.3). Several courses are currently available online, and some offer a certificate that can be submitted to the instructor as evidence of completion.

Plagiarism has been shown to be positively correlated with procrastination (Roig & DeTommaso, 1995); that is, students are more likely to plagiarize if they have not left

---

Box 6.3 Online Plagiarism Courses

http://teachpsych.org/Resources/Documents/otrp/resources/plagiarism/Educating%20
    Students%20about%20Plagiarism.pdf
https://www.indiana.edu/~academy/firstPrinciples/choice.html
http://www.umuc.edu/current-students/learning-resources/academic-integrity/tutorial/
    index.cfm
https://plagiarism.duke.edu/

---

enough time to review what they have written and to carefully cite their source materials. Thus, in addition to educating students about plagiarism, instructors can reduce its incidence by designing their assignments to discourage procrastination. Procrastination over writing assignments appears to be extremely common in undergraduates. For example, Fritzsche, Rapp Young, & Hickson (2003) reported that 40% of students self-reported procrastinating over papers. If an instructor scaffolds an assignment to require drafts of different parts of the paper to be turned in at specified dates throughout the semester, students will be forced to manage their time more effectively. This approach was effective in reducing plagiarism in Biological Psychology courses (Grose-Fifer & Davis-Ferreira, 2018; Grose-Fifer, Davis, & Pryiomka, 2014).

Also, students are less likely to plagiarize when they are given a unique assignment in which they are asked to think critically about a particular issue, as opposed to an "all-about" term paper. For example, instead of asking students to write four pages about schizophrenia, Belter and du Pré (2009) gave students short clinical case vignettes and asked them to discuss the cases from a theoretical perspective using at least four credible sources. The authors found evidence of plagiarism in about 25% of student papers, which is considerably below the national average of 62% (McCabe, 2005). Moreover, Belter and du Pré (2009) found that students who were required to take an online unit on plagiarism and pass a quiz (100% correct) early on in their course were less likely to plagiarize than students who had not received this instruction (6 vs. 25%).

6.5 Lowering the Stakes in Writing Assignments

The writing assignments described in Section 6.2 are typically high-stakes. As we have emphasized, they should be scaffolded appropriately so that students' writing improves over the semester. The WAC movement promotes the idea that writing deepens knowledge of content materials and fosters CT. Bean (2011) has likened low-stakes exploratory writing to "thinking on paper," and advocates for assignments where the emphasis is on producing quality thinking rather than quality writing. Informal, low-stakes assignments have the advantage over high-stakes assignments in that they do not produce grading overload for instructors. Also, because they are brief, they can be assigned frequently, and as we and others have advocated, the more writing practice students get, the more likely they are to improve their skills.

Low-stakes or writing-to-learn assignments carry much less of the final course grade, and are typically short pieces of writing that require minimal time investment from the student and minimal grading effort from the instructor (e.g., pass/fail). They have been shown to help students understand and retain content, and to promote deeper thinking (Butler et al., 2001; Connor-Greene, 2000b; Conrad, 2013; Drabick et al., 2007; Nevid et al., 2012; Stewart et al., 2010). Some assignments may fall between the two levels, such as those described in the following subsection; these can be designated as high- or low-stakes depending on how the grade is assigned. In addition to the examples provided in this chapter, Chapter 8 outlines online assignments, such as blogging and wikis, while Chapter 3 describes Wikipedia editing—all of which utilize multimedia to engage students in writing.

6.5.1 Small Paper Writing

Although traditionally many instructors require students to write a lengthy term paper and allow them free choice over their topic, this may not be the most effective way of helping them learn to write (Bean, 2011). Students often find it very difficult to know where to start in these types of assignment, and this may inadvertently encourage plagiarism, especially if they look to the Internet for sample papers or leave starting the assignment to the last minute. Instead, Bean (2011) has suggested that it is more helpful for students to write smaller papers that have a more constrained course-related focus. Bean suggests that these types of assignment should require that students develop a thesis and provide support for their argument. Smaller writing assignments may also be more "instructor-friendly," by making it more feasible to give feedback in a timely manner. Assigning a series of short papers is very effective in increasing the amount of writing in a course. As we have already suggested, students frequently lack the expertise needed to read primary source research articles; in assigning short papers, instructors should take care to match their students' expertise with the types of source they want them to reference. For example, Zehr (1998) found that articles in *Current Directions in Psychological Science* were relatively easy for most students to understand and summarize. Even less technical readings could include chapters from Hock's (2012) *Forty studies that changed psychology* and articles from *Scientific American* or *American Psychologist*.

Marek et al. (2005) provide a model of how to effectively utilize a small paper writing assignment in an Introductory Psychology class. They designed their assignment to encourage students to relate psychological concepts to their everyday lives, and so focused on sleep deprivation and body image. Students were required to gather four non-academic articles from pre-assigned reputable websites, selected to insure that they accessed articles pitched at an appropriate developmental level. Students also gathered data about their own relevant behavior (e.g., their sleeping or eating habits) by completing a self-report instrument. They then wrote a brief (three- or four-page) paper in which they answered a series of assigned questions, expressed their opinions about the topic, and evaluated their own behaviors. They reported that writing these papers affected how they thought about the topics, which suggests that the assignment was effective in helping them relate course materials to their personal behaviors and lives (Marek et al., 2005).

Bean (2011) has suggested that writing persuasive pieces, such as a news article or a letter to a relative, may help students think more clearly about complex issues. Such assignments require students to describe psychological phenomena in "plain English," thus separating key concepts from the scientific jargon. Along these lines, Vipond (1993) reported that students felt that they learned a lot from having to write informational pamphlets to help ninth graders grasp basic psychological concepts.

6.5.2 Minute Papers

Ungraded low-stakes, in-class writing exercises like minute papers, in which students simply write down a main point of the class, help students organize their thoughts and consolidate what they have just learned (Angelo & Cross, 1993). These types of exercise can be used either during or at the end of class to assess student understanding (Orr, 2005; see Box 2.3 for suggestions on how to use low-stakes writing for formative assessment). Instructors can then adjust their lesson plans to provide better learning experiences for their students. Similarly, asking students to write their responses to readings or assignments in class can provide a concrete place to begin a discussion (Bean, 2011). When students write their thoughts down before they speak, it helps organize them and encourages a more considered discussion and questioning of topics; it can also be used to encourage shyer or less vocal students to contribute to the discussion (Orr, 2005). Recently, Sawyer et al. (2017) found that students who first critiqued a model minute paper and then wrote their own minute papers about fundamental concepts in Developmental Psychology performed better on test items on these constructs than students who participated in a Think–Pair–Share.

Content knowledge in Introductory Psychology classes can be increased when students engage in low-stakes, brief writing exercises either in class (Butler et al., 2001; Drabick et al., 2007; Gingerich et al., 2014) or as homework (Nevid et al., 2012). Butler et al. (2001) asked students to write for about 1 minute in response to a question about a psychology concept that had just been covered in a lecture. Students then engaged in a Think–Pair–Share (Lyman, 1981, 1987; see also Box 4.2) by discussing their answers with a peer, and then participated in a short class discussion in which the best answer (if there was one) was revealed. This was a quick-and-easy 5-minute exercise to do in a large class and required minimal grading (complete/incomplete). Importantly, when tested on multiple-choice examinations, students had higher scores for items that were similar in content to the questions they had written about (Butler et al., 2001). Drabick et al. (2007) also found that 5-minute writing papers in recitation sections helped to improve Introductory Psychology students' content knowledge, as evidenced by gains on multiple-choice test scores. Students who wrote for 5 minutes about a psychological concept benefitted more than students who spent the same amount of time thinking about the topic. Note that in both cases, students later engaged in a 10-minute discussion about the concept (Drabick et al., 2007). Both of these studies (Butler et al., 2001; Drabick et al., 2007) reported that the in-class writing exercises were associated with better student attendance, perhaps because the in-class assignments were associated with credit toward the final grade, and/or because students felt more actively engaged in the class.

Nevid et al. (2012) also reported benefits for Introductory Psychology students who completed brief "writing to learn" exercises as homework. Students who wrote one or two paragraphs on a concept from a chapter of the textbook (one assignment per chapter) performed better on multiple-choice items that were related to the writing assignments (16 items) than on items that they had not written about (195 items). The type of writing assignment—*write about what you learned* or *write about this in the context of your life*—had no significant effect on the test scores, nor did the number of words that students wrote (which averaged only 97 words) (Nevid et al., 2012).

In all three of these studies (Butler et al., 2001; Drabick et al., 2007; Nevid et al., 2012), students were awarded credit for completing the assignments. Each assignment carried a small number of points, but as there were many assignments over the course of the semester, they significantly affected students' final grades. In two of the studies, the low-stake assignments carried quite a bit of collective weight: 10% for Nevid et al. (2012) and 25% for Butler et al. (2001); such cumulative weighting of low-stakes writing is likely to be important, as students may lack motivation to complete assignments that are not associated with any credit (Janzow & Eison, 1990; but see also Gingerich et al., 2014). It is important to note that the instructors in these studies spent little time grading student writing for content: Nevid et al. (2012) simply asked students to write a short paragraph that was related to the topic and assessed their work on a pass/fail basis; similarly Drabick et al. (2007) used a grading scheme of complete/incomplete.

More recently, Gingerich et al. (2014) found that low-stakes writing helped non-psychology majors in an Introductory Psychology class (N = 924) to remember course content. They found that when students spent a few minutes of class time writing their own examples of psychological concepts, or their own explanations of concepts, they performed better on multiple-choice exams than when they copied instructor-generated information from a slide (see also Bertsch, Pesta, Wiscott, & McDaniel, 2007 for a meta-analytic review of evidence on the benefits of generating information for long-term retention). Furthermore, Gingerich et al. (2014) found that performance differences were present 6 weeks after the end of the semester when students took an online test, which underscores how a quick in-class writing-to-learn exercise helps students to "think on paper." Although the effect size was relatively small, with a mean difference of 4% on the aggregated test scores, cumulatively these assignments could have a substantial impact on students' final grades.

6.5.3 Microthemes

Microthemes are more formal than other types of writing-to-learn assignments (Bean, 2011). These are short (100–500-word) essays that are relatively easy to grade, but require students to think deeply to come up with their answers. Students must develop a clear and concise, evidence-based argument about an assigned topic or question. As Bean (2011) points out, these papers can reveal which concepts students are struggling to understand. Stewart et al. (2010) showed that requiring students to write 12-minute in-class graded microthemes in a Psychology of Women course helped them remember the information better, as evidenced by higher multiple-choice test scores. Additionally, the quality of student writing was higher for those in the writing group as compared to those in the control group, presumably because the students were required to write regularly (a total of 10 times during the semester). Waller (1994) used a similar approach in a History of Psychology class. After a short half-hour lecture in which he highlighted two radically different viewpoints on a psychology topic (e.g., free will versus determinism), he asked students to take a personal position and to write to a peer about that position. He went on to use their essays as a springboard for in-class debates, with students providing feedback to their peers (see also Section 4.3.2 on Debates). Students subsequently used their microthemes as the basis for a critical analysis essay in which they explored similar themes in greater depth. Students reported that these exercises deepened their level of understanding of the material, thus illustrating another way in which low-stakes assignments can be used to scaffold more complex, higher-stakes papers.

6.5.4 Reflection Papers

Reflection papers typically explore connections between course material and students' own experiences. Instructors may also ask students whether they found specific concepts to be surprising and why. Conrad (2013) found that first-year students in a Psychology of Memory class who wrote three one-page reflections about how memory-related concepts connected to their own lives showed greater content knowledge than students who were required to write a three-page final paper based on an article about memory. Students in the reflection paper group also outperformed the control group on a cumulative final exam. Conrad (2013) suggested that spreading out the writing assignments over the course of the semester gave students the benefits of distributed practice with key concepts, which is typically more effective than massed practice for deep learning (Seabrook, Brown, & Solity, 2005; see Section 7.1.2 for further discussion of the spacing effect on learning).

6.5.5 Creative Writing Assignments in Psychology

Many students in introductory-level classes struggle with remembering content related to biological psychology. Grose-Fifer (unpublished) instituted an extra-credit assignment in which Introductory Psychology students were required to write a poem, rap, or song that contained at least three "facts" that they had not known previously. The assignment was due on the day of the test and was successful in increasing student performance on test questions pertaining to biological psychology. Similarly, in an Abnormal Psychology class, writing a poem was more effective than writing an essay or short story in terms of deepening students' understanding of what it would be like to suffer from schizophrenia (Gorman, Gorman, & Young, 1986).

6.5.6 Journaling

One very popular low-stakes assignment across different disciplines is semi-structured journal writing, in which students are asked to think deeply about course materials, usually by relating them to their own lives or by reflecting on what they have learned in class (or at an internship or fieldwork site) (Bean, 2011). Kenyon (1989) used journaling to help math students develop their metacognitive skills; students were encouraged to use their entries to troubleshoot and clarify their thinking by considering questions like, *Why am I stuck?* Similarly, Keeler (1997) reported that graduate students in a Statistics class found that journaling increased their understanding of how they reasoned and approached problems. Asking students to write journal entries that relate psychological concepts to their everyday lives (Bolin, Khramtsova, & Saarnio, 2005; Hettich, 1990) is similar to the medium-stakes assignment (Marek et al., 2005) described in Section 6.5.1 on Small Paper Writing. In contrast to a small paper assignment, journaling is more frequent (i.e., it provides more distributed practice) and gives students a historical record of how their learning and thinking have developed in the course of a class (Bolin et al., 2005; Hettich, 1990). This may provide excellent material for them to use in writing metacognitive reflective essays on their personal and academic growth across a semester.

Benefits of journaling have been demonstrated in a variety of psychology courses. For example, Bolin et al. (2005) asked students in an Introductory Psychology class to keep a journal, in which they had to respond to at least 10 prompts over the course of the semester that asked them to connect a course concept to their own lives. Students reported that journaling helped to make the material more personally relevant and contributed to their personal growth over the semester. The authors suggested that this may have increased the students' motivation and enthusiasm for the course in general (Bolin et al., 2005). Hettich (1990) used a very similar journaling assignment across a variety of psychology classes (N = 440 students), with students generating weekly one-page entries over the course of a semester. Hettich provided more extensive feedback than Bolin et al. (2005), and he graded students on the variety and number of entries, depth of thinking, and quality of writing. In Hettich's study, the journal entries were worth 15–20% of the final grade (depending on the course). Therefore, in some ways, the journal could be considered a high- or medium-stakes assignment, even though each entry carried only a small percentage of the grade. Hettich's journaling assignments also had an additional facet: students re-read and classified their entries within the context of Bloom's Taxonomy, which helped them to practice their analytical skills. Overall, 95% of students reported that they preferred journaling over writing a term paper, and students generally agreed that it helped to improve their CT. As a caveat, however, Hettich (1990) suggested that the grading structure (which evaluated the depth of thinking and the quality of the writing) might be too laborious for classes with enrollments of more than 25 students. Note that the grading structure used by Hettich differed from that of Bolin et al. (2005), who graded journal entries for effort rather than accuracy. Importantly, in both studies, journaling appeared to be effective in increasing student learning and engagement, which suggests that benefits may accrue to students without burdening the instructor.

Connor-Greene (2000b) investigated how journaling (and the frequency of journaling) impacted learning in a Theories of Personality course. In each entry, students explained how the behavior of an individual (chosen from a variety of different sources, ranging from books to real life) illustrated a concept put forward by one of the prominent personality theorists. Students in sections with this assignment performed better on tests compared to those in the control section. One important note, especially for instructors teaching large classes: test scores did not differ between students who wrote frequent, weekly entries and those who were required to submit five entries over the course of the semester. Connor-Greene graded the assignments using a three-point scale, based on the accuracy of the description of the concept and the relevance of the example. Although this grading approach may be more labor-intensive than simple pass/fail or complete/incomplete, it seems feasible to implement in classes of various sizes.

6.6   Summary

1) Writing assignments in psychology classes improve students' content knowledge and critical thinking (CT).
2) Writing assignments need to be pitched at the appropriate developmental level, ideally using rubrics to convey expectations and guidelines.
3) High-stakes writing assignments need appropriate scaffolding, and should be graded incrementally (i.e., with feedback provided as students complete each step of the process).
4) Low-stakes assignments reduce the grading burden, but still yield multiple benefits for student learning.

7

Enhancing Learning Through Testing, Metacognitive Development, and Psychosocial Interventions

7.1   Why Use Tests in Student-Centered Teaching?

As discussed in Chapter 2, the diverse learners in your class will be best supported when you use a variety of assessments to determine how well they are learning and how effectively you are teaching them. Frequent low-stakes formative assessments of students' knowledge and skills will allow you to adjust your lesson plans to better meet your students' needs and improve their learning outcomes. Similarly, the extent to which students have attained the learning outcomes in your particular class will need to be evaluated using *summative assessments* at the end of a unit or course. Summative assessments may include relatively high-stakes midterm and final exams, papers, multimedia projects, and portfolios (see also Chapter 2). This multifaceted assessment approach acknowledges the breadth of learning goals you will have in your classes and represents a sharp departure from more traditional models in which course grades are heavily influenced by final examination scores. Somewhat ironically, as colleges depend less on high-stakes testing for summative assessment (O'Brien, 2010), there is a renewed emphasis on testing within K–12 education. Educational reforms such as the No Child Left Behind Act (2001), the Race to the Top program (2009), and the Common Core State Standards Initiative (2013) mandate standardized testing as a form of outcomes assessment in K–12 education. High-stakes assessments are also widely used in determining access to top-tier schools and colleges. High-stakes testing in K–12 schools has led to curriculum narrowing (teaching to the test) and greater use of teacher-centered methods (Au, 2007). Perhaps not surprisingly, there have been expressions of considerable frustration and anger among parents and educators over this (Au & Tempel, 2012; Hagopian, 2014; Hursh, 2008; Jones, Jones, & Hargrove, 2003; Nichols & Berliner, 2007), as well as increased test anxiety among school-aged children (Segool, Carlson, Goforth, von der Embse, & Barterian, 2013). In light of these trends, many have come to view testing as potentially harmful and lacking in validity—especially for individuals who perform poorly on tests due to anxiety (Chapell et al., 2005; Hembree, 1988; Seipp, 1991; von der Embse & Hasson, 2012; von der Embse & Witmer, 2014) and/or negative self-concepts about their abilities (Nguyen & Ryan, 2008; Steele & Aronson, 1995).

Counter to the view that testing should be minimized or eliminated altogether, cognitive psychology research has demonstrated pervasive benefits of frequent testing in

Teaching Psychology: An Evidence-Based Approach, First Edition. Jillian Grose-Fifer, Patricia J. Brooks, and Maureen O'Connor.
© 2019 John Wiley & Sons, Inc. Published 2019 by John Wiley & Sons, Inc.
Companion website: www.wiley.com/go/Grose-Fifer/teaching-psychology

enhancing long-term retention of information. When students are able to easily retrieve information about basic concepts in psychological science, it frees up more cognitive resources for higher-order thinking, such as complex problem solving (see, e.g., Section 5.4.4 on Team-Based Learning). In team-based learning, testing is used to ensure students have mastered basic concepts before they begin to solve more sophisticated problems with their team/classmates. Relatedly, upper-level classes can only deepen students' understanding of psychological science if the students are able to remember key concepts from their introductory and intermediate-level classes. In this chapter, we therefore argue that in addition to other forms of formative assessment (see Box 2.3), student-centered classes should include frequent low-stakes quizzes and higher-stakes tests. Quizzes and tests give students practice in retrieving information and help to identify gaps in their knowledge, skills, and abilities that future instruction should cover. For students to learn effectively, it is helpful if they understand how memory works, and consequently which study habits are best and why (Bjork, Dunlosky, & Kornell, 2013). Students also should be aware of the impact of cognitive biases that affect their learning and of the critical role of meta-cognition in overcoming such biases (Bjork et al., 2013; see Section 7.3). We conclude this chapter with a discussion of various psychosocial factors, including mindset, that influence student attitudes and engagement in the learning process, and we provide evidence for ways in which motivation to learn can be fostered through psychosocial interventions.

7.1.1 Benefits of Retrieval Practice

Although tests are often given for the purpose of evaluating students and assigning grades, what is more important, from the perspective of student-centered teaching, is that they also improve students' long-term retention of information. Testing creates opportunities for learners to practice retrieving information from long-term memory, which promotes reconsolidation of the memory trace, increasing the likelihood that information will be accessible in the future (Finn & Roediger, 2011). Frequent testing also provides invaluable preparation for high-stakes tests, such as the GRE, that a student may encounter in their academic journey. The phenomenon of memory enhancement for previously tested information is referred to in the literature as the "testing effect" (McDaniel, Anderson, Derbish, & Morrisette, 2007).

The basic finding that practice in retrieving information from long-term memory leads to superior performance on subsequent tests compared to simply re-studying the material has been demonstrated in hundreds of studies (for review, see Roediger, Putnam, & Smith, 2011). In a meta-analysis of 61 well-controlled studies (i.e., with control groups having equivalent exposure to the information tested), Rowland (2014) documented stronger testing effects when tests required recall rather than recognition of information. This suggests that expending additional effort to actually retrieve information from memory is especially advantageous for long-term retention, which is consistent with work documenting the "generation effect," whereby information actively generated by students is more memorable than information that is passively read (cf. Bertsch, Pesta, Wiscott, & McDaniel, 2007; Slamecka & Graf, 1978). Despite the advantage of recall over recognition tests, all forms of test produced better performance than re-study (Rowland, 2014; see also Bjork, Soderstrom, & Little, 2015 for a review of studies utilizing multiple-choice tests). The testing effect is stronger when learners are given feedback, demonstrating the power of learning from mistakes (Rowland, 2014). Also, explaining why answers are correct (or not) has been shown to be more beneficial for memory retention than simply indicating whether they were right or wrong (Butler, Godbole, & Marsh, 2013). Feedback is particularly critical for multiple-choice tests, as incorrect answers can be perpetuated on future tests because they seem familiar (Brown, Schilling, & Hockensmith, 1999; Butler, Karpicke, & Roediger, 2008; Roediger & Marsh, 2005).

A second benefit of testing is that it can identify gaps in knowledge. Such information is as critical for teachers as it is for students. It allows instructors to engage in more effective lesson planning via "just-in-time teaching" (Simkins & Maier, 2010). This approach uses formative assessments (like quiz and test scores and student feedback) to design classes and assignments that remedy misunderstandings and other potential obstacles to student progress and incrementally build on what students have already grasped. Thus, students use their prior knowledge to provide essential toeholds when they tackle new material (Hattie, 2015; Willingham, 2009). For students, gaining awareness of gaps in their understanding is a crucial form of *meta-cognition*: an awareness and understanding of their own thought processes and knowledge (Schraw & Moshman, 1995). As will be discussed in Section 7.3, having an accurate grasp of one's abilities and knowledge base is not only important for knowing which specific topics require more study (Roediger, Putnam, & Smith, 2011), but also allows students to adjust their encoding and retrieval strategies (Bahrick & Hall, 2005) and to overcome any illusions of knowing, such as unwarranted overconfidence, which are detrimental for learning.

Retrieval practice also results in *test-potentiated learning*: an improved ability to learn during a subsequent study session. Multiple retrieval practice sessions better potentiate learning than does a single session (Arnold & McDermott, 2013a, 2013b; Izawa, 1966). Receiving feedback after answering a question incorrectly or not knowing an answer appears to make a topic more accessible for future learning and reconsolidation. This may be because failures are often more memorable and provide stronger catalysts for learning than positive experiences (Baumeister, Bratslavsky, Finkenauer, & Vohs, 2001; Izawa, 1967; Parlow & Berlyne, 1971; Richland, Kornell, & Kao, 2009). Several other explanations have been offered as to why testing potentiates future learning. For instance, testing leads to better organization of information, which makes future study more effective (Arnold & McDermott, 2013a). During free-recall tests, participants have been shown to remember information in clusters of related items, and this categorization process improves with subsequent testing (Zaromb & Roediger, 2010). Testing may also increase a person's metacognitive accuracy about what they were unable to remember and so may improve or change their retrieval strategies (Roediger & Karpicke, 2006). Also, during initial testing, retrieval cues activate a network of related concepts (among which is the correct answer), and so when the answer is retrieved from memory, or provided from an external source (e.g., looking it up or receiving feedback), the associative links between the cue and the answer become strengthened, making it easier to recall the answer in the future (Kornell, Klein, & Rawson, 2015).

7.1.2   Importance of Distributing and Interleaving Practice

Long-term retention of information, as well as skill learning, is increased more by practice (study or testing) that is spaced or distributed over time than by massed practice:

studying for the same amount of time in one sitting (Cepeda, Vul, Rohrer, Wixted, & Pashler, 2008; Dempster, 1989; Dunlosky, Rawson, Marsh, Nathan, & Willingham, 2013; Schmidt & Bjork, 1992). There are several possible explanations for why distributed practice is particularly beneficial for memory (for reviews, see Benjamin & Tullis, 2010; Healy, Kole, & Bourne, 2014). For example, accurate metacognition about the efficacy of one's retrieval strategies takes time to develop. If materials are re-reviewed after only a brief period, then retrieval is relatively easy because there has been little time for memory decay to occur—but the information is not yet consolidated in long-term memory. Consequently, students may develop a false sense of confidence that they already know the materials because they seem familiar. It is also likely that more effort and/or different encoding strategies are required when longer intervals occur between practice sessions, increasing the likelihood of memory consolidation. Indeed, during spaced practice, the initially learned information has already been at least partially con-solidated, and so the second study session serves to strengthen the memory trace.

The optimal spacing between practice intervals depends on how long you want your students to remember the information. Cepeda et al. (2008) found that optimal spacing varied nonlinearly with retention interval and test type. Practice intervals of 1 day (14% of retention interval) were optimal for recognizing or recalling information a week later, but optimal intervals varied when participants had to remember information for longer periods: to retain information for 70 or 350 days, the optimal practice interval was 21 days for recall tests and 7 or 21 days, respectively, for recognition tests (Cepeda et al., 2008). Another advantage of spacing practice is that students are exposed to other types of information and/or the use of different skills in between practicing. Although interleaved practice, which involves mixing up different types of problem (e.g., in a Statistics course) or a variety of topics (e.g., in an introductory-level survey course) within a lesson or a study session, is more difficult than sticking with the same problem type or topic, it ultimately leads to better learning (Dunlosky et al., 2013). Thus, students should be aware that creating what are often described in the literature as "desirable difficulties" during studying (Bjork & Bjork, 2011) may feel less effective, but it in fact boosts learning (see Section 7.4). Retrieving information from disparate topics helps students to better organize their knowledge and increases their ability to discriminate among different concepts or problem types (Dunlosky et al., 2013). College students in remedial math classes who were exposed to cumulative interleaved practice quizzes outperformed other students who simply reviewed the materials or practiced only one rule at a time (Mayfield & Chase, 2002). Pedagogical practices that capitalize on using distributed, interleaved practice in classes are also likely to enhance long-term retention of information and skills. For example, mini-reviews, conducted in class or as homework assignments, help to re-engage students with the material and make it more likely they will remember the information for longer (Carpenter, Cepeda, Rohrer, Kang, & Pashler, 2012).

7.2   Using Quizzes in Your Classes

An increasing number of Scholarship of Teaching and Learning (SoTL) studies have investigated the applicability of the testing effect in classroom settings (for review, see Nguyen & McDaniel, 2015). Several have confirmed that distributed quizzing improves performance on summative tests in college students (Agarwal, D'Antonio, Roediger, McDermott, & McDaniel, 2014; Batsell, Perry, Hanley, & Hostetter, 2017; Connor-Greene, 2000a; Daniel & Broida, 2004; Glass, 2009; Hopkins, Lyle, Hieb, & Ralston, 2016; Jensen, McDaniel, Woodard, & Kummer, 2014; Lyle & Crawford, 2011; Maki & Maki, 2001; McDaniel, Wildman, & Anderson, 2012). Interspersing quiz questions between other instructional activities in your classes is one way to provide your students with distributed, interleaved retrieval practice, which is likely to promote learning and allows you to gauge their level of understanding. Frequent informal quizzing has also been shown to lessen students' test anxiety (Szpunar, Moulton, & Schacter, 2013). You may be concerned that this sounds like a lot of work, but as discussed in Chapter 3, if quiz questions are administered using student response systems (SRSs) like clickers, this increases class participation (as every student responds) without requiring additional grading. Furthermore, students may be more likely to attend class knowing that they will be better prepared for future tests.

Pre-class quizzes incentivize students to complete assignments such as reading before class (Marchant, 2002; Narloch, Garbin, & Turnage, 2006), improve final exam scores, and encourage students to engage in higher-order thinking during class (Narloch et al., 2006). However, in middle- and high-school students, quizzes given at the end of classes and review quizzes administered just before a test were found to increase test scores more than pre-class quizzes (McDaniel, Thomas, Agarwal, McDermott, & Roediger, 2013; McDermott, Agarwal, D'antonio, Roediger, & McDaniel, 2014; Roediger, Agarwal, McDaniel, & McDermott, 2011). One way to administer review quizzes is to use slideware (e.g., PowerPoint) to create games like Jeopardy (see Sections 3.1.2 and 5.5). To maximize the benefits, give students prior notification to allow them time to study and be prepared for such games (Gibson, 1991). Not only do students enjoy playing games, but Massey, Brown, and Johnston (2005) found that students had higher exam scores for questions that were related to a Jeopardy review game they had played than for unrelated questions.

Course management systems (CMSs) can be used to administer online quizzes, either before class to encourage reading compliance or after class. Post-class quizzes are particularly beneficial in promoting long-term retention of information (Agarwal et al., 2014; McDaniel et al., 2013; McDermott et al., 2014; Roediger, Agarwal, et al., 2011). In a CMS, students can take a test multiple times, increasing the likelihood that they will attain mastery of concepts by virtue of the successive relearning effect (Dunlosky & Rawson, 2015; Rawson, Dunlosky, & Sciartelli, 2013) and thereby improve their performance on summative tests. When using in-class and online quizzes, try to explain why answers are correct (or not), as this increases learning better than just indicating that they are correct (Butler et al., 2013). Finally, students can support one another's learning when they use a CMS (or other platform) to create study guide wikis in preparation for an upcoming test (see Section 8.3.3 on Using Wikis to Improve Writing, Critical Thinking, and Information Literacy).

7.2.1 Quiz and Test Design

Given the American Psychological Association (APA)'s five broad goals for the undergraduate major (American Psychological Association, 2013), it is likely that you will need to use a variety of assessments (not just tests) to adequately capture the depth and breadth of your students' learning gains, particularly in higher-order thinking and communication skills (see also Chapters 4 and 6). Consistent with backward course design, both summative and formative test items need to align with the learning objectives (LOs) of your course or unit (Wiggins & McTighe, 2005). You will also need to decide whether your tests should be open-book (OB), where students have access to study materials (e.g., textbook, notes, the Internet), or closed-book (CB), where they must rely solely on their memory. There are arguments and evidence supporting the use of either format (Durning et al., 2016), and your decision will be guided by your course LOs. LOs that focus on increasing students' basic knowledge about psychological science for use in their future academic, professional, and personal lives will probably be better served by CB tests. CB tests require more effort in retrieving information from memory than OB tests, and so lead to longer-term retention (Agarwal, Karpicke, Kang, Roediger, & McDermott, 2008; Agarwal & Roediger, 2011; Gharib, Phillips, & Mathew, 2012). Also, students seem to prepare differently for OB compared to CB tests. It has been suggested that students may study less for OB tests because they believe that they will have time to look up what they will need to know during the test itself (Gharib et al., 2012; Weber, McBee, & Krebs, 1983). Indeed, a review of 37 studies found that although some studies showed no difference in student preparation time between OB and CB tests, many others showed a relative reduction in studying (or decreased class attendance) before an OB test (Durning et al., 2016). However, critics of CB tests argue that they simply test students' ability to quickly recall basic facts that can be learned through rote memorization, and are measuring surface rather than deep transferrable learning (Wiggins, 2011; Williams & Wong, 2009). There may be some truth to this. Anderson and Walvoord (1998) found that 91% of college exam questions assessed lower-order thinking skills. However, the ability to quickly remember essential information (the first level of Bloom's taxonomy) should not be fully discounted as unimportant, as it may be the first step toward deeper understanding and learning (Hattie, 2015). When information is retrieved efficiently, it lessens cognitive load, allowing students to devote greater attentional resources to higher-order thinking (Hattie & Yates, 2014).

Proponents of OB tests suggest that such tests assess higher-order thinking on authentic tasks that are more representative of the kinds of problems students will face in the workplace (Wiggins, 2011; Williams & Wong, 2009). It is difficult to compare OB and CB test scores or study strategies without knowing the exact format of the test used and whether students were familiar with OB tests and how to prepare for them. For example, Eilertsen and Valdermo (2000) found that students needed appropriate training to prepare effectively for OB tests. Indeed, in a comprehensive review by Durning et al. (2016), although many studies showed reduced study time with OB tests, some showed that they increased the likelihood of students using study strategies that promote deep learning. It is possible that differences in student preparedness across studies may explain in part why some studies found higher scores for OB compared to CB tests, some found the opposite, and some found no difference even for test items purported to probe critical thinking (CT) (Durning et al., 2016). If you do decide to use an OB test, it should be designed to assess learning outcomes related to authentic problem solving, and you will need to adequately prepare students for how to solve these problems and take this kind of test. Also, it is helpful to know that although in general OB tests have been shown to reduce test anxiety (Broyles, Cyr, & Korsen, 2005; Gharib et al., 2012; Green, Ferrante, & Heppard, 2016; Myyry & Joutsenvirta, 2015;

Theophilides & Koutselini, 2000; Weber et al., 1983), they may actually increase anxiety among students who are unfamiliar with the format (Eilertsen & Valdermo, 2000) or who are worried about the use of technology, if the test is administered online (Myyry & Joutsenvirta, 2015).

Research shows that the testing effect is more pronounced for cued recall than for recognition (Rowland, 2014), so short-answer and fill-in-the-blank questions are likely to promote better retention of information on quizzes and tests than multiple-choice formats. That said, we acknowledge that multiple-choice formats are easier to administer and that their scoring is quicker and more objective, which is probably why they are so widely used in higher education. Regardless of the format, writing a good test with many questions is time-consuming. Before you start, it is advisable to create a table of concepts that you want to test at the various levels of Bloom's taxonomy (Anderson et al., 2001), to ensure questions span across different levels. Questions need to test whether LOs have been reached and so should focus on important concepts rather than peripheral minutia. There should be a clear rationale behind each one, and they should be unambiguous and culturally neutral.

When designing quizzes and tests, it is better to use questions that elicit higher-order thinking than ones that simply require rote memorization. When summative test items probed basic knowledge (the lowest tier of Bloom's taxonomy), testing effects were found if quiz items were very similar or were related to the same concept (Daniel & Broida, 2004; Lyle & Crawford, 2011; McDaniel et al., 2012). However, lab-based studies using educationally relevant materials found that some quiz items (those that were related only at the broader topic level) did not enhance later recall of related but previously untested information (Wooldridge, Bugg, McDaniel, & Liu, 2014), and in some circumstances they actually caused retrieval-induced forgetting—a failure to remember previously known but non-tested information (Carroll, Campbell-Ratcliffe, Murnane, & Perfect, 2007; Little, Bjork, Bjork, & Angello, 2012). In general, giving feedback and increasing the time interval between the quiz and the test has been shown to eliminate this negative testing effect (Little & Bjork, 2015; Little et al., 2012). However, quizzing may have no benefits if quiz and test items are only related at a broad domain level rather than at a more specific conceptual level. For example, using a short-answer quiz question such as, "What term is given to describe a pre-operational child's tendency to see the world only from their own perspective?" (Answer: egocentricity), is unlikely to improve a student's ability to answer a subsequent test question that asks, "What is the term used to describe the Piagetian developmental stage during which children primarily explore the world using their senses? (Answer: sensorimotor stage). Both questions are about Piaget's stages of development, and so they are broadly, but not specifically, related. Nguyen and McDaniel (2015) caution that the use of ancillary products provided by textbook publishers may exacerbate this problem, as the quiz items available to students may not align with those in test banks provided to instructors for the creation of tests. One way to mitigate this—so that the unstudied, but conceptually related information also benefits from the testing effect—is to ensure that students integrate thinking about other related concepts when they are being quizzed. Little and colleagues found that this could be achieved by using multiple-choice test questions in which the incorrect answers were plausible (i.e., they were related to, but did not answer the question), and so required greater processing to differentiate them from the correct answer (Little & Bjork, 2015; Little et al., 2012). For example, to prompt students to think in a more integrative way about Piaget's developmental stages, instead of the short-answer quiz question just described, you could instead use a multiple-choice question that asks, "Which of Piaget's developmental stages describes children as egocentric? A) sensori-motor stage, B) formal operational stage, C) preoperational stage, D) concrete operational stage?" All of the answers are somewhat plausible, because they correctly describe Piaget's four developmental stages, so one needs to know what is happening during each stage to answer the question. Also, requiring students to apply knowledge rather than remember basic facts makes quizzes more difficult, but improves transfer of knowledge, and thus has a greater impact on summative test scores (Bailey, Jensen, Nelson, Wiberg, & Bell, 2017; Jensen et al., 2014; Nguyen & McDaniel, 2015).

Unfortunately, various analyses of test-bank questions and tests across different disciplines have shown that multiple-choice tests often probe only the lowest (knowledge) level of Bloom's taxonomy and tend to be poorly written (DiBattista & Kurzawa, 2011; Downing, 2005; Jozefowicz et al., 2002; Tarrant, Knierim, Hayes, & Ware, 2006). If using multiple-choice quizzes, it is important to use empirically based guidelines for well-written questions that also tap higher-order thinking (Haladyna, Downing, & Rodriguez, 2002), because poorly constructed questions have been shown to impact student test scores and course pass rates (Downing, 2005; Tarrant & Ware, 2008). Some best principles for good test construction are simple to apply; for example, although many multiple-choice tests are constructed with four answers, a meta-analysis has shown that three is optimal (Rodriguez, 2005). Common problems to avoid include using stems (first part of the question) that fail to actually pose a question or are not meaningful in themselves (e.g., "Which of the following is true?"), or that include irrelevant material. These types of question are unlikely to align with LOs and/or may impose unnecessary high amounts of cognitive load (Brame, 2013). Also, students have difficulty understanding negative stems (e.g., "Which of the following is not representative of classical conditioning?"). Because students can answer "all of the above" or "none of the above" response options with partial knowledge, such options should be avoided (DiBattista & Kurzawa, 2011; Downing, 2005; Hansen & Dexter, 1997; Masters et al., 2001; Tarrant et al., 2006). Further evidence-based best practices for multiple-choice test construction are described by Haladyna and colleagues (Haladyna, 2012; Haladyna et al., 2002), and examples can also be found at Vanderbilt University's Center for Teaching (Brame, 2013).

7.2.2 Helping Students to Use Quiz and Test Feedback to Enhance Learning

Testing with feedback has been shown to improve long-term retention considerably more than testing without it, but there is some disagreement about the optimal timing for its provision. Recent meta-analytical data from both laboratory and classroom studies show that delayed feedback led to better long-term recall than did immediate feedback (Rowland, 2014). There are various explanations for this: first, it takes time for the memory trace of incorrect answers to fade following an initial test (Kulhavy, 1977); second, delayed feedback constitutes a form of distributed practice where exposure to information occurs at varied intervals (Cepeda et al., 2008; Dempster, 1989; Schmidt & Bjork, 1992); and third, in laboratory studies, delayed feedback on a first test is typically given closer in time to a second test than is immediate feedback, and it is the proximity of the feedback to the second test that enhances memory on that test

(Metcalfe, Kornell, & Finn, 2009). Importantly, an earlier meta-analysis highlighted that although delayed feedback led to better recall than immediate feedback in laboratory studies, classroom studies tended to show the opposite phenomenon (Kulik & Kulik, 1988). Butler, Karpicke, and Roediger (2007) suggested that these differences might be attributable to differences in depth of processing of the feedback across study types. Laboratory studies require participants to pay attention to the feedback they receive, regardless of whether it is delayed or immediate. However, when students take a test and then get it back a few days later, they may pay more attention to their grade than to the feedback, and classroom studies do not manipulate depth-of-feedback processing. On the other hand, in classroom situations where immediate feedback is typically provided, such as when answering clicker questions, taking an Immediate Feedback Assessment Technique (IF-AT) test in team-based learning (see Section 5.4.4), or doing an online quiz, students are likely to pay attention to their correct answers as well as any corrective feedback. Administering frequent clicker quizzes in class has the added benefit of reducing test anxiety among college students (Szpunar et al., 2013). The idea that attention to feedback is important for subsequent memory is supported by research showing that participants pay particular attention to feedback for low-confidence correct answers (Kulhavy, 1977) and high-confidence errors (Butterfield & Metcalfe, 2006), so both are more likely to be remembered in future than other items that attract less attention (Butler et al., 2008; Butterfield & Metcalfe, 2006). Therefore, it seems likely that if students are given incentives to review both correct answers and corrective feedback, they will benefit more when tests are corrected and returned to them a few days later. Cumulative tests could be used to encourage this behavior.

7.2.3 Cumulative Tests

Cumulative tests are not popular with students (Lawrence, 2013), but they enhance memory retention more than noncumulative versions, particularly among introductory-level (Khanna, Brack, & Finken, 2013) and low-performing students (Beagley & Capaldi, 2016; Lawrence, 2013). Students who take cumulative tests benefit from the use of distributed, interleaved practice, and such tests increase the likelihood that they will remember materials even after the course is over. Across various core psychology courses, students who took cumulative tests performed better than those who took noncumulative versions, and this advantage persisted on tests taken 2 months (but only among low-performing students; Lawrence, 2013) and 18 months (Khanna et al., 2013) after the course had ended. Increasing your students' awareness about these studies may help to decrease their resistance toward taking cumulative tests.

7.3 Students' Metacognitive Biases

People tend to overestimate both their social and their intellectual abilities (Kruger & Dunning, 1999; Zell & Krizan, 2014). This tendency is greatest among unskilled individuals—a phenomenon known as the *Dunning–Kruger effect* (Dunning, 2011). Dunning and Kruger proposed that unskilled people suffer the "double curse" of lacking knowledge and lacking metacognitive awareness of this deficit. Experts, in contrast, are often acutely aware of what they do not yet grasp, and can strategically seek out sources of information to remedy their gaps in knowledge and skills (Dunning, 2011; Kruger & Dunning, 1999). Relatedly, students with less than average test scores have been shown to be less accurate in predicting their test performance than those with higher scores (Dunning, Heath, & Suls, 2004; Hacker, Bol, Horgan, & Rakow, 2000; Miller & Geraci, 2011a, 2011b; Shaughnessy, 1979; Sinkavich, 1995). However, Miller and Geraci (2011b) found that low-performing students were not particularly confident in their judgments, suggesting that their metacognitive awareness was not as low as Dunning and Kruger would suggest. Miller and Geraci (2011a) found that showing students data about test performance accuracy and discussing metacognition with them helped low-performing students to predict their test scores more accurately, although it did not improve the scores.

Students' metacognitive inaccuracies in judging what they know (also known as "metamemory") have also been linked to suboptimal study habits (Bjork et al., 2013; Koriat & Bjork, 2005, 2006). Laboratory studies have shown that participants tended to show a *stability bias* after a short study period, in that they were skeptical that further study would improve their recall and were confident that their current state of knowledge would remain largely unchanged (Kornell & Bjork, 2009). This kind of overconfidence in a real-life setting is likely to lead to students curtailing their studying prematurely. In a study designed to better understand the mechanisms behind inaccurate metamemory, Koriat and Bjork (2005) found that problems with metamemory are exacerbated by a mismatch between study and test conditions. Although participants in this study felt confident that they had learned an association between two words when they saw them together, they often failed to recall the target word when the cue word was presented by itself on a test. In a similar experiment, Nelson and Dunlosky (1991) found that participants were most accurate in judging whether they had learned the association between two words if the cue word was presented by itself and the judgment was made after a delay, rather than immediately. In other words, metamemory was more accurate in situations that were more like the testing condition. Koriat and Bjork (2005) extrapolated these data to explain students' overconfidence during studying. Students often prepare for a test by re-reading their notes or the textbook. Re-reading is an ineffective study strategy that creates false confidence and an illusion of knowing (i.e., everything seems so clear and familiar, it must already be known; Glenberg, Wilkinson, & Epstein, 1982). The illusion of knowing makes it difficult for students to shift their perspective to the future test. That is, they often fail to realize that it will be much more difficult to remember information when they are given only part of it (Koriat & Bjork, 2005). Another problem that commonly arises is that information that seems particularly familiar (usually from having heard it multiple times) is often mistakenly remembered as true (Hasher, Goldstein, & Toppino, 1977), because it is readily activated in memory. Such "illusory truths" include pseudoscientific myths (e.g., "People use only 10% of their brains"; "Vaccines cause autism"; "People differ in their learning styles"). Fazio, Brashier, Payne, and Marsh (2015) found that showing false statements multiple times in an experiment (e.g., "The largest ocean in the world is the Atlantic") increased the probability that participants would identify them as true answers, even if they produced the correct answer when asked the question directly (e.g., "What is the largest ocean in the world?"). This helps explain in part, why pseudoscientific myths are so resistant to change (Benassi & Goldstein, 2006).

7.3.1 Instructors' Metacognitive Biases

Instructors also have metacognitive biases that affect their ability to function as effective teachers. Like our students, we probably overestimate our abilities and are prone to the Dunning–Kruger effect. We are likely to think that we are better teachers than we actually are (Cross, 1977). Consistent with the *superiority illusion* or *better-than-average effect* (Alicke, Klotz, Breitenbecher, Yurak, & Vredenburg, 1995), more than 66% of professors at a college in Nebraska rated themselves in the top quartile of teachers, and 90% thought they were above average (Cross, 1977). Price (2006) suggests that this belief may be exacerbated if we fail to collaborate and discuss our teaching with our colleagues, or if we do not acknowledge criticism from our students. Such perceptions of being above-average teachers may stem in part from the "curse of knowledge" (Birch, 2005; Camerer, Loewenstein, & Weber, 1989), which makes it difficult to imagine what our classes might look like from the student's perspective (Wieman, 2007). In particular, as experts, it may be hard for us to deconstruct some of our well-engrained habits, such as knowing how to read journal articles and write papers, or how to explain psychological scientific principles in a way that students find relatable. It is also easy for us to forget that students may experience cognitive overload when bombarded with new information, as processing new information takes considerable effort and attention can only be maintained for relatively short periods of time (Risko, Anderson, Sarwal, Engelhardt, & Kingstone, 2012; Sweller, 1994; see also Chapter 3 on "death by PowerPoint" and the perils of lecturing to your students).

7.4 Building Study Habits

Very few students are trained in how to study for tests (Kornell & Bjork, 2007), and they often have misperceptions about the most effective way to study (Bjork et al., 2013). A comprehensive review of laboratory and classroom studies by Dunlosky et al. (2013) showed that the two most effective study techniques were retrieval practice (quizzing) and distributed practice. However, most students prepare for tests by re-reading their textbook or notes (Gurung, 2005; Hartlep & Forsyth, 2000; Hartwig & Dunlosky, 2012; Karpicke, Butler, & Roediger, 2009; Kornell & Bjork, 2007; McCabe, 2011; Susser & McCabe, 2013), a practice that has been shown to have little effect on test performance (Dunlosky et al., 2013). Although some students are unaware of the merits of testing as a study technique (Karpicke et al., 2009), the frequency with which students use quizzing to study has been shown to correlate with final exam scores (Gurung, Weidert, & Jeske, 2012) and GPA (Gurung, 2005; Hartwig & Dunlosky, 2012). Students also tend to cram their study into the day or night before the exam rather than distributing their practice over time (Hartwig & Dunlosky, 2012; McCabe, 2011; Taraban, Maki, & Rynearson, 1999; Wissman, Rawson, & Pyc, 2012); this may be due in part to poor time management, especially in low-performing students (Hartwig & Dunlosky, 2012). However, it may also be due to the misperception that cramming is an effective study technique (McCabe, 2011). Even in studies where students performed better after distributed compared to massed practice, they continued to think that massed practice was more effective (Arnott & Dust, 2012; Kornell, 2009).

Bjork et al. (2013) have suggested that distributed or interleaved practice may feel less effective to students because they make more mistakes compared to when they practice for longer blocks of time and information is still fresh in their memory. Indeed, many students think that learning can be achieved quickly (Schommer-Aikins & Easter, 2006) and so fail to realize that some difficulty is actually desirable for greater learning. However, even when students indicated that under ideal circumstances they would space their study before an exam, most reported that they would be unlikely to do so in reality (Susser & McCabe, 2013). Students reported that they would be more likely to use distributed practice before a test if they were interested in the material or thought it was particularly relevant to them, if there was a lot of material to learn or the material was difficult, and if they were going to take a short-answer or essay-format test. Perhaps not surprisingly, students reported that they would be unlikely to use distributed practice on weeks when they had many other academic commitments. This is congruent with other studies showing that relatively few students actually plan out their studying in advance of an exam (Hartwig & Dunlosky, 2012; Kornell & Bjork, 2007), although high-performing students are more likely to do so (Hartwig & Dunlosky, 2012).

Students with poor time-management skills are more likely to have low grades (Britton & Tesser, 1991; Gortner Lahmers & Zulauf, 2000; Trueman & Hartley, 1996), particularly if they have difficulties with short-term planning or feel that they are not in control of their time (Buehler, Griffin, & Ross, 1994). Time-management issues are particularly prevalent among first-generation college students (Collier & Morgan, 2008; Reid & Moore, 2008; Terenzini, Springer, Yaeger, Pascarella, & Nora, 1996), who are also more likely to have considerable demands on their time outside of school (see Chapter 1 for a discussion about the challenges today's students face). One way to help students to develop better time-management strategies is to have them set goals using SMART (Specific, Measurable, Achievable, Realistic, and Timely) action plans (see Section 5.2.5) or other similar techniques, such as those described by Oettingen, Kappes, Guttenberg, and Gollwitzer (2015). These authors reported that using a reflection/planning intervention improved time-management skills. Students had to first vividly imagine accomplishing a future academic goal and then think about the reality of their current situation and the obstacles that might prevent it from occurring, before finally deciding how best to overcome the obstacles (Oettingen et al., 2015).

In sum, the studies reviewed in this section underscore the need to help students develop more effective study habits and more accurate metacognition so that they can more accurately assess what they know, as well as the efficacy of their habits. Cognitive psychology and educational research has underscored the superiority of deep, elaborative processing over shallow encoding for enhancing learning (Craik & Lockhart, 1972; Dunlosky et al., 2013), yet students may be unaware of effective ways of encoding new information. Relatedly, studying is more effective when we focus on one thing at a time and block out other distractions (Fernandes & Moscovitch, 2000). Multitasking, such as emailing, listening to music, watching TV, or dealing with interruptions while studying is common among students, but has been associated with lower exam scores and GPA (Allen, Lerner, & Hinrichsen, 1972; Hartwig & Dunlosky, 2012; Michaels & Miethe, 1989). So, how can we persuade students to use more effective study habits? One method is to give explicit instruction about the science that shows which study techniques are most effective and why (for reviews of optimal study habits, see Dunlosky & Rawson, 2015; Dunlosky et al., 2013; Gurung, 2005; Gurung & McCann, 2012; Roediger

& Pyc, 2012). The direct-instruction approach has been shown to be effective in a variety of different disciplines in terms of improving both study habits and, in some cases, test scores (Cardinale & Johnson, 2017; Cathey, Visio, Whisenhunt, Hudson, & Shoptaugh, 2016; Cook, Kennedy, & McGuire, 2013; Zhao, Wardeska, McGuire, & Cook, 2014). Notably, most of these studies provided this instruction *after* the first test in a course, with the rationale that students would be more receptive to changing their studying strategies if they performed worse than they had anticipated (Cathey et al., 2016; Cook et al., 2013; Zhao et al., 2014). However, Chew (2010) suggests that learning about superior study habits is a good way to kick off any course. In courses where you will be covering the topic of memory anyway (e.g., Introductory Psychology, Cognitive Psychology), you can simply begin with this topic of learning and memory, making sure to include effective study habits. Chew has posted five short "How to Get the Most Out of Studying" videos to YouTube, which could be good starting points for class discussion and other activities aimed at heightening students' awareness about which study skills are most effective. Cardinale and Johnson (2017) used these videos as part of a metacognitive intervention, in which students learned about memory, study habits, and the malleability of the brain. Students kept journals about what they had learned and how it impacted their study habits, as well as their beliefs about the ability for intelligence to improve over time (see also Section 7.5). Another potentially useful resource is Elizabeth Bjork's Lasting Learning website (http://www.lastinglearning.com/author/elizabeth-bjork/).

In-class demonstrations, in which students generate, analyze, and discuss data illustrating effective study practices, may also help persuade students of the utility of effortful study to enhance learning. For example, Balch (2006) was able to convince students of the benefits of distributed practice by using an in-class demonstration of the spacing effect. He presented lists of words, in which some were repeated either consecutively or after the presentation of several others. After a short interval of time, students were asked to recall the words, and Balch was able to demonstrate that those that were presented nonconsecutively (distributed practice) were recalled more frequently than those presented consecutively (massed practice). Students' test scores improved after the demonstration, and more students reported using distributed practice while studying. Similarly, Chew (2010) used a variant of Craik and Tulving's (1975) classic experiment as a class demonstration to show that deep processing results in better memory than shallow processing. This demonstration employed an Intention to Learn $(2) \times$ Depth of Processing (2) design, with the class divided into four groups, each with a different set of written instructions. A list of words was read one at a time, with half of the students indicating whether a particular letter was present (shallow processing) and the other half indicating whether the word was pleasant (deep processing). This was followed by a recall test that was expected by half the students (Intention to Learn group) but a surprise to the others (No Intention to Learn group). After aggregating the data, students could see that deep processing was superior to shallow processing, regardless of whether they were trying to remember words for an upcoming recall test. Students could then reflect on how they might use the principle of deep processing to study more effectively.

Students often need help in learning how to engage in deep processing when studying; this can be encouraged by teaching specific ways to encode information at a deeper level. For example, teaching students the CRIME mnemonic (Chunking, Rehearsing,

Imagery, Mnemonics, Elaboration) provides strategies they might use in various combinations when trying to encode different types of information (Hattie & Yates, 2014). Berry and Chew (2008) found that having students generate questions about a topic increased scores on subsequent tests, especially for low-performing students—presumably because generating questions increased encoding of the information. This may be likened to the technique of elaborative interrogation described by Dunlosky et al. (2013), which they found to have moderate utility in promoting long-term memory. With elaborative interrogation, students ask and answer questions about a topic, such as why something is true or makes sense. Elaborating freely (i.e., generating one's own questions) has been shown to be more effective than using cued elaboration in promoting memory (for a review, see Dunlosky et al., 2013). Dunlosky and colleagues also found evidence that the related technique of self-explanation, where students think out loud in the learning process (e.g., by explaining the rationale for steps in a math problem), was a moderately effective study technique.

Similarly, teaching students to organize materials graphically using concept maps, which highlight inter-relationships between concepts, has been associated with improved exam scores (Berry & Chew, 2008; see also Nesbit & Adesope, 2006) for meta-analytical data indicating that concept maps can improve learning. Students benefit from using multiple effective study strategies: Blunt and Karpicke (2014) found that redrawing concept maps from memory produced better long-term memory retention than simply creating the initial maps, demonstrating the importance of the testing effect.

Flash cards, which have a question on one side and the corresponding answer on the other, make use of cued recall, which as already summarized, is a powerful learning tool. Cards are typically re-reviewed many times, and so students are likely to experience test-potentiated or successive relearning, such that it becomes increasingly easy to answer each question. A lab-based experiment using materials from psychology textbook passages found that quizzing students (using cued recall) until they were able to answer each question correctly boosted long-term retention of the information (Rawson & Dunlosky, 2011). The data showed that the optimal study technique was to answer each question correctly three times and then to do three subsequent but well-spaced quizzes, where each question had to be answered correctly once. This study schedule might be particularly difficult for students, but the good news is that the authors were also able to show improved performance on course exams when Introductory Psychology students used electronic flash cards in only two quiz sessions (Rawson et al., 2013). In the first session, students had to answer each question correctly three times, but in the second only one correct answer was required (Rawson et al., 2013). In addition to using your CMS or slideware to create electronic flash cards, apps like Quizlet, Study Blue, and Flash Card Machine can also be used and might be helpful to your students. It is possible that students will need to be trained on how to use flash cards properly. For example, it is tempting to turn over the card and read the answer without actually retrieving it from memory first; in this case, the use of flash cards may create an illusion of knowing, as the answer will likely seem familiar. A lack of consistency in the way students use flash cards may explain why some studies have found no correlation between flash card use and academic performance (Hartwig & Dunlosky, 2012), while others have demonstrated improved learning outcomes (Golding, Wasarhaley, & Fletcher, 2012; Senzaki, Hackathorn, Appleby, & Gurung, 2017). Senzaki et al. (2017)

suggested that their students' flash card usage may have been particularly successful because they trained them to create flash cards with three separated answers, each corresponding to each of the first three levels of Bloom's Taxonomy (Remember–Understand–Apply). The first answer was copied verbatim from the textbook; the second was rewritten in the students' own words; and the third was based on a real-life example. Students were also advised to space their practice.

In their review of 10 frequently used study habits, Dunlosky et al. (2013) reported that the least effective were highlighting, summarizing, re-reading, and using imagery and key word mnemonics. It should be noted, however, that of the many known mnemonic devices, Dunlosky and colleagues assessed the efficacy of only the key word one, which relies heavily on visual imagery. Mnemonics do not increase students' understanding of material, but they can help to organize information so that it is easier to retrieve in the future (Brown, Roediger, & McDaniel, 2014). For example, students can benefit by taking the first letter of every word in a list to create an acronym (e.g., OCEAN or CANOE for the Big Five personality traits; Stalder, 2005) or an acrostic (e.g., when learning the names of the cranial nerves; Bloom & Lamkin, 2006). Relatedly, memory champions often use the method of loci (sometimes referred to as a "memory palace") to remember long sequences of items (Maguire, Valentine, Wilding, & Kapur, 2003), and the frequency of mnemonic usage has been shown to be predictive of exam grades among Introductory Psychology students (Gurung, 2005; Stalder, 2005) and accounting students (Laing, 2010). It is possible that summarizing and highlighting may have greater utility if students are adequately trained in the use of these techniques. In support of this supposition, Smith, Holliday, & Austin (2010) found that the quality of summaries written as study aids predicted college students' scores on recall tests (Smith et al., 2010). Similarly, Leutner, Leopold, & den Elzen-Rump (2007) found that students who were trained to highlight critical items remembered more of the tested material than those who were not (Leutner et al., 2007). In real-world situations, many students highlight indiscriminately, but in a lab study, Yue and colleagues found students to be relatively selective and effective when asked to highlight key elements in a text. However, compared to students who were anti-highlighting, those who endorsed highlighting as a helpful review practice highlighted more words but remembered less of the material (Yue, Storm, Kornell, & Bjork, 2015). This adds credence to the suggestion that the low utility of highlighting found by Dunlosky et al. (2013) may be attributable to poor techniques.

7.5   Mindsets around Testing and Learning

As already detailed, regular testing has multiple benefits for students. In addition, throughout this book we provide other examples of best practices for optimizing student learning. However, adopting these practices is not always enough to ensure student success. Indeed, in a synthesis of over 1000 meta-analyses, 50% of the variance in learning among K–12 and college students was attributed to student variables, while teacher variables contributed 20–25% (Hattie, 2015). There is a large volume of research showing that students' perceptions about themselves as learners greatly impact motivation, which in turn influences grades and retention in college (e.g., see Fong et al., 2017; Harackiewicz & Priniski, 2018; Honicke & Broadbent, 2016; Lazowski & Hulleman, 2016;

Richardson, Abraham, & Bond, 2012; Robbins et al., 2004; Valentine, DuBois, & Cooper, 2004). The influences of psychosocial factors are often amplified among students from under-represented groups and first-generation college students, who may feel that they do not belong in college (Aronson, Fried, & Good, 2002). Awareness of or belief in negative stereotypes about oneself has been shown to have detrimental effects on test performance (Gonzales, Blanton, & Williams, 2002; Steele, 1997; Steele & Aronson, 1995). Similarly, doubts about belongingness or academic abilities can set up negative self-fulfilling prophesies. Believing that failure is inevitable often elicits detrimental "helpless" strategies (Dweck, 1975), such as avoiding studying for a test or procrastinating over an assignment.

There is considerable research showing that social-cognitive factors impact how students deal with academic challenges in college (for review, see Harackiewicz & Priniski, 2018; Lazowski & Hulleman, 2016). Dweck and colleagues have extensively investigated how people's beliefs about the malleability of intelligence affect learning (for a review, see Yeager & Dweck, 2012), while others have focused on attribution theory (Perry & Hamm, 2017; Weiner, 1985) or self-concepts, such as self-efficacy (Richardson et al., 2012; Robbins et al., 2004), to explain how different students perceive and react to various academic challenges. These lines of research conclusively demonstrate that students' misinformed beliefs often lead to maladaptive behaviors.

Dweck and colleagues have shown that children and adults typically endorse one of two general beliefs about the malleability of intelligence (and other abilities), and that these predict how students approach schoolwork and handle challenges. Those with a "growth" or "incremental" mindset believe that intelligence can be fostered, while those with a "fixed" or "entity" mindset believe that it is static (for review, see Yeager & Dweck, 2012). Students with a growth mindset are more likely to endorse mastery goals; that is, they value the process of learning over getting a good grade. Such students believe that their performance is dependent on their effort and are less likely to be derailed by low grades or feedback suggesting that improvement is warranted. Consequently, students with growth mindsets are more resilient to academic setbacks and challenging transitions. In contrast, students with fixed mindsets are more likely to focus on grades and outperforming their peers (performance goals), and may avoid challenging tasks in order not to "look stupid" (for review, see Burnette, O'Boyle, VanEpps, Pollack, & Finkel, 2013; Yeager & Dweck, 2012). A meta-analysis by Burnette et al. (2013) showed that students with growth mindsets are less likely to experience anxiety and negative affect than students with fixed mindsets, which may facilitate learning. Moreover, students who feel that their academic success is beyond their control typically attribute poor performance to low ability (which they assume is immutable), rather than low effort (Perry, 2003; Perry & Hamm, 2017). Fortunately, as we summarize in the next section, it is possible to change students' mindsets and attributions about learning and academic success using some relatively simple interventions.

7.5.1 Overcoming Student Anxiety and Increasing Motivation for Learning

Test anxiety is a pervasive problem in both schools and colleges; students who perceive test taking and other forms of evaluation as stressful often underperform (Chapell et al., 2005; Hembree, 1988; Seipp, 1991). Test anxiety is more prevalent among female undergraduates than males, and is negatively correlated with cumulative GPA (Chapell et al., 2005;

Hembree, 1988; Seipp, 1991). Meta-analytical data show that students with high test anxiety have poorer study skills and less self-control than students with low test anxiety (Hembree, 1988). Test anxiety is typically described as consisting of both emotional (physiological arousal) and cognitive (worrying, which interferes with studying/retrieval) components. Helping students to reappraise physiological arousal before or during a test as normal and potentially helpful to performance was found to increase scores on a practice GRE exam (Jamieson, Mendes, Blackstock, & Schmader, 2010); therefore, teaching your students about this approach may help to alleviate some aspects of test anxiety. However, meta-analyses have also shown that the cognitive component of test anxiety affects academic performance more than the emotional part (Hembree, 1988; Seipp, 1991). Relatedly, therapists often use expressive writing to help reduce intrusive thoughts associated with anxiety-related rumination. Park, Ramirez, & Beilock (2014) successfully adopted this technique to reduce math anxiety among undergraduates in a lab study. Students with high math anxiety who wrote for 7 minutes on how they felt about taking an upcoming math test had higher test scores than math-anxious students who did not receive the intervention (Park et al., 2014).

Naveh-Benjamin, McKeachie, & Lin (1987) suggest that two types of students may experience test anxiety: for both, anxiety inhibits retrieval during test taking, but one group has good study habits while the other does not (Naveh-Benjamin et al., 1987). Indeed, a meta-analysis by Ergene (2003) found that improving study habits had a moderate effect on reducing test anxiety (although it should also be noted that interventions such as systemic desensitization had much larger effects). Not surprisingly, test-anxious students with good study skills do much better on low- than on high-stakes assignments, whereas those with poor study skills perform poorly on both (Naveh-Benjamin et al., 1987). High-stakes, time-pressured testing is particularly anxiety-provoking. Even highly skilled people can "choke" under pressure, especially on tasks that rely heavily on working memory (Beilock, 2008; Beilock & Carr, 2005). Very high-stakes tests, such as final exams that carry a high percentage of the course grade and which are administered with little time for reflective thinking, are likely to increase anxiety and reduce performance (Onwuegbuzie & Seaman, 1995). To the extent possible, such very high-stakes tests should be avoided, as they may assess students' ability to cope with high levels of stress rather than what they have learned.

Some academic disciplines, such as mathematics, are often perceived by students to be especially challenging, and therefore anxiety-provoking, which may decrease motivation and performance. Undergraduates studying psychology and other social sciences frequently suffer from statistics anxiety (Onwuegbuzie & Wilson, 2003; Zeidner, 1991). Active learning, instructor immediacy, and the solving of real-world problems in a relaxed atmosphere where humor is often used all help to reduce statistics anxiety (for review, see Chew & Dillon, 2014). Students with high levels of statistics anxiety often lack math experience and fail to see the value of statistics (Baloğlu, 2003). Therefore, another approach is to use a "utility-value" intervention, in which students write briefly about the utility of a subject or task in their own lives or in fulfilling their life goals (Harackiewicz & Priniski, 2018). Like many other psychosocial interventions, this approach relies on the "*saying is believing*" principle; that is, if students discuss or write about a topic, they are more likely to internalize those beliefs. Utility-value interventions have been shown to be effective in improving student interest, exam scores, and persistence in statistics (Acee & Weinstein, 2010), Introductory Psychology

(Hulleman, Godes, Hendricks, & Harackiewicz, 2010; Hulleman, Kosovich, Barron, & Daniel, 2017), and the sciences (Canning & Harackiewicz, 2015; Harackiewicz, Canning, Tibbetts, Priniski, & Hyde, 2016). Furthermore, these interventions have been shown to be particularly effective for low-performing students (Harackiewicz et al., 2016; Hulleman et al., 2010, 2017) and among first-generation students who are members of under-represented groups (Harackiewicz et al., 2016).

7.5.2 Dealing with Failure and Building Resilience

Students might fail a test or do poorly on an assignment for any number of reasons (e.g., extenuating circumstances that affected them on the day of the test, allocating insufficient time to studying, failure to attend class, maladaptive study habits, difficulties understanding the material). To help a student deal with failure, we first have to find out why they *think* they failed. The way that they bounce back will depend heavily on whether they believe they will be able to remedy the problem. In some cases, a student's personal life, disability, or health might be the primary reason for their difficulties, in which case referral to the appropriate student support service(s) is the best route (see also Chapter 9 on the subject of Behavioral Intervention Teams). In other cases, it is advisable to help the student identify and fix the problem. Students often feel emotionally vulnerable after doing poorly on a test or assignment, so it is important that they feel supported so they can move on to discussing and remedying the problem. Reassurance that they can improve their standing in a course can be facilitated by strategies such as adopting a course policy where the lowest exam score is dropped. Alternatively, you might consider allowing students to submit corrected answers to a test (detailing where they found the information) and awarding partial credit.

As already discussed, students who attribute poor performance to low effort rather than poor ability are more likely to be resilient. Thus, helping students to develop a growth mindset that allows them to reframe their attributions about academic performance is likely to have an enduring impact. Instructors should examine their own biases about their students' potential to learn, as these may affect how they give feedback and could influence students' perceptions about their ability to improve in a class. Rattan, Good, & Dweck (2012) found that graduate teaching assistants (TAs) who endorsed fixed mindsets about math ability were more likely than those with growth mindsets to console a hypothetical student with a low test score by suggesting that "math isn't for everyone" and that they probably have "other strengths." Students receiving this kind of feedback from a hypothetical teacher felt less supported and had lower motivation and expectations about their future performance than students who received feedback suggesting that they needed to change their study strategies (Rattan et al., 2012).

Fortunately, considerable evidence (originating from research in middle and high schools) demonstrates that low-cost interventions can increase motivation and build resilience by changing the way students think about themselves and their abilities. Such interventions have been shown to improve academic performance and student persistence, especially among at-risk students, such as those from under-represented groups and first-generation college students (for reviews, see Bjork & Bjork, 2011; Harackiewicz & Priniski, 2018; Lazowski & Hulleman, 2016). In many cases, they focus on helping students adopt adaptive mindsets about how they learn. Reading and writing about the malleability of intelligence and the plasticity of the brain increases the likelihood that students will adopt a growth mindset (Dweck & Leggett, 1988; Yeager & Dweck, 2012).

Aronson et al. (2002) found that three 1-hour interventions (at 10-day intervals) were effective in promoting growth mindsets in college students and helped to reduce stereotype threat in African American students. Participants were led to believe they were participating in a mentoring program. They were given a letter, purportedly from a struggling middle-school student, and were asked to respond in an encouraging manner. Students in the intervention group were told that intelligence changes with experience, and were shown a video depicting how the brain makes new neural connections during learning. The students were asked to use this information in their mentoring letter, along with examples from their own lives showing that intelligence can increase over time. They wrote a similar letter in the second session, while in the third, they wrote and recorded a short speech about the malleability of intelligence. Students in the control group performed similar tasks, but they learned about multiple intelligences and were told to encourage the student to whom they were writing to find their particular area of strength. Compared to the controls, the intervention group had higher end-of-year GPAs and were more likely to endorse an incremental mindset; these effects were greater for African American than for White students (Aronson et al., 2002). Paunesku, Yeager, Romero, and Walton (unpublished manuscript cited in Yeager & Dweck, 2012) used a slightly modified form of this intervention with community-college students in a developmental (i.e., pre-college-level) math class. Students read and then wrote about an article on the malleability of intelligence and the brain, which emphasized that the brain could be changed by practicing and learning new math methods, even in people with prior difficulties in math. Prior focus groups had revealed that students in these classes often spent a lot of time on math problems but were not using the correct approach. Therefore, the article stressed that learning was dependent on effort, as well as on using the right techniques and seeking help when needed. Yeager et al. (2016) found that similar online summer training for high-school graduates entering college increased persistence among students from under-represented groups.

Wilson and Linville (1982, 1985) used attributional reframing to help build resilience in first-year students who were concerned about their grades. During the intervention, students looked at statistical data demonstrating that grades at their university typically improved over time, and watched interviews with more senior students describing how their grades had improved and why. Students who received the intervention were more likely to persist in college, and a year later had higher GPAs compared to controls. Similarly, long-term GPAs were found to improve when first-year students were first exposed to information (via handouts or videos) emphasizing that poor grades are often attributable to low effort and/or poor strategies, and then reflected on this information, either in writing or through discussion (for review, see Haynes, Perry, Stupnisky, & Daniels, 2009).

Other interventions help foster resiliency among students who are transitioning to a new environment and feel out of place, by helping them to realize that their feelings are common and likely to improve over time (Kreniske, 2017; Walton & Cohen, 2011). In typical social belongingness interventions, students first hear more senior students describe their academic journeys, and then use this information to write about the temporary nature of their feelings about not belonging. These types of intervention have been shown to improve GPAs and persistence among female engineering students

(Walton, Logel, Peach, Spencer, & Zanna, 2015) and first-generation undergraduates who are members of minoritized racial groups (Yeager et al., 2016). Importantly, focus groups help to refine the precise contents of these interventions to ensure that student concerns are covered. Stephens, Townsend, Hamedani, Destin, & Manzo (2015) used a similar approach with first-year, first-generation students, who listened to panels of other students describing the obstacles that they had faced and overcome in college. Students who heard panelists describe their experiences in the context of whether they were first-generation students earned better grades, were more likely to persist, and exhibited fewer signs of stress than students who listened to panelists who did not disclose information about their parents' level of education (Stephens, Hamedani, & Destin, 2014; Stephens et al., 2015).

Finally, personal-value interventions, which are grounded in self-affirmation theory (Steele, 1988), are designed to promote resilience by boosting self-worth, particularly among individuals who feel threatened in certain settings or situations (Cohen, Garcia, Apfel, & Master, 2006). Writing about (or listing) some things that they personally value, once or twice during the semester, has been shown to be successful in boosting course grades among women in physics classes (Miyake et al., 2010) and first-generation students in biology classes (Harackiewicz et al., 2014), and to increase overall GPA in Latinx students (Brady et al., 2016), first-generation students (Tibbetts et al., 2016), and students who feel that they do not belong in college (Layous et al., 2017).

7.6   Summary

1) Testing provides opportunities for students to practice retrieving information from memory, which improves long-term retention and increases awareness of knowledge and skills. Without such awareness, students may fall prey to illusions of knowing or false confidence that stems from underdeveloped metacognition.
2) Testing helps instructors to evaluate their students' needs and to support their learning.
3) Today's students often enter college without effective study strategies and require training in retrieval practice, reflection, and elaboration.
4) Using psychosocial interventions to foster a growth mindset and other adaptive beliefs may help assuage students' negative self-beliefs about their academic ability and their place in college, and can help to foster better learning.

8

Gearing Up to Teach Online

8.1   The Continuum of Online Instruction

For a multitude of reasons, online instruction (also known as distance education) is becoming increasingly common in higher education. In 2015, nearly six million (30%) undergraduates reported taking at least one online course, with about two-thirds of them enrolled at public institutions (Digital Learning Compass Partnership, 2017). Given current trends in higher education (Allen & Seaman, 2016; Digital Learning Compass Partnership, 2017), it is quite likely that as an instructor you will teach an online course at some point in your career. One of the major advantages of online instruction is that students and faculty do not have to be in the same physical location for teaching and learning to occur; this flexibility should make higher education more accessible to a wider range of people. Indeed, online courses may be especially appealing to adult learners with children and other significant work commitments (Conway, Wladis, & Hachey, 2011; Pontes, Hasit, Pontes, Lewis, & Siefring, 2010). However, a class divide still exists with regard to access to technology. Large numbers of people only have access to the Internet via their phones, while others have no Internet access at all (Anderson, 2017; The Pew Research Center, 2015). There is growing enthusiasm for mobile learning (i.e., being able to use mobile devices to support learning) among students (Dahlstrom, Brooks, & Bichsel, 2014), but research to support its efficacy is still in its infancy (Han & Shin, 2016).

Web-based learning occurs along a continuum, including *fully online* courses, where all instruction occurs in an online environment; *blended* or *hybrid courses*, in which some of the face-to-face (F2F) class time is moved online; and *Web-enhanced classes* (including *flipped classes*), where there is no reduction in F2F time, but learning is enhanced through the use of online tools. Online teaching is inherently student-centered (Yang & Cornelious, 2005), and much of the material in this book can be adapted for online courses. However, we strongly recommend that new instructors start at the lowest end of the continuum and get familiar with online teaching tools by Web-enhancing their F2F classes. The next step might then be to "flip" some F2F classes by having students review Web-based materials before coming to class and then spend class time working on more in-depth problems. Using this incremental approach allows instructors more time to hone key skills, such as creating videos and podcasts and developing student-centered learning environments using a course management system (CMS;

Teaching Psychology: An Evidence-Based Approach, First Edition. Jillian Grose-Fifer, Patricia J. Brooks, and Maureen O'Connor.
© 2019 John Wiley & Sons, Inc. Published 2019 by John Wiley & Sons, Inc.
Companion website: www.wiley.com/go/Grose-Fifer/teaching-psychology

alternatively called a learning management system or LMS), before moving large portions of a course (or all of it) online. We have laid out this chapter with this general framework in mind, starting with a discussion of how CMSs can be used to enhance learning in F2F classes, moving to the flipped classroom, and ending with advice for teaching hybrid and fully online classes.

8.2 How Course Management Systems can Make Face-to-Face Classes More Student-Centered

The vast majority of higher-education institutions subscribe to a Web-based CMS, such as Blackboard or Canvas, or use open-source systems, such as Moodle, Sakai, and Google Classroom (Dahlstrom et al., 2014). These systems frequently serve as platforms for online instruction, but they also have considerable utility in F2F classes. In 2013–14, 60% of faculty from hundreds of institutions reported that their CMS was critical to their teaching (Dahlstrom et al., 2014). In general, students also view CMSs positively (Arkorful & Abaidoo, 2015; Dahlstrom et al., 2014; Papastergiou, 2006); several studies have shown that they feel that use of a CMS enhances both their learning and their motivation (for review, see Papastergiou, 2006). Although students widely use CMSs in their classes, a large percentage feel that they could be more skilled in *how* to use them, which underscores the need for training both at the start of class and as you introduce new assignments that require students to interact with the CMS in novel ways (Dahlstrom et al., 2014). Despite the fact that most CMSs have free downloadable apps, many students avoid accessing them using their mobile devices because they feel that they lack sufficient training to do so (Chen, Seilhamer, Bennett, & Bauer, 2015). Furthermore, mobile CMS use may be challenging if a device has poor screen resolution, small screen size, slow download speeds, and limited memory (Elias, 2011), especially when trying to view complex images or videos.

Of course, you too will need to learn how to use your CMS (if you don't already know) in order to support your students. Most institutions offer training sessions for instructors, as well as guides and helplines for instructors and students alike. There are also a wealth of YouTube videos that provide step-by-step guides for various CMS functions; some are aimed at instructors, while others are designed to help students. Be assured that you do not have to be an expert in using your CMS when you first start Web-enhancing your F2F classes. We suggest that you get familiar with some basic functions, such as uploading readings and posting grades, and move to using more complex features once you become more comfortable.

At a basic level, CMSs act as course repositories that provide students with access to digital course materials at their convenience and allow instructors to easily recycle or adapt these materials across multiple sections and/or semesters. CMSs enable instructors to post, receive, and grade a variety of multimedia assignments, to conduct assessments using surveys and quizzes, and to send announcements and emails to students. In addition, they provide platforms for students to collaborate with one another and forums that permit interactions among peers and with instructional staff. CMSs are also useful for organizing courses, performing administrative tasks, and archiving student work and performance. They can facilitate the use of best teaching practices (Chickering & Gamson, 1987), as they enable instructors to post feedback and grades quickly and confidentially. Archiving grades online in a CMS grade-book helps instructors to keep track of their students' progress, and the online grade-book can also be effortlessly exported into spreadsheet programs such as Excel. For any given assignment, it is quick and easy to sort the corresponding column of grades in order to identify particular groups of students and email them about their progress in the class. For instance, you might congratulate students on a job well done, including if they have made a marked improvement, or you might note that they seem to be struggling and/or missing assignments and offer to meet them to help. Archiving grades online may also encourage students to monitor their class performance more closely. Geddes (2009) found that first-year business school students who checked their CMS grade-book regularly had better final course grades than those who did not, suggesting this practice may have encouraged better self-regulation. Relationships between students and faculty can also be cultivated by using the CMS to facilitate communication. For example, office hours can be conducted online (Lage, Platt, & Treglia, 2000); this may be particularly useful for students who spend relatively little time on campus because of other commitments in their lives. Clearly, CMSs can be used to make classes more student-centered in this way.

Regular use of a CMS can also increase students' technological skills, by allowing them to engage in innovative multimedia assignments that foster other core skills for psychology majors, such as effective collaboration, communication, and critical thinking (CT) (Papastergiou, 2006). In a Web-enhanced F2F classroom, CMSs are commonly used to post multimedia learning materials (e.g., readings, videos, links to websites), which may be accompanied by short-answer writing prompts aimed at encouraging CT and deeper learning (see Yuksel, 2017, for an example using TED talks). Reviewing online learning materials and writing brief reflections as homework prior to class may enhance students' understanding of concepts or spark a class discussion (Dahlstrom et al., 2014). Note, however, that online homework may need to count as a substantial portion of the course grade in order to motivate students to access and use the learning materials posted to the CMS (Machado, 2011; Powers, Brooks, Galazyn, & Donnelly, 2016).

One advantage of posting course materials to a CMS is that students can access them whenever they want (i.e., activity can be asynchronous), allowing them to work at their own pace (or within the time constraints imposed by the instructor). This flexibility has been associated with greater student satisfaction and decreased levels of stress (for review, see Arkorful & Abaidoo, 2015); it is also consistent with the principles of Universal Design for Learning (UDL) (Burgstahler, 2015; Connell et al., 1997; see also Section 2.5 on Universal Design). Posting digitized texts within the CMS allows students to look up the pronunciation and meaning of words as they read, providing invaluable support for those who may struggle with reading comprehension, such as English-language learners (Padrón, Waxman, & Rivera, 2002). Importantly, all digital materials should be in accessible formats so that students with disabilities are able to use them; this is relatively easy to do with digitized formats (see the Web Content Accessibility Guidelines [WCAG] 2.0). CMSs can also be used to administer quizzes to check for reading compliance and to assess understanding of course materials. When students take tests or quizzes in the CMS, they can receive immediate, automated feedback, which is one of the basic tenets of good pedagogical practice, as it is likely to enhance learning (Chickering & Gamson, 1987; Rowland, 2014; see also Chapter 7, which describes the benefits of testing in enhancing long-term retention of information). Students' mastery of a subject can be fostered further if they have the opportunity to take (or retake) tests until they reach a certain performance threshold (Boggs, Shore, & Shore, 2004). Alternatively, an instructor can use the information from pre-class quiz scores to focus their upcoming classes on the issues with which students seem to be struggling (Woods, Baker, & Hopper, 2004)—this technique is known as "just-in-time teaching" (Simkins & Maier, 2010).

8.3   Using Online Tools to Facilitate Writing, Collaboration, and Critical Thinking

One very common use of CMSs is to increase students' engagement with one another. In 2013–14, about 41% of thousands of faculty surveyed at over 150 institutions used CMSs to promote interactions among students in their classes, primarily through asynchronous posts to discussion forums (Dahlstrom et al., 2014). In online classes, discussion boards provide a critical forum for student interaction, but they have also been used to strengthen students' engagement with learning materials in F2F classes. For example, requiring students to post to a discussion board about pre-class readings increased the likelihood that they would complete those readings in F2F classes (Lineweaver, 2010). Curtis and Lawson (2001) suggested that discussions that take place online via a CMS may be of a higher quality than those in F2F classes. They posited that this was because the act of writing encourages thinking (see also Chapter 6); moreover, students tend to take more time to reflect on their contributions when they are written. Indeed, Guiller, Durndell, and Ross (2008) found that students assigned to online discussion groups engaged in more CT in their discussions than those assigned to F2F groups. Online discussions typically include a wider range of perspectives than those that occur in the classroom because even students who are reluctant to speak in class are likely to have the confidence to post online (DenBeste, 2003; King, 2002). Reading one another's posts helps students to learn from their classmates (DenBeste, 2003; King, 2002) and strengthens the depth of any subsequent in-class discussions (Dietz-Uhler & Bishop-Clark, 2001; King, 2002; Vess, 2005). However, online discussions may be viewed unfavorably by students if they feel this is "busy work" that does not enhance their learning (Howland & Moore, 2002). Therefore, it is important for assignments to link specifically and transparently to the learning objectives (LOs) of the course or unit (see Chapter 2).

   It is important to provide students with clear guidelines on how to create high-quality posts and work collaboratively with others online (for an example of an online discussion rubric, see Rovai, 2007). Establishing class rules for appropriate behavior in online environments (often referred to as "netiquette") is just as important as when these interactions occur in person (see also Chapter 5). Students are more likely to post to an online discussion if it counts toward their final grade (Palmer, Holt, & Bray, 2008; Rovai, 2003), and using a structured grading system that rewards higher-order thinking gives rise to better-quality posts (Bryant, 2005). The content and quality of student discussion has been shown to be largely determined by the initial guiding question (Dennen & Wieland, 2007; Guldberg & Pilkington, 2007; Hara, Bonk, & Angeli, 2000). More probing questions are likely to elicit deeper thinking, and although questions that focus solely on students' personal experiences are likely to result in lengthy posts, they elicit little interaction between students (Guldberg & Pilkington, 2007). Students benefit from modeling and instruction on how to construct good posts. For example, when students were given scaffolded instruction related to argumentation, they produced more evidence in their posts than when no instruction was given (Oh & Jonassen, 2007). Wang and Chen (2008) provide a list of "rules" that promote engagement in interactive, higher-order thinking in online discussions. These include always providing evidence to back up an argument, keeping posts brief, referring to and building on other students' posts by quoting or paraphrasing, being constructive and encouraging, playing the devil's advocate (but making it clear that this is the intent), and using questions to encourage deeper thinking. Others have suggested that assigning specific roles leads to more fruitful discussions; these roles might include a starter who provides the initial direction of the discussion, an elaborator who encourages students to think more deeply, a synthesizer who pulls information from posts to direct the discussion, and a wrapper who summarizes the discussion (for more roles, see Wise, Saghafian, & Padmanabhan, 2012). As we have discussed in Chapter 4, the way in which an instructor facilitates the discussion is a key determinant of whether students engage in CT and interact constructively with one another (Dennen & Wieland, 2007). When comparing discussion board posts from two different classes, Dennen and Wieland (2007) found that the quality of students' posts and interactions was significantly higher for the class in which the instructor posed initial guiding questions and then asked probing questions to help students expand on their posts than for the class where the instructor rarely provided an initial question and restricted themselves mostly to making evaluative comments or responding with mini-lectures.

Although many studies have examined students' perceptions of online discussion, few have investigated whether online discussion affects learning outcomes. According to social learning theory, one would expect that writing in a discussion board, where students can construct knowledge with their peers, should have even greater benefits than writing-to-learn exercises carried out alone (see also Section 6.5). Several studies have shown that high-achieving students post more to discussion boards than their lower-performing peers (Cheng, Paré, Collimore, & Joordens, 2011; Davies & Graff, 2005; Krentler & Willis-Flurry, 2005; Romero, López, Luna, & Ventura, 2013; Stacey & Rice, 2002; Webb, Jones, Barker, & van Schaik, 2004). However, correlation is not causation, and this finding may simply reflect that more proficient students are more likely to post (and complete other assignments). A handful of other studies suggest that engagement in online discussion does in fact boost learning. For example, both students' weighted average marks (this is similar to GPA but takes into account credits per class) and the number of discussion posts they made contributed about equal variance to their final grade, but these two predictors were not correlated with each other (Palmer et al., 2008). This suggests that, regardless of ability, engaging in online discussion increased learning. Greater post-test compared to pre-test gains in a massive open online course (MOOC) have been found to be correlated with the number of discussion posts relating to main points in the materials or asking clarifying questions (Wang, Yang, Wen, Koedinger, & Rosé, 2015). Furthermore, in a study of over 1000 students, Cheng and colleagues introduced online discussions partway through a course, and found that improvements in exam scores subsequent to the online discussions (i.e., changes in final exam relative to midterm exam scores) correlated with students' use of the discussion board (Cheng et al., 2011). In contrast, Picciano (2002) found that the quality of discussion board posts was correlated with students' writing assignment grades but not their exam scores. Finally, medical students who participated in an online discussion forum outperformed those who did not participate, on a final physiology exam (Taradi, Taradi, Radić, & Pokrajac, 2005).

Online discussion boards have also been used to build a sense of community among commuter students who spend relatively little time on campus (DenBeste, 2003; King, 2002). Perhaps not surprisingly, the most significant predictor of a student's sense of community in online classes has been shown to be the degree of skill with which the instructor facilitates the discussion (Wang & Chen, 2008). Setting up the structure of an online discussion is also important, as discussion may be ineffective if students have to wade through large numbers of posts to construct any meaning. Information overload can be prevented by dividing students into small groups so that the number of posts that they have to read and interact with becomes more manageable (Bliss & Lawrence, 2009; Bryant, 2005; Kim, 2013). Breaking larger classes into small groups (10–20 students) for online discussions increases participation (Bliss & Lawrence, 2009; Kim, 2013), elicits more higher-order thinking (Bliss & Lawrence, 2009), and encourages elaborative interaction with other students (Kim, 2013). Most CMS platforms have a group feature that can help you to organize groups for a variety of collaborative assignments, such as writing and commenting on blogs and wikis and performing peer review on assignments.

Brief online writing formats (such as blogs and wikis) have gained in popularity as a means of engaging students in collaborative writing. As described in more detail in the next section, blogs are typically diary-like entries (e.g., https://blogs.scientificamerican.com or https://teachpsych.org/E-xcellence-in-Teaching-Blog). They can be personal or informational, and they are typically written by one person, although others can add comments. In contrast, wikis are usually informational, and are collaboratively constructed (e.g., Wikipedia or http://psychjobsearch.wikidot.com/, which provides a summary of academic jobs in psychology). Even though today's younger students tend to be digital natives, having grown up in a world with nearly continuous access to the Internet via personal computers and mobile devices (Prensky, 2001), it is likely that many have never created a blog (Jones, Johnson-Yale, Millermaier, & Perez, 2009; Jones, Johnson-Yale, Millermaier, & Seoane Perez, 2009b) or edited a wiki (Schweitzer, 2008). It is therefore important to lay the appropriate groundwork and to support them as they learn these new skills. Students are unlikely to post to a wiki or a blog, or cooperate with other students, if it does not impact their grade or if they do not understand why doing so is important. To strengthen student buy-in for novel multimedia assignments, it is important to make the links between the course LOs and the assignments very transparent. For the majority of students, learning to use these technologies will increase their comfort with new technology in general. Wiki and blog assignments also have the potential to improve students' group work, CT, communication, and information literacy skills (see also Chapter 3 on the benefits of Wikipedia editing assignments).

To develop the skills needed for wiki or blog assignments, we suggest running workshops in a computer lab or a classroom where students have access to computers (e.g., their own, or borrowed laptops or other devices if your college has a loaner program). Such workshops give students the opportunity to work with others and ask questions as they gain familiarity with the technology. For a first assignment, you might invite them to write an "all about me" entry in a blog or wiki (depending on which one you are using), where they can have fun with self-expression while giving the class (and your-self) a chance to get to know them better (O'Bannon & Britt, 2011). Inviting your class to contribute to an interactive blog where students discuss college issues and experi-ences has been shown to be an effective way of building supportive relationships (Kreniske & Todorova, 2017), bearing in mind that it is important for the class to estab-lish ground rules about effective ways to respectfully interact with one another.

We also suggest that when you first try wiki or blog assignments, you host them within your CMS. One advantage of doing this is that student contributions are logged directly into a grade-book, which simplifies grading; another is that because only mem-bers of the class see these products, it provides a safe space to explore topics without having to worry about potential hostile comments from the general public. The down-side of using such a platform is that wikis and blogs are usually posted publicly; this may be a key motivator for students to produce their best work (Ducate & Lomicka, 2008; Lowe & Williams, 2004), and hosting them privately means that the authenticity of the assignment is lessened. Another important issue is that the students will no longer be able to access the wiki or blog once the class is over. For these reasons, in Sections 8.3.2 and 8.3.3 we provide suggestions for more public Web hosts for both types of assign-ments, many of which allow the site administrator (i.e., the instructor) to limit who can view or post to them. Despite the caveats regarding hosting the assignments in a CMS, students can still benefit from reviewing one another's work (Cho & Cho, 2011). Peer review by multiple students typically results in more substantive content changes than when an instructor gives feedback (Cho, Schunn, & Wilson, 2006; Cho & Cho, 2011; see also Chapter 6).

Blogs and wikis typically have links to external webpages, articles, and news items, and often include embedded images and videos, which make them visually appealing as well as potentially useful sources of information (Oravec, 2002). Students should be aware of the issues around the fair use of images, music, and other elements that they may want to use in their multimedia projects in general (for a comprehensive review, see McGrail & McGrail, 2010). The librarians at your college are likely to have expertise in copyright use (Colleran, 2013), and you may be able to enlist their help in designing a workshop to introduce your students to Creative Commons (creativecommons.org) and to regulations pertaining to the fair use of copyright-protected material. Materials within Creative Commons have three general levels of use: some can be used freely in student online work as long as the source is attributed, some require a license if the material is to be modified, and some require a license if it is to be used for commercial purposes. Davis and McGrail (2017) provide a comprehensive guide to teaching stu-dents about fair use in the context of blogging, and the Media Education Lab at Temple University offers a number of relevant lesson plans (see https://mediaeducationlab. com/sites/default/files/TEACHING%2520ABOUT%2520COPYRIGHT%2520AND %2520FAIR%2520USE%2520final_1.pdf).

8.3.1 What Kinds of Blog Assignment Work?

Blogs (derived from "Web log") are webpages on which posts are displayed in reverse chronological order (Downes, 2004; Nardi, Schiano, & Gumbrecht, 2004). They are often used as outlets for people to express their personal ideas and opinions to the pub-lic (Downes, 2004; Nardi et al., 2004). Receiving comments from interested readers is thought to motivate the blogger to post on a regular basis (Sim & Hew, 2010). For class assignments, a blog is typically written by an individual student (although instructors have used both group and class blogs), with other students commenting on the entries (Oravec, 2002).

The brevity and informality of a blog post provides excellent opportunities for students to engage in low-stakes writing on a regular basis. To our knowledge, few publications discuss the use of blog assignments in psychology courses, but assignments in many other disciplines are eminently adaptable (for review, see Sim & Hew, 2010). Blogs often reflect and expand on what students have learned in a particular class, reading, or public event (Davi, Frydenberg, & Gulati, 2007; Ellison & Wu, 2008; Wang & Hsu, 2008). They typically engage larger numbers of students than in-class discussions (Downes, 2004), and so provide a wider range of perspectives (Wang & Hsu, 2008). Yang and Chang (2012) suggest that dialoging with peers within a blog helps to create zones of proximal development (Vygotsky, 1978), which foster learning. In support of this, students have reported that reading other people's blogs and having to synthesize the information and express their own opinion on what they had read enhanced their learning more than writing their own blog or a traditional paper because it exposed them to a greater variety of ideas (Ellison & Wu, 2008). Davi et al. (2007) found that most students in their study thought that pre-class blogging about a reading stimulated class discussion. For each class period, an assigned subset of students used the class blog to post questions or reflections related to the readings, and their classmates commented on them. When blogging about course-related topics, students have multiple opportunities to practice and develop their skills in using credible evidence to justify their thoughts and opinions (Oravec, 2002).

Student blogs (and discussion board posts) about what was covered in class can also provide instructors with insightful formative assessments of their students' understanding of the course material (Paulus et al., 2009). In just-in-time teaching (Simkins & Maier, 2010), this information is used to guide the focus of the upcoming class. Blog posts can also provide valuable information about students' epistemological development. For example, when nutrition students posted their reactions to a class on nutritional supplements, Paulus et al. (2009) found that some were skeptical about what they had been told. These kinds of activities may be helpful for instructors who want to gauge their students' misconceptions about psychology (especially pseudoscience) so that they can focus their efforts accordingly. Blogs can also be used to identify individual students who are struggling and provide them with greater support (Robertson, 2011).

Blogging has also been used to create a sense of community among students on internships (Chu, Chan, & Tiwari, 2012; Deng & Yuen, 2012), in large classes (Farmer, Yue, & Brooks, 2008; Halic, Lee, Paulus, & Spence, 2010), on online courses (Kerawalla, Minocha, Kirkup, & Conole, 2009), and in first-year cohorts (Kreniske & Todorova, 2017; Robertson, 2011). Students in a large nutrition class who contributed to group blogs about how current events applied to what they were learning in class reported that blogging gave them a greater sense of community and enhanced their learning (Halic et al., 2010). On a slightly different note, student-teachers found it helpful to blog about their feelings regarding their teaching experiences and to exchange advice with their classmates (Deng & Yuen, 2012). Similarly, blogging about their internships and reading other students' blogs increased discipline-specific knowledge in information management and nursing students (Chu et al., 2012). Nursing students also found that blogging helped to improve their problem-solving abilities (Chu et al., 2012). Students involved in psychology-related service-learning courses and internships may experience similar benefits from blogging about them.

Robertson (2011) used a blogging assignment in a class of first-year students to encourage self-expression and metacognition related to academic progress. Students reflected on how their thinking, planning, and emotions had developed over the course of the semester. Commenting on one another's blogs helped students to feel socially supported within the class, and increased the likelihood that students would try out new ideas suggested by their peers. This type of assignment is especially well suited for introductory courses, first-year seminars, and learning communities, where there is a heavy emphasis on personal development and acculturation to college life (see also Kreniske, 2017).

Several studies have shown that students perceive blogging in a favorable light and think that it increases learning (e.g., Bennett, Bishop, Dalgarno, Waycott, & Kennedy, 2012; Chu et al., 2012; Churchill, 2009; Davi et al., 2007; Ducate & Lomicka, 2008; Ellison & Wu, 2008; Halic et al., 2010). In addition, studies of English-language learners have shown that blogging helps improve the use of vocabulary and complex sentence structures (Arslan & Şahin-Kızıl, 2010; Miyazoe & Anderson, 2010; Sun, 2010). Davi et al. (2007) found that the quality of writing and CT in student blogs on course readings in three (non-language-centered) courses improved over a semester; they attributed this to the sustained reading and writing practice that is associated with frequent blogging (see other examples of writing-to-learn assignments in Chapter 6).

8.3.2 How to Set Up a Successful Blog Assignment

Once you have ensured that your blog assignment aligns with your LOs, you need to decide where to host the blog and to become familiar with the nuances of its utilities. Blogs can be hosted within a CMS, but if the primary goal of creating them is to "give away psychology" to the public or to connect students in more than one section of a course, then it is better to use an external site, like Tumblr, Wordpress, or Blogger. Like CMS-hosted blogs, all three of these sites allow bloggers to set up individual or group blogs, and although blog access can be limited to the class (or subgroups), it can also be widened for a more public audience. As we mentioned at the outset of this section, it is very important to scaffold blogging assignments. Several studies have shown that when students are unsure about how to use blogging technology or are unclear about what to post, they may not post at all (for review, see Kerawalla et al., 2009). Other studies suggest that students may need guidance on how to give feedback to their peers (Ellison & Wu, 2008). Reading other blogs (including the instructor's own, if available) can provide students with valuable models before they begin their own (Ducate & Lomicka, 2008). You might consider assigning students to follow a blog on *Scientific American* (https://blogs.scientificamerican.com), for example, which currently has psychology-relevant topics ranging from *Beautiful Minds* ("Insights into intelligence, creativity, and the mind") to *Dog Spies* ("Explore the science behind the dog in your bed"). For a Developmental Psychology course, you might assign *The Baby Scientist* at *Psychology Today* (https://www.psychologytoday.com/us/blog/the-baby-scientist).

Freeman and Brett (2012) cautioned that students need to feel a sense of ownership to be motivated to blog on a regular basis and that this can be stifled if there are too many rules. In support of this, Chu et al. (2012) found that nursing students who were not awarded credit or given mandates about how frequently to post blogged as regularly (about once a week) about their internships as information management students who were required to post every 1–2 days for 30% of their final grade. The rules you decide to implement for your students' blogs should depend on the characteristics of your students and the other demands on their time. In the majority of studies, blog activities *do* count toward the final grade and students are required to make a certain number of posts and comments over the course of the semester, often on a weekly basis (for review, see Sim & Hew, 2010). Across a variety of institutions, Lunsford (2011) found that when the blog activity was worth 20–30% of the final grade, it was reasonable to expect students to write four to six blog posts over the course of a semester, in addition to extending the discussion by commenting on other students' posts.

Finally, if you are worried that commenting on student blogs will take up too much of your time, be reassured that part of the beauty of blogging is that it is a low-stakes assignment and much of the work of reading and commenting is done by other students. Grading can also be crowd-sourced among students (Davidson, 2011). However, if you have a very large class, consider creating a single class blog to which everyone contributes. This has the advantage that you and your students only have to look in one place for new posts. Alternatively, you could use Halic et al.'s (2010) design of dividing students into blog groups (i.e., each group of 7–14 students had its own blog), which would reduce the total number of blogs you (and your students) would need to monitor. Introducing students to the concept of Rich Site Summary (RSS) feeds also allows them to monitor their own and other students' blogs, as they are automatically informed about updates.

8.3.3   Using Wikis to Improve Writing, Critical Thinking, and Information Literacy

A wiki is a group of webpages that multiple users can edit collaboratively using a Web browser (Wikipedia is probably the best-known example; see Chapter 3). The term "wiki" comes from the Hawaiian word *wikiwiki*, meaning "speedy" (https://en.wiktionary.org/wiki/wikiwiki#Verb), and reflects the speed with which information can be Web-published and made visible to others. Wikis can be set up on a CMS and used for various administrative activities within a course (e.g., students can sign up for appointments, organize themselves into groups, or volunteer for different activities using different wikis). Students can also share information among themselves, such as their contact information or their availability to meet and work on group projects or in study groups. More importantly, wikis provide students with opportunities to work together on assignments in a personally accountable way. Student work is visible to other students in the wiki, which circumvents the need for drafts of assignments to be circulated via email and the instructor can track individual contributions (Duffy & Bruns, 2006). When creating assignments, it is helpful to know that wikis have more organizational flexibility than blogs, with entries typically organized by content areas rather than the order in which information was added (Barton & Cummings, 2009). Hyperlinks are frequently used to cross-reference different pages or to link to content on external websites.

Parker and Chao (2007) provide many suggestions as to how wikis can be used in educational settings. For example, they can facilitate peer editing of student papers.

When students post their papers on individual pages within a group wiki, peers can edit or comment on them (see also Section 6.3.2 on Using Peer Review to Give Feedback). The wiki history helps both the instructor and the students evaluate how a piece of writing has evolved over time, and if a student does not agree with a change that someone else has made, they can revert the document to a former version. While many of these features are available in Google Docs and other collaborative editing software, the wikis in standard CMS platforms may make it easier to track the contributions of individual students, which becomes critical when assigning grades. On the other hand, unlike Google Docs, most wikis do not support simultaneous editing.

Wikis can also be used as repositories of knowledge when students work collaboratively in groups or as a class to explain and expand on concepts within a particular topic. As such, wikis provide excellent opportunities for cooperative learning, where students assist rather than compete with one another (see also Chapter 5 on Group Work). The synergistic nature of wiki assignments allows students to tackle large projects that could not be done individually, such as creating a professional-looking webpage about a psychological construct or writing a study guide for an upcoming test. In designing wiki assignments, one must be mindful that editing will need to be done sequentially (most wikis only allow one person to work on the document at a time), and students will need to coordinate their time accordingly.

To crowd-source materials for a wiki study guide, we recommend that the instructor provide sets of key questions or concepts and assign students to add explanations and definitions, links to helpful videos, and other aids (Powers, Brooks, McCloskey, Sekerina, & Cohen, 2013). Students can divide the work by focusing on different topics; other students can take turns in editing their peers' contributions while working collaboratively to create an extensive document (Lending, 2010; O'Bannon & Britt, 2011). This type of assignment might also be a good way to introduce students to the use of a wiki so that they can grasp the technological aspects before engaging in creating more extensive wikis. O'Bannon and Britt (2011) found that pre-service teachers who worked in pairs to contribute to a study guide on Internet tools felt the assignment increased their knowledge, and most continued to use the guide even after the assignment was over. Lending (2010) also found that most students in a course on information management thought that creating a class wiki study guide for the final exam was helpful; final exam scores were 5% higher than in previous classes that did not use a wiki. In this class, students added content, revised material, and edited the wiki every few days in the 3–4 weeks before the final exam, with contributions counting toward their final grade. Lending (2010) provides a useful rubric for grading wiki participation, with an emphasis on quantity rather than quality, since this is a much less time-demanding way to grade.

Giving students both technological assistance and guidance about how to collaborate with others is likely to result in the greatest learning gains for wiki assignments (De Wever, Hämäläinen, Voet, & Gielen, 2015). Without sufficient guidance, students may fail to post to the wiki (Cole, 2009) or to collaborate effectively with their classmates (Judd, Kennedy, & Cropper, 2010). Some students are reticent to edit their peers' work or have others edit their writing (Wheeler, Yeomans, & Wheeler, 2008), so it is important to train students in how to revise one another's work in a socially responsible and constructive way. Positive relationships among peers can be nurtured by having students use the wiki commenting feature to summarize and explain edits, ask for clarification, and provide recognition of a job well done. De Wever et al. (2015) found that students who were trained on how to collaborate effectively felt greater responsibility for the final product and were less likely to say that they had written most of a page than students who were not trained. Having students edit one another's work not only improves the quality of their writing, but also broadens each student's exposure to concepts outside their own theme, especially if they have to read some of the background literature in order to edit a section (De Wever et al., 2015). A similar collaborative editing design was also found to be successful in a small Special Topics in Psychology class, in which students created a "Relationships for Dummies" wiki that connected media portrayals of relationships to psychological theories (Slotter, 2010). Each of the nine students produced their own page in the class wiki, but they also edited and commented on their classmates' outlines and contributed additional material to their pages. Students indicated that they enjoyed the activity and felt that they learned a lot from it. In terms of more objective measures of student learning, as mentioned in Section 3.4.1, studies have shown that Wikipedia editing leads to increased information literacy (Shane-Simpson, Che, & Brooks, 2016), as well as improvements in students' research and writing skills (Brooks, Che, Walters, & Shane-Simpson, 2017; Edwards, 2015; Evans, Mabey, & Mandiberg, 2015).

Like blogs, wiki assignments can be set up using a CMS (which can track the number of words/edits and can easily link to a grade-book) or external sites, such as pbworks. com, education.weebly.com, or wikidot.com/education. External sites, like pbworks, often have a variety of privacy settings. For example, it is possible to make a wiki visible to the public but only allow designated editors (i.e., contributing students) to make changes. This may make an assignment more manageable to grade, but even if people outside the course do make edits (such as in a Wikipedia editing assignment), the wiki generates a history of changes for each page, so it remains possible to assess students' contributions. This feature is important, because individual accountability is a key component of cooperative learning (Johnson & Johnson, 2009a; Slavin, 2011).

8.4   Teaching in a Flipped Classroom

Once you feel that you have attained sufficient mastery of your CMS, you might consider "flipping" one or two class periods in one or more of your courses, and then even an entire course as you gain confidence. As you embark on new techniques such as teaching online, remember to gather formative assessment data to help you tweak your design! A flipped (or inverted) class is so-named because lower-order thinking such as going over basic concepts, which was traditionally done in the classroom, is moved to an online environment and completed as homework, while higher-order thinking such as applying concepts, which was traditionally embedded in homework assignments, is flipped into class time, where students work collaboratively to co-construct knowledge together (Lage et al., 2000). The rationale for the design is that it provides students with better support for more challenging activities and helps to create a more inclusive and interactive classroom environment. One important aspect of the flipped class is that F2F time is not reduced; it is simply restructured to be more collaborative and student-centered.

The flipped classroom model is becoming increasingly common in K–12 education (Horn & Staker, 2011) and has grown in popularity in colleges (O'Flaherty & Phillips, 2015). Hussey, Richmond, and Fleck (2015) offer a useful primer for designing flipped psychology courses; additionally, several studies report on the effects of flipping courses in the psychology major, including Statistics (Hussey, Fleck, & Richmond, 2014; Peterson, 2016; Wilson, 2013), Research Methods (Cummins-Sebree & White, 2014), and Physiological Psychology (Talley & Scherer, 2013).

Student perceptions of flipped classes are generally positive (Bishop & Verleger, 2013; Cummins-Sebree & White, 2014; Pierce & Fox, 2012; Wilson, 2013); nevertheless, students may need to adjust their course expectations, as they have to take greater responsibility for their own learning than in traditional classes. Student buy-in can be increased by explaining the rationale for the change in pedagogy and making reference to studies that show that active learning trumps traditional lecturing (Freeman et al., 2014). Several studies have shown that students in flipped classes (including those in the psychology major) perform better on exams and assignments (Cummins-Sebree & White, 2014; Foldnes, 2016; Peterson, 2016; Pierce & Fox, 2012; Talley & Scherer, 2013; Wilson, 2013; Wong, Ip, Lopes, & Rajagopalan, 2014) and collaborate more with peers (Burke & Fedorek, 2017) than students in traditional lecture classes. However, Morton and Colbert-Getz (2017) suggested that significant improvements related to flipping may be visible only when exam items probe beyond the foundational knowledge level of Bloom's taxonomy (see Figure 2.1). In their study, they found that medical students who took a flipped class in Anatomy outperformed students in a traditional class on test items that required them to apply their knowledge, but that there was no significant group difference for items that tested information at the more basic level of remembering. Morton and Colbert-Getz (2017) suggest that the level of learning (i.e., application vs. remembering) might explain why some studies have not found significantly better learning outcomes for students in flipped classes, even when the students perceived that they had learned more effectively than their peers in traditional classes (e.g., McLaughlin et al., 2013). Since the benefits of the flipped classroom relate to increased active learning, it is not surprising that students in classes with high amounts of active learning perform similarly to those in flipped classes (Jensen, Kummer, & Godoy, 2015; Lape et al., 2014). In other words, the benefits of flipping come from an increase in student-centered teaching rather than the use of technology per se. Flipping classes may have the added benefit of improving student retention: Fautch (2015) found that fewer students withdrew from her highly challenging Organic Chemistry course when it was flipped. However, she found no improvement in class grades or exam scores in comparison to students in her previous non-flipped classes. This null finding was probably because a greater number of lower-performing students persisted in the flipped class than in the traditional one.

One of the challenges of flipping a course is making sure that students are adequately prepared for class. This preparation might include reading the textbook or other sources of information, or watching videos or listening to podcasts (Wilson, 2013). To this end, instructors often create mini video lectures, sometimes referred to as content-acquisition podcasts (CAPs) (Kennedy et al., 2016). CAPs can be created from narrated PowerPoint slideshows exported as video files and uploaded to YouTube (see Box 8.1). Alternatively, you might want to use one of the many publicly available psychology-related videos. For example, Wilson (2013) asked her Statistics students to watch Khan

---

Box 8.1 Tips for Creating Online Video Podcasts

One very easy way to create a video podcast is to use a narrated PowerPoint show:

1) Create a short slide show using Mayer's principles of multimedia design (Mayer, 2014a, 2014b), consisting mostly of graphics.
2) Record narration on each slide, in conjunction with pointer movements to highlight key aspects (you will need a sound card in your computer and a microphone).
3) Export as a video.
4) Upload the video to YouTube as an unlisted file.
5) Post a link to the video on your CMS.

Academy (www.khanacademy.org) videos in preparation for working through problems in class. If you choose videos that feature an expert on a topic, you will not only save yourself a lot of preparation time, but can also expose your students to a "big name" in the field. Critics have argued that using this approach perpetuates the use of lecturing (albeit online) as an instructional technique and therefore is based on flawed pedagogy (Ash, 2012). However, most flipped classes have evolved beyond simply providing video recordings of lectures (Hadjianastasis & Nightingale, 2016). Pre-class videos should be succinct (Bishop & Verleger, 2013) and should follow best principles of multimedia design, such as featuring lots of graphics and animations, and using analogies to simpler concepts to explain complex ones (Mayer, 2014a, 2014b; see also Chapter 3). The goal of these instructional materials is to draw students' attention to important points and to clarify concepts that they are likely to have difficulty understanding. The ability to pause and rewind videos is helpful in terms of allowing students to review materials at their own pace (Bergmann & Sams, 2012), and using a variety of media is consistent with the principles of UDL (Burgstahler, 2015; Connell et al., 1997; see also Section 2.5 on Universal Design). Relatedly, international students for whom English is not their native language report that online videos enhance their learning, presumably because they can watch them at their own pace (Evans, 2008).

As we mentioned in Section 2.4.1, several studies have reported that many students in traditional courses fail to complete reading assignments before coming to class (Clump, Bauer, & Breadley, 2004; Hobson, 2004; Hoeft, 2012; Sikorski et al., 2002). This also poses a problem in flipped classes, but students who are particularly overextended in terms of their time (such as commuter students, students with jobs or significant family responsibilities, and student athletes) may prefer watching concise videos that summarize the most salient issues to reading lengthy textbook chapters. Furthermore, there is evidence to suggest that watching videos/vodcasts may be more effective in enhancing student learning than reading a textbook. In a meta-analysis, Ginns (2005) found that students learn better from graphics with audio recordings than graphics with text, which suggests that they may retain more from a video than from the textbook. Gross, Pietri, Anderson, Moyano-Camihort, and Graham (2015) found that students in a Physical Chemistry hybrid class who watched video lectures online had better test scores than those in a traditional class, with the performance differences being particularly marked for women and members of minoritized groups. They attributed this to the fact that students who were struggling in the class benefitted from being able to review the materials covered in the lectures at their own pace. Another advantage of posting mini-videos online (including videos that provide detailed instructions for assignments) is that it supports students who may have missed a class and saves the instructor from having to go over basic points with multiple students (Bergmann & Sams, 2012). We have also found this to be helpful for students enrolling in classes after the semester has begun.

That said, issues with noncompliance have also been reported in some flipped classes (Mellefont & Fei, 2014). Exam performance has been shown to be correlated with the amount of time students spend watching online videos (Gross et al., 2015), and compliance is maximized when pre-class assignments are not overly lengthy. Therefore, videos/vodcasts should not be more than 30 minutes long and should be of reasonably high production quality (Milman, 2012). In general, students prefer to watch 10–20-minute videos over longer ones (Zappe, Leicht, Messner, Litzinger, & Lee, 2009); it is no coincidence that TED Talks all last 18 minutes or less. While watching videos, students should be encouraged to take notes and generate questions (Bergmann & Sams, 2012).

Students are more likely to complete their pre-class assignments if they are quizzed on them (Bishop & Verleger, 2013). Quizzing can occur online or in the classroom, but research has shown that embedding quizzes within videos using specialized software such as Camtasia or Adobe Captivate is particularly effective in enhancing learning (Zhang, Zhou, Briggs, & Nunamaker, 2006). Alternatively, students could post reflections, write summaries, or answer guiding questions prior to class. They are more likely to complete their pre-class assignments if they count toward the final grade. Each class can then begin in addressing any questions they might have in relation to their assignments. Such questions often serve as valuable feedback that can be used to improve existing resources for future classes (Bergmann & Sams, 2012).

8.4.1 Activities for the Flipped Classroom

Many of the classroom activities that we suggested in Chapters 4 and 5 are suitable for encouraging CT in a flipped-classroom session. These include class discussions, debates, role-plays, analyses of case studies, collection of data in experimental simulations, problem-based learning, and team-based learning, where students work in groups on open-ended real-life problems (Sweet & Michaelsen, 2012). In the flipped classroom, the goal is to guide students as they work collaboratively to support one another's learning in zones of proximal development (Vygotsky, 1978). The flipped class allows students to spend more time engaged in experiential learning, which may be particularly beneficial in classes in which the LOs focus heavily on the development of skills, such as Research Methods and Statistics courses, where students learn to design research and analyze data in order to address their questions of interest. Flipped classes can provide more time for students to collect and analyze data, which fosters scientific literacy while making abstract psychological concepts more accessible. We have found flipping to be particularly beneficial in courses like Sensation and Perception, where students struggle to understand how psychophysical experiments work in the absence of hands-on experience. When students collaborate in groups to analyze and interpret data collected through online experiments, they gain a better understanding of the research methods used to study sensation and perception, as well as the theories behind the experiments. Another advantage of teaching in a flipped class is that it allows instructors to provide more individualized instruction by spending more time with students who need extra help (Bergmann & Sams, 2012).

In flipped classes, students are able to engage in more sophisticated problem solving than in traditional classes. Not only are they better prepared by virtue of the pre-class assignments, but they can also benefit from the collective knowledge and skills of their classmates. Students profit especially from engaging in real-life problem solving, where they get to practice thinking like a psychologist (Wallace, Walker, Braseby, & Sweet, 2014). The National Center for Case Study Teaching in Science (NCCSTS; http://sciencecases.lib.buffalo.edu/cs/), funded by the National Science Foundation (NSF), provides a host of peer-reviewed instructor case studies in psychology (as well as other disciplines) that can be used for this very purpose. Each case study begins with a short story about a topical dilemma that tends to evoke empathy in the reader (Herreid, 1997). For example, one asks the reader to take the perspective of a defense attorney who is representing a young Black man charged with assault. The attorney has to weigh all the evidence and decide whether they should take on the considerable expense of hiring an expert witness to cast doubt on the testimony of the eyewitnesses in the case. Students then have to think deeply and collaborate with their classmates to come to a consensual decision. The case studies include pre-class materials, scaffolded activities, and assessment suggestions, all for a nominal fee.

8.5   Transitioning to Teaching Fully Online

Teaching institutions often require that instructors take a training course before they teach online for the first time, and many of these are offered in online formats. Not only does taking such a course better prepare you to teach, but actually taking it online (especially if you have never taken an online course before) can help you understand your students' experiences and potential frustrations. In this book, we have stressed the importance of backward design and careful course planning (see Chapter 2), but this process is especially paramount in online classes (Dykman & Davis, 2008). Online courses typically require more up-front planning than F2F classes, as students will need very clear expectations from the outset in order to succeed. Be particularly aware of research that shows that teaching online (especially for the first time) typically takes much more time than teaching F2F classes (National Education Association, 2000; Zuckweiler, Schniederjans, & Ball, 2004), although it may afford greater flexibility in terms of when and where you can teach. One of the potential pitfalls of online teaching is that it may be more difficult to assist students who are struggling or who get behind in their work (Dykman & Davis, 2008). In F2F classes, there are many opportunities for instructors to directly engage with the student; if all communication is done electronically, students may ignore offers of help until it is too late (Dykman & Davis, 2008). Indeed, attrition rates are generally higher in online than in F2F classes (Frydenberg, 2007; Moody, 2004), especially among first-year students (Cochran, Campbell, Baker, & Leeds, 2014).

As with F2F classes, you will begin planning for an online course with your broader LOs and then break these down into more specific objectives for each topic or class period. You will need to make decisions about whether all work will be completed asynchronously (i.e., where students have some flexibility in terms of when they work, as long as they are in compliance with deadlines for completion of assignments) or whether you will arrange synchronous meetings using affordable and reliable software such as Zoom, Blackboard Collaborate, GotoMeeting, Adobe Connect, or Skype. Synchronous meetings are ideal for group work and other in-class activities (e.g., role-plays, debates) where students take turns speaking and listening (see Chapter 5). Using the chat function, students can write down questions or comments and be called upon in turn. Classes can also be split into small "break-out" groups for a specific activity (e.g., see Section 5.4.5), with the instructor making periodic visits to each group before reassembling the class. This feature is particularly valuable in programs and courses where students benefit from practice with interviewing or other skills that may be relevant to their professional life (Snow, Lamar, Hinkle, & Speciale, 2018). Given the opportunities for F2F interaction via teleconferencing software, the dynamics of synchronous online classes are very different from those of asynchronous ones, which emphasize independent study of course material via homework and quizzing, although these too, can make use of discussion boards, blogs, and wikis.

Ideally, all of the tools we have described for creating a Web-enhanced course will apply directly to teaching a course fully online. In addition to the standard tools available on your CMS, if you are teaching an introductory or mid-level course with a standard textbook, you might also want to consider adopting one of the online learning platforms available through textbook publishers to supplement your lesson plans: MyLab Psychology (Pearson), LaunchPad (Worth Publishers—McMillan Learning), or WileyPLUS Learning Space (Wiley). These online course supplements encompass sets of student resources, such as video tool-kits, short-answer questions, and multiple-choice quizzes, as well as instructor resources, such as a calendar and grade-book. As a means of cost-saving for students, the online course packs are typically packaged for use with an e-book, with student resources aligned with each textbook chapter. Although it may seem cumbersome for students to access online work on two platforms (i.e., your college CMS and the publisher-provided course pack and e-book), the most widely used CMSs (e.g., Blackboard, Canvas) integrate fully with the publisher platforms. Note, however, that students will need training and support to use the publisher-provided materials effectively, and may become frustrated when technical difficulties arise (Powers et al., 2013).

Many recent books and articles focus exclusively on teaching fully online courses. We have provided a list of useful resources for instructors who want to teach online (see Box 8.2), although it is not exhaustive and we would encourage you to expand your own knowledge in this area. We also provide a list of peer-reviewed journals that focus on online teaching (see Box 8.3), with the caveat that more are likely to emerge in the near future.

Box 8.2 Resources for Planning to Teach Online

American Psychological Association (2013). Guide to establishing an online teaching program. Retrieved from https://www.apa.org/ed/precollege/undergrad/ptacc/online-teaching.pdf.

Bailey, C. J., & Card, K. A. (2009). Effective pedagogical practices for online teaching: Perception of experienced instructors. *The Internet and Higher Education*, 12(3), 152–155.

Baran, E., Correia, A. P., & Thompson, A. (2013). Tracing successful online teaching in higher education: Voices of exemplary online teachers. *Teachers College Record*, 115(3), 1–41.

Boettcher, J. V., & Conrad, R.-M. (2016). *The online teaching survival guide: Simple and practical pedagogical tips*. San Francisco, CA: Jossey Bass.

Brinthaupt, T. M., Fisher, L. S., Gardner, J. G., Raffo, D. M., & Woodward, J. B. (2011). What the best online teachers should do. *MERLOT Journal of Online Learning and Teaching*, 7(4). Retrieved from http://jewlscholar.mtsu.edu/bitstream/handle/mtsu/5180/what%20the%20best%20online%20teachers%20should%20do.pdf?sequence=1.

Jayakumar, R., & Krishnakumar, R. (2014). E-tivities: An active online learning with conceptual background resources. *International Journal of Applied Research*, 1(1), 25–30.

Keengwe, J., & Kidd, T. T. (2010). Towards best practices in online learning and teaching in higher education. *Journal of Online Learning and Teaching*, 6(2), 533. Retrieved from http://jolt.merlot.org/vol6no2/keengwe_0610.pdf.

Ko, S., & Rossen, S. (2017). *Teaching online: A practical guide*. New York, NY: Taylor & Francis.

Miller, M. D. (2014). *Minds online: Teaching effectively with technology*. Cambridge, MA: Harvard University Press.

Neff, K. S., & Donaldson, S. I. (2013). *Teaching psychology online: Tips and strategies for success*. New York, NY: Psychology Press.

Northern Illinois University. Video tutorials for preparing to teach online. Retrieved from https://www.niu.edu/facdev/resources/onlineteaching/preparing-to-teach.shtml.

Palloff, R. M., & Pratt, K. (2013). *Lessons from the virtual classroom: The realities of online teaching*. San Francisco, CA: Jossey Bass.

Teaching and Learning Services. (2014) Online course design: Time on task. Rhode Island Institute of Technology. July. Retrieved from: http://www.rit.edu/academicaffairs/tls/sites/rit.edu.academicaffairs.tls/files/docs/Course%20Design_Online_Time%20%20on%20Task_v1.5.pdf.

Box 8.3 Lists of Journals Focusing on Online Teaching

---

https://depd.wisc.edu/html/mags3.htm
http://empowerteaching.usu.edu/journalsforteachingandlearning
http://www.fctl.ucf.edu/researchandscholarship/sotl/journals/—see those under "Individual SoTL Journals (Technology Focus)"

8.6   Summary

1) Online tools available through CMSs can be utilized effectively in student-centered F2F courses to improve communication and help students prepare for classes.
2) Blogs and wikis offer opportunities for students to write collaboratively and engage in peer editing and revision of work.
3) Flipping your classes through the use of videos or CAPs assigned as homework helps to make them more student-centered.
4) Gaining experience with e-learning in F2F and hybrid courses can help make the transition to teaching fully online manageable.

9

Becoming an Effective and Fulfilled Teacher

This concluding chapter is designed to support your thinking about the ethical issues associated with teaching and how to foster a career as a teacher of psychology. In the final section of this chapter, we cover ways to self-reflect, document, and showcase your teaching to others, and describe opportunities to engage in further professional development to enhance your pedagogy.

9.1   Ethical Teaching Using an Evidence-Based Approach

Various bodies, including the Society for Teaching and Learning in Higher Education (STLHE, 1996), the American Association of University Professors (AAUP, 2009), the American Psychological Association (APA, 2017a), and the National Education Association (NEA, 2010) have created guidelines as to what constitutes ethical teaching (Hill & Zinsmeister, 2012; Murray, Gillese, Lennon, Mercer, & Robinson, 1996). In general, they all suggest that instructors are duty-bound to encourage learning and to treat students equitably and with respect. Therefore, these bodies advise that instructors should be knowledgeable and current in the fields that they are teaching, *as well as in the best ways to teach*. Thus, it is clear that ethical teachers should adopt a scientist-educator evidence-based approach (Bernstein et al., 2010). As we have underscored many times throughout this book, there is overwhelming evidence that a student-centered active learning approach is the most effective pedagogy for maximizing learning; it is no longer ethically acceptable to simply lecture to students (Freeman et al., 2014; Johnson, Johnson, & Stanne, 2000).

As we laid out in Chapter 1, understanding our students' identities and where they are in their academic journey is an important first step in our ethical duty to foster learning. Using an unbiased student-centered approach and creating safe learning environments for "difficult" discussions of sensitive, complex, and/or controversial societal and personal issues will help students to connect their coursework with their lived experiences. Furthermore, encouraging students to bring their diverse talents, perspectives, and backgrounds to the class will enrich the learning experience for all. Teaching in a culturally responsive way is predicated on frequent self-reflection on how your worldviews and implicit biases could potentially impact

Teaching Psychology: An Evidence-Based Approach, First Edition. Jillian Grose-Fifer, Patricia J. Brooks, and Maureen O'Connor.
© 2019 John Wiley & Sons, Inc. Published 2019 by John Wiley & Sons, Inc.
Companion website: www.wiley.com/go/Grose-Fifer/teaching-psychology

the way you teach (Sue & Sue, 2016). In addition, using a variety of methods and assessments with structured developmentally appropriate assignments and ample practice validates and empowers all students to learn, regardless of their preparedness and abilities. Universal Design for Learning (UDL) recommends that you be clear and transparent in conveying your expectations in terms of learning outcomes, assessments, and how courses will be taught (see Chapter 2 for more on UDL). This approach is also consistent with the APA's ethical guidelines for educators (American Psychological Association, 2017a) and the basic principles of backward course design (as described in Chapter 2).

By eschewing a teacher-centered approach that places undue focus on the passive transmission of content knowledge, student-centered teachers focus more on developing students' academic skills and personal growth. This more holistic approach to teaching is endorsed by the Association of American Colleges and Universities (AACU, 2015) and in the five broad APA goals for the psychology undergraduate major (American Psychological Association, 2013). Developing content knowledge in the field of psychology is only *one* of the APA's five goals; as summarized in Chapter 2, the other four focus on critical thinking (CT) and scientific inquiry, being ethically and socially responsible in a diverse world, communication, and professional development. In the past, teacher-centered instructors may have *felt* that they had implicitly addressed many of these—for instance, believing that students' CT develops when they are exposed to challenging course materials in readings and lectures, that their writing improves when they write a term paper, and that their skills in group work improve when they give a presentation with other students. Unfortunately, this approach often fails to give adequate instructional emphasis to the development of the underlying skills, and so leads to hit-or-miss success in terms of the overarching learning objectives (LOs). Targeted instruction with timely feedback is much more effective in producing gains in CT than assuming that students will "pick it up as they go" (Abrami et al., 2008; Ennis, 1989); scaffolded assignments that deconstruct how to read and summarize a primary source article lead to better papers than simply assigning students to "write a paper using primary sources" (Grose-Fifer & Davis-Ferreira, 2018; Grose-Fifer, Davis, & Pryiomka, 2014); teaching students about group dynamics and structuring group activities to foster positive interdependency produce greater learning gains across multiple domains than simply asking students to "work together" on an assignment (Johnson, Johnson, & Smith, 2014).

As just outlined, throughout this book we have offered practical advice on how to structure meaningful learning experiences that will foster the skills necessary for students to attain broad academic abilities that will enable lifelong learning. Using this more holistic approach to teaching inevitably means that you will not cover everything in your course textbook (if, indeed, a textbook is even appropriate for your course). But, rest assured, when you adopt this approach, your students are more likely to develop the critical skills they will need to compete in today's workforce and to lead engaged lives as active contributors to their communities.

As pointed out by the organizations cited at the beginning of this chapter, it is important to be impartial in your treatment of your students; this is particularly salient when conducting assessments. Subjectivity can easily creep in based on prior interactions with students. For example, Malouff, Emmerton, and Schutte (2013) found that when grading a written assignment, instructors were influenced by how well their students had performed on a prior oral presentation. Using rubrics and grading de-identified student work can help increase objectivity and mitigate problems with fairness when performing assessments; work can easily be de-identified when students upload it to a course management system (CMS). CMSs also allow for the provision of timely, confidential feedback about student performance on exams and assignments, other important elements of ethical instruction.

Relatedly, it is important to be equitable when students present extenuating circumstances regarding missed or late exams or assignments. Most of today's students can be considered non-traditional (see Chapter 1), and as Keith-Spiegel, Whitley, Balogh, Perkins, and Wittig (2002) have pointed out, when students have complicated lives, you may need to have a flexible make-up policy in order for them to do well in your class. To better support students who had conflicting responsibilities, Nelson (1996) instituted a policy of writing two different versions of each exam and administering them 2 weeks apart; students could then choose on which date to take the exam—or, if they elected to take both, they were awarded the higher of their two scores. Other approaches that might be even simpler to administer are to have a policy of dropping the lowest test score or offering an additional "optional" cumulative final exam that may be used either to make up a missed exam or to replace a poor grade on an earlier exam. In Section 7.5.2, we discuss in more detail how to address the problem of poor performance on exams and other assignments.

When students are struggling in a class, they often ask for extra-credit assignments to help boost their grade. It is helpful to deal with this potential (and very common) situation at the beginning of the semester by explaining that it would be unfair to offer extra credit to students on an individual basis. However, providing extra-credit opportunities to the whole class may serve to reduce anxiety and increase motivation; extra-credit assignments can also provide powerful learning experiences if they increase mastery of a skill or topic (Weimer, 2003). For example, if you are assigning an online study-guide wiki (as described in Section 8.3.3), you could offer extra credit for students who contribute substantially more than the minimal requirement (i.e., rewarding those who will be better prepared for the upcoming exam).

Finally, ethical teachers nurture the whole student. If a student is struggling in your class, it may be that they need additional support. In our experience, new instructors, as well as anyone teaching in a new institution or working part-time, can be reluctant to reach out for support in dealing with student issues or may simply be unaware how or whether to do so. Invariably, if a student is struggling in your class, that student will have issues in other classes or situations as well, and so would benefit from outreach to the appropriate student support service(s). You cannot and should not feel you have to solve all students' problems on your own. If you are not sure where to refer your student for help, you might want to seek advice from your more experienced colleagues. It is also a good idea to find out whether your college is one of the many that has a multidisciplinary Behavioral Intervention Team (BIT; see the National Behavioral Intervention Team Association [NABITA] website at https://nabita.org/behavioral-intervention-teams for some alternative names). Your BIT can advise you as to how best to support your student. In some cases, it may contact the student directly to provide assistance. If you do not have a BIT, then contact the Office of the Dean of Student Affairs or the Counseling Center when you need advice on how to support your students.

9.2   Ethical Classroom Management

As we mentioned at the start of this chapter, instructors have an ethical responsibility to create safe, respectful learning environments that foster personal as well as academic development. We have made specific suggestions about how to do this throughout the book (see especially Sections 1.5.1 and 4.3.1). Another important aspect of classroom management is ensuring that students do not prevent one another from learning by engaging in disruptive behaviors, such as having side conversations with peers, making inappropriate comments to the instructor or other students, surfing the Internet, texting, arriving late/leaving early, or falling asleep, any of which can contribute to an inhospitable learning environment (Black, Wygonik, & Frey, 2011). We will all encounter students who engage in disruptive behaviors in our teaching careers. Interestingly, though, in a 5-year study of classroom behaviors, Boice (1996) found such incivilities are most likely to occur when students perceive that the instructor has a negative attitude, is inattentive, or is condescending, or when they fail to intervene when students behave inappropriately. Lack of instructor immediacy, warmth, and interest during the first weeks of class was the most common trigger for persistent classroom incivilities among students (Boice, 1996), underscoring the importance of establishing rapport with your students (Frisby & Martin, 2010; Wilson & Ryan, 2013).

Sharing your research interests and background can lessen the psychological distance between you and your students and is a first step toward personalizing your relationship (Fritschner, 2000); at the same time, it provides an opportunity to reveal your teaching qualifications in a non-defensive way (Alexander-Snow, 2004). We have found that students particularly appreciate it when we reveal our interest and research in pedagogy, because it underscores that we are personally invested in their learning and development.

Another strategy to help avoid disruptive behavior is to devote a portion of the first class period to allowing students to co-construct rules for classroom interactions and other important classroom management issues. Operationalizing incivilities helps to circumnavigate the problem that students often engage in inappropriate behavior because they don't realize it is disruptive (Nordstrom, Bartels, & Bucy, 2009). Also, involving students in making the ground rules increases their sense of agency; see also Davidson (2017), who encourages instructors to leave part of the syllabus open to allow students to take the lead in designing some aspect of their course.

Incivilities are less likely to occur when students are actively engaged in learning than they are in teacher-centered classes, where expectations for student participation are minimal to non-existent (Alberts, Hazen, & Theobald, 2010). Halpern and Desrochers (2005) applied social psychological theories to explain why student-centered teaching reduces the likelihood of incivilities. They stressed that making students more accountable in class reduces the undesirable behaviors typically associated with student anonymity and de-individuation. Some of the ways to do this include learning your students' names, setting up expectations for total participation using techniques like Think–Write–Pair–Share (T-W-P-S), and randomly calling on students during your classes. Halpern also found that making 15-minute out-of-class appointments (for extra credit) to get to know her students helped to create rapport (Halpern & Desrochers, 2005). Active learning increases student engagement more than traditional lectures, but even so, students sometimes get distracted. Sorcinelli (2003) suggests that students who are off-task can often be reoriented by making eye contact with them and asking them direct questions. One of us routinely asks students who appear to be distracted by something on their laptops to look up information for the class. Randomly calling on students with laptops is often effective in getting the class to put them away. If the student continues to be inattentive, talking to them after class may help them to understand that their behavior was disruptive and decrease the likelihood of its persisting in future classes (Boice, 1996).

Sometimes, students might question the value of an assignment or task in a confrontational way. The likelihood of this occurring can be reduced by being as transparent as possible about the purpose of in-class activities and assignments, and how they contribute to students' academic and professional development. Sorcinelli (2003) suggests that instructors should remain calm and respond to any challenge in a good-natured, explanatory way. If a student continues to question your authority, Feldmann (2001) suggests asking to meet them after class to discuss the issue further (and to explain why their behavior was troublesome). If, despite all your best efforts, you find that some students continue to be disruptive, there are multiple resources to call on. Remember that you are not alone. Consult with your BIT, which will guide you as to what to do and, where necessary, will intervene with a student. If you do not have a BIT at your college, then contact your Department Chair or the Dean of Student Affairs.

On rare occasions, when students become hostile or threatening, your safety and that of your students is paramount. It is important to remain calm. If possible, try to explain that you are happy to discuss the matter further but cannot do so if they are unable to control themselves. If they cannot calm themselves then you can ask them to leave the classroom. If they refuse to do so, it is appropriate to tell them that you are going to call Campus Public Safety/Security. Again, report any serious disruptions to the BIT, or if you do not have one, to your Department Chair and the Dean of Student Affairs, who will help you deal with the situation. Similarly, if you are concerned about a student's mental health or if they are behaving erratically in the classroom, speak to them quietly, offer to escort them to the Wellness/Counseling Center, or call the Campus Public Safety/Security office if you feel that their safety, your own, or that of other members of your class is threatened.

Another important duty of an ethically responsible instructor is to educate students about academic dishonesty (Hill & Zinsmeister, 2012). As we noted in Section 6.4, students are often unaware what behaviors (like plagiarism) are considered academically dishonest; hence, the likelihood of such behaviors occurring can be reduced by training them in their avoidance using examples and exercises. However, it is still important to include your college's statement about academic dishonesty in your syllabus and to explain any consequences imposed by the institution if your students overstep the boundaries that you set.

9.3 Closing the Loop: Evaluating the Effectiveness of Your Instruction

Throughout this book, we offer evidence-based suggestions for teaching diverse learners. As scientist-educators, we are ethically obliged to assess whether the pedagogical practices we use in our classes are effective for our *particular* students, and to close the assessment loop by making necessary adjustments if they are not meeting the course LOs (Angelo & Cross, 1993; Halpern et al., 1998; Richmond et al., 2014). As discussed in Chapter 2, if students are struggling to meet your LOs then you may need to reassess your teaching methods, consider whether your expectations are developmentally appropriate, or reevaluate whether your assessment is sufficiently aligned with a particular outcome to reliably measure student learning gains (see Chapter 4). Notably, multifaceted skills, such as CT, are notoriously difficult to assess. For example, Burke, Sears, Kraus, and Roberts-Cady (2014) found that students who improved their ability to debunk pseudoscience failed to show improvements on classical tests of CT; hence, the latter were clearly not suitable for assessing gains in psychological literacy. Regularly evaluating your choice of assessments and the way you teach increases the likelihood that you will use valid and reliable methods to assess student learning, and may spur you to try out a new technique.

To maximize the likelihood for positive change in your pedagogy, assessment of the efficacy of any new teaching intervention should be approached as systematically as any other line of scientific inquiry. This means focusing on one specific targeted change at a time; changing lots of different things at the same time creates too many independent variables and makes it difficult to identify which one made a significant difference in your course. Furthermore, you will need to consider the most suitable way to evaluate whether your intervention had a beneficial effect on student learning (i.e., the dependent variables). Although student and faculty perceptions often differ widely with regard to what constitutes good teaching (for review, see Spooren, Brockx, & Mortelmans, 2013), collecting information from your students about the perceived efficacy of an activity, demonstration, or assignment can be very informative (see Section 2.7). The Society for the Teaching of Psychology (STP) has published a useful e-book that lays out best practices for developing such assessments, as well as providing a compendium of scales designed to assess students' perceptions across a multitude of domains, including CT, metacognition, academic self-efficacy and self-regulation, and procrastination, to name but a few (Jhangiani, Troisi, Fleck, Legg, & Hussey, 2015).

In addition to measuring students' perceptions, it is also wise to use objective assessments to evaluate whether they have benefitted from an intervention, using a control group (between-subjects design) or condition (within-subjects design). Again, the dependent variables that you choose should measure the targeted intervention as specifically as possible. We suggest you look back to Chapters 2 and 7 for suggestions on different ways to assess learning. Exam/test scores and assignment grades are often the most obvious candidates, but consider analyzing them in greater depth (e.g., by focusing on answers to questions that are particularly relevant to the intervention, or by using a rubric to target a particular way of thinking/communicating). The issue of finding a suitable control can be potentially tricky, as many instructors feel that it is unethical to use between-subjects designs where a potentially beneficial teaching intervention is used in one section of a class but not in another (Smith, 2008). One way to get around this is to compare performance with a class from a previous semester (before you had your great idea for the intervention), or with students in another instructor's section of the same course. Alternatively, you could use a within-subjects design and look at changes in pre- and post-test assessments related to the intervention, or compare test scores for intervention-related items to those on unrelated items (Smith, 2008).

9.4   The Scholarship of Teaching and Learning

When scientist-educators systematically assess their pedagogical practices (as laid out in Section 9.3), they are often only one step away from engaging in the scholarship of teaching and learning (SoTL). SoTL is formal research that culminates in public dissemination of the findings; that is, publications in peer-reviewed journals and conference presentations (Gurung, Ansburg, Alexander, Lawrence, & Johnson, 2008; Pan, 2009; see Box 9.1 for a list of journals that publish SoTL research). As with all scientific studies, SoTL research is guided by theoretical frameworks, and so is hypothesis-driven and rigorously designed with adequate statistical power and control/baseline conditions (Wilson-Doenges & Gurung, 2013). By definition, when designing a SoTL study, there is an intent to publish, and so you will need to apply to your campus's Institutional Review Board (IRB) for the Protection of Human Subjects for approval or exemption to conduct the study (Martin, 2013). For the IRB to categorize a protocol as exempt, the data must be de-identified prior to any analysis, and the measures must not extend beyond those normally collected in the course, such as exam grades, assignments, and other previously instituted assessments. Note that you may also request an exemption to analyze measures of learning from previously taught courses. Some SoTL projects may also constitute institutionally mandated course assessment, as required by accreditation agencies such as the Middle States Commission on Higher Education or the Western Association of Schools and Colleges. When submitting an application to conduct a SoTL project where the data collected may also be used for departmental or college assessment purposes, it is helpful to include a letter of cooperation from your Department Chair in the IRB application.

Often, you might want to collect data outside of the realm of:

> "Research conducted in established or commonly accepted educational settings, involving normal educational practices, such as: (i) research on regular and special education instructional strategies, or (ii) research on the effectiveness of or the comparison among instructional techniques, curricula, or classroom management methods."
>
> *(U.S. Department of Health & Human Services,*
> *Office for Human Research Protections (n.d.),*
> *Exempt Categories 45 CFR 46.101)*

In such cases, your research will not meet the criteria for exemption (Martin, 2013). The priority of the IRB is to protect your students and ensure that they are not harmed in any way, and you should consult with the IRB when planning your project to ensure that it meets its approval. In particular, your application should carefully explain the precautions that you will take to ensure that students do not feel coerced to participate (e.g., delaying any analysis of the data until after the completion of the semester, when grades have been submitted). You (or, better, an assistant or colleague who is not responsible for any element of grading in the course) will need to explain the nature of the research and obtain informed consent from your students. In exceptional circumstances, your experimental design might necessitate withholding some information about the research in the consent form if it has the potential to affect students' behavior and thus the results. In this case, students should be debriefed after the research

---

Box 9.1 Scholarship of Teaching and Learning Journals

Applied Cognitive Psychology
Assessment & Evaluation in Higher Education
British Journal of Educational Psychology
Chronicle of Higher Education
Cognition and Instruction
College Teaching
Computers & Education
Computers and Composition
Computers in Human Behavior
Contemporary Educational Psychology
Education Research Review
Educational Psychologist
Educational Psychology: An International Journal of Experimental Educational Psychology
Educational Research and Evaluation
Frontiers in Education
Frontiers in Psychology
Higher Education Review
Higher Education: The International Journal of Higher Education Research
International Journal for the Scholarship of Teaching and Learning
International Journal of Pedagogies and Learning
Journal of College Student Development
Journal of Computer-Assisted Learning
Journal of Computers in Education
Journal of Curriculum and Pedagogy
Journal of Diversity in Higher Education
Journal of Educational Psychology
Journal of Higher Education
Journal of Instructional Psychology
Journal of Interactive Technology and Pedagogy
Journal of Pedagogy
Journal of Scholarship in Teaching and Learning
Journal on Excellence in College Teaching
Learning and Individual Differences
Learning and Instruction
Metacognition and Learning
Pedagogies: An International Journal
Pedagogy: Critical Approaches to Teaching Literature, Language, Composition, & Culture
Psychology Learning and Teaching
Research and Practice in College Teaching
Research in Higher Education
Review of Educational Research
Scholarship and Learning in Psychology
Studies in Higher Education
Teaching in Higher Education
Teaching of Psychology

has been completed (i.e., at the end of the semester). If the research is not exempt, you must also give students the option to choose not to participate. For example, they might decide not to fill out any assessments that were only added to measure the efficacy of the intervention (Fleck & Ropp, 2014; Linder, Elek, & Calderon, 2014). In this case, if you decide to award extra credit or course points for student participation in your SoTL project, it is important to also create alternatives so that students who opt out are not penalized (Fleck & Ropp, 2014). Occasionally, the potential for using data for a SoTL study may emerge after a course has ended, in which case it could be very difficult to obtain informed consent. This may not be an issue if the data are de-identified and the IRB deems that the protocol is exempt, but Family Educational Rights and Privacy Act (FERPA) regulations mean that you will not be able to disseminate portions of a student's work (e.g., writing quotes, presentations, podcasts) without their express permission, even if it is de-identified, which could limit the scope of the project (Fleck & Ropp, 2014).

There is a rich array of resources to support instructors who want to engage in SoTL. The STP has two SoTL-related e-books (Jhangiani et al., 2015; Smith & Schwartz, 2015), which are free to download from its website (http://teachpsych.org/ebooks/index.php). Recently, with support from the Association for Psychological Science (APS), the Hub for Introductory Psychology & Pedagogical Research (HIPPR; http://hippr.uwgb.org/) was created to support instructors (including graduate students) who are interested in collaborating on the development of research studies that have more diverse and larger samples than they would be capable of generating alone. The STP also provides a consulting service, where you can ask for SoTL advice, and an annual SoTL workshop (see the STP website for more information, https://teachpsych.org/). In addition to hosting the Annual Conference on Teaching (ACT), the STP also has satellite meetings associated with several large conferences, such as the Association for Psychological Science/Society for the Teaching of Psychology (APS-STP) Teaching Institute, the APA Annual Convention, and the Society for Personality and Social Psychology (SPSP), to name but a few (see Box 9.2 for a list of

---

Box 9.2 Conferences Featuring SoTL Research

- APS-STP Teaching Institute
  http://teachpsych.org/STP-@APS
- STP Annual Conference on Teaching (ACT)
  http://teachpsych.org/conferences/act.php
- National Institute on the Teaching of Psychology
  http://nitop.org
- Lilly Conferences on College and University Teaching and Learning
  http://lillyconferences.com
- Teaching Professor conferences
  http://teachingprofessor.com/conferences
- Directory of national and international conferences from the Center for Excellence in Teaching and Learning at Kennesaw State University
  https://cetl.kennesaw.edu/conferences

conferences where SoTL is welcomed). Within the STP, the Graduate Student Teaching Association (GSTA) and Early Career Psychologists Committee (ECP) also frequently organize workshops, symposia, and meet-ups at various conferences. As a graduate student, you will automatically become a member of the GSTA by joining the STP for a nominal fee. Members are encouraged to contribute teaching tips, activities, demonstrations, and new SoTL research findings to the GSTA blog (http://teachpsych. org/page-1784686).

In addition to attending international, national, and regional conferences on teaching and learning, you might also think about presenting your work to your colleagues within your department or institution. Taking part in faculty development workshops is another way to spread the word about your research, and may serve to improve student learning at your home institution. Many colleges now have Teaching and Learning Centers that encourage faculty presentations and workshops, in addition to providing other valuable resources to support teaching (see Box 1.2 on Locating Resources for Student-Centered Teaching). Attending conferences and reading SoTL articles contributes to your professional development as a teacher and underscores your commitment to stay current in the field. Attending conferences also provides opportunities to interact and potentially develop collaborations with like-minded people who value SoTL, and so often acts as a catalyst for new research projects (Lawrence & Wilson, 2014).

In the past, SoTL research was relatively undervalued in comparison to research in other subdisciplines of psychology (this may be due in part to the relatively low impact factors of journals that publish SoTL), but growing numbers of higher education institutions are now recognizing its validity as a scholarly activity (Bartsch & Dickson, 2015; Hutchings, Huber, & Ciccone, 2011; Ruchensky & Huss, 2015). Consequently, at many institutions, SoTL bears increasing weight in hiring, tenure, and promotion decisions (Bartsch & Dickson, 2015; Hutchings et al., 2011; Ruchensky & Huss, 2015). Bartsch and Dickson (2015) make the point that engaging in SoTL not only demonstrates your prowess as a scholar, but also highlights your efficacy and commitment as a teacher, as well as your willingness to engage in the assessment process in general, which may make you a highly sought-after colleague. When presenting your application to a personnel committee, it is often helpful to contextualize the importance of your scholarly achievements. Ruchensky and Huss (2015) suggest, for example, that committees may view a publication in a journal like *Teaching of Psychology*, which has a relatively low impact factor, more favorably if you report that the journal's rejection rate is 80% and that SoTL is a specialized subfield.

Several researchers have noted a shift in SoTL, and those taking an activist-constructivist stance have helped move the role of undergraduates from research participants to members of the SoTL research team, which is consistent with the spirit of participatory action research (Allin, 2014; Felten et al., 2013; McKinney, 2012; Werder & Otis, 2010). Felten et al. (2013) point out that collaborating with students in SoTL projects may not only empower and motivate them to be more involved in the evolution of their learning, but should also increase the richness of SoTL by including their perspectives and priorities, and using their expertise to refine instruments and methodologies (Werder, Thibou, & Kaufer, 2012). Undergraduates have participated in SoTL research as paid interns (Butcher & Maunder, 2014; Partridge & Sandover, 2010) and as consultants (Burke, 2013; Cohen et al., 2013; Weller, Domarkaite, Lam, & Metta, 2013; Werder et al., 2012).

These studies found that student involvement facilitated the research process and yielded multiple benefits for the students, including increased agency for their learning and a better understanding of research in general.

9.5   Mentoring Student Research

Alternatively, students may get involved in instructor-mentored research in areas outside of SoTL. Students often engage in research after taking a related class with a particular instructor. Many start by volunteering as a research assistant; others enroll in research-related independent study courses, and may work on a capstone project or honors thesis. Engaging in instructor-mentored research increases the amount of student–faculty contact, and so is considered a high-impact practice and has been linked to increased student retention (Kuh, 2008). Undergraduates who participate in mentored research activities across various disciplines have been shown to have increased awareness and interest in related careers, and higher graduation rates; the impact is particularly high for members of under-represented groups (for review, see Thiry, Weston, Laursen, & Hunter, 2012).

When students join a lab, they become part of a research community in which mentoring is shared among a network of people, including more experienced undergraduates and graduate students (Thiry & Laursen, 2011). Students new to research often benefit from working with more experienced students in zones of proximal development, where their knowledge and skills are developed incrementally through hands-on experiences (Vygotsky, 1978). Such experiences allow students to engage in authentic tasks and to develop an appreciation that research is a collaborative and iterative process that requires a great deal of patience and perseverance (Thiry et al., 2012). Students engaging in undergraduate research assistantships in psychology in particular have reported that this experience improved their abilities to analyze data, use statistical programs, and write papers, as well as their teamwork, leadership, and time-management skills and self-confidence (Landrum & Nelsen, 2002).

The exact nature of the mentoring relationship often depends on the number of students that the instructor is mentoring. Graduate students are likely to have more frequent interactions with their mentees than are faculty members, who have to oversee entire labs. In either case, students do best when they work closely with at least one other person who provides direct guidance and helps them to see how their role fits into the larger research project (Thiry & Laursen, 2011). After reviewing 60 studies investigating students' perceptions of their research experiences, Linn, Palmer, Baranger, Gerard, and Stone (2015) recommended that mentors focus on understanding the expectations of their mentees at the outset of the research experience, in addition to encouraging students to formally reflect on their development as scientists. Colbert-White and Simpson (2017) provide a potentially useful workbook for structuring goals and reflections for mentees engaging in a program of supervised research. They suggest that research mentors should meet with mentees at least three times during the semester to ensure that they are progressing and are receiving enough support, with the goal that the mentees become increasingly autonomous as they learn about as many aspects of the research process as possible. The three meetings suggested by Colbert-White and Simpson (2017) correspond to an early-semester meeting to establish expectations, set goals, and work out a timeline, a mid-semester meeting to reevaluate goals, set new goals, and discuss the student's experiences, and a final meeting to reassess goals, discuss accomplishments, share constructive feedback, and discuss future goals. These would be in addition to other meetings where the mentee learns the ropes of working in the lab and completes assigned tasks.

When advising students, you might want to share information about the National Science Foundation (NSF) Research Experiences for Undergraduates (REU) program, which funds summer-long research internships at many institutions, as well as grants for undergraduate research that are available through the Psi Chi International Honor Society in Psychology and other organizations. At many institutions, undergraduate research is supported through the Ronald E. McNair Postbaccalaureate Achievement program. This U.S. Department of Education program provides financial support for students from disadvantaged backgrounds who demonstrate strong academic potential for doctoral studies (https://www2.ed.gov/programs/triomcnair/index.html). In addition to working closely with a faculty mentor on a research project, McNair scholars also receive other supports that increase the likelihood of their admission to a doctoral program.

Students can benefit from presenting at research conferences that are especially tailored for first-time junior presenters; these include undergraduate research conferences (e.g., the National Conference on Undergraduate Research, the National Collegiate Honors Council Conference) and regional conferences that have special poster sessions for undergraduate research (e.g., the Eastern Psychological Association). Some journals also specialize in publishing undergraduate research, and so provide students a chance to increase their cultural capital as research scientists (e.g., *Psi Chi Journal of Psychological Research, Journal of Psychology and the Behavioral Sciences*); for a comprehensive list, see https://www.cur.org/resources/students/undergraduate_journals/.

9.6   Self-Assessment

As we have pointed out, engaging in systematic, meaningful self-reflection about your teaching efficacy is one of the hallmarks of a scientist-educator (Richmond et al., 2014). A first step in this process might be to keep a teaching diary, in which you write brief notes after every class documenting how the class went and noting improvements that are needed in the future. A second step would be to use these to create developmental or formative portfolios for each course that you teach, in which you summarize your reflections. These can provide the foundations for a summative teaching portfolio (see Section 9.7) that showcases your efficacy as an instructor across several courses (Gross Davis, 2009). Course portfolios are relatively concise (10–12 pages, plus appendices), and include the course's objectives and content (supported by related artifacts like the syllabus, assignments, etc.), a record of how it was structured to achieve those objectives, and a reflection on each of these elements (Bernstein, Burnett, Goodburn, & Savory, 2006).

Assessing whether students met a course's LOs is an excellent way to begin the creation of a course portfolio; for each LO, provide a description of the relevant activities/assignments, samples of student work (preferably with your feedback), and summaries of the grades achieved, along with the student feedback you have collected. Then write an evaluative commentary with suggestions for improvements. Engaging in this kind of self-assessment benefits you (and your future students) in several ways, foremost by fostering a sense of responsibility for your students' learning (Smith & Tillema, 2001). Self-assessment will encourage you to adopt a more student-centered approach to teaching and help you to monitor your growth as a professional (De Rijdt, Tiquet, Dochy, & Devolder, 2006). As you develop your course portfolio, you may want to share it with colleagues, who can offer insights for further improvement; alternatively, they might use it as a model to teach similar courses (Schafer, Hammer, & Berntsen, 2012). Developing a course portfolio can also be the prelude to planning a SoTL research study within your class (Bernstein, 2010), where you intentionally set out to study whether an intervention has benefits by comparing student performance before and after its implementation (e.g., by analyzing exam results, papers, journals, and other assignments; for more information on SoTL, see Section 9.4).

9.7 Developing a Teaching Portfolio

Several authors (e.g., Bernstein et al., 2006; Seldin, Miller, & Seldin, 2010) have suggested that although teaching can take a great deal of time, it is often less valued in academia compared to research activities. One reason for this is that teaching excellence is often hard to evaluate, whereas research excellence is measurable by tangible products, such as publications and grants. One suggested solution is for instructors to create summative teaching portfolios that evaluate and showcase their teaching efficacy in a systematic and scholarly way (Bernstein et al., 2006; Seldin et al., 2010). Summative portfolios are increasingly valued by committees making hiring, tenure, promotion, and teaching award decisions (Seldin et al., 2010).

As we suggested in Section 9.6, as you grow your teaching practice, your developmental or formative course portfolios (indicating how you made changes in your courses over time) can be used to build a more comprehensive evaluative portfolio (Gross Davis, 2009). Like their formative counterparts, summative portfolios should be concise documents that reflect on the intention and design of your courses and the efficacy of your instructional methods, with artifacts (collated in appendices) to provide supporting evidence (Bernstein et al., 2006). Information should be summarized in a clear and concise fashion; see Seldin et al. (2010) for many excellent examples of how to do this. Teaching portfolios reflect your goals as an instructor, and will change over time as you increase your mastery; hence, no two portfolios are the same (Ouellett, 2007). That said, there are some basic elements that should be present in your teaching portfolio (see Box 9.3). Of particular importance is the inclusion of a statement of your teaching philosophy, which is a self-reflective, authentic, and deeply considered written statement describing your approach to teaching. We provide advice about writing a teaching philosophy statement in the next and final section of this chapter.

9.8 Writing a Teaching Philosophy Statement

Your teaching philosophy statement is probably the most critical component of your teaching portfolio with respect to the academic job market. In their survey of online job postings in the 2004–05 academic year, Meizlish and Kaplan (2008) found that nearly one-third of postings across six disciplines (including psychology) requested some form

---

Box 9.3 Creating a Summative Teaching Portfolio

Sample graduate student teaching portfolios
http://www.ctl.uga.edu/pages/portfolio-program
http://cte.virginia.edu/resources/developing-a-teaching-portfolio/

Elements to include in a teaching portfolio
These items often reflect the past 4 years of teaching:

- Table of contents
- Teaching philosophy statement
- Summary of courses taught (include course names, numbers, and average enrollments) and students mentored
- Explanation of how courses are constructed, with illustrative examples from course syllabi
- Course syllabi (in appendix)
- Evidence of teaching efficacy, including peer observations, summative student evaluations, statement by Department Chair, and teaching awards
- Evidence of student learning, including summary of course and assignment grades and distributions, samples of student work (often with instructor feedback), and list of student successes (awards, co-authored student conference presentations and publications, and graduate school acceptance/attendance)
- Reflective commentary on innovations and changes made to courses, with evidence of their success
- Evidence of commitment to professional development, such as SoTL publications and conference presentations, and attendance at pedagogy-related conferences and workshops
- Goals for future teaching

(LaVelle, 1999; Seldin, Miller, & Seldin, 2010)

---

of written evidence of the candidate's approach to teaching; follow-up surveys of search committees revealed that nearly 57% required a statement of teaching philosophy at some point in the process, as they felt that such as statement was an important way to assess a candidate's teaching ability and potential. Even when teaching philosophy statements were not explicitly requested, search committees responded favorably to having them in the applicant's file (Meizlish & Kaplan, 2008).

There is, however, an even more important audience for a teaching philosophy statement—namely, you! Self-reflection is a key feature of being a scientist-educator, and formalizing your teaching philosophy in a succinct written format allows you to reflect critically and holistically on the evolution of your teaching practice (University of Minnesota Center for Educational Innovation, n.d.). Teaching philosophies typically improve with experience, but even new instructors can benefit from writing a statement before stepping into the classroom for the first time, for the following reasons:

- It encourages you to think more deeply about how students learn, which helps to shift the focus from what you are teaching to what your students are learning.
- It encourages you to think about the diversity of students in your classes, and how instruction should be designed to engage all students and to build more inclusive and respectful communities.

- It provides an orienting framework to guide you in making the myriad and minute decisions that are required to develop and teach a course, by keeping the focus on the needs of your students.
- It forces you to ask why certain topics need to be included while others may be excluded in the overall scheme of how a course is taught.
- It encourages you to consider what sorts of skills and knowledge you expect students to gain in your classes. Making learning goals explicit helps students to see beyond the next exam and creates a coherent rationale for what you are asking them to do.
- It guides the manner in which you develop specific assignments. Prioritizing learning goals allows you to consider the value of multiple assessments in relation to those goals.
- It sets the foundation for thinking about your teaching as a process and not a product, which leads to increased awareness that *how* you teach changes in different circumstances, and evolves over time.
- If you are a graduate student or are early in your career, it helps you to consider possible answers to interviewer questions about prior teaching experiences and how to support student learning.
- It directs attention to the types of institutions that are compatible with your perspectives and interests in teaching.

Despite the benefits of developing a teaching philosophy prior to teaching a college course for the first time, we recognize that this may be a daunting task if you have not yet had a chance to try out and adapt evidence-based active teaching methods yourself. However, going through the steps that we suggest below can help you to develop your own voice—one that is sufficiently confident to craft an authentic statement about who you are (or hope to be) as a teacher. Remember to first think deeply about how you will cultivate a student-centered learning environment, then worry about developing your teaching philosophy into a written statement. There are myriad resources designed to assist in the process of writing a teaching philosophy statement. Many institutional teaching and learning centers make materials and tutorials publicly available that chronicle suggested steps for developing a philosophy (see Box 9.4).

One way to start writing a teaching statement is by asking some big-picture questions regarding what you want your students to learn (Goodyear & Alchin, 1998; O'Neal, Meizlish, & Kaplan, 2007). These should reflect the disciplinary context; for example,

---

Box 9.4 Resources for Writing a Statement of Teaching Philosophy

Guidance on Writing Your Teaching Philosophy, from the University of Minnesota Center for Educational Innovation: https://cei.umn.edu/writing-your-teaching-philosophy.

Kaplan, M., O'Neal, C., Meizlish, D., Carillo, R., & Kardia, D. (2005). Rubric for statements of teaching philosophy, from the University of Michigan Center for Research on Learning and Teaching: http://www.crlt.umich.edu/sites/default/files/resource_files/TeachingPhilosophyRubric.pdf.

Kearns, K. D., & Sullivan, C. S. (2011). Resources and practices to help graduate students and postdoctoral fellows write statements of teaching philosophy. *Advances in Physiology Education*, 35(2), 136–145.

Teaching Philosophy Rubric, from the University of Minnesota Center for Educational Innovation: https://drive.google.com/file/d/0B5x7J1Vso_k6dE52LTdKclhqaEk/view.

the APA's (2013) five overarching learning goals for the psychology major, and the STP's taskforce emphasis on the development of scientific literacy and other competencies that you would expect in a liberal arts college, such as oral and written communication skills (Richmond et al., 2014). It is often helpful to articulate these goals by describing how the student walking out of the final exam of your course is different from the one who entered your class on the first day of class (Lang, 2010). Some big-picture questions that you might consider in thinking about your philosophy include:

- What is the value of a college degree today?
- What are essential skills for success in today's economy?
- How can training in psychological science advance those skills?
- How might training in psychology address current public policy concerns?

The next step is to provide concrete examples of how you (will) teach in a student-centered class. From a practical standpoint, the approaches you will use in any particular class will be determined by the level of the class and the foundational preparation of the students, the size of the class, and the modality of the course (e.g., in-class, on-line, hybrid) (Lang, 2010). Try to describe why you believe the selected methods will lead to the desired learning outcomes (O'Neal et al., 2007). Avoid using generic language about "the importance of active learning"; a statement written at this level of abstraction is less likely to be taken seriously by your readers, because it suggests a lack of in-depth analysis of your teaching practices (Kaplan, Meizlish, O'Neal, & Wright, 2007). Instead, provide examples of how a particular construct readily lends itself to group work or hands-on exploration. If you have taught your own classes or have been a teaching assistant for another instructor, you will have experience to draw on when making the link between your own values and your goals for your students. The more specific examples you can provide, the better (Lang, 2010). For example, you might allow students an opportunity to respond to feedback on an early draft of an assignment because you value mastery over performance goals and you view enhancing written communication as an important goal. Even if you have not yet taught your own class, you can still draw on your own experiences as a student to illustrate how you plan to approach a certain topic (e.g., "Ever since a class in which I created a podcast about the functions of neurons, I have had a clear grasp of that challenging construct"). Selectively tell stories of great and perhaps not-so-great moments in your classes (Kearns & Sullivan, 2011). Reflect on how the good moments became deep learning experiences for your students (and, perhaps, for you as well); writing about these in conjunction with what you learned from your less successful moments demonstrates the ways in which your current teaching practices are evidence-based.

Given the increased diversity in today's college population, it is increasingly important that instructors describe how they create inclusive learning environments in the teaching statement (O'Neal et al., 2007). Again, give specific examples—such as having students sit in a circle instead of in rows because you value an inclusive and participatory classroom. Describe how you create a safe environment for students to engage in difficult dialogs about race, gender, sexual orientation, social class, and privilege, and demonstrate how you teach in ways that are culturally sensitive. Articulate the ways in which you use Universal Design (UD) by describing in detail how the needs of the most vulnerable students are met in your classes, and how this approach benefits all of your students.

Consistent with backward course design, your teaching philosophy should show explicit links between your goals for student learning and how you assess learning outcomes. Provide the rationale for your decisions, along with illustrative examples of the different types of formative assessment (e.g., weekly quizzes, homework assignments, discussion prompts, journal entries) that you use to encourage student learning (Kearns & Sullivan, 2011). Also, describe your use of summative assessments, such as class projects and presentations, short-answer exam questions, and podcasts, to illustrate that, consistent with the flexibility principle of UD, you use a variety of methods to assess student learning. The teaching philosophy statement also provides an opportunity for you to demonstrate how acting as a mentor to undergraduates in a research lab environment, or in other outside-of-the-classroom experiences such as service learning, volunteer work, or a psychology club, has contributed to your students' learning. Finally, include examples of how you have used assessment data to modify a teaching method or assignment to demonstrate your efforts to "close the assessment loop" (Angelo & Cross, 1993) and showcase your use of a scientist-educator approach.

Once you have thought through your underlying teaching philosophy, the next step is to record the statement in written form. Basic principles of strong writing apply. Focus on the structure, rhetoric, and language of your statement, as you would for any published work (O'Neal et al., 2007). The resources listed in Box 9.4 provide more explicit guidance about structuring the written product. For example, Kearns and Sullivan (2011) suggest developing a metaphor for your teaching in the opening paragraph of your statement and advancing it with specific examples throughout the document. Other resources emphasize principles of good writing, such as keeping the statement concise (Montell, 2003) and checking for grammar, spelling, and organization (Kaplan et al., 2007). Most importantly, make sure your statement reflects clearly who you are, with humility and accuracy (Korn, 2012).

While your students will clearly experience your teaching philosophy through your course syllabus, class activities, assignments, and choice of assessments, we suggest that you share it with them explicitly by making your written teaching philosophy statement available to them (perhaps via the CMS), and by referring to it in your syllabus and when introducing activities and assignments. This approach shows that you respect your students' intelligence and that you care deeply about teaching and about their personal development (Goodyear & Alchin, 1998).

9.9   Summary

1) Ethical teachers maximize student learning by adopting a scientist-educator approach to teaching and using evidence-based teaching methods.
2) Scientist-educators engage in professional development to ensure that they are current in the fields that they are teaching, as well as in the scholarship of teaching and learning.
3) Scientist-educators assess and self-reflect about the efficacy of their pedagogy and institute and evaluate new practices to enhance student learning and personal development.

References

Abrami, P. C., Bernard, R. M., Borokhovski, E., Wade, A., Surkes, M. A., Tamim, R., & Zhang, D. (2008). Instructional interventions affecting critical thinking skills and dispositions: A stage 1 meta-analysis. *Review of Educational Research*, 78(4), 1102–1134.

Academy for Co-Teaching and Collaboration at St. Cloud State University. (2012). Collaboration self-assessment tool. Retrieved from https://www.stcloudstate.edu/oce/_files/documents/coteaching/CollaborationtoolCSAT.pdf.

Acee, T. W., & Weinstein, C. E. (2010). Effects of a value-reappraisal intervention on statistics students' motivation and performance. *Journal of Experimental Education*, 78(4), 487–512.

Adam, A., & Manson, T. M. (2014). Using a pseudoscience activity to teach critical thinking. *Teaching of Psychology*, 41(2), 130–134.

Adams, C. (2006). PowerPoint, habits of mind, and classroom culture. *Journal of Curriculum Studies*, 38(4), 389–411.

Adams, M. J., & Umbach, P. D. (2012). Nonresponse and online student evaluations of teaching: Understanding the influence of salience, fatigue, and academic environments. *Research in Higher Education*, 53(5), 576–591.

Agarwal, P. K., D'Antonio, L., Roediger, H. L. III, McDermott, K. B., & McDaniel, M. A. (2014). Classroom-based programs of retrieval practice reduce middle school and high school students' test anxiety. *Journal of Applied Research in Memory and Cognition*, 3(3), 131–139.

Agarwal, P. K., Karpicke, J. D., Kang, S. H., Roediger, H. L. III, & McDermott, K. B. (2008). Examining the testing effect with open- and closed-book tests. *Applied Cognitive Psychology*, 22(7), 861–876.

Agarwal, P. K., & Roediger, H. L. III (2011). Expectancy of an open-book test decreases performance on a delayed closed-book test. *Memory*, 19(8), 836–852.

Aggarwal, P., & O'Brien, C. L. (2008). Social loafing on group projects: Structural antecedents and effect on student satisfaction. *Journal of Marketing Education*, 30, 255–264.

Alberts, H. C., Hazen, H. D., & Theobald, R. B. (2010). Classroom incivilities: The challenge of interactions between college students and instructors in the U.S. *Journal of Geography in Higher Education*, 34(3), 439–462.

Alexander-Snow, M. (2004). Dynamics of gender, ethnicity, and race in understanding classroom incivility. *New Directions for Teaching and Learning*, 2004(99), 21–31.

Teaching Psychology: An Evidence-Based Approach, First Edition. Jillian Grose-Fifer, Patricia J. Brooks, and Maureen O'Connor.
© 2019 John Wiley & Sons, Inc. Published 2019 by John Wiley & Sons, Inc.
Companion website: www.wiley.com/go/Grose-Fifer/teaching-psychology

Alfieri, L., Brooks, P. J., Aldrich, N. J., & Tenenbaum, H. R. (2011). Does discovery-based instruction enhance learning? *Journal of Educational Psychology*, 103(1), 1–18.

Aliaga, M., Cobb, G., Cuff, C., Garfield, J., Gould, R., Lock, R., … Utts, J. (2005). Guidelines for assessment and instruction in statistics education (GAISE): college report. Retrieved from http://www.amstat.org/education/gaise/GaiseCollege_Full.pdf.

Alicke, M. D., Klotz, M. L., Breitenbecher, D. L., Yurak, T. J., & Vredenburg, D. S. (1995). Personal contact, individuation, and the better-than-average effect. *Journal of Personality and Social Psychology*, 68(5), 804–825.

Allen, G. J., Lerner, W. M., & Hinrichsen, J. J. (1972). Study behaviors and their relationships to test anxiety and academic performance. *Psychological Reports*, 30(2), 407–410.

Allen, I. E., & Seaman, J. (2016). Online report card: Tracking online education in the United States. Babson Park, MA: Babson Survey Research Group. Retrieved from the Education Advisory Board website: http://onlinelearningsurvey.com/reports/onlinereportcard.pdf.

Allen, M., Berkowitz, S., Hunt, S., & Louden, A. (1999). A meta-analysis of the impact of forensics and communication education on critical thinking. *Communication Education*, 48(1), 18–30.

Alley, M., Schreiber, M., Ramsdell, K., & Muffo, J. (2006). How the design of headlines in presentation slides affects audience retention. *Technical Communication*, 53(2), 225–234.

Allin, L. (2014). Collaboration between staff and students in the scholarship of teaching and learning: The potential and the problems. *Teaching and Learning Inquiry*, 2(1), 95–102.

Alter, C., & Adkins, C. (2006). Assessing student writing proficiency in graduate schools of social work. *Journal of Social Work Education*, 42(2), 337–354.

Ambler, M. (1998). Land-based colleges offer science students a sense of place. *Tribal College*, 10(1), 6–8.

American Assocation of University Professors. (2014). On trigger warnings. Retrieved from https://www.aaup.org/report/trigger-warnings.

American Association of University Professors. (2009). Statement of professional ethics. Retrieved from the American Association of University Professors website: https://www.aaup.org/report/statement-professional-ethics#b1.

American College Health Association. (2016). National college health assessment II: Reference group executive summary fall 2016. Hanover, MD: American College Health. Retrieved from http://www.acha-ncha.org/docs/NCHA-II_FALL_2016_REFERENCE_GROUP_EXECUTIVE_SUMMARY.pdf.

American Psychological Association. (2012). Guidelines for psychological practice with lesbian, gay, and bisexual clients. Retrieved from http://www.apa.org/pubs/journals/features/amp-a0024659.pdf.

American Psychological Association. (2013). APA guidelines for the undergraduate psychology major. Version 2.0. Retrieved from http://www.apa.org/ed/precollege/about/psymajor-guidelines.pdf.

American Psychological Association. (2015). Guidelines for psychological practice with transgender and gender nonconforming clients. Retrieved from http://www.apa.org/practice/guidelines/transgender.pdf.

American Psychological Association. (2017a). Ethical principles of psychologists and code of conduct. Retrieved from the American Psychological Association website: http://www.apa.org/ethics/code/ethics-code-2017.pdf.

American Psychological Association. (2017b). Multicultural guidelines: An ecological approach to context, identity, and intersectionality. Retrieved from http://www.apa.org/about/policy/multicultural-guidelines.pdf.

American Psychological Association, Center for Workforce Studies. (2014). Frequently asked questions about psychology workforce. Retrieved from http://www.apa.org/workforce/about/faq.aspx#II.3.

Ames, C. (1992). Classrooms: Goals, structures, and student motivation. *Journal of Educational Psychology*, 84(3), 261–271.

Anderson, D. D. (1992). Using feature films as tools for analysis in a psychology and law course. *Teaching of Psychology*, 19(3), 155–158.

Anderson, L., Kinnair, D., Hardy, P., & Sumner, T. (2012). They just don't get it: Using digital stories to promote meaningful undergraduate reflection. *Medical Teacher*, 34(7), 597–598.

Anderson, L. W. E., Krathwohl, D. R. E., Airasian, P. W., Cruikshank, K. A., Mayer, R. E., Pintrich, P. R., ... Wittrock, M. C. (2001). *A taxonomy for learning, teaching, and assessing: A revision of Bloom's taxonomy of educational objectives*. New York, NY: Longman.

Anderson, M. (2017). Digital divide persists even as lower-income Americans make gains in tech adoption. Pew Research Center. Retrieved from http://www.pewresearch.org/fact-tank/2017/03/22/digital-divide-persists-even-as-lower-income-americans-make-gains-in-tech-adoption/.

Anderson, V., & Walvoord, B. (1998). *Effective grading: A tool for learning and assessment*. San Francisco, CA: Jossey Bass.

Andrade, H. G. (1997). Understanding rubrics. *Educational Leadership*, 54(4), 14–17.

Angelo, T. A., & Cross, K. P. (1993). *Classroom assessment techniques*. San Francisco, CA: Jossey-Bass.

Anthis, K. (2011). Is it the clicker, or is it the question? Untangling the effects of student response system use. *Teaching of Psychology*, 38(3), 189–193.

Arkorful, V., & Abaidoo, N. (2015). The role of e-learning, advantages and disadvantages of its adoption in higher education. *International Journal of Instructional Technology and Distance Learning*, 12(1), 29–42.

Arnold, K. M., & McDermott, K. B. (2013a). Free recall enhances subsequent learning. *Psychonomic Bulletin and Review*, 20(3), 507–513.

Arnold, K. M., & McDermott, K. B. (2013b). Test-potentiated learning: Distinguishing between direct and indirect effects of tests. *Journal of Experimental Psychology: Learning, Memory, and Cognition*, 39(3), 940–945.

Arnott, E., & Dust, M. (2012). Combating unintended consequences of in-class revision using study skills training. *Psychology Learning and Teaching*, 11(1), 99–104.

Aronson, E., Blaney, N., Stephin, C., Sikes, J., & Snapp, M. (1978). *The jigsaw classroom*. Beverly Hills, CA: Sage Publishing Company.

Aronson, J., Fried, C. B., & Good, C. (2002). Reducing the effects of stereotype threat on African American college students by shaping theories of intelligence. *Journal of Experimental Social Psychology*, 38(2), 113–125.

Arslan, R. Ş., & Şahin-Kızıl, A. (2010). How can the use of blog software facilitate the writing process of English language learners? *Computer Assisted Language Learning*, 23(3), 183–197.

Arum, R., & Roksa, J. (2011). *Academically adrift: Limited learning on college campuses*. Chicago, IL: University of Chicago Press.

Ash, K. (2012). Educators view 'flipped' model with a more critical eye. *Education Week*, 32(2), S6–S7.

Ash, S. L., & Clayton, P. H. (2009). Generating, deepening, and documenting learning: The power of critical reflection in applied learning. *Journal of Applied Learning in Higher Education*, 1, 25–48.

Association for Psychological Science (2013). What we know now: How psychological science has changed over a quarter century. *APS Observer*, 26, Retrieved from http://www.psychologicalscience.org/index.php/publications/observer/2013/november-13/what-we-know-now-how-psychological-science-has-changed-over-a-quarter-century.html.

Association of College and Research Libraries. (2015). Framework for information literacy for higher education. Document ID: b910a6c4-6c8a-0d44-7dbc-a5dcbd509e3f. Retrieved from http://www.ala.org/acrl/standards/ilframework.

Association of American Colleges and Universities. (2015). Essential learning outcomes. Retrieved from http://www.aacu.org/sites/default/files/files/LEAP/IntroToLEAP2015.pdf.

Au, W. (2007). High-stakes testing and curricular control: A qualitative metasynthesis. *Educational researcher*, 36(5), 258–267.

Au, W., & Tempel, M. B. (Eds.) (2012). *Pencils down: Rethinking high-stakes testing and accountability in public schools*. Milwaukee, WI: Rethinking Schools.

Avery, R. J., Bryant, W. K., Mathios, A., Kang, H., & Bell, D. (2006). Electronic course evaluations: Does an online delivery system influence student evaluations? *Journal of Economic Education*, 37(1), 21–37.

Badura, A. S. (2002). Capturing students' attention: Movie clips set the stage for learning in abnormal psychology. *Teaching of Psychology*, 29(1), 58–60.

Bahrick, H. P., & Hall, L. K. (2005). The importance of retrieval failures to long-term retention: A metacognitive explanation of the spacing effect. *Journal of Memory and Language*, 52(4), 566–577.

Bailey, E., Jensen, J., Nelson, J., Wiberg, H., & Bell, J. (2017). Weekly formative exams and creative grading enhance student learning in an introductory biology course. *CBE-Life Sciences Education*, 16(1), ar2.

Bain, K. (2011). *What the best college teachers do*. Boston, MA: Harvard University Press.

Baker, A., Goodman, J. D., & Mueller, B. (2015, June 13). Beyond the chokehold: The path to Eric Garner's death. *The New York Times*. Retrieved from https://www.nytimes.com/2015/06/14/nyregion/eric-garner-police-chokehold-staten-island.html.

Balch, W. R. (2006). Encouraging distributed study: A classroom experiment on the spacing effect. *Teaching of Psychology*, 33(4), 249–252.

Baloğlu, M. (2003). Individual differences in statistics anxiety among college students. *Personality and Individual Differences*, 34(5), 855–865.

Barefoot, B. O. (Ed.) (1993). *Exploring the evidence: Reporting outcomes of freshman seminars. The freshman year experience. (monograph series no. 11)*. Columbia, SC: National Resource Center for the Freshman Year Experience, University of South Carolina.

Barkley, E. F., Cross, K. P., & Major, C. H. (2014). *Collaborative learning techniques: A handbook for college faculty*. San Francisco, CA: Jossey Bass.

Barr, R. B., & Tagg, J. (1995). From teaching to learning—A new paradigm for undergraduate education. *Change: The Magazine of Higher Learning*, 27(6), 12–26.

Barr, T. F., Dixon, A. L., & Gassenheimer, J. B. (2005). Exploring the "lone wolf" phenomenon in student teams. *Journal of Marketing Education*, 27(1), 81–90.

Barrett, H. (2006). Researching and evaluating digital storytelling as a deep learning tool. In *Society for Information Technology & Teacher Education (SITE) international conference* (Vol. 1) (pp. 647). Orlando, FL. Retrieved from https://www.learntechlib.org/p/22117/.

Barrows, H. S. (1996). Problem-based learning in medicine and beyond: A brief overview. *New Directions for Teaching and Learning*, 1996(68), 3–12.

Bartels, J. M., Milovich, M. M., & Moussier, S. (2016). Coverage of the Stanford prison experiment in introductory psychology courses: A survey of introductory psychology instructors. *Teaching of Psychology*, 43(2), 136–141.

Bartholomae, D. (1980). The study of error. *College Composition and Communication*, 31(3), 253–269.

Barton, M., & Cummings, R. (2009). *Wiki writing: Collaborative learning in the college classroom*. Ann Arbor, MI: University of Michigan Press.

Bartsch, R. A., & Dickson, K. (2015). How SoTL can aid in the academic job search. In R. Smith, & B. Schwartz (Eds.), *Using SoTL to enhance your academic position*. Retrieved from the Society for the Teaching of Psychology website: http://teachpsych.org/ebooks/.

Bates, J. A. (1991). Teaching hypothesis testing by debunking a demonstration of telepathy. *Teaching of Psychology*, 18(2), 94–97.

Batsell, W. R. Jr., Perry, J. L., Hanley, E., & Hostetter, A. B. (2017). Ecological validity of the testing effect: The use of daily quizzes in introductory psychology. *Teaching of Psychology*, 44(1), 18–23.

Baumeister, R. F., Bratslavsky, E., Finkenauer, C., & Vohs, K. D. (2001). Bad is stronger than good. *Review of General Psychology*, 5(4), 323–370.

Beagley, J. E., & Capaldi, M. (2016). The effect of cumulative tests on the final exam. *Problems, Resources, and Issues in Mathematics*, 26(9), 878–888.

Bean, J. C. (2011). *Engaging ideas: The professor's guide to integrating writing, critical thinking, and active learning in the classroom*. San Francisco, CA: John Wiley & Sons.

Beason, L. (1993). Feedback and revision in writing across the curriculum classes. *Research in the Teaching of English*, 27(4), 395–422.

Beatty, I. D., & Gerace, W. J. (2009). Technology-enhanced formative assessment: A research-based pedagogy for teaching science with classroom response technology. *Journal of Science Education and Technology*, 18(2), 146–162.

Beatty, I. D., Gerace, W. J., Leonard, W. J., & Dufresne, R. J. (2006). Designing effective questions for classroom response system teaching. *American Journal of Physics*, 74(1), 31–39.

Bedard, K., & Kuhn, P. (2008). Where class size really matters: Class size and student ratings of instructor effectiveness. *Economics of Education Review*, 27(3), 253–265.

Beemyn, G., & Rankin, S. R. (2011). Introduction to the special issue on "LGBTQ campus experiences." *Journal of Homosexuality*, 58(9), 1159–1164.

Beilock, S. L. (2008). Math performance in stressful situations. *Current Directions in Psychological Science*, 17(5), 339–343.

Beilock, S. L., & Carr, T. H. (2005). When high-powered people fail: Working memory and "choking under pressure" in math. *Psychological Science*, 16(2), 101–105.

Beins, B. C. (1993). Using the Barnum effect to teach about ethics and deception in research. *Teaching of Psychology*, 20(1), 33–35.

Beins, B. C., & Beins, A. M. (2011). *Effective writing in psychology: Papers, posters, and presentations*. Hoboken, NJ: John Wiley & Sons.

Beins, B. C., Smith, R. A., & Dunn, D. S. (2010). Writing for psychology majors as a developmental process. In D. S. Dunn, B. C. Beins, M. A. McCarthy, & G. A. Hill, IV (Eds.),

Best practices for teaching beginnings and endings in the psychology major: Research, cases, and recommendations (pp. 253–278). New York, NY: Oxford University Press.

Bell, J. H. (2000). When hard questions are asked: Evaluating writing centers. *The Writing Center Journal*, 21(1), 7–28.

Belous, C. K., & Bauman, M. L. (2017). What's in a name? Exploring pansexuality online. *Journal of Bisexuality*, 17(1), 58–72.

Belter, R. W., & du Pré, A. (2009). A strategy to reduce plagiarism in an undergraduate course. *Teaching of Psychology*, 36(4), 257–261.

Benassi, V. A., & Goldstein, G. S. (2006). Students' beliefs about paranormal claims: Implications for teaching introductory psychology. In D. S. Dunn, & S. L. Chew (Eds.), *Best practices for teaching introduction to psychology* (pp. 225–243). Mahwah, NJ: Erlbaum.

Benedict, L., & Pence, H. E. (2012). Teaching chemistry using student-created videos and photo blogs accessed with smartphones and two-dimensional barcodes. *Journal of Chemical Education*, 89(4), 492–496.

Benjamin, A. S., & Tullis, J. (2010). What makes distributed practice effective? *Cognitive Psychology*, 61(3), 228–247.

Bennett, S., Bishop, A., Dalgarno, B., Waycott, J., & Kennedy, G. (2012). Implementing web 2.0 technologies in higher education: A collective case study. *Computers and Education*, 59(2), 524–534.

Bensley, D. A., Crowe, D. S., Bernhardt, P., Buckner, C., & Allman, A. L. (2010). Teaching and assessing critical thinking skills for argument analysis in psychology. *Teaching of Psychology*, 37(2), 91–96.

Bensley, D. A., & Haynes, C. (1995). The acquisition of general purpose strategic knowledge for argumentation. *Teaching of Psychology*, 22(1), 41–45.

Bensley, D. A., & Murtagh, M. P. (2012). Guidelines for a scientific approach to critical thinking assessment. *Teaching of Psychology*, 39(1), 5–16.

Bergmann, J., & Sams, A. (2012). *Flip your classroom: Reach every student in every class every day*. Eugene, OR: International Society for Technology in Education.

Berk, R. A. (2009). Multimedia teaching with video clips: TV, movies, YouTube, and mtvU in the college classroom. *International Journal of Technology in Teaching and Learning*, 5(1), 1–21.

Berk, R. A. (2011). Research on PowerPoint®: From basic features to multimedia. *International Journal of Technology in Teaching and Learning*, 7(1), 24–35.

Bernstein, D. J. (2010). Finding your place in the scholarship of teaching and learning. *International Journal for the Scholarship of Teaching and Learning*, 4(2), 4.

Bernstein, D. J., Addison, W., Altman, C., Hollister, D., Komarraju, M., Prieto, L., ... Shore, C. (2010). Toward a scientist-educator model of teaching psychology. In D. Halpern (Ed.), *Undergraduate education in psychology: A blueprint for the future* (pp. 29–46). Washington, DC: American Psychological Association.

Bernstein, D. J., Burnett, A. N., Goodburn, A. M., & Savory, P. (2006). *Making teaching and learning visible: Course portfolios and the peer review of teaching*. San Francisco, CA: Jossey Bass.

Berry, J. W., & Chew, S. L. (2008). Improving learning through interventions of student-generated questions and concept maps. *Teaching of Psychology*, 35(4), 305–312.

Berry, T., Cook, L., Hill, N., & Stevens, K. (2010). An exploratory analysis of textbook usage and study habits: Misperceptions and barriers to success. *College Teaching*, 59(1), 31–39.

Bertsch, S., Pesta, B. J., Wiscott, R., & McDaniel, M. A. (2007). The generation effect: A meta-analytic review. *Memory and Cognition*, 35(2), 201–210.

Beyer, A. M. (2011). Improving student presentations: Pecha Kucha and just plain powerpoint. *Teaching of Psychology*, 38(2), 122–126.

Birch, S. A. (2005). When knowledge is a curse: Children's and adults' reasoning about mental states. *Current Directions in Psychological Science*, 14(1), 25–29.

Birkett, M., & Hughes, A. (2013). A collaborative project to integrate information literacy skills into an undergraduate psychology course. *Psychology Learning and Teaching*, 12(1), 96–100.

Birkett, M., Neff, L., & Pieper, S. (2012). Using personal interest portfolios to promote engagement and improve student learning in a large undergraduate course. *Journal on Excellence in College Teaching*, 23(2), 49–67.

Birmingham, C., & McCord, M. (2004). Group process research: Implications for using learning groups. In L. K. Michaelsen, A. B. Knight, & L. D. Fink (Eds.), *Team-based learning: A transformative use of small groups in college teaching* (pp. 73–93). Sterling, VA: Stylus.

Bishop, J. L., & Verleger, M. A. (2013). The flipped classroom: A survey of the research. In American Society for Engineering Education (ASEE) National Conference Proceedings, Atlanta, GA (Vol. 30, pp. 1–18).

Bishop, W. (1990). Bringing writers to the center: Some survey results, surmises, and suggestions. *The Writing Center Journal*, 10(2), 31–44.

Bjork, E. L., & Bjork, R. A. (2011). Making things hard on yourself, but in a good way: Creating desirable difficulties to enhance learning. In M. A. Gernsbacher, R. W. Pew, L. M. Hough, & J. R. Pomerantz (Eds.), *Psychology and the real world: Essays illustrating fundamental contributions to society* (pp. 56–64). New York, NY: Worth.

Bjork, E. L., Soderstrom, N. C., & Little, J. L. (2015). Can multiple-choice testing induce desirable difficulties? Evidence from the laboratory and the classroom. *American Journal of Psychology*, 128(2), 229–239.

Bjork, R. A., Dunlosky, J., & Kornell, N. (2013). Self-regulated learning: Beliefs, techniques, and illusions. *Annual Review of Psychology*, 64, 417–444.

Black, L. J., Wygonik, M. L., & Frey, B. A. (2011). Faculty-preferred strategies to promote a positive classroom environment. *Journal on Excellence in College Teaching*, 22, 109–134.

Bleske-Rechek, A. L. (2001). Obedience, conformity, and social roles: Active learning in a large introductory psychology class. *Teaching of Psychology*, 28(4), 260–262.

Blessing, S. B., & Blessing, J. S. (2010). PsychBusters: A means of fostering critical thinking in the introductory course. *Teaching of Psychology*, 37(3), 178–182.

Blessing, S. B., & Blessing, J. S. (2015). Using a movie as a capstone activity for the introductory course. *Teaching of Psychology*, 42(1), 51–55.

Bliss, C. A., & Lawrence, B. (2009). Is the whole greater than the sum of its parts? A comparison of small group and whole class discussion board activity in online classes. *Journal of Asynchronous Learning Networks*, 13(4), 25–39.

Bloom, C. M., & Lamkin, D. M. (2006). The Olympian struggle to remember the cranial nerves: Mnemonics and student success. *Teaching of Psychology*, 33(2), 128–129.

Blouin, D. D., & Perry, E. M. (2009). Whom does service learning really serve? Community-based organizations' perspectives on service learning. *Teaching Sociology*, 37(2), 120–135.

Bloxham, S., & Campbell, L. (2010). Generating dialogue in assessment feedback: Exploring the use of interactive cover sheets. *Assessment and Evaluation in Higher Education*, 35(3), 291–300.

Blunt, J. R., & Karpicke, J. D. (2014). Learning with retrieval-based concept mapping. *Journal of Educational Psychology*, 106(3), 849–858.

Bodi, S. (2002). How do we bridge the gap between what we teach and what they do? Some thoughts on the place of questions in the process of research. *Journal of Academic Librarianship*, 28(3), 109–114.

Boggs, S., Shore, M., & Shore, J. (2004). Using e-learning platforms for mastery learning in developmental mathematics courses. *Mathematics and Computer Education*, 38(2), 213–220.

Boice, B. (1996). Classroom incivilities. *Research in Higher Education*, 37(4), 453–486.

Bolin, A. U., Khramtsova, I., & Saarnio, D. (2005). Using student journals to stimulate authentic learning: Balancing Bloom's cognitive and affective domains. *Teaching of Psychology*, 32(3), 154–159.

Bolt, M. (2013). *Instructors resources to accompany Myers, D. Psychology* (10th ed.). New York, NY: Worth.

Bower, G. H., & Clark, M. C. (1969). Narrative stories as mediators for serial learning. *Psychonomic Science*, 14(4), 181–182.

Bowles, S., Cunningham, C. J., De La Rosa, G. M., & Picano, J. (2007). Coaching leaders in middle and executive management: Goals, performance, buy-in. *Leadership and Organization Development Journal*, 28(5), 388–408.

Bowles-Terry, M. (2012). Library instruction and academic success: A mixed-methods assessment of a library instruction program. *Evidence Based Library and Information Practice*, 7(1), 82–95.

Bowman, N., Brandenberger, J., Lapsley, D., Hill, P., & Quaranto, J. (2010). Serving in college, flourishing in adulthood: Does community engagement during the college years predict adult well-being? *Applied Psychology: Health and Well-Being*, 2(1), 14–34.

Boyatzis, C. J. (1994). Using feature films to teach social development. *Teaching of Psychology*, 21(2), 99–101.

Boyce, T. E., & Hineline, P. N. (2002). Interteaching: A strategy for enhancing the user-friendliness of behavioral arrangements in the college classroom. *The Behavior Analyst*, 25(2), 215–226.

Boyd, R. (2008). Do people use only 10 percent of their brains? What's the matter with only exploiting a portion of our gray matter? *Scientific American*, Retrieved from https://www.scientificamerican.com/article/do-people-only-use-10-percent-of-their-brains/.

Boysen, G. A. (2012). A guide to writing learning objectives for teachers of psychology. Retrieved from the Society for the Teaching of Psychology website: http://teachpsych.org/resources/Documents/otrp/resources/boysen12.pdf.

Boysen, G. A. (2017). Evidence-based answers to questions about trigger warnings for clinically-based distress: A review for teachers. *Scholarship of Teaching and Learning in Psychology*, 3(2), 163.

Boysen, G. A., & Prieto, L. R. (2018). Trigger warnings in psychology: Psychology teachers' perspectives and practices. *Scholarship of Teaching and Learning in Psychology*, 4(1), 16.

Brady, S. T., Reeves, S. L., Garcia, J., Purdie-Vaughns, V., Cook, J. E., Taborsky-Barba, S., ... Cohen, G. L. (2016). The psychology of the affirmed learner: Spontaneous self-affirmation in the face of stress. *Journal of Educational Psychology*, 108(3), 353–373.

Brame, C. (2013). Writing good multiple choice test questions. Retrieved from https://cft.vanderbilt.edu/guides-sub-pages/writing-good-multiple-choice-test-questions/.

Braxton, J. M., & McClendon, S. A. (2001). The fostering of social integration and retention through institutional practice. *Journal of College Student Retention: Research, Theory and Practice*, 3(1), 57–71.

Braxton, J. M., Milem, J. F., & Sullivan, A. S. (2000). The influence of active learning on the college student departure process: Toward a revision of Tinto's theory. *Journal of Higher Education*, 71(5), 569–590.

Bringle, R. G., Ruiz, A. I., Brown, M. A., & Reeb, R. N. (2016). Enhancing the psychology curriculum through service learning. *Psychology Learning and Teaching*, 15(3), 294–309.

Britton, B. K., & Tesser, A. (1991). Effects of time-management practices on college grades. *Journal of Educational Psychology*, 83(3), 405–410.

Brooks, P. J., Che, E. S., Walters, S., & Shane-Simpson, C. (2017). Launching PSYCH+feminism to engage undergraduates in Wikipedia editing. In R. Obeid, A. M. Schwartz, C. Shane-Simpson, & P. J. Brooks (Eds.), *How we teach now: The GSTA guide to student-centered teaching* (pp. 296–309). Retrieved from the Society for the Teaching of Psychology website: http://teachpsych.org/ebooks/howweteachnow.

Broton, K., & Goldrick-Rab, S. (2016). The dark side of college (un) affordability: Food and housing insecurity in higher education. *Change: The Magazine of Higher Learning*, 48(1), 16–25.

Brown, A. S., Schilling, H. E., & Hockensmith, M. L. (1999). The negative suggestion effect: Pondering incorrect alternatives may be hazardous to your knowledge. *Journal of Educational Psychology*, 91(4), 756–764.

Brown, M. J. (2008). Student perceptions of teaching evaluations. *Journal of Instructional Psychology*, 35(2), 177–182.

Brown, P. C., Roediger, H. L. III, & McDaniel, M. A. (2014). *Make it stick.* Cambridge, MA: Harvard University Press.

Broyles, I. L., Cyr, P. R., & Korsen, N. (2005). Open book tests: Assessment of academic learning in clerkships. *Medical Teacher*, 27(5), 456–462.

Bruffee, K. A. (1995). Sharing our toys: Cooperative learning versus collaborative learning. *Change: The Magazine of Higher Learning*, 27(1), 12–18.

Bruner, J. S. (1990). *Acts of meaning.* Cambridge, MA: Harvard University Press.

Brunken, R., Plass, J. L., & Leutner, D. (2003). Direct measurement of cognitive load in multimedia learning. *Educational Psychologist*, 38(1), 53–61.

Brunner, D. D. (1992). Dislocating boundaries in our classrooms. *Feminist Teacher*, 6, 18–24.

Bryant, B. K. (2005). Electronic discussion sections: A useful tool in teaching large university classes. *Teaching of Psychology*, 32(4), 271–275.

Budesheim, T. L., & Lundquist, A. R. (1999). Consider the opposite: Opening minds through in-class debates on course-related controversies. *Teaching of Psychology*, 26(2), 106–110.

Buehler, R., Griffin, D., & Ross, M. (1994). Exploring the "planning fallacy": Why people underestimate their task completion times. *Journal of Personality and Social Psychology*, 67(3), 366–381.

Bunce, D. M., Flens, E. A., & Neiles, K. Y. (2010). How long can students pay attention in class? A study of student attention decline using clickers. *Journal of Chemical Education*, 87(12), 1438–1443.

Burdo, J. R. (2012). Wikipedia neuroscience stub editing in an introductory undergraduate neuroscience course. *Journal of Undergraduate Neuroscience Education*, 11(1), A1–A5.

Burgstahler, S. (2001). Universal design of instruction. Retrieved from http://files.eric.ed.gov/fulltext/ED468709.pdf.

Burgstahler, S. (2015). Universal design of instruction (UDI): Definitions, principles, guidelines, and examples. Retrieved from http://www.washington.edu/doit/universal-design-instruction-udi-definition-principles-guidelines-and-examples.

Burke, A. S., & Fedorek, B. (2017). Does "flipping" promote engagement?: A comparison of a traditional, online, and flipped class. *Active Learning in Higher Education*, 18(1), 11–24.

Burke, B. L., Sears, S. R., Kraus, S., & Roberts-Cady, S. (2014). Critical analysis: A comparison of critical thinking changes in psychology and philosophy classes. *Teaching of Psychology*, 41(1), 28–36.

Burke, H. (2013). Legitimizing student expertise in student-faculty partnerships. *Teaching and Learning Together in Higher Education*, 1(10), 6. Retrieved from http://repository.brynmawr.edu/tlthe/vol1/iss10/6.

Burnette, J. L., O'Boyle, E. H., VanEpps, E. M., Pollack, J. M., & Finkel, E. J. (2013). Mind-sets matter: A meta-analytic review of implicit theories and self-regulation. *Psychological Bulletin*, 139(3), 655–701.

Buskist, W., & Irons, J. G. (Eds.) (2008). *Simple strategies for teaching your students to think critically*. Malden, MA: Wiley-Blackwell.

Butcher, J., & Maunder, R. (2014). Going URB@ N: Exploring the impact of undergraduate students as pedagogic researchers. *Innovations in Education and Teaching International*, 51(2), 142–152.

Butler, A., Phillmann, K.-B., & Smart, L. (2001). Active learning within a lecture: Assessing the impact of short, in-class writing exercises. *Teaching of Psychology*, 28(4), 257–259.

Butler, A. C., Godbole, N., & Marsh, E. J. (2013). Explanation feedback is better than correct answer feedback for promoting transfer of learning. *Journal of Educational Psychology*, 105(2), 290–298.

Butler, A. C., Karpicke, J. D., & Roediger, H. L. III (2007). The effect of type and timing of feedback on learning from multiple-choice tests. *Journal of Experimental Psychology: Applied*, 13(4), 273–281.

Butler, A. C., Karpicke, J. D., & Roediger, H. L. III (2008). Correcting a metacognitive error: Feedback increases retention of low-confidence correct responses. *Journal of Experimental Psychology: Learning, Memory, and Cognition*, 34(4), 918–928.

Butler, L. D., Carello, J., & Maguin, E. (2017). Trauma, stress, and self-care in clinical training: Predictors of burnout, decline in health status, secondary traumatic stress symptoms, and compassion satisfaction. *Psychological Trauma: Theory, Research, Practice, and Policy*, 9(4), 416.

Butterfield, B., & Metcalfe, J. (2006). The correction of errors committed with high confidence. *Metacognition and Learning*, 1(1), 69–84.

Buzzetto-More, N. (2010). Assessing the efficacy and effectiveness of an e-portfolio used for summative assessment. *Interdisciplinary Journal of e-Learning and Learning Objects*, 6(1), 61–85.

Cabrera, A. F., Crissman, J. L., Bernal, E. M., Nora, A., Terenzini, P. T., & Pascarella, E. T. (2002). Collaborative learning: Its impact on college students' development and diversity. *Journal of College Student Development*, 43(1), 20–34.

Caldwell, J. E. (2007). Clickers in the large classroom: Current research and best-practice tips. *CBE Life Sciences Education*, 6(1), 9–20.

Calhoon, S., & Becker, A. (2008). How students use the course syllabus. *International Journal for the Scholarship of Teaching and Learning*, 2(1), 6.

Camerer, C., Loewenstein, G., & Weber, M. (1989). The curse of knowledge in economic settings: An experimental analysis. *Journal of Political Economy*, 97(5), 1232–1254.

Canning, E. A., & Harackiewicz, J. M. (2015). Teach it, don't preach it: The differential effects of directly-communicated and self-generated utility–value information. *Motivation Science*, 1(1), 47–71.

Cardinale, J. A., & Johnson, B. C. (2017). Metacognition modules: A scaffolded series of online assignments designed to improve students' study skills. *Journal of Microbiology and Biology Education*, 18(1), 18.1.13.

Carello, J., & Butler, L. D. (2015). Practicing what we teach: Trauma-informed educational practice. *Journal of Teaching in Social Work*, 35(3), 262–278.

Carless, D. (2006). Differing perceptions in the feedback process. *Studies in Higher Education*, 31(2), 219–233.

Carmichael, P., & MacMillan, M. (2011). Teaching source credibility evaluation to undergraduates: A reflective dialogue. *Transformative Dialogues: Teaching and Learning Journal*, 4(3), 1–8.

Carnevale, A. P., Smith, N., & Strohl, J. (2010). *Help wanted: Projections of job and education requirements through 2018*. Washington, DC: Center on Education and the Workforce.

Carpenter, S. K., Cepeda, N. J., Rohrer, D., Kang, S. H., & Pashler, H. (2012). Using spacing to enhance diverse forms of learning: Review of recent research and implications for instruction. *Educational Psychology Review*, 24(3), 369–378.

Carroll, D. W. (1986). Use of the jigsaw technique in laboratory and discussion classes. *Teaching of Psychology*, 13(4), 208–210.

Carroll, M., Campbell-Ratcliffe, J., Murnane, H., & Perfect, T. (2007). Retrieval-induced forgetting in educational contexts: Monitoring, expertise, text integration, and test format. *European Journal of Cognitive Psychology*, 19(4–5), 580–606.

Carter, A. M. (2015). Teaching with trauma: Trigger warnings, feminism, and disability pedagogy. *Disability Studies Quarterly*, 35(2), 9. Retrieved from http://dsq-sds.org/article/view/4652/3935.

Case, K. A. (2007). Raising white privilege awareness and reducing racial prejudice: Assessing diversity course effectiveness. *Teaching of Psychology*, 34(4), 231–235.

Case, K. A. (2011). The class interview: Student engagement in courses covering sensitive topics. *Psychology Learning and Teaching*, 10(1), 52–56.

Case, K. A. (2017). Toward an intersectional pedagogy model: Engaged learning for social justice. In K. A. Case (Ed.), *Intersectional pedagogy: Complicating identity and social justice* (pp. 1–24). New York, NY: Routledge.

Case, K. A., Miller, A., & Jackson, S. (2012). We talk about race too much in this class! Complicating the essentialized woman through intersectional pedagogy. In S. Pliner, & C. Banks (Eds.), *Teaching, learning, and intersecting identities in higher education* (pp. 32–48). New York, NY: Peter Lang Publishing.

CAST. (2018). Universal design for learning guidelines version 2.2. Retrieved from http://udlguidelines.cast.org.

Cathey, C. L., Visio, M. E., Whisenhunt, B. L., Hudson, D. L., & Shoptaugh, C. F. (2016). Helping when they are listening: A midterm study skills intervention for introductory psychology. *Psychology Learning and Teaching*, 15(3), 250–267.

Caulfield, M. (2017). Web literacy for student fact-checkers… and other people who care about facts. Retrieved from https://webliteracy.pressbooks.com/.

Celio, C. I., Durlak, J., & Dymnicki, A. (2011). A meta-analysis of the impact of service-learning on students. *Journal of Experiential Education*, 34(2), 164–181.

Cepeda, N. J., Vul, E., Rohrer, D., Wixted, J. T., & Pashler, H. (2008). Spacing effects in learning: A temporal ridgeline of optimal retention. *Psychological Science*, 19(11), 1095–1102.

Cestone, C. M., Levine, R. E., & Lane, D. R. (2008). Peer assessment and evaluation in team-based learning. *New Directions for Teaching and Learning*, 2008(116), 69–78.

Chandler, C. J., & Gregory, A. S. (2010). Sleeping with the enemy: Wikipedia in the college classroom. *The History Teacher*, 43(2), 247–257.

Chapdelaine, A., & Chapman, B. L. (1999). Using community-based research projects to teach research methods. *Teaching of Psychology*, 26(2), 101–105.

Chapell, M. S., Blanding, Z. B., Silverstein, M. E., Takahashi, M., Newman, B., Gubi, A., & McCann, N. (2005). Test anxiety and academic performance in undergraduate and graduate students. *Journal of Educational Psychology*, 97(2), 268–274.

Chapman, K. J., & Van Auken, S. (2001). Creating positive group project experiences: An examination of the role of the instructor on students' perceptions of group projects. *Journal of Marketing Education*, 23(2), 117–127.

Chen, B., Seilhamer, R., Bennett, L., & Bauer, S. (2015). Students' mobile learning practices in higher education: A multi-year study. *Educause Review*, 7. Retrieved from http://er.educause.edu/articles/2015/6/students-mobile-learning-practices-in-higher-education-a-multiyear-study.

Chen, J. C. (2017). Nontraditional adult learners: The neglected diversity in postsecondary education. *SAGE Open*, 7(1), 1–12.

Cheng, C. K., Paré, D. E., Collimore, L.-M., & Joordens, S. (2011). Assessing the effectiveness of a voluntary online discussion forum on improving students' course performance. *Computers and Education*, 56(1), 253–261.

Chenoweth, N. A., & Hayes, J. R. (2001). Fluency in writing generating text in L1 and L2. *Written Communication*, 18(1), 80–98.

Cherney, I. D. (2008). The effects of active learning on students' memories for course content. *Active Learning in Higher Education*, 9(2), 152–171.

Chesney, T. (2006). An empirical examination of Wikipedia's credibility. *First Monday*, 11(11). Retrieved from http://firstmonday.org/ojs/index.php/fm/article/viewArticle/1413.

Chew, P. K., & Dillon, D. B. (2014). Statistics anxiety update: Refining the construct and recommendations for a new research agenda. *Perspectives on Psychological Science*, 9(2), 196–208.

Chew, S. L. (2010). Improving classroom performance by challenging student misconceptions about learning. *APS Observer*, 23(4), 51–54.

Chiang, C., Lewis, C., Wright, M., Agapova, S., Akers, B., Azad, T., … Chen, J. (2012). Learning chronobiology by improving Wikipedia. *Journal of Biological Rhythms*, 27(4), 333–336.

Chickering, A. W., & Gamson, Z. F. (1987). Seven principles for good practice in undergraduate education. *American Association for Higher Education Bulletin*, 39, 2–6.

Chien, Y.-T., Chang, Y.-H., & Chang, C.-Y. (2016). Do we click in the right way? A meta-analytic review of clicker-integrated instruction. *Educational Research Review*, 17, 1–18.

Cho, K., & MacArthur, C. (2010). Student revision with peer and expert reviewing. *Learning and Instruction*, 20(4), 328–338.

Cho, K., Schunn, C. D., & Wilson, R. W. (2006). Validity and reliability of scaffolded peer assessment of writing from instructor and student perspectives. *Journal of Educational Psychology*, 98(4), 891–901.

Cho, Y. H., & Cho, K. (2011). Peer reviewers learn from giving comments. *Instructional Science*, 39(5), 629–643.

Christopher, A. N., Walter, J., Marek, P., & Koenig, C. S. (2004). Using a "new classic" film to teach about stereotyping and prejudice. *Teaching of Psychology*, 31(3), 199–202.

Christopher, A. N., & Walter, M. I. (2006). An assignment to help students learn to navigate primary sources of information. *Teaching of Psychology*, 33(1), 42–45.

Chu, S. K., Chan, C. K., & Tiwari, A. F. (2012). Using blogs to support learning during internship. *Computers and Education*, 58(3), 989–1000.

Chu, Y., & Walters, L. M. (2013). The question-asking behavior of Asian students in an American university classroom. *Journal of English as an International Language*, 8(2), 10–29.

Churchill, D. (2009). Educational applications of Web 2.0: Using blogs to support teaching and learning. *British Journal of Educational Technology*, 40(1), 179–183.

Clark, I. L. (1985). Leading the horse: The writing center and required visits. *The Writing Center Journal*, 5(2/1), 31–34.

Clayson, D. E. (2009). Student evaluations of teaching: Are they related to what students learn? A meta-analysis and review of the literature. *Journal of Marketing Education*, 31(1), 16–30.

Cleary, A. M. (2008). Using wireless response systems to replicate behavioral research findings in the classroom. *Teaching of Psychology*, 35(1), 42–44.

Cleveland, M. (2011). A practical guide to using YouTube in the classroom. In D. S. Dunn, J. H. Wilson, J. Freeman, & J. R. Stowell (Eds.), *Best practices for technology-enhanced teaching and learning: Connecting to psychology and the social sciences* (pp. 197–206). Oxford, U.K.: Oxford University Press.

Clump, M. A. (2012). More than just stepping away from the podium: A jigsaw classroom. In J. Holmes, S. C. Baker, & J. R. Stowell (Eds.), *Essays from e-xcellence in teaching* (Vol. XI) (pp. 15–19). Retrieved from the Society for the Teaching of Psychology website: http://teachpsych.org/ebooks/eit2011/index.php.

Clump, M. A., Bauer, H., & Breadley, C. (2004). The extent to which psychology students read textbooks: A multiple class analysis of reading across the psychology curriculum. *Journal of Instructional Psychology*, 31(3), 227–232.

Cochran, J. D., Campbell, S. M., Baker, H. M., & Leeds, E. M. (2014). The role of student characteristics in predicting retention in online courses. *Research in Higher Education*, 55(1), 27–48.

Coffin, C., Curry, M. J., Goodman, S., Hewings, A., Lillis, T., & Swann, J. (2005). *Teaching academic writing: A toolkit for higher education*. New York, NY: Routledge.

Cohen, G. L., Garcia, J., Apfel, N., & Master, A. (2006). Reducing the racial achievement gap: A social-psychological intervention. *Science*, 313(5791), 1307–1310.

Cohen, J., Cook-Sather, A., Lesnick, A., Alter, Z., Awkward, R., Decius, F., … Mengesha, L. (2013). Students as leaders and learners: Towards self-authorship and social change on a college campus. *Innovations in Education and Teaching International*, 50(1), 3–13.

Cohen, P. A. (1981). Student ratings of instruction and student achievement: A meta-analysis of multisection validity studies. *Review of Educational Research*, 51(3), 281–309.

Colbeck, C. L., Campbell, S. E., & Bjorklund, S. A. (2000). Grouping in the dark: What college students learn from group projects. *Journal of Higher Education*, 71, 60–83.

Colbert, K. (1987). The effects of CEDA and NDT debate on critical thinking. *Journal of theAmerican Forensic Association*, 23, 194–201.

Colbert-White, E., & Simpson, E. (2017). A workbook for scaffolding mentored undergraduate research experiences in the social and behavioral sciences. *International Journal of Teaching and Learning in Higher Education*, 29(2), 309–380.

Cole, M. (2009). Using wiki technology to support student engagement: Lessons from the trenches. *Computers and Education*, 52(1), 141–146.

Colleran, E. W. (2013). Desperately seeking copyright. Copyright on campus: Librarians remain at the head of the class. *Against the Grain*, 15(5), 34.

Collier, P. J., & Morgan, D. L. (2008). "Is that paper really due today?": Differences in first-generation and traditional college students' understandings of faculty expectations. *Higher Education*, 55(4), 425–446.

Conboy, C., Fletcher, S., Russell, K., & Wilson, M. (2012). An evaluation of the potential use and impact of Prezi, the zooming editor software, as a tool to facilitate learning in higher education. *Innovations in Practice*, 7, 31–45.

Connell, B. R., Jones, M., Mace, R., Mueller, J., Mullick, A., Ostroff, E., … Vanderheiden, G. (1997). The principles of universal design. Retrieved from www.ncsu.edu/ncsu/design/cud/about_ud/udprinciplestext.htm.

Conner, D. B. (1996). From Monty Python to Total recall: A feature film activity for the cognitive psychology course. *Teaching of Psychology*, 23(1), 33–35.

Connor-Greene, P. A. (2000a). Assessing and promoting student learning: Blurring the line between teaching and testing. *Teaching of Psychology*, 27(2), 84–88.

Connor-Greene, P. A. (2000b). Making connections: Evaluating the effectiveness of journal writing in enhancing student learning. *Teaching of Psychology*, 27(1), 44–46.

Connor-Greene, P. A. (2002). Problem-based service learning: The evolution of a team project. *Teaching of Psychology*, 29(3), 193–197.

Connor-Greene, P. A. (2007). Observation or interpretation? Demonstrating unintentional subjectivity and interpretive variance. *Teaching of Psychology*, 34(3), 167–171.

Connor-Greene, P. A., & Greene, D. J. (2002). Science or snake oil? Teaching critical evaluation of "research" reports on the internet. *Teaching of Psychology*, 29(4), 321–324.

Conrad, N. J. (2013). Practicing what is preached: Self-reflections on memory in a memory course. *Teaching of Psychology*, 40(1), 44–47.

Conway, J. M., Amel, E. L., & Gerwien, D. P. (2009). Teaching and learning in the social context: A meta-analysis of service learning's effects on academic, personal, social, and citizenship outcomes. *Teaching of Psychology*, 36(4), 233–245.

Conway, K., Wladis, C., & Hachey, A. (2011). Minority student access in the online environment. *HETS Online Journal*, 2(1), 52–78.

Conzemius, A., & O'Neill, J. (2005). *The power of SMART goals: Using goals to improve student learning*. Bloomington, IN: Solution Tree Press.

Cook, E., Kennedy, E., & McGuire, S. Y. (2013). Effect of teaching metacognitive learning strategies on performance in general chemistry courses. *Journal of Chemical Education*, 90(8), 961–967.

Cook, K. E., & Murowchick, E. (2014). Do literature review skills transfer from one course to another? *Psychology Learning and Teaching*, 13(1), 3–11.

Cooper, J. L., MacGregor, J., Smith, K. A., & Robinson, P. (2000). Implementing small-group instruction: Insights from successful practitioners. *New Directions for Teaching and Learning*, 2000(81), 63–76.

Cooper, J. L., & Robinson, P. (2000). The argument for making large classes seem small. *New Directions for Teaching and Learning*, 2000(81), 5–16.

Coutinho, S. (2008). Self-efficacy, metacognition, and performance. *North American Journal of Psychology*, 10(1), 165.

Covarrubias, R., & Fryberg, S. A. (2015). Movin' on up (to college): First-generation college students' experiences with family achievement guilt. *Cultural Diversity and Ethnic Minority Psychology*, 21(3), 420–429.

Covarrubias, R., Gallimore, R., & Okagaki, L. (2016). "I know that I should be here." Lessons learned from the first-year performance of borderline university applicants. *Journal of College Student Retention: Research, Theory and Practice*, 20(1), 92–115.

Covarrubias, R., Herrmann, S. D., & Fryberg, S. A. (2016). Affirming the interdependent self: Implications for Latino student performance. *Basic and Applied Social Psychology*, 38(1), 47–57.

Cox, P. L., & Bobrowski, P. E. (2000). The team charter assignment: Improving the effectiveness of classroom teams. *Journal of Behavioral and Applied Management*, 1(1), 92–103.

Craik, F. I., & Lockhart, R. S. (1972). Levels of processing: A framework for memory research. *Journal of Verbal Learning and Verbal Behavior*, 11(6), 671–684.

Craik, F. I., & Tulving, E. (1975). Depth of processing and the retention of words in episodic memory. *Journal of Experimental Psychology: General*, 104(3), 268–294.

Crone, T. S., & Portillo, M. C. (2013). Jigsaw variations and attitudes about learning and the self in cognitive psychology. *Teaching of Psychology*, 40(3), 246–251.

Cross, K. P. (1977). Not can, but will college teaching be improved? *New Directions for Higher Education*, 1977(17), 1–15.

Cross, K. P., & Steadman, M. H. (1996). *Classroom research: Implementing the scholarship of teaching*. San Francisco, CA: Jossey-Bass.

Crouch, C. H., & Mazur, E. (2001). Peer instruction: Ten years of experience and results. *American Journal of Physics*, 69(9), 970–977.

Cumiskey, K. (2015). Towards a liberation classroom: The power of difficult discussions and participatory practices in a psychology course. Paper presented at the 6th Annual Pedagogy Day Conference on the Teaching of Psychology, New York, NY.

Cummins-Sebree, S. E., & White, E. (2014). Using the flipped classroom design: Student impressions and lessons learned. *Association for University Regional Campuses of Ohio Journal*, 20, 113–129.

Curtis, D. D., & Lawson, M. J. (2001). Exploring collaborative online learning. *Journal of Asynchronous Learning Networks*, 5(1), 21–34.

Dahlstrom, E., Brooks, D. C., & Bichsel, J. (2014). *The current ecosystem of learning management systems in higher education: Student, faculty, and IT perspectives: Research report*. Louisville, CO: ECAR, September 2014. Retrieved from http://library.educause.edu/~/media/files/library/2014/9/ers1414-pdf.pdf.

Dancer, D., & Kamvounias, P. (2005). Student involvement in assessment: A project designed to assess class participation fairly and reliably. *Assessment and Evaluation in Higher Education*, 30(4), 445–454.

Daniel, D. (2011). Practical PowerPoint. In D. S. Dunn, J. H. Wilson, J. Freeman, & J. R. Stowell (Eds.), *Best practices for technology-enhanced teaching and learning: Connecting to psychology and the social sciences*. New York, NY: Oxford University Press.

Daniel, D. B., & Broida, J. (2004). Using web-based quizzing to improve exam performance: Lessons learned. *Teaching of Psychology*, 31(3), 207–208.

Daniel, F., Gaze, C. M., & Braasch, J. L. G. (2015). Writing cover letters that address instructor feedback improves final papers in a research methods course. *Teaching of Psychology*, 42(1), 64–68.

Davi, A., Frydenberg, M., & Gulati, G. J. (2007). Blogging across the disciplines: Integrating technology to enhance liberal learning. *MERLOT Journal of Online Learning and Teaching*, 3(3), 222–233.

Davidson, C. N. (2011). Collaborative learning for the digital age. *The Chronicle of Higher Education*, 26. Retrieved from http://www.chronicle.com/article/Collaborative-Learning-for-the/128789.

Davidson, C. N. (2017). *The new education: How to revolutionize the university to prepare for a world in flux*. New York, NY: Basic Books.

Davies, J., & Graff, M. (2005). Performance in e-learning: Online participation and student grades. *British Journal of Educational Technology*, 36(4), 657–663.

Davies, P. L., Schelly, C. L., & Spooner, C. L. (2013). Measuring the effectiveness of Universal Design for Learning intervention in postsecondary education. *Journal of Postsecondary Education and Disability*, 26(3), 195–220.

Davis, A., & McGrail, E. (2017). *Student blogs: How online writing can transform your classroom*. Lanham, MD: Rowman and Littlefield.

De Rijdt, C., Tiquet, E., Dochy, F., & Devolder, M. (2006). Teaching portfolios in higher education and their effects: An explorative study. *Teaching and Teacher Education*, 22(8), 1084–1093.

De Wever, B., Hämäläinen, R., Voet, M., & Gielen, M. (2015). A wiki task for first-year university students: The effect of scripting students' collaboration. *The Internet and Higher Education*, 25, 37–44.

Debowski, S., Wood, R. E., & Bandura, A. (2001). Impact of guided exploration and enactive exploration on self-regulatory mechanisms and information acquisition through electronic search. *Journal of Applied Psychology*, 86(6), 1129–1141.

Dede, C. (2010). Comparing frameworks for 21st century skills. In J. Bellanca, & R. Brandt (Eds.), *21st century skills: Rethinking how students learn* (pp. 51–76). Bloomington, IN: Solution Tree Press.

Deil-Amen, R. (2011). Socio-academic integrative moments: Rethinking academic and social integration among two-year college students in career-related programs. *Journal of Higher Education*, 82(1), 54–91.

Dempster, F. N. (1989). Spacing effects and their implications for theory and practice. *Educational Psychology Review*, 1(4), 309–330.

DenBeste, M. (2003). PowerPoint, technology and the web: More than just an overhead projector for the new century? *The History Teacher*, 36(4), 491–504.

Deng, L., & Yuen, A. H. (2012). Understanding student perceptions and motivation towards academic blogs: An exploratory study. *Australasian Journal of Educational Technology*, 28, 48–66.

Dennen, V. P., & Wieland, K. (2007). From interaction to intersubjectivity: Facilitating online group discourse processes. *Distance Education*, 28(3), 281–297.

Deslauriers, L., Schelew, E., & Wieman, C. (2011). Improved learning in a large-enrollment physics class. *Science*, 332(6031), 862–864.

Dewey, J. (1933). *How we think: A restatement of the relation of reflective thinking to the educative process*. Lexington, MA: Heath.

Diamond, M. R. (2004). The usefulness of structured mid-term feedback as a catalyst for change in higher education classes. *Active Learning in Higher Education*, 5(3), 217–231.

DiBattista, D., & Kurzawa, L. (2011). Examination of the quality of multiple-choice items on classroom tests. *Canadian Journal for the Scholarship of Teaching and Learning*, 2(2), Article 4.

DiClementi, J. D., & Handelsman, M. M. (2005). Empowering students: Class-generated course rules. *Teaching of Psychology*, 32(1), 18–21.

Dietz-Uhler, B., & Bishop-Clark, C. (2001). The use of computer-mediated communication to enhance subsequent face-to-face discussions. *Computers in Human Behavior*, 17(3), 269–283.

Digital Learning Compass Partnership. (2017). Distance education enrollment report. Retrieved from www.digitallearningcompass.org.

Dommeyer, C. J. (2007). Using the diary method to deal with social loafers on the group project: Its effects on peer evaluations, group behavior, and attitudes. *Journal of Marketing Education*, 29(2), 175–188.

Dorris, W., & Ducey, R. (1978). Social psychology and sex roles in films. *Teaching of Psychology*, 5(3), 168–169.

Dow, E. A. A., Kukucka, J., Galazyn, M., Powers, K. L., & Brooks, P. (2013). A five slide-model for pedagogy. In Proceedings of the Farmingdale State College: Teaching of Psychology: Ideas and Innovations. 27th Annual Conference, Tarrytown, NY. Retrieved from http://files.eric.ed.gov/fulltext/ED543391.pdf.

Downes, S. (2004). Educational blogging. *Educause Review*, 39(5), 14–26.

Downing, S. M. (2005). The effects of violating standard item writing principles on tests and students: The consequences of using flawed test items on achievement examinations in medical education. *Advances in Health Sciences Education*, 10(2), 133–143.

Drabick, D. A. G., Weisberg, R., Paul, L., & Bubier, J. L. (2007). Keeping it short and sweet: Brief, ungraded writing assignments facilitate learning. *Teaching of Psychology*, 34(3), 172–176.

Dragga, S. (2010). The effects of praiseworthy grading on students and teachers. *Journal of Teaching Writing*, 7(1), 41–50.

Draper, S. W., & Brown, M. I. (2004). Increasing interactivity in lectures using an electronic voting system. *Journal of Computer Assisted Learning*, 20(2), 81–94.

D'Souza, C. (2013). Debating: A catalyst to enhance learning skills and competencies. *Education and Training*, 55(6), 538–549.

Ducate, L. C., & Lomicka, L. L. (2008). Adventures in the blogosphere: From blog readers to blog writers. *Computer Assisted Language Learning*, 21(1), 9–28.

Duell, O. K., & Schommer-Aikins, M. (2001). Measures of people's beliefs about knowledge and learning. *Educational Psychology Review*, 13(4), 419–449.

Duffy, P. D., & Bruns, A. (2006). The use of blogs, wikis and RSS in education: A conversation of possibilities. In Proceedings Online Learning and Teaching Conference 2006 (pp. 31–38), Brisbane, Australia. Retrieved from http://eprints.qut.edu.au/5398/1/5398.pdf.

Dundes, L. (2001). Small group debates: Fostering critical thinking in oral presentations with maximal class involvement. *Teaching Sociology*, 29, 237–243.

Dunlap, M. R. (1998). Adjustment and developmental outcomes of students engaged in service learning. *Journal of Experiential Education*, 21(3), 147–153.

Dunlosky, J., & Rawson, K. A. (2015). Practice tests, spaced practice, and successive relearning: Tips for classroom use and for guiding students' learning. *Scholarship of Teaching and Learning in Psychology*, 1(1), 72–78.

Dunlosky, J., Rawson, K. A., Marsh, E. J., Nathan, M. J., & Willingham, D. T. (2013). Improving students' learning with effective learning techniques: Promising directions from cognitive and educational psychology. *Psychological Science in the Public Interest*, 14(1), 4–58.

Dunn, D. S. (1997). Identifying imagoes: A personality exercise on myth, self, and identity. *Teaching of Psychology*, 24(3), 193–195.

Dunning, D. (2011). The Dunning–Kruger effect: On being ignorant of one's own ignorance. *Advances in Experimental Social Psychology*, 44, 247–296.

Dunning, D., Heath, C., & Suls, J. M. (2004). Flawed self-assessment: Implications for health, education, and the workplace. *Psychological Science in the Public Interest*, 5(3), 69–106.

Durning, S. J., Dong, T., Ratcliffe, T., Schuwirth, L., Artino, A. R., Boulet, J. R., & Eva, K. (2016). Comparing open-book and closed-book examinations: A systematic review. *Academic Medicine*, 91(4), 583–599.

Dweck, C. S. (1975). The role of expectations and attributions in the alleviation of learned helplessness. *Journal of Personality and Social Psychology*, 31(4), 674–685.

Dweck, C. S., & Leggett, E. L. (1988). A social-cognitive approach to motivation and personality. *Psychological Review*, 95(2), 256–273.

Dwyer, C. A., Millett, C. M., & Payne, D. G. (2006). *A culture of evidence: Postsecondary assessment and learning outcomes. Recommendations to policymakers and the higher education community*. Princeton, NJ: Educational Testing Service.

Dykman, C. A., & Davis, C. K. (2008). Online education forum: Part two—Teaching online versus teaching conventionally. *Journal of Information Systems Education*, 19(2), 157–164.

Eaton, J., & Uskul, A. K. (2004). Using the Simpsons to teach social psychology. *Teaching of Psychology*, 31, 277–278.

Eckes, S. E., & Ochoa, T. A. (2005). Students with disabilities: Transitioning from high school to higher education. *American Secondary Education*, 33, 6–20.

Edwards, J. C. (2015). Wiki women: Bringing women into Wikipedia through activism and pedagogy. *The History Teacher*, 48(3), 409–436.

Eilertsen, T. V., & Valdermo, O. (2000). Open-book assessment: A contribution to improved learning? *Studies in Educational Evaluation*, 26(2), 91–103.

Einarson, M. K., & Clarkberg, M. E. (2010). Race differences in the impact of students' out-of-class interactions with faculty. *Journal of the Professoriate*, 3(2), 101–136.

Eisenberg, M. B. (2008). Information literacy: Essential skills for the information age. *DESIDOC Journal of Library and Information Technology*, 28(2), 39–47.

Eisenberg, M. B., & Berkowitz, R. E. (1990). *Information problem solving: The big six skills approach to library and information skills instruction*. Norwood, NJ: Ablex Publishing Company.

Elam, C., Stratton, T., & Gibson, D. D. (2007). Welcoming a new generation to college: The millennial students. *Journal of College Admission*, 195, 20–25.

Elbow, P., & Sorcinelli, M. D. (2011). Using high-stakes and low-stakes writing to enhance learning. In M. Svinicki, & W. McKeachie (Eds.), *McKeachie's teaching tips* (13th ed.) (pp. 213–234). Belmont, CA: Wadsworth.

Elias, T. (2011). Universal instructional design principles for mobile learning. *The International Review of Research in Open and Distributed Learning*, 12(2), 143–156.

Ellison, N. B., & Wu, Y. (2008). Blogging in the classroom: A preliminary exploration of student attitudes and impact on comprehension. *Journal of Educational Multimedia and Hypermedia*, 17(1), 99–122.

Elwood, S. (2009). Integrating participatory action research and GIS education: Negotiating methodologies, politics and technologies. *Journal of Geography in Higher Education*, 33(1), 51–65.

Engle, J., & Tinto, V. (2008). Moving beyond access—College success for low-income, first-generation students. Retrieved from the Pell Institute website: http://www.pellinstitute. org/publications-Moving_Beyond_Access_2008.shtml.

Ennis, R. H. (1989). Critical thinking and subject specificity: Clarification and needed research. *Educational Researcher*, 18(3), 4–10.

Erez, A., Lepine, J. A., & Elms, H. (2002). Effects of rotated leadership and peer evaluation on the functioning and effectiveness of self-managed teams: A quasi-experiment. *Personnel Psychology*, 55(4), 929–948.

Ergene, T. (2003). Effective interventions on test anxiety reduction: A meta-analysis. *School Psychology International*, 24(3), 313–328.

Ericsson, K. A., Krampe, R. T., & Tesch-Römer, C. (1993). The role of deliberate practice in the acquisition of expert performance. *Psychological Review*, 100(3), 363–406.

Estow, S., Lawrence, E. K., & Adams, K. A. (2011). Practice makes perfect: Improving students' skills in understanding and avoiding plagiarism with a themed methods course. *Teaching of Psychology*, 38(4), 255–258.

Evans, C. (2008). The effectiveness of m-learning in the form of podcast revision lectures in higher education. *Computers and Education*, 50(2), 491–498.

Evans, S., Mabey, J., & Mandiberg, M. (2015). Editing for equality: The outcomes of the art+ feminism Wikipedia edit-a-thons. *Art Documentation: Journal of the Art Libraries Society of North America*, 34(2), 194–203.

Everson, H. T., & Tobias, S. (1998). The ability to estimate knowledge and performance in college: A metacognitive analysis. *Instructional Science*, 26(1), 65–79.

Eyler, J. (2002). Reflection: Linking service and learning—Linking students and communities. *Journal of Social Issues*, 58(3), 517–534.

Facione, P. A., Facione, N. C., & Giancarlo, C. A. F. (2001). *California critical thinking disposition inventory: CCTDI*. La Cruz, CA: Academic Press.

Faidley, J., Evensen, D. H., Salisbury-Glennon, J., Glenn, J., & Hmelo, C. E. (2000). How are we doing? Methods of assessing group processing in a problem-based learning context. In D. H. Evensen, & C. E. Hmelo (Eds.), *Problem-based learning: A research perspective on learning interactions* (pp. 109–135). Mahwah, NJ: Lawrence Erlbaum Associates.

Fallahi, C. R., Wood, R. M., Austad, C. S., & Fallahi, H. (2006). A program for improving undergraduate psychology students' basic writing skills. *Teaching of Psychology*, 33(3), 171–175.

Farmer, B., Yue, A., & Brooks, C. (2008). Using blogging for higher order learning in large cohort university teaching: A case study. *Australasian Journal of Educational Technology*, 24(2), 123–136.

Fautch, J. M. (2015). The flipped classroom for teaching organic chemistry in small classes: Is it effective? *Chemistry Education Research and Practice*, 16(1), 179–186.

Fazio, L. K., Brashier, N. M., Payne, B. K., & Marsh, E. J. (2015). Knowledge does not protect against illusory truth. *Journal of Experimental Psychology: General*, 144(5), 993–1002.

Feichtner, S. B., & Davis, E. A. (1984). Why some groups fail: A survey of students' experiences with learning groups. *Journal of Management Education*, 9(4), 58–73.

Feldmann, L. J. (2001). Classroom civility is another of our instructor responsibilities. *College Teaching*, 49(4), 137–140.

Felten, P., Bagg, J., Bumbry, M., Hill, J., Hornsby, K., Pratt, M., & Weller, S. (2013). A call for expanding inclusive student engagement in SoTL. *Teaching and Learning Inquiry*, 1(2), 63–74.

Fernald, L. D. (1989). Tales in a textbook: Learning in the traditional and narrative modes. *Teaching of Psychology*, 16(3), 121–124.

Fernandes, M. A., & Moscovitch, M. (2000). Divided attention and memory: Evidence of substantial interference effects at retrieval and encoding. *Journal of Experimental Psychology: General*, 129(2), 155–176.

Fields, J., Thompson, K. C., & Huisma, S. (2015). Lives-as-text: Assigning self-narrative to inform learning. In K. Brakke, & J. A. Houska (Eds.), *Telling stories: The art and science of storytelling as an instructional strategy*. Retrieved from the Society for the Teaching of Psychology website: http://teachpsych.org/ebooks/.

Filipiak, S. N., Rehfeldt, R. A., Heal, N. A., & Baker, J. C. (2010). The effects of points for preparation guides in interteaching procedures. *European Journal of Behavior Analysis*, 11, 115–132.

Fink, L. D. (2007). The power of course design to increase student engagement and learning. *Peer Review*, 9(1), 13–17.

Fink, L. D. (2013). *Creating significant learning experiences: An integrated approach to designing college courses, revised and updated*. San Francisco, CA: Jossey-Bass.

Finn, B., & Roediger, H. L. III (2011). Enhancing retention through reconsolidation: Negative emotional arousal following retrieval enhances later recall. *Psychological Science*, 22(6), 781–786.

Fleck, B. K. B., Hussey, H. D., & Rutledge-Ellison, L. (2017). Linking class and community. *Teaching of Psychology*, 44(3), 232–239.

Fleck, B. K. B., & Ropp, A. (2014). Using students as participants: Gaining IRB approval for SoTL research. In W. S. Altman, L. Stein, & J. R. Stowell (Eds.), *Essays from e-xcellence in teaching* (Vol. 14). Retrieved from the Society for the Teaching of Psychology website: http://teachpsych.org/ebooks/eit2014/index.php.

Fleming, M. Z., Piedmont, R. L., & Hiam, C. M. (1990). Images of madness: Feature films in teaching psychology. *Teaching of Psychology*, 17(3), 185–187.

Fletcher, C., & Cambre, C. (2009). Digital storytelling and implicated scholarship in the classroom. *Journal of Canadian Studies*, 43(1), 109–130.

Foldnes, N. (2016). The flipped classroom and cooperative learning: Evidence from a randomised experiment. *Active Learning in Higher Education*, 17(1), 39–49.

Fong, C. J., Davis, C. W., Kim, Y., Kim, Y. W., Marriott, L., & Kim, S. (2017). Psychosocial factors and community college student success: A meta-analytic investigation. *Review of Educational Research*, 87(2), 388–424.

Forehand, M. (2005). Bloom's taxonomy: Original and revised. In M. Orey (Ed.), *Emerging perspectives on learning, teaching, and technology* (pp. 41–47). Retrieved from http://projects.coe.uga.edu/epltt/.

Forer, B. R. (1949). The fallacy of personal validation: A classroom demonstration of gullibility. *Journal of Abnormal and Social Psychology*, 44(1), 118–123.

Fortney, J. C., Curran, G. M., Hunt, J. B., Cheney, A. M., Lu, L., Valenstein, M., & Eisenberg, D. (2016). Prevalence of probable mental disorders and help-seeking behaviors among veteran and non-veteran community college students. *General Hospital Psychiatry*, 38, 99–104.

Freeman, M., Blayney, P., & Ginns, P. (2006). Anonymity and in class learning: The case for electronic response systems. *Australasian Journal of Educational Technology*, 22(4), 568–580.

Freeman, S., Eddy, S. L., McDonough, M., Smith, M. K., Okoroafor, N., Jordt, H., & Wenderoth, M. P. (2014). Active learning increases student performance in science, engineering, and mathematics. *Proceedings of the National Academy of Sciences of the United States of America*, 111(23), 8410–8415.

Freeman, W., & Brett, C. (2012). Prompting authentic blogging practice in an online graduate course. *Computers and Education*, 59(3), 1032–1041.

Freire, P. (1996). *Pedagogy of the oppressed (revised)*. New York, NY: Continuum.

Freudenberg, N., Manzo, L., Mongiello, L., Jones, H., Boeri, N., & Lamberson, P. (2013). Promoting the health of young adults in urban public universities: A case study from City University of New York. *Journal of American College Health*, 61(7), 422–430.

Frisby, B. N., & Martin, M. M. (2010). Instructor–student and student–student rapport in the classroom. *Communication Education*, 59(2), 146–164.

Fritschner, L. M. (2000). Inside the undergraduate college classroom: Faculty and students differ on the meaning of student participation. *Journal of Higher Education*, 71(3), 342–362.

Fritzsche, B. A., Rapp Young, B., & Hickson, K. C. (2003). Individual differences in academic procrastination tendency and writing success. *Personality and Individual Differences*, 35(7), 1549–1557.

Frydenberg, J. (2007). Persistence in university continuing education online classes. *The International Review of Research in Open and Distributed Learning*, 8(3), 1–15.

Frymier, A. B., & Shulman, G. M. (1995). "What's in it for me?": Increasing content relevance to enhance students' motivation. *Communication Education*, 44(1), 40–50.

Fuller, M. B., Skidmore, S. T., Bustamante, R. M., & Holzweiss, P. C. (2016). Empirically exploring higher education cultures of assessment. *The Review of Higher Education*, 39(3), 395–429.

Gamst, G., & Freund, J. S. (1978). Effects of subject-generated stories on recall. *Bulletin of the Psychonomic Society*, 12(3), 185–188.

Garavalia, L. S., Hummel, J., Wiley, L., & Huitt, W. (2000). Constructing the course syllabus: Faculty and student perceptions of important syllabus components. *Journal of Excellence in College Teaching*, 10, 5–22.

Gardner, H. (October, 16, 2013). Howard Gardner: "Multiple intelligences" are not "learning styles." *Washington Post*. Retrieved from https://www.washingtonpost.com/news/answer-sheet/wp/2013/10/16/howard-gardner-multiple-intelligences-are-not-learning-styles/?utm_term=.db90500643fe.

Garfield, J., & Ben-Zvi, D. (2009). Helping students develop statistical reasoning: Implementing a statistical reasoning learning environment. *Teaching Statistics*, 31(3), 72–77.

Garner, M. (2005). Faculty consultations: An extra dimension to the university of Wyoming writing center. *Praxis: A Writing Center Journal*, 3(1). Retrieved from https://repositories.lib.utexas.edu/bitstream/handle/2152/62223/Garner_3.1WhomWeServe-3.pdf?sequence=2.

Garside, C. (1996). Look who's talking: A comparison of lecture and group discussion teaching strategies in developing critical thinking skills. *Communication Education*, 45(3), 212–227.

Gates, G. J. (2017). In U.S., more adults identifying as LGBT. Retrieved from http://news.gallup.com/poll/201731/lgbt-identification-rises.aspx.

Gazarian, P. K. (2010). Digital stories: Incorporating narrative pedagogy. *Journal of Nursing Education*, 49(5), 287–290.

Geddes, D. (2009). How am I doing? Exploring on-line gradebook monitoring as a self-regulated learning practice that impacts academic achievement. *Academy of Management Learning and Education*, 8(4), 494–510.

Georgakopoulos, A., & Guerrero, L. K. (2010). Student perceptions of teachers' nonverbal and verbal communication: A comparison of best and worst professors across six cultures. *International Education Studies*, 3(2), 3–16.

Gharib, A., Phillips, W., & Mathew, N. (2012). Cheat sheet or open-book? A comparison of the effects of exam types on performance, retention, and anxiety. *Psychology Research*, 2(8), 469–478.

Gibson, B. (1991). Research methods jeopardy: A tool for involving students and organizing the study session. *Teaching of Psychology*, 18(3), 176–177.

Giles, H. C. (2014). Risky epistemology: Connecting with others and dissonance in community-based research. *Michigan Journal of Community Service Learning*, 20(2), 65–78.

Giles, J. (2005). Internet encyclopaedias go head to head. *Nature*, 438(7070), 900–901.

Gingerich, K. J., Bugg, J. M., Doe, S. R., Rowland, C. A., Richards, T. L., Tompkins, S. A., & McDaniel, M. A. (2014). Active processing via write-to-learn assignments: Learning and retention benefits in introductory psychology. *Teaching of Psychology*, 41(4), 303–308.

Ginns, P. (2005). Meta-analysis of the modality effect. *Learning and Instruction*, 15(4), 313–331.

Ginsberg, M. B., & Wlodkowski, R. J. (2009). *Diversity and motivation: Culturally responsive teaching in college*. San Francisco, CA: Jossey Bass.

Glad, K. A., Hafstad, G. S., Jensen, T. K., & Dyb, G. (2017). A longitudinal study of psychological distress and exposure to trauma reminders after terrorism. *Psychological Trauma: Theory, Research, Practice, and Policy*, 9(S1), 145.

Glass, A. L. (2009). The effect of distributed questioning with varied examples on exam performance on inference questions. *Educational Psychology*, 29(7), 831–848.

Gleaves, A., & Walker, C. (2013). Richness, redundancy or relational salience? A comparison of the effect of textual and aural feedback modes on knowledge elaboration in higher education students' work. *Computers and Education*, 62(0), 249–261.

Glenberg, A. M., Wilkinson, A. C., & Epstein, W. (1982). The illusion of knowing: Failure in the self-assessment of comprehension. *Memory and Cognition*, 10(6), 597–602.

Goddard, P. (2003). Implementing and evaluating a writing course for psychology majors. *Teaching of Psychology*, 30(1), 25–29.

Golding, J. M., Wasarhaley, N. E., & Fletcher, B. (2012). The use of flashcards in an introduction to psychology class. *Teaching of Psychology*, 39(3), 199–202.

Gonzales, P. M., Blanton, H., & Williams, K. J. (2002). The effects of stereotype threat and double-minority status on the test performance of Latino women. *Personality and Social Psychology Bulletin*, 28(5), 659–670.

Goodyear, G. E., & Alchin, D. (1998). Statements of teaching philosophy. In M. Kaplan (Ed.), *To improve the academy* (Vol. 17) (pp. 103–122). Stillwater, OK: New Forums Press.

Gordon, B. L. (2008). Requiring first-year writing classes to visit the writing center: Bad attitudes or positive results? *Teaching English in the Two Year College*, 36(2), 154–163.

Gordon, S. P., & Gordon, F. S. (2009). Visualizing and understanding probability and statistics: Graphical simulations using Excel. *PRIMUS*, 19(4), 346–369.

Gorman, M. E., Gorman, M. E., & Young, A. (1986). Poetic writing in psychology. In A. Young, & T. Fulwiler (Eds.), *Writing across the disciplines: Research into practice* (pp. 139–159). Upper Montclair, NJ: Boynton/Cook.

Gortner Lahmers, A., & Zulauf, C. R. (2000). Factors associated with academic time use and academic performance of college students: A recursive approach. *Journal of College Student Development*, 41(5), 544–556.

Goto, K., & Schneider, J. (2009). Interteaching: An innovative approach to facilitate university student learning in the field of nutrition. *Journal of Nutrition Education and Behavior*, 41(4), 303–304.

Graesser, A. C., Hauft-Smith, K., Cohen, A. D., & Pyles, L. D. (1980). Advanced outlines, familiarity, and text genre on retention of prose. *Journal of Experimental Education*, 48(4), 281–290.

Graff, N. (2011). "An effective and agonizing way to learn": Backwards design and new teachers' preparation for planning curriculum. *Teacher Education Quarterly*, 38(3), 151–168.

Grahe, J. (2017). Authentic research projects benefit students, their instructors, and science. In R. Obeid, A. M. Schwartz, C. Shane-Simpson, & P. J. Brooks (Eds.), *How we teach now: The GSTA guide to student-centered teaching* (pp. 351–367). Retrieved from the Society for the Teaching of Psychology website: http://teachpsych.org/ebooks/howweteachnow.

Grant, J. M., Mottet, L., Tanis, J. E., Harrison, J., Herman, J., & Keisling, M. (2011). *Injustice at every turn: A report of the national transgender discrimination survey*. Washington, DC: National Center for Transgender Equality and The National Gay and Lesbian Task Force.

Green, S. G., Ferrante, C. J., & Heppard, K. A. (2016). Using open-book exams to enhance student learning, performance, and motivation. *Journal of Effective Teaching*, 16(1), 19–35.

Grobman, K. H. (2015). Antsy students impatient to leave class and faculty captive in NPR driveway moments? Enhancing science classes with personal stories. In K. Brakke, & J. A. Houska (Eds.), *Telling stories: The art and science of storytelling as an instructional strategy*. Retrieved from the Society for the Teaching of Psychology website: http://teachpsych.org/ebooks/index.php.

Grose-Fifer, J. (2017). Using role play to enhance critical thinking about ethics in psychology. In R. Obeid, A. M. Schwartz, C. Shane-Simpson, & P. J. Brooks (Eds.), *How we teach now: The GSTA guide to student-centered teaching* (pp. 213–223). Retrieved from the Society for the Teaching of Psychology website: http://teachpsych.org/ebooks/howweteachnow.

Grose-Fifer, J., Davis, C., & Pryiomka, K. (2014). Guided reading and writing assignments in biological psychology courses. Paper presented at the Annual Meeting of the Eastern Psychological Association, Boston, MA.

Grose-Fifer, J., & Davis-Ferreira, C. (2018). Improved student outcomes in biological psychology courses through scaffolded reading and writing assignments. In T. Kuther (Ed.), *Integrating writing into the college classroom*. Retrieved from the Society for the Teaching of Psychology website: http://teachpsych.org/.

Grose-Fifer, J., Helmer, K. A., & Zottoli, T. M. (2014). Interdisciplinary connections and academic performance in Psychology–English learning communities. *Teaching of Psychology*, 41(1), 57–62.

Gross, D., Pietri, E. S., Anderson, G., Moyano-Camihort, K., & Graham, M. J. (2015). Increased preclass preparation underlies student outcome improvement in the flipped classroom. *CBE-Life Sciences Education*, 14(4), ar36.

Gross Davis, B. (2009). *Tools for teaching*. (pp. 481–488). San Franciso, CA: Jossey Bass.

Gross, M., Armstrong, B., & Latham, D. (2012). The analyze, search, evaluate (ASE) process model: Three steps toward information literacy. *Community and Junior College Libraries*, 18(3–4), 103–118.

Gross, M., & Latham, D. (2012). What's skill got to do with it?: Information literacy skills and self-views of ability among first-year college students. *Journal of the American Society for Information Science and Technology*, 63(3), 574–583.

Gross, M., & Latham, D. (2013). Addressing below proficient information literacy skills: Evaluating the efficacy of an evidence-based educational intervention. *Library and Information Science Research*, 35(3), 181–190.

Gross, M., Latham, D., & Armstrong, B. (2012). Improving below-proficient information literacy skills: Designing an evidence-based educational intervention. *College Teaching*, 60(3), 104–111.

Guiller, J., Durndell, A., & Ross, A. (2008). Peer interaction and critical thinking: Face-to-face or online discussion? *Learning and Instruction*, 18(2), 187–200.

Guldberg, K., & Pilkington, R. (2007). Tutor roles in facilitating reflection on practice through online discussion. *Journal of Educational Technology and Society*, 10(1).

Gurung, R. A. (2005). How do students really study (and does it matter)? *Teaching of Psychology*, 32, 239–241.

Gurung, R. A., Ansburg, P. I., Alexander, P. A., Lawrence, N. K., & Johnson, D. E. (2008). The state of the scholarship of teaching and learning in psychology. *Teaching of Psychology*, 35(4), 249–261.

Gurung, R. A., & Martin, R. C. (2011). Predicting textbook reading the textbook assessment and usage scale. *Teaching of Psychology*, 38(1), 22–28.

Gurung, R. A., & McCann, L. I. (2012). How should students study? In B. M. Schwartz, & R. A. R. Gurung (Eds.), *Evidence-based teaching for higher education*. Washington, DC: American Psychological Association.

Gurung, R. A., Weidert, J., & Jeske, A. (2012). Focusing on how students study. *Journal of the Scholarship of Teaching and Learning*, 10(1), 28–35.

Habanek, D. V. (2005). An examination of the integrity of the syllabus. *College Teaching*, 53(2), 62–64.

Hacker, D. J., Bol, L., Horgan, D. D., & Rakow, E. A. (2000). Test prediction and performance in a classroom context. *Journal of Educational Psychology*, 92(1), 160–170.

Hadjianastasis, M., & Nightingale, K. P. (2016). Podcasting in the STEM disciplines: The implications of supplementary lecture recording and "lecture flipping." *FEMS Microbiology Letters*, 363(4), fnw006.

Haggis, T. (2006). Pedagogies for diversity: Retaining critical challenge amidst fears of "dumbing down". *Studies in Higher Education*, 31(5), 521–535.

Hagopian, J. (Ed.) (2014). *More than a score: The new uprising against high-stakes testing.* Chicago, IL: Haymarket Books.

Haladyna, T. M. (2012). *Developing and validating multiple-choice test items.* New York, NY: Routledge.

Haladyna, T. M., Downing, S. M., & Rodriguez, M. C. (2002). A review of multiple-choice item-writing guidelines for classroom assessment. *Applied Measurement in Education*, 15(3), 309–333.

Halic, O., Lee, D., Paulus, T., & Spence, M. (2010). To blog or not to blog: Student perceptions of blog effectiveness for learning in a college-level course. *The Internet and Higher Education*, 13(4), 206–213.

Hall, D., & Buzwell, S. (2012). The problem of free-riding in group projects: Looking beyond social loafing as reason for non-contribution. *Active Learning in Higher Education*, 14(1), 37–49.

Halonen, J. S. (2008). Measure for measure: The challenge of assessing critical thinking. In D. S. Dunn, J. S. Halonen, & R. A. Smith (Eds.), *Teaching critical thinking in psychology* (pp. 59–75). Malden, MA: Wiley-Blackwell.

Halonen, J. S., Dunn, D. S., McCarthy, M. A., & Baker, S. C. (2012). Are you really above average? Documenting your teaching effectiveness. In B. M. Schwartz, & R. A. R. Gurung (Eds.), *Evidence-based teaching for higher education* (pp. 131–149). Washington, DC: American Psychological Association.

Halpern, D. F. (1998). Teaching critical thinking for transfer across domains: Disposition, skills, structure training, and metacognitive monitoring. *American Psychologist*, 53(4), 449–455.

Halpern, D. F. (1999). Teaching for critical thinking: Helping college students develop the skills and dispositions of a critical thinker. *New Directions for Teaching and Learning*, 1999(80), 69–74.

Halpern, D. F., & Desrochers, S. (2005). Social psychology in the classroom: Applying what we teach as we teach it. *Journal of Social and Clinical Psychology*, 24(1), 51–61.

Halpern, D. F., Smothergill, D. W., Allen, M., Baker, S., Baum, C., Best, D., … Hester, M. (1998). Scholarship in psychology: A paradigm for the twenty-first century. *American Psychologist*, 53(12), 1292–1297.

Hammann, L. A., & Stevens, R. J. (2003). Instructional approaches to improving students' writing of compare-contrast essays: An experimental study. *Journal of Literacy Research*, 35(2), 731–756.

Hammer, E. A. (2009). Using service learning to promote critical thinking. In D. S. Dunn, J. S. Halonen, & R. A. Smith (Eds.), *Teaching critical thinking in psychology: A handbook of best practices.* Chichester, U.K.: John Wiley and Sons.

Han, I., & Shin, W. S. (2016). The use of a mobile learning management system and academic achievement of online students. *Computers and Education*, 102, 79–89.

Hansen, J. D., & Dexter, L. (1997). Quality multiple-choice test questions: Item-writing guidelines and an analysis of auditing testbanks. *Journal of Education for Business*, 73(2), 94–97.

Hara, N., Bonk, C. J., & Angeli, C. (2000). Content analysis of online discussion in an applied educational psychology course. *Instructional Science*, 28(2), 115–152.

Harackiewicz, J. M., Canning, E. A., Tibbetts, Y., Giffen, C. J., Blair, S. S., Rouse, D. I., & Hyde, J. S. (2014). Closing the social class achievement gap for first-generation students in undergraduate biology. *Journal of Educational Psychology*, 106(2), 375–389.

Harackiewicz, J. M., Canning, E. A., Tibbetts, Y., Priniski, S. J., & Hyde, J. S. (2016). Closing achievement gaps with a utility-value intervention: Disentangling race and social class. *Journal of Personality and Social Psychology*, 111(5), 745–765.

Harackiewicz, J. M., & Priniski, S. J. (2018). Improving student outcomes in higher education: The science of targeted intervention. *Annual Review of Psychology*, 69, 409–435.

Hargittai, E., & Shaw, A. (2015). Mind the skills gap: The role of internet know-how and gender in differentiated contributions to Wikipedia. *Information, Communication and Society*, 18(4), 424–442.

Harlow, L. L. (2013). Teaching quantitative psychology. In T. D. Little (Ed.), *The Oxford handbook of quantitative methods* (Vol. 1)Foundations (pp. 105–117). New York, NY: Oxford University Press.

Hartlep, K. L., & Forsyth, G. A. (2000). The effect of self-reference on learning and retention. *Teaching of Psychology*, 27(4), 269–271.

Hartwig, M. K., & Dunlosky, J. (2012). Study strategies of college students: Are self-testing and scheduling related to achievement? *Psychonomic Bulletin and Review*, 19(1), 126–134.

Hasher, L., Goldstein, D., & Toppino, T. (1977). Frequency and the conference of referential validity. *Journal of Verbal Learning and Verbal Behavior*, 16(1), 107–112.

Haswell, R. H. (1983). Minimal marking. *College English*, 45(6), 600–604.

Haswell, R. H. (2005). NCTE/CCCC's recent war on scholarship. *Written Communication*, 22(2), 198–223.

Hatch, D. L., Zschau, T., Hays, A., McAllister, K., Harrison, M., Cate, K. L., ... Lloyd, S. A. (2014). Of mice and meth: A new media-based neuropsychopharmacology lab to teach research methods. *Teaching of Psychology*, 41(2), 167–174.

Hattie, J. (2015). The applicability of visible learning to higher education. *Scholarship of Teaching and Learning in Psychology*, 1(1), 79–91.

Hattie, J., & Timperley, H. (2007). The power of feedback. *Review of Educational Research*, 77(1), 81–112.

Hattie, J., & Yates, G. C. (2014). *Visible learning and the science of how we learn*. Abingdon, U.K.: Routledge.

Hayes, J. R. (2006). New directions in writing theory. *Handbook of Writing Research*, 2, 28–40.

Haynes, T. L., Perry, R. P., Stupnisky, R. H., & Daniels, L. M. (2009). A review of attributional retraining treatments: Fostering engagement and persistence in vulnerable college students. In J. Smart (Ed.), *Higher education: Handbook of theory and research* (pp. 227–272). Dordrecht, NL: Springer.

Head, A. J., & Eisenberg, M. B. (2009). Lessons learned: How college students seek information in the digital age. Retrieved from the Social Science Research Network website: http://papers.ssrn.com/sol3/papers.cfm?abstract_id=2281478.

Head, A. J., & Eisenberg, M. B. (2010). How today's college students use Wikipedia for course-related research. *First Monday*, 15(3). Retrieved from the Social Science Research Network website: https://ssrn.com/abstract=2281527.

Healy, A., Kole, J., & Bourne, L. (2014). Training principles to advance expertise. *Frontiers in Psychology*, 5(131).

Hembree, R. (1988). Correlates, causes, effects, and treatment of test anxiety. *Review of Educational Research*, 58(1), 47–77.

Hemenover, S. H., Caster, J. B., & Mizumoto, A. (1999). Combining the use of progressive writing techniques and popular movies in introductory psychology. *Teaching of Psychology*, 26(3), 196–198.

Henslee, A. M., Burgess, D. R., & Buskist, W. (2006). Student preferences for first day of class activities. *Teaching of Psychology*, 33(3), 189–191.

Henson, R., & Stephenson, S. (2009). Writing consultations can effect quantifiable change: One institution's assessment. Writing Lab Newsletter, p. 1. Retrieved from http://link.galegroup.com/apps/doc/A204036307/AONE?u=cuny_johnjay&sid=AONE&xid=26fb6863.

Heo, M. (2009). Digital storytelling: An empirical study of the impact of digital storytelling on pre-service teachers' self-efficacy and dispositions towards educational technology. *Journal of Educational Multimedia and Hypermedia*, 18(4), 405–428.

Hermann, A. D., Foster, D. A., & Hardin, E. E. (2010). Does the first week of class matter? A quasi-experimental investigation of student satisfaction. *Teaching of Psychology*, 37(2), 79–84.

Herreid, C. F. (1997). What makes a good case? *Journal of College Science Teaching*, 27(3), 163–165.

Hertel, J. P., & Millis, B. J. (Eds.) (2002). *Using simulations to promote learning in higher education: An introduction.* Sterling, VA: Stylus Publishing.

Hettich, P. (1990). Journal writing: Old fare or nouvelle cuisine? *Teaching of Psychology*, 17(1), 36–39.

Higbee, J. L. (Ed.) (2003). *Curriculum transformation and disability: Implementing universal design in higher education.* Minneapolis, MN: University of Minnesota, Center for Research on Developmental Education and Urban Literacy.

Hill, A., Arford, T., Lubitow, A., & Smollin, L. M. (2012). "I'm ambivalent about it": The dilemmas of PowerPoint. *Teaching Sociology*, 40(3), 242–256.

Hill, B. M., & Shaw, A. (2013). The Wikipedia gender gap revisited: Characterizing survey response bias with propensity score estimation. *PLoS One*, 8(6), e65782.

Hill, G. W. IV, & Zinsmeister, D. D. (2012). Becoming an ethical teacher. In W. Buskist, & V. A. Benassi (Eds.), *Effective college and university teaching: Strategies and tactics for the new professoriate* (pp. 125–137). Thousand Oaks, CA: Sage.

Himmele, P., & Himmele, W. (2011). *Total participation techniques: Making every student an active learner.* Alexandria, VA: ASCD.

Hmelo-Silver, C. E. (2004). Problem-based learning: What and how do students learn? *Educational Psychology Review*, 16(3), 235–266.

Hobson, E. H. (2004). Getting students to read: Fourteen tips. *Idea Paper*, 40, 1–10.

Hock, R. R. (2012). *Forty studies that changed psychology* (7th ed.). Upper Saddle River, NJ: Pearson.

Hoeft, M. E. (2012). Why university students don't read: What professors can do to increase compliance. *International Journal for the Scholarship of Teaching and Learning*, 6(2), 12.

Holzl, J. (1997). Twelve tips for effective PowerPoint presentations for the technologically challenged. *Medical Teacher*, 19(3), 175–179.

Honicke, T., & Broadbent, J. (2016). The influence of academic self-efficacy on academic performance: A systematic review. *Educational Research Review*, 17, 63–84.

Hopkins, R. F., Lyle, K. B., Hieb, J. L., & Ralston, P. A. (2016). Spaced retrieval practice increases college students' short-and long-term retention of mathematics knowledge. *Educational Psychology Review*, 28(4), 853–873.

Horn, M. B., & Staker, H. (2011). The rise of K–12 blended learning. San Mateo, CA: Innosight Institute. Retrieved from http://leadcommission.org/sites/default/files/The%20Rise%20of%20K-12%20Blended%20Learning_0.pdf.

Howard, R. M. (1999). *Standing in the shadow of giants: Plagiarists, authors, collaborators.* Santa Barbara, CA: Greenwood Publishing Group.

Howland, J. L., & Moore, J. L. (2002). Student perceptions as distance learners in internet-based courses. *Distance Education*, 23(2), 183–195.

Hulleman, C. S., Godes, O., Hendricks, B. L., & Harackiewicz, J. M. (2010). Enhancing interest and performance with a utility value intervention. *Journal of Educational Psychology*, 102(4), 880–895.

Hulleman, C. S., Kosovich, J. J., Barron, K. E., & Daniel, D. B. (2017). Making connections: Replicating and extending the utility value intervention in the classroom. *Journal of Educational Psychology*, 109(3), 387–404.

Hunsu, N. J., Adesope, O., & Bayly, D. J. (2016). A meta-analysis of the effects of audience response systems (clicker-based technologies) on cognition and affect. *Computers and Education*, 94, 102–119.

Hursh, D. W. (2008). *High-stakes testing and the decline of teaching and learning: The real crisis in education* (Vol. 1). Lanham, MD: Rowman and Littlefield.

Hurtado, S., & Ruiz, A. (2012). The climate for underrepresented groups and diversity on campus. *American Academy of Political and Social Science*, 634(1), 190–206.

Hussey, H. D., Fleck, B. K., & Richmond, A. S. (Eds.) (2014). *Promoting active learning through a flipped course design.* Hershey, PA: IGI Global.

Hussey, H. D., Richmond, A. S., & Fleck, B. (2015). A primer for creating a flipped psychology course. *Psychology Learning and Teaching*, 14(2), 169–185.

Hutchings, P., Huber, M. T., & Ciccone, A. (2011). *The scholarship of teaching and learning reconsidered: Institutional integration and impact* (Vol. 21). Chichester, U.K.: John Wiley and Sons.

Iannarelli, B. A., Bardsley, M. E., & Foote, C. J. (2010). Here's your syllabus, see you next week: A review of the first day practices of outstanding professors. *Journal of Effective Teaching*, 10(2), 29–41.

Institute of International Education. (2017). *Open Doors 2017*. Retrieved from https://www.iie.org/Research-and-Insights/Open-Doors/Open-Doors-2017-Media-Information.

Ishiyama, J. T., & Hartlaub, S. (2002). Does the wording of syllabi affect student course assessment in introductory political science classes? *Political Science and Politics*, 35(03), 567–570.

Izawa, C. (1966). Reinforcement-test sequences in paired-associate learning. *Psychological Reports*, 18(3), 879–919.

Izawa, C. (1967). Function of test trials in paired-associate learning. *Journal of Experimental Psychology*, 75(2), 194–209.

Jamieson, J. P., Mendes, W. B., Blackstock, E., & Schmader, T. (2010). Turning the knots in your stomach into bows: Reappraising arousal improves performance on the GRE. *Journal of Experimental Social Psychology*, 46(1), 208–212.

Janzow, F., & Eison, J. (1990). Grades: Their influence on students and faculty. *New Directions for Teaching and Learning*, 1990(42), 93–102.

Jehangir, R. (2010). *Higher education and first-generation students: Cultivating community, voice, and place for the new majority*. New York, NY: Palgrave Macmillan.

Jensen, J. L., Kummer, T. A., & Godoy, P. D. d. M. (2015). Improvements from a flipped classroom may simply be the fruits of active learning. *CBE-Life Sciences Education*, 14(1), ar5.

Jensen, J. L., McDaniel, M. A., Woodard, S. M., & Kummer, T. A. (2014). Teaching to the test… or testing to teach: Exams requiring higher order thinking skills encourage greater conceptual understanding. *Educational Psychology Review*, 26(2), 307–329.

Jhangiani, R., Troisi, J., Fleck, B., Legg, A., & Hussey, H. (2015). A compendium of scales for use in the scholarship of teaching and learning. Retrieved from the Society for the Teaching of Psychology website: http://teachpsych.org/Resources/Documents/ebooks/compscalesstl.pdf#page=20.

Johnson, D. W., & Johnson, F. P. (1989). *Cooperation and competition: Theory and research*. Edina, MN: Interaction Book Company.

Johnson, D. W., & Johnson, F. P. (2005). New developments in social interdependence theory. *Genetic, Social, and General Psychology Monographs*, 131(4), 285–358.

Johnson, D. W., & Johnson, F. P. (2009a). An educational psychology success story: Social interdependence theory and cooperative learning. *Educational Researcher*, 38(5), 365–379.

Johnson, D. W., & Johnson, F. P. (2009b). Energizing learning: The instructional power of conflict. *Educational Researcher*, 38(1), 37–51.

Johnson, D. W., & Johnson, F. P. (2009c). *Joining together: Group theory and group skills* (10th ed.). Upper Saddle River, NJ: Pearson.

Johnson, D. W., Johnson, F. P., & Smith, K. A. (1998). Cooperative learning returns to college what evidence is there that it works? *Change: The Magazine of Higher Learning*, 30(4), 26–35.

Johnson, D. W., Johnson, F. P., & Smith, K. A. (2000). Constructive controversy. *Change*, 32(1), 28–37.

Johnson, D. W., Johnson, F. P., & Smith, K. A. (2014). Cooperative learning: Improving university instruction by basing practice on validated theory. *Journal on Excellence in College Teaching*, 25, 85–118.

Johnson, D. W., Johnson, F. P., & Stanne, M. E. (2000). *Cooperative learning methods: A meta-analysis*. Minneapolis, MN: University of Minnesota Press.

Johnson, D. W., & Johnson, R. T. (2002). Learning together and alone: Overview and meta-analysis. *Asia Pacific Journal of Education*, 22(1), 95–105.

Johnson, D. W., Johnson, R. T., & Smith, K. A. (1991). *Active learning: Cooperation in the college classroom*. Edina, MN: Interaction Book Company.

Johnson, E., & Carton, J. (2006). Introductory psychology without the big book. In D. Dunn, & S. Chew (Eds.), *Best practices for teaching introduction to psychology* (pp. 83–92). Mahwah, NJ: Lawrence Erlbaum Associates.

Johnson, E. J., Tuskenis, A. D., Howell, G. L., & Jaroszewski, K. (2011). Development and effects of a writing and thinking course in psychology. *Teaching of Psychology*, 38(4), 229–236.

Jones, C. (2001). The relationship between writing centers and improvement in writing ability: An assessment of the literature. *Education*, 122(1), 3–21.

Jones, C., Connolly, M., Gear, A., & Read, M. (2001). Group interactive learning with group process support technology. *British Journal of Educational Technology*, 32(5), 571–586.

Jones, G. M., Jones, B. D., & Hargrove, T. (2003). *The unintended consequences of high-stakes testing*. Lanham, MD: Rowman and Littlefield Publishers.

Jones, S., Johnson-Yale, C., Millermaier, S., & Perez, F. S. (2009). U.S. college students' internet use: Race, gender and digital divides. *Journal of Computer-Mediated Communication*, 14(2), 244–264.

Jones, S., Johnson-Yale, C., Millermaier, S., & Seoane Perez, F. (2009). Everyday life, online: U.S. college students' use of the internet. *First Monday*, 14(10). doi:10.5210/fm.v14i10.2649.

Jonsson, A., & Svingby, G. (2007). The use of scoring rubrics: Reliability, validity and educational consequences. *Educational Research Review*, 2(2), 130–144.

Jordan, L. A., & Papp, R. (2013). PowerPoint®: It's not "yes" or "no"—It's "when" and "how." *Research in Higher Education Journal*, 22, 1–12.

Jorgensen, T. D., & Marek, P. (2013). Workshops increase students' proficiency at identifying general and APA-style writing errors. *Teaching of Psychology*, 40(4), 294–299.

Jozefowicz, R. F., Koeppen, B. M., Case, S., Galbraith, R., Swanson, D., & Glew, R. H. (2002). The quality of in-house medical school examinations. *Academic Medicine*, 77(2), 156–161.

Judd, T., Kennedy, G., & Cropper, S. (2010). Using wikis for collaborative learning: Assessing collaboration through contribution. *Australasian Journal of Educational Technology*, 26(3), 341–354.

Kaddoura, M. (2013). Think pair share: A teaching learning strategy to enhance students' critical thinking. *Educational Research Quarterly*, 36(4), 3–24.

Kagan, S. (2014). Kagan structures, processing, and excellence in college teaching. *Journal on Excellence in College Teaching*, 25, 119–138.

Kahneman, D. (2011). *Thinking fast and slow*. New York: Farrar, Straus and Giroux.

Kang, S. H., McDermott, K. B., & Roediger, H. L. III (2007). Test format and corrective feedback modify the effect of testing on long-term retention. *European Journal of Cognitive Psychology*, 19(4–5), 528–558.

Kaplan, M., Meizlish, D. S., O'Neal, C., & Wright, M. C. (2007). A research-based rubric for developing statements of teaching philosophy. In D. R. Robertson, & L. B. Nilson (Eds.), *To improve the academy: Resources for faculty, instructional and organizational development* (Vol. 26) (pp. 242–262). San Francisco, CA: Jossey-Bass.

Karau, S. J., & Williams, K. D. (1993). Social loafing: A meta-analytic review and theoretical integration. *Journal of Personality and Social Psychology*, 65(4), 681–706.

Karp, M. M., O'Gara, L., & Hughes, K. L. (2008). Do support services at community colleges encourage success or reproduce disadvantage? An exploratory study of students in two community colleges. CCRC Working Paper No. 10. NewYork, NY: Community College Research Center, Teacher's College, Columbia University.

Karpiak, C. P. (2011). Assessment of problem-based learning in the undergraduate statistics course. *Teaching of Psychology*, 38(4), 251–254.

Karpicke, J. D., Butler, A. C., & Roediger, H. L. III (2009). Metacognitive strategies in student learning: Do students practise retrieval when they study on their own? *Memory*, 17(4), 471–479.

Katz, J., DuBois, M., & Wigderson, S. (2014). Learning by helping? Undergraduate communication outcomes associated with training or service-learning experiences. *Teaching of Psychology*, 41(3), 251–255.

Kazis, R., Callahan, A., Davidson, C., McLeod, A., Bosworth, B., Choitz, V., & Hoops, J. (2007). Adult learners in higher education: Barriers to success and strategies to improve results. Employment and Training Administration. Occasional Paper 2007–03. Washington, DC: U.S. Department of Labor, Employment and Training Administration, Office of Policy Development and Research.

Kearns, K. D., & Sullivan, C. S. (2011). Resources and practices to help graduate students and postdoctoral fellows write statements of teaching philosophy. *Advances in Physiology Education*, 35(2), 136–145.

Keeler, C. (1997). Portfolio assessment in graduate level statistics courses. In I. Gal, & J. B. Garfield (Eds.), *The assessment challenge in statistics education* (pp. 165–178). Amsterdam: IOS Press.

Keeley, J., Furr, R. M., & Buskist, W. (2009). Differentiating psychology students' perceptions of teachers using the teacher behavior checklist. *Teaching of Psychology*, 37(1), 16–20.

Keith-Spiegel, P., Whitley, B. E. Jr., Balogh, D. W., Perkins, D. V., & Wittig, A. F. (2002). *The ethics of teaching: A casebook*. Mahwah, NJ: Lawrence Erlbaum Associates.

Kelley, S., & Calkins, S. (2006). Evaluating popular portrayals of memory in film. *Teaching of Psychology*, 33(3), 191–194.

Kellogg, R. T. (1994). *The psychology of writing*. New York, NY: Oxford University Press.

Kellogg, R. T., & Raulerson, B. A. (2007). Improving the writing skills of college students. *Psychonomic Bulletin and Review*, 14(2), 237–242.

Kelting-Gibson, L. M. (2005). Comparison of curriculum development practices. *Educational Research Quarterly*, 29(1), 26–36.

Kena, G., Hussar, W., McFarland, J., de Brey, C., Musu-Gillette, L., Wang, X., … Dunlop Velez, E. (2016). The condition for education 2016 (NCES 2016–144). National Center for Education Statistics. Retrieved from https://nces.ed.gov/pubsearch/.

Kennedy, M. J., Hirsch, S. E., Dillon, S. E., Rabideaux, L., Alves, K. D., & Driver, M. K. (2016). Using content acquisition podcasts to increase student knowledge and to reduce perceived cognitive load. *Teaching of Psychology*, 43(2), 153–158.

Kennedy, P. W., Sheckley, B. G., & Kehrhahn, M. T. (2000). The dynamic nature of student persistence: Influence of interactions between student attachment, academic adaptation, and social adaptation. Paper presented at the Annual Meeting of the Association for Institutional Research, Cincinnati, OH.

Kennedy, R. (2007). In-class debates: Fertile ground for active learning and the cultivation of critical thinking and oral communication skills. *International Journal of Teaching and Learning in Higher Education*, 19(2), 183–190.

Kenyon, R. (1989). Writing is problem solving. In P. Connolly, & T. Vilardi (Eds.), *Writing to learn mathematics and science*. New York, NY: Teachers College Press.

Kerawalla, L., Minocha, S., Kirkup, G., & Conole, G. (2009). An empirically grounded framework to guide blogging in higher education. *Journal of Computer Assisted Learning*, 25(1), 31–42.

Ketterlin-Geller, L. R., & Johnstone, C. (2006). Accommodations and universal design: Supporting access to assessments in higher education. *Journal of Postsecondary Education and Disability*, 19(2), 163–172.

Keutzer, C. S. (1993a). Jeopardy© in abnormal psychology. *Teaching of Psychology*, 20(1), 45–46.

Keutzer, C. S. (1993b). Midterm evaluation of teaching provides helpful feedback to instructors. *Teaching of Psychology*, 20(4), 238–240.

Khanna, M. M., Brack, A. S. B., & Finken, L. L. (2013). Short-and long-term effects of cumulative finals on student learning. *Teaching of Psychology*, 40, 175–182.

Kim, E. (2009). Navigating college life: The role of peer networks in first-year college adaptation experience of minority immigrant students. *Journal of The First-Year Experience and Students in Transition*, 21(2), 9–34.

Kim, J. (2013). Influence of group size on students' participation in online discussion forums. *Computers and Education*, 62, 123–129.

King, K. P. (2002). Identifying success in online teacher education and professional development. *The Internet and Higher Education*, 5(3), 231–246.

King, P. M., & Kitchener, K. S. (2004). Reflective judgment: Theory and research on the development of epistemic assumptions through adulthood. *Educational Psychologist*, 39(1), 5–18.

Kirschner, P. A., Sweller, J., & Clark, R. E. (2006). Why minimal guidance during instruction does not work: An analysis of the failure of constructivist, discovery, problem-based, experiential, and inquiry-based teaching. *Educational Psychologist*, 41(2), 75–86.

Kirsh, S. (1998). Using animated films to teach social and personality development. *Teaching of Psychology*, 25(1), 49–51.

Kitchener, K. S. (1994). Assessing reflective thinking within curricular contexts. Retrieved from http://files.eric.ed.gov/fulltext/ED415751.pdf.

Knowles, M. S., Holton, E. F. III, & Swanson, R. A. (2012). *The adult learner*. New York, NY: Routledge.

Kocaman-Karoglu, A. (2016). Personal voices in higher education: A digital storytelling experience for pre-service teachers. *Education and Information Technologies*, 21(5), 1153–1168.

Kolar, D., & McBride, C. (2003). Creating problems to solve problems: An interactive teaching technique for statistics courses. *Teaching of Psychology*, 30(1), 67–68.

Kolb, D. A. (2014). *Experiential learning: Experience as the source of learning and development*. Upper Saddle River, NJ: Pearson.

Koriat, A., & Bjork, R. A. (2005). Illusions of competence in monitoring one's knowledge during study. *Journal of Experimental Psychology: Learning, Memory, and Cognition*, 31(2), 187–194.

Koriat, A., & Bjork, R. A. (2006). Illusions of competence during study can be remedied by manipulations that enhance learners' sensitivity to retrieval conditions at test. *Memory and Cognition*, 34(5), 959–972.

Korn, J. H. (2012). Writing and developing your philosophy of teaching. In W. Buskist, & V. A. Benassi (Eds.), *Effective college and university teaching: Strategies and tactics for the new professoriate* (pp. 71–79). Thousand Oaks, CA: Sage.

Kornell, N. (2009). Optimising learning using flashcards: Spacing is more effective than cramming. *Applied Cognitive Psychology*, 23(9), 1297–1317.

Kornell, N., & Bjork, R. A. (2007). The promise and perils of self-regulated study. *Psychonomic Bulletin and Review*, 14(2), 219–224.

Kornell, N., & Bjork, R. A. (2009). A stability bias in human memory: Overestimating remembering and underestimating learning. *Journal of Experimental Psychology: General*, 138(4), 449–468.

Kornell, N., Klein, P. J., & Rawson, K. A. (2015). Retrieval attempts enhance learning, but retrieval success (versus failure) does not matter. *Journal of Experimental Psychology: Learning, Memory, and Cognition*, 41(1), 283–294.

Kosslyn, S. M. (2007). *Clear and to the point: 8 psychological principles for compelling PowerPoint presentations.* New York, NY: Oxford University Press.

Kramer, T. J., & Korn, J. H. (1999). Class discussions: Promoting participation and preventing problems. In B. Perlman, L. I. McCann, S. H. McFadden, & E. Yago (Eds.), *Lessons learned: Practical advice for the teaching of psychology.* Washington, DC: The American Psychological Society.

Kraus, R. (2008). You must participate: Violating research ethical principles through role-play. *College Teaching,* 56(3), 131–136.

Kreiner, D. S. (1997). Guided notes and interactive methods for teaching with videotapes. *Teaching of Psychology,* 24(3), 183–185.

Kreiner, D. S. (2009). Problem-based group activities for teaching sensation and perception. *Teaching of Psychology,* 36(4), 253–256.

Kreniske, P. (2017). Developing a culture of commenting in a first-year seminar. *Computers in Human Behavior,* 72, 724–732.

Kreniske, P., & Todorova, R. (2017). Using blogs to engage first-generation college students. In R. Obeid, A. M. Schwartz, C. Shane-Simpson, & P. J. Brooks (Eds.), *How we teach now: The GSTA guide to student-centered teaching* (pp. 282–295). Retrieved from the Society for the Teaching of Psychology website: http://teachpsych.org/ebooks/howweteachnow.

Krentler, K. A., & Willis-Flurry, L. A. (2005). Does technology enhance actual student learning? The case of online discussion boards. *Journal of Education for Business,* 80(6), 316–321.

Kretchmar, M. D. (2001). Service learning in a general psychology class: Description, preliminary evaluation, and recommendations. *Teaching of Psychology,* 28(1), 5–10.

Krogstad, J. M. (2016). 5 facts about Latinos and education. Retrieved from the Pew Research Center website: http://www.pewresearch.org/fact-tank/2016/07/28/5-facts-about-latinos-and-education/.

Kruger, J., & Dunning, D. (1999). Unskilled and unaware of it: How difficulties in recognizing one's own incompetence lead to inflated self-assessments. *Journal of Personality and Social Psychology,* 77(6), 1121–1134.

Kubitz, K., & Lightner, R. (2012). Application exercises. Challenges and strategies in the psychology classroom. In M. Sweet, & L. K. Michaelsen (Eds.), *Team-based learning in the social sciences and humanities: Group work that works to generate critical thinking and engagement* (pp. 65–80). Sterling, VA: Stylus Publishing.

Kuh, G. D. (2003). What we're learning about student engagement from NSSE: Benchmarks for effective educational practices. *Change: The Magazine of Higher Learning,* 35(2), 24–32.

Kuh, G. D. (2008). *High-impact educational practices: What they are, who has access to them, and why they matter.* Washington, DC: Association of American Colleges and Universities.

Kuh, G. D., Cruce, T. M., Shoup, R., Kinzie, J., & Gonyea, R. M. (2008). Unmasking the effects of student engagement on first-year college grades and persistence. *Journal of Higher Education,* 79(5), 540–563.

Kuhlthau, C. C. (1999). Accommodating the user's information search process: Challenges for information retrieval system designers. *Bulletin of the American Society for Information Science and Technology,* 25(3), 12–16.

Kuhlthau, C. C. (2004). *Seeking meaning: A process approach to library and information services* (2nd ed.). Westport, CT: Libraries Unlimited Incorporated.

Kuhn, D., Cheney, R., & Weinstock, M. (2000). The development of epistemological understanding. *Cognitive Development*, 15(3), 309–328.

Kuhn, D., Pease, M., & Wirkala, C. (2009). Coordinating the effects of multiple variables: A skill fundamental to scientific thinking. *Journal of Experimental Child Psychology*, 103(3), 268–284.

Kulhavy, R. W. (1977). Feedback in written instruction. *Review of Educational Research*, 47(2), 211–232.

Kulik, J. A., & Kulik, C.-L. C. (1988). Timing of feedback and verbal learning. *Review of Educational Research*, 58(1), 79–97.

Kurtiş, T., & Adams, G. (2017). Decolonial intersectionality. Implications for theory, research, and pedagogy. In K. A. Case (Ed.), *Intersectional pedagogy: Complicating identity and social justice* (pp. 46–59). New York, NY: Routledge.

Lage, M. J., Platt, G. J., & Treglia, M. (2000). Inverting the classroom: A gateway to creating an inclusive learning environment. *Journal of Economic Education*, 31(1), 30–43.

Laing, G. K. (2010). An empirical test of mnemonic devices to improve learning in elementary accounting. *Journal of Education for Business*, 85(6), 349–358.

Lambert, J. (2010). *Digital storytelling cookbook*. Berkely, CA: Digital Diner Press.

Lamoreaux, M., Darnell, K., Sheehan, E., & Tusher, C. (2012). Educating students about plagiarism. Retrieved from the Office of Teaching Resources in Psychology for Society for the Teaching of Psychology website: https://teachpsych.org/Resources/Documents/otrp/resources/plagiarism/Educating%20Students%20about%20Plagiarism.pdf.

Lampert, L. (2005). "Getting psyched" about information literacy: A successful faculty-librarian collaboration for educational psychology and counseling. *The Reference Librarian*, 43(89–90), 5–23.

Landau, J. D., Druen, P. B., & Arcuri, J. A. (2002). Methods for helping students avoid plagiarism. *Teaching of Psychology*, 29(2), 112–115.

Landrum, R. E. (2012). Selection of textbooks or readings for your course. In B. M. Schwartz, & R. A. R. Gurung (Eds.), *Evidence-based teaching for higher education* (pp. 117–129). Washington, DC: American Psychological Association.

Landrum, R. E. (2013). Writing in APA style: Faculty perspectives of competence and importance. *Psychology Learning and Teaching*, 12(3), 259–265.

Landrum, R. E., Gurung, R. A., & Spann, N. (2012). Assessments of textbook usage and the relationship to student course performance. *College Teaching*, 60(1), 17–24.

Landrum, R. E., & Nelsen, L. R. (2002). The undergraduate research assistantship: An analysis of the benefits. *Teaching of Psychology*, 29(1), 15–19.

Landrum, R. E., & Smith, R. A. (2007). Creating syllabi for statistics and research methods courses. In D. S. Dunn, R. A. Smith, & B. C. Beins (Eds.), *Best practices for teaching statistics and research methods in the behavioral sciences* (pp. 45–57). Mahwah, NJ: Lawrence Erlbaum.

Lang, J. M. (2010). Four steps to a memorable teaching philosophy. *Chronicle of Higher Education*.
Retrieved from http://www.chronicle.com/article/4-Steps-to-a-Memorable/124199.

Lape, N. K., Levy, R., Yong, D., Haushalter, K., Eddy, R., & Hankel, N. (2014). Probing the inverted classroom: A controlled study of teaching and learning outcomes in undergraduate Engineering and Mathematics. Paper presented at the 121st American Association of Engineering Education (ASEE) Annual Conference and Exposition,

Indianapolis, IN. Retrieved from https://peer.asee.org/probing-the-inverted-classroom-a-controlled-study-of-teaching-and-learning-outcomes-in-undergraduate-engineering-and-mathematics.pdf.

Larkin, J. E., & Pines, H. A. (2005). Developing information literacy and research skills in introductory psychology: A case study. *Journal of Academic Librarianship*, 31(1), 40–45.

Latané, B., Williams, K., & Harkins, S. (1979). Many hands make light the work: The causes and consequences of social loafing. *Journal of Personality and Social Psychology*, 37(6), 822–832.

Lattuca, L. R., Voigt, L. J., & Fath, K. Q. (2004). Does interdisciplinarity promote learning? Theoretical support and researchable questions. *The Review of Higher Education*, 28(1), 23–48.

LaVelle, M. (1999). Building a teaching portfolio. *Anthropology News*, 40(3), 37–38.

Lawrence, N. K. (2013). Cumulative exams in the introductory psychology course. *Teaching of Psychology*, 40(1), 15–19.

Lawrence, N. K., Serdikoff, S. L., Zinn, T. E., & Baker, S. C. (2009). Have we demystified critical thinking. In D. S. Dunn, J. S. Halonen, & R. A. Smith (Eds.), *Teaching critical thinking in psychology: A handbook of best practices* (pp. 23–33). Oxford, U.K: Wiley-Blackwell.

Lawrence, N. K., & Wilson, J. H. (2014). On the importance of attending teaching conferences. In J. N. Busler, B. C. Beins, & W. Buskist (Eds.), *Preparing the new psychology professoriate: Helping graduate students become competent teachers* (2nd ed.). Retrieved from the Society for the Teaching of Psychology website: http://teachpsych.org.

Lawrence, S. M., & Tatum, B. D. (1999). White racial identity and anti-racist education: A catalyst for change. In E. Lee, D. Menkart, & M. Okazawa-Rey (Eds.), *Beyond heroes and holidays: A practical guide to K–12 anti-racist, multicultural education and staff development* (pp. 45–51). Washington, DC: Network of Educators on the Americas.

Lawson, T. J. (1999). Assessing psychological critical thinking as a learning outcome for psychology majors. *Teaching of Psychology*, 26, 207–209.

Lawson, T. J., Bodle, J. H., Houlette, M. A., & Haubner, R. R. (2006). Guiding questions enhance student learning from educational videos. *Teaching of Psychology*, 33(1), 31–33.

Lawson, T. J., Bodle, J. H., & McDonough, T. A. (2007). Techniques for increasing student learning from educational videos: Notes versus guiding questions. *Teaching of Psychology*, 34(2), 90–93.

Lawson, T. J., & Crane, L. L. (2014). Dowsing rods designed to sharpen critical thinking and understanding of ideomotor action. *Teaching of Psychology*, 41(1), 52–56.

Lawson, T. J., Jordan-Fleming, M. K., & Bodle, J. H. (2015). Measuring psychological critical thinking: An update. *Teaching of Psychology*, 42(3), 248–253.

Layous, K., Davis, E. M., Garcia, J., Purdie-Vaughns, V., Cook, J. E., & Cohen, G. L. (2017). Feeling left out, but affirmed: Protecting against the negative effects of low belonging in college. *Journal of Experimental Social Psychology*, 69, 227–231.

Lazowski, R. A., & Hulleman, C. S. (2016). Motivation interventions in education: A meta-analytic review. *Review of Educational Research*, 86(2), 602–640.

Leahy, R. (1990). What the college writing center is—And isn't. *College Teaching*, 38(2), 43–48.

Lehman, D. R., & Nisbett, R. E. (1990). A longitudinal study of the effects of undergraduate training on reasoning. *Developmental Psychology*, 26(6), 952–960.

Lemov, D. (2015). *Teach like a champion 2.0: 62 techniques that put students on the path to college.* John Wiley and Sons.

Lending, D. (2010). Using a wiki to collaborate on a study guide. *Journal of Information Systems Education*, 21(1), 5–13.

Leon, S. M. (2008). Slowing down, talking back, and moving forward: Some reflections on digital storytelling in the humanities curriculum. *Arts and Humanities in Higher Education*, 7(2), 220–223.

Lerner, L. D. (1995). Making student groups work. *Journal of Management Education*, 19(1), 123–125.

Leutner, D., Leopold, C., & den Elzen-Rump, V. (2007). Self-regulated learning with a text-highlighting strategy. *Zeitschrift für Psychologie/Journal of Psychology*, 215(3), 174–182.

Levasseur, D. G., & Kanan Sawyer, J. (2006). Pedagogy meets PowerPoint: A research review of the effects of computer-generated slides in the classroom. *The Review of Communication*, 6(1–2), 101–123.

Lewandowski, G. W., Jr. (2003). Classroom demonstration for teaching threats to internal validity. Poster presented at 17th Annual Meeting on Undergraduate Teaching of Psychology Ideas and Innovations, Ellenville, NY. Retrieved from http://www.teachpsychscience.org/files/pdf/56201061709AM_1.PDF.

Lewis, K. G. (2001). Using midsemester student feedback and responding to it. *New Directions for Teaching and Learning*, 2001(87), 33–44.

Lilienfeld, S. O., Lohr, J. M., & Morier, D. (2001). The teaching of courses in the science and pseudoscience of psychology: Useful resources. *Teaching of Psychology*, 28(3), 182–191.

Lilienfeld, S. O., Lynn, S. J., Ruscio, J., & Beyerstein, B. L. (2010). The top ten myths of popular psychology. *Skeptic Magazine*, 15, 36–43.

Lim, R. F., Diamond, R. J., Chang, J. B., Primm, A. B., & Lu, F. G. (2008). Using non-feature films to teach diversity, cultural competence, and the DSM-IV-TR outline for cultural formulation. *Academic Psychiatry*, 32(4), 291–298.

Lim, S. (2009). How and why do college students use Wikipedia? *Journal of the American Society for Information Science and Technology*, 60(11), 2189–2202.

Linder, K. E., Elek, E. D., & Calderon, L. (2014). SoTL and the institutional review board: Considerations before navigating the application process for classroom research in higher education. *Journal of the Scholarship of Teaching and Learning*, 14(2), 1–14.

Lineweaver, T. T. (2010). Online discussion assignments improve students' class preparation. *Teaching of Psychology*, 37(3), 204–209.

Linn, M. C., Palmer, E., Baranger, A., Gerard, E., & Stone, E. (2015). Undergraduate research experiences: Impacts and opportunities. *Science*, 347(6222), 1261757.

Lipsitz, A. (2000). Research methods with a smile: A gender difference exercise that teaches methodology. *Teaching of Psychology*, 27(2), 111–113.

Little, J. L., & Bjork, E. L. (2015). Optimizing multiple-choice tests as tools for learning. *Memory and Cognition*, 43(1), 14–26.

Little, J. L., Bjork, E. L., Bjork, R. A., & Angello, G. (2012). Multiple-choice tests exonerated, at least of some charges: Fostering test-induced learning and avoiding test-induced forgetting. *Psychological Science*, 23(11), 1337–1344.

Logan, R. D. (1988). Using a film as a personality case study. *Teaching of Psychology*, 15(2), 103–104.

LoSchiavo, F. M., Buckingham, J. T., & Yurak, T. J. (2002). First-day demonstration for social psychology courses. *Teaching of Psychology*, 29(3), 216–219.

Lotkowski, V. A., Robbins, S. B., & Noeth, R. J. (2004). The role of academic and non-academic factors in improving college retention. ACT Policy Report. Retrieved from http://files.eric.ed.gov/fulltext/ED485476.pdf.

Lou, Y., Abrami, P. C., & Spence, J. C. (2000). Effects of within-class grouping on student achievement: An exploratory model. *Journal of Educational Research*, 94(2), 101–112.

Lou, Y., Abrami, P. C., Spence, J. C., Poulsen, C., Chambers, B., & d'Apollonia, S. (1996). Within-class grouping: A meta-analysis. *Review of Educational Research*, 66(4), 423–458.

Lowe, C., & Williams, T. (2004). Moving to the public: Weblogs in the writing classroom. Into the Blogopshere. Retrieved from http://conservancy.umn.edu/bitstream/handle/11299/172819/Lowe-Williams_Moving%20to%20the%20Public.pdf?sequence=1&isAllowed=y.

Lowman, J., Judge, A. M., & Wiss, C. (2010). Lurking on the internet: A small-group assignment that puts a human face on psychopathology. *Teaching of Psychology*, 37(4), 267–270.

Lundberg, C. A., & Schreiner, L. A. (2004). Quality and frequency of faculty-student interaction as predictors of learning: An analysis by student race/ethnicity. *Journal of College Student Development*, 45(5), 549–565.

Lundy, B. L. (2007). Service learning in life-span developmental psychology: Higher exam scores and increased empathy. *Teaching of Psychology*, 34(1), 23–27.

Lunsford, L. G. (2011). Learning to blog—Blogging to learn. Instructor resources for psychology. Office of Teaching Resources in Psychology. Retrieved from http://teachpsych.org/resources/Documents/otrp/resources/lunsford11.pdf.

Lyle, K. B., & Crawford, N. A. (2011). Retrieving essential material at the end of lectures improves performance on statistics exams. *Teaching of Psychology*, 38(2), 94–97.

Lyman, F. (1981). The responsive class discussion. In A. S. Anderson (Ed.), *Mainstreaming Digest*. College Park, MD: College of Education, University of Maryland.

Lyman, F. (1987). Think-pair-share: An expanding teaching technique. *MAA-CIE Cooperative News*, 1(1), 1–2.

Lynch, R. T., & Gussel, L. (1996). Disclosure and self-advocacy regarding disability-related needs: Strategies to maximize integration in postsecondary education. *Journal of Counseling and Development*, 74(4), 352–357.

Lyons, M. J., Bradley, C., & White, J. (1984). Video taping and abnormal psychology: Dramatized clinical interviews. *Teaching of Psychology*, 11(1), 41–42.

Machado, C. (2011). Gender differences in student discourse on discussion board and blogs: An instructor's quest to create a level playing field in a hybrid classroom. *Journal of Interactive Online Learning*, 10(1), 36–48.

Madigan, R., Johnson, S., & Linton, P. (1995). The language of psychology: APA style as epistemology. *American Psychologist*, 50(6), 428–436.

Maguire, E. A., Valentine, E. R., Wilding, J. M., & Kapur, N. (2003). Routes to remembering: The brains behind superior memory. *Nature Neuroscience*, 6(1), 90–95.

Maki, W. S., & Maki, R. H. (2001). Mastery quizzes on the Web: Results from a Web-based introductory psychology course. *Behavior Research Methods, Instruments, and Computers*, 33(2), 212–216.

Malouff, J. M., & Emmerton, A. J. (2014). Students can give psychology away: Oral presentations on YouTube. *Psychology Learning and Teaching*, 13(1), 38–42.

Malouff, J. M., Emmerton, A. J., & Schutte, N. S. (2013). The risk of a halo bias as a reason to keep students anonymous during grading. *Teaching of Psychology*, 40(3), 233–237.

Malouff, J. M., & Shearer, J. J. (2016). How to set up assignments for students to give oral presentations on video. *College Teaching*, 64(3), 97–100.

Mangold, W. D., Bean, L. G., Adams, D. J., Schwab, W. A., & Lynch, S. M. (2002). Who goes who stays: An assessment of the effect of a freshman mentoring and unit registration program on college persistence. *Journal of College Student Retention: Research, Theory and Practice*, 4(2), 95–122.

Marchant, G. J. (2002). Student reading of assigned articles: Will this be on the test? *Teaching of Psychology*, 29, 49–51.

Marcis, J. G., & Carr, D. R. (2004). The course syllabus in the principles of economics: A national survey. *Atlantic Economic Journal*, 32(3), 259–259.

· Marek, P., Christopher, A., Koenig, C., & Reinhart, D. (2005). Writing exercises for introductory psychology. *Teaching of Psychology*, 32(4), 244–246.

Marmolejo, E. K., Wilder, D. A., & Bradley, L. (2004). A preliminary analysis of the effects of response cards on student performance and participation in an upper division university course. *Journal of Applied Behavior Analysis*, 37(3), 405–410.

Marsh, H. W. (1987). Students' evaluations of university teaching: Research findings, methodological issues, and directions for future research. *International Journal of Educational Research*, 11(3), 253–388.

Martin, R. C. (2013). Navigating the IRB: The ethics of SoTL. *New Directions for Teaching and Learning*, 2013(136), 59–71.

Massey, A. P., Brown, S. A., & Johnston, J. D. (2005). It's all fun and games… Until students learn. *Journal of Information Systems Education*, 16(1), 9–14.

Masters, J. C., Hulsmeyer, B. S., Pike, M. E., Leichty, K., Miller, M. T., & Verst, A. L. (2001). Assessment of multiple-choice questions in selected test banks accompanying text books used in nursing education. *Journal of Nursing Education*, 40(1), 25–32.

Mayer, R. E. (2014a). *Cognitive theory of multimedia learning.* Cambridge, U.K.: Cambridge University Press.

Mayer, R. E. (2014b). Research-based principles for designing multimedia instruction. In V. A. Benassi, C. E. Overson, & C. M. Hakala (Eds.), *Applying science of learning in education: Infusing psychological science into the curriculum*. Retrieved from the Society for the Teaching of Psychology website: http://teachpsych.org/ebooks/asle2014/index.php.

Mayer, R. E., & Moreno, R. (2003). Nine ways to reduce cognitive load in multimedia learning. *Educational Psychologist*, 38(1), 43–52.

Mayer, R. E., Stull, A., DeLeeuw, K., Almeroth, K., Bimber, B., Chun, D., … Zhang, H. (2009). Clickers in college classrooms: Fostering learning with questioning methods in large lecture classes. *Contemporary Educational Psychology*, 34(1), 51–57.

Mayfield, K. H., & Chase, P. N. (2002). The effects of cumulative practice on mathematics problem solving. *Journal of Applied Behavior Analysis*, 35(2), 105–123.

Mayo, J. (2006). Colleague swap revisited: The use of peer critique to improve student writing skills. *Psychology Teacher Network*, 16(2), 7.

Mazur, E. (1997). Peer instruction: Getting students to think in class. In *AIP conference proceedings* (Vol. 399) (pp. 981–988). Woodbury, NY.

Mazur, E. (2009). Farewell, lecture? *Science*, 323(5910), 50–51.

McCabe, D. L. (2005). Cheating among college and university students: A North American perspective. *International Journal for Educational Integrity*, 1(1). doi:10.21913/IJEI. v21911i21911.21914.

McCabe, J. (2009). Racial and gender microaggressions on a predominantly-white campus: Experiences of black, latina/o and white undergraduates. *Race, Gender and Class*, 16, 133–151.

McCabe, J. (2011). Metacognitive awareness of learning strategies in undergraduates. *Memory and Cognition*, 39(3), 462–476.

McCarthy, J. P., & Anderson, L. (2000). Active learning techniques versus traditional teaching styles: Two experiments from history and political science. *Innovative Higher Education*, 24(4), 279–294.

McConnell, W., Albert, R. G., & Marton, J. P. (2008). Involving college students in social science research. *Transformative Dialogues, Teaching and Learning Journal*, 2(1), 2–8.

McConnell, W., & Marton, J. P. (2011). Introducing students to social science research. *Transformative Dialogues: Teaching and Learning Journal*, 5(1), 1–9.

McCullough, M., & Holmberg, M. (2005). Using the Google search engine to detect word-for-word plagiarism in Master's theses: A preliminary study. *College Student Journal*, 39(3), 435–444.

McDaniel, M. A., Anderson, J. L., Derbish, M. H., & Morrisette, N. (2007). Testing the testing effect in the classroom. *European Journal of Cognitive Psychology*, 19(4–5), 494–513.

McDaniel, M. A., Thomas, R. C., Agarwal, P. K., McDermott, K. B., & Roediger, H. L. III (2013). Quizzing in middle-school science: Successful transfer performance on classroom exams. *Applied Cognitive Psychology*, 27(3), 360–372.

McDaniel, M. A., Wildman, K. M., & Anderson, J. L. (2012). Using quizzes to enhance summative-assessment performance in a web-based class: An experimental study. *Journal of Applied Research in Memory and Cognition*, 1(1), 18–26.

McDermott, K. B., Agarwal, P. K., D'antonio, L., Roediger, H. L. III, & McDaniel, M. A. (2014). Both multiple-choice and short-answer quizzes enhance later exam performance in middle and high school classes. *Journal of Experimental Psychology: Applied*, 20(1), 3–21.

McFarland, J., Hussar, B., de Brey, C., Snyder, T., Wang, X., Wilkinson-Flicker, S., … Hinz, S. (2017). The condition of education 2017 (NCES 2017–144). National Center for Education Statistics. Retrieved from https://nces.ed.gov/pubsearch/pubsinfo.asp?pubid=2017144.

McGrail, E., & McGrail, J. P. (2010). Copying right and copying wrong with Web 2.0 tools in the teacher education and communications classrooms. *Contemporary Issues in Technology and Teacher Education*, 10(3), 257–274.

McGrew, S., Ortega, T., Breakstone, J., & Wineburg, S. (2017). The challenge that's bigger than fake news: Teaching students to engage in civic online reasoning. *American Educator*. Retrieved from https://www.aft.org/sites/default/files/periodicals/ae_fall2017_mcgrew.pdf.

McKeachie, W., & Svinicki, M. (2013). *McKeachie's teaching tips* (13th ed.). Belmont, CA: Cengage Learning.

McKendall, M. (2000). Teaching groups to become teams. *Journal of Education for Business*, 75(5), 277–282.

McKinney, K. (2012). Making a difference: Application of SoTL to enhance learning. *Journal of the Scholarship of Teaching and Learning*, 12(1), 1–7.

McLaughlin, J. E., Griffin, L. M., Esserman, D. A., Davidson, C. A., Glatt, D. M., Roth, M. T., ... Mumper, R. J. (2013). Pharmacy student engagement, performance, and perception in a flipped satellite classroom. *American Journal of Pharmaceutical Education*, 77(9), 196.

McLean, C. P., & Miller, N. A. (2010). Changes in critical thinking skills following a course on science and pseudoscience: A quasi-experimental study. *Teaching of Psychology*, 37(2), 85–90.

McNally, R. J. (September 13, 2016). If you need a trigger warning, you need PTSD treatment. *The New York Times*. Retrieved from https://www.nytimes.com/roomfordebate/2016/09/13/do-trigger-warnings-work/if-you-need-a-trigger-warning-you-need-ptsd-treatment.

McNicoll, P. (1999). Issues in teaching participatory action research. *Journal of Social Work Education*, 35(1), 51–62.

McTighe, J., & Wiggins, G. P. (2012). Understanding by design framework. White paper. ASCD. Retrieved from http://www.ascd.org/ASCD/pdf/siteASCD/publications/UbD_WhitePaper0312.pdf.

Meizlish, D., & Kaplan, M. (2008). Valuing and evaluating teaching in academic hiring: A multidisciplinary, cross-institutional study. *Journal of Higher Education*, 79(5), 489–512.

Melchiori, K. J., & Mallett, R. K. (2015). Using Shrek to teach about stigma. *Teaching of Psychology*, 42(3), 260–265.

Mellefont, L., & Fei, J. (2014). Using Echo360 personal capture software to create a "flipped" classroom for microbiology laboratory classes. In Proceedings of the ASCILITE 2014 Conference (pp. 534–538), Dunedin, New Zealand. Retrieved from http://ascilite2014.otago.ac.nz/files/concisepapers/159-Mellefont.pdf.

Meriam Library. (2010). Evaluating information—Applying the CRAAP test. Retrieved from http://www.csuchico.edu/lins/handouts/eval_websites.pdf.

Metcalfe, J., Kornell, N., & Finn, B. (2009). Delayed versus immediate feedback in children's and adults' vocabulary learning. *Memory and Cognition*, 37(8), 1077–1087.

Metzger, M. J., & Flanagin, A. J. (2013). Credibility and trust of information in online environments: The use of cognitive heuristics. *Journal of Pragmatics*, 59, 210–220.

Meyer, C. L., Harned, M., Schaad, A., Sunder, K., Palmer, J., & Tinch, C. (2016). Inmate education as a service learning opportunity for students. *Teaching of Psychology*, 43(2), 120–125.

Michaels, J. W., & Miethe, T. D. (1989). Academic effort and college grades. *Social Forces*, 68(1), 309–319.

Michaelsen, L. K., Fink, L. D., & Knight, A. (1997). Designing effective group activities: Lessons for classroom teaching and faculty development. *To Improve the Academy*, 385. Retrieved from http://digitalcommons.unl.edu/podimproveacad/385.

Michaelsen, L. K., & Sweet, M. (2008). The essential elements of team-based learning. *New Directions for Teaching and Learning*, 2008(116), 7–27.

Milgram, S. (1963). Behavioral study of obedience. *Journal of Abnormal and Social Psychology*, 67(4), 371–378.

Miller, J. (2014). Building academic literacy and research skills by contributing to Wikipedia: A case study at an Australian university. *Journal of Academic Language and Learning*, 8(2), A72–A86.

Miller, J. E., Groccia, J. E., & Wilkes, J. M. (1996). Providing structure: The critical element. *New Directions for Teaching and Learning*, 67, 17–30.

Miller, T. M., & Geraci, L. (2011a). Training metacognition in the classroom: The influence of incentives and feedback on exam predictions. *Metacognition and Learning*, 6(3), 303–314.

Miller, T. M., & Geraci, L. (2011b). Unskilled but aware: Reinterpreting overconfidence in low-performing students. *Journal of Experimental Psychology: Learning, Memory, and Cognition*, 37(2), 502–506.

Millis, K. K. (2001). Comparing two collaborative projects in a cognitive psychology course. *Teaching of Psychology*, 28(4), 263–265.

Milman, N. B. (2012). The flipped classroom strategy: What is it and how can it best be used? *Distance Learning*, 9(3), 85–87.

Miyake, A., Kost-Smith, L. E., Finkelstein, N. D., Pollock, S. J., Cohen, G. L., & Ito, T. A. (2010). Reducing the gender achievement gap in college science: A classroom study of values affirmation. *Science*, 330(6008), 1234–1237.

Miyazoe, T., & Anderson, T. (2010). Learning outcomes and students' perceptions of online writing: Simultaneous implementation of a forum, blog, and wiki in an EFL blended learning setting. *System*, 38(2), 185–199.

Montell, G. (2003). How to write a statement of teaching philosophy. The Chronicle of Higher Education. Retrieved from https://www.chronicle.com/article/How-to-Write-a-Statement-of/45133.

Moody, J. (2004). Distance education: Why are the attrition rates so high? *Quarterly Review of Distance Education*, 5(3), 205–210.

Moreno, R. (2004). Decreasing cognitive load for novice students: Effects of explanatory versus corrective feedback in discovery-based multimedia. *Instructional Science*, 32(1–2), 99–113.

Morling, B., McAuliffe, M., Cohen, L., & DiLorenzo, T. M. (2008). Efficacy of personal response systems ("clickers") in large, introductory psychology classes. *Teaching of Psychology*, 35(1), 45–50.

Morton, D. A., & Colbert-Getz, J. M. (2017). Measuring the impact of the flipped anatomy classroom: The importance of categorizing an assessment by Bloom's taxonomy. *Anatomical Sciences Education*, 10(2), 170–175.

Moule, P., Judd, M., & Girot, E. (1998). The poster presentation: What value to the teaching and assessment of research in pre-and post-registration nursing courses? *Nurse Education Today*, 18(3), 237–242.

Muehlenkamp, J. J., Weiss, N., & Hansen, M. (2015). Problem-based learning for introductory psychology: Preliminary supporting evidence. *Scholarship of Teaching and Learning in Psychology*, 1(2), 125–136.

Muir, G. M., & Cleary, A. M. (2011). Interactive classroom demonstrations. In D. S. Dunn, J. H. Wilson, J. Freeman, & J. R. Stowell (Eds.), *Best practices for technology-enhanced teaching and learning: Connecting to psychology and the social sciences*. New York, NY: Oxford University Press.

Murdock, B. B. Jr. (1962). The serial position effect of free recall. *Journal of Experimental Psychology*, 64(5), 482–488.

Murray, F. S. (1974). Effects of narrative stories on recall. *Bulletin of the Psychonomic Society*, 4(6), 577–579.

Murray, H., Gillese, E., Lennon, M., Mercer, P., & Robinson, M. (1996). Ethical principles for college and university teaching. *New Directions for Teaching and Learning*, 1996(66), 57–63.

Musselman, E. G. (2004). Using structured debate to achieve autonomous student discussion. *History Teacher*, 37, 335–349.

Myers, D., Gray, P., Kalat, J. W., Morris, C. G., Tavris, C., Wade, C., … Weiten, W. (2010). Changes in psychological science: Perspectives from textbook authors. *APS Observer*, 23, 18–24.

Myhre, S. K. (2012). Using the CRAAP test to evaluate websites. Retrieved from https://scholarspace.manoa.hawaii.edu/handle/1012.

Myyry, L., & Joutsenvirta, T. (2015). Open-book, open-web online examinations: Developing examination practices to support university students' learning and self-efficacy. *Active Learning in Higher Education*, 16(2), 119–132.

Nadal, K. L., Wong, Y., Griffin, K. E., Davidoff, K., & Sriken, J. (2014). The adverse impact of racial microaggressions on college students' self-esteem. *Journal of College Student Development*, 55(5), 461–474.

Nardi, B. A., Schiano, D. J., & Gumbrecht, M. (2004). Blogging as social activity, or, would you let 900 million people read your diary? In Proceedings of the 2004 ACM Conference on Computer Supported Cooperative Work (pp. 222–231), Chicago, IL. Retrieved from https://dl.acm.org/citation.cfm?id=1031643.

Narloch, R., Garbin, C. P., & Turnage, K. D. (2006). Benefits of prelecture quizzes. *Teaching of Psychology*, 33(2), 109–112.

Nash, J. C. (2008). Teaching statistics with Excel 2007 and other spreadsheets. *Computational Statistics and Data Analysis*, 52(10), 4602–4606.

National Association of Colleges and Employers. (2014). The skills/qualities employers want in new college graduate hires. Retrieved from http://www.naceweb.org/about-us/press/class-2015-skills-qualities-employers-want.aspx.

National Center for Education Statistics. (2016a). Characteristics of postsecondary students. Retrieved from https://nces.ed.gov/programs/coe/indicator_csb.asp.

National Center for Education Statistics. (2016b). Fast Facts. Race/ethnicity of college faculty. Retrieved from https://nces.ed.gov/fastfacts/display.asp?id=61.

National Center for Education Statistics. (2018). Digest of education statistics 2016 (NCES 2017–094). National Center for Education Statistics. Retrieved from https://nces.ed.gov/programs/digest/d16/index.asp.

National Conference of State Legislatures. (2011). Investing in higher education for Latinos: Trends in Latino college access and success. Retrieved from http://www.ncsl.org/documents/educ/trendsinlatinosuccess.pdf.

National Education Association (2000). *A survey of traditional and distance learning higher education members*. Washington, DC: National Education Association.

National Education Association. (2010). Code of ethics of the education profession. Retrieved from National Education Association website: http://www.nea.org/assets/docs/2013-NEA-Handbook-Code-of-Ethics.pdf.

National Science Foundation. (2017). Program provides blueprint for recruiting minorities to science and engineering. Retrieved from https://www.nsf.gov/news/news_summ.jsp?cntn_id=110124.

National Survey of Student Engagement. (2013). A fresh look at student engagement. Annual Results. Retrieved from http://nsse.iub.edu/NSSE_2013_Results/pdf/NSSE_2013_Annual_Results.pdf.

National Survey of Student Engagement. (2015). Topical Module: Experiences with information literacy. Retrieved from http://nsse.indiana.edu/2015_institutional_report/pdf/Modules/NSSE15%20Module%20Summary-Experiences%20with%20Information%20Literacy.pdf.

Naveh-Benjamin, M., McKeachie, W. J., & Lin, Y.-G. (1987). Two types of test-anxious students: Support for an information processing model. *Journal of Educational Psychology*, 79(2), 131–136.

Nelson, C. E. (1996). Student diversity requires different approaches to college teaching, even in math and science. *American Behavioral Scientist*, 40(2), 165–175.

Nelson, J. S., Range, L. M., & Ross, M. B. (2012). A checklist to guide graduate students' writing. *International Journal of Teaching and Learning in Higher Education*, 24(3), 376–382.

Nelson, T. O., & Dunlosky, J. (1991). When people's judgments of learning (JOLs) are extremely accurate at predicting subsequent recall: The "delayed-JOL effect". *Psychological Science*, 2(4), 267–271.

Nesbit, J. C., & Adesope, O. O. (2006). Learning with concept and knowledge maps: A meta-analysis. *Review of Educational Research*, 76(3), 413–448.

Nestojko, J. F., Bui, D. C., Kornell, N., & Bjork, E. L. (2014). Expecting to teach enhances learning and organization of knowledge in free recall of text passages. *Memory & Cognition*, 42(7), 1038–1048.

Nevid, J. S., Pastva, A., & McClelland, N. (2012). Writing-to-learn assignments in introductory psychology: Is there a learning benefit? *Teaching of Psychology*, 39(4), 272–275.

Neville, A. J., & Norman, G. R. (2007). PBL in the undergraduate MD program at McMaster University: Three iterations in three decades. *Academic Medicine*, 82(4), 370–374.

Newton, P. M. (2015). The learning styles myth is thriving in higher education. *Frontiers in Psychology*, 6, 1908.

Newton, S. E., Eberly, M. B., & Wiggins, R. A. (2001). The syllabus as a tool for student-centered learning. *Journal of General Education*, 50(1), 56–74.

Nguyen, H.-H. D., & Ryan, A. M. (2008). Does stereotype threat affect test performance of minorities and women? A meta-analysis of experimental evidence. *Journal of Applied Psychology*, 93(6), 1314–1334.

Nguyen, K., & McDaniel, M. A. (2015). Using quizzing to assist student learning in the classroom: The good, the bad, and the ugly. *Teaching of Psychology*, 42(1), 87–92.

Nichols, S. L., & Berliner, D. C. (2007). *Collateral damage: How high-stakes testing corrupts America's schools*. Cambridge, MA: Harvard Education Press.

Nicol, D. (2010). From monologue to dialogue: Improving written feedback processes in mass higher education. *Assessment and Evaluation in Higher Education*, 35(5), 501–517.

Nietfeld, J. L., Cao, L., & Osborne, J. W. (2005). Metacognitive monitoring accuracy and student performance in the postsecondary classroom. *Journal of Experimental Education*, 74, 7–28.

Nieto, A. M., & Saiz, C. (2008). Evaluation of Halpern's "structural component" for improving critical thinking. *The Spanish Journal of Psychology*, 11(1), 266–274.

Nissim-Sabat, D. (1979). The teaching of abnormal psychology through the cinema. *Teaching of Psychology*, 6(2), 121–123.

Nix, E. M. (2010). Wikipedia: How it works and how it can work for you. *The History Teacher*, 43(2), 259–264.

Nodine, B. F. (2002). Writing: Models, examples, teaching advice, and a heartfelt plea. In S. F. Davis, & W. Buskist (Eds.), *The teaching of psychology: Essays in honor of Wilbert J. McKeachie and Charles L. Brewer* (pp. 107–120). Mahwah, NJ: Lawrence Erlbaum Associates.

Nordstrom, A. H. (2014). The voices project: Reducing white students' racism in introduction to psychology. *Teaching of Psychology*, 42, 43–50.

Nordstrom, C. R., Bartels, L. K., & Bucy, J. (2009). Predicting and curbing classroom incivility in higher education. *College Student Journal*, 43(1), 74–86.

North, S. M. (1984). The idea of a writing center. *College English*, 46(5), 433–446.

Norton, L. (2004). Psychology Applied Learning Scenarios (PALS): A practical introduction to problem-based learning using vignettes for psychology lecturers. Retrieved from http://78.158.56.101/archive/psychology/docs/pdf/p20040422_pals.pdf.

Norton, L. (2009). *Action research in teaching and learning: A practical guide to conducting pedagogical research in universities*. Abingdon, U.K.: Routledge.

Norton, L., Clifford, R., Hopkins, L., Toner, I., & Norton, J. (2002). Helping psychology students write better essays. *Psychology Learning and Teaching*, 2(2), 116–126.

Novak, J. D., & Cañas, A. J. (2006). *The theory underlying concept maps and how to construct them (technical report no. IHMC CmapTools 2006-01)*. Pensacola, FL: Institute for Human and Machine Cognition.

Novak, J. D., & Gowin, D. B. (1984). *Learning how to learn*. Cambridge, U.K.: Cambridge University Press.

Novak, J. M., Markey, V., & Allen, M. (2007). Evaluating cognitive outcomes of service learning in higher education: A meta-analysis. *Communication Research Reports*, 24(2), 149–157.

Noyd, R. K., & The Staff of The Center for Educational Excellence. (2010). A primer on writing effective learning-centered course goals. Retrieved from http://www.designlearning.org/wp-content/uploads/2010/03/Writing-Good-Learning-Goals-by-Robert-Noyd-US-Air-Force-Academy.pdf.

Nuhfer, E. B. (2010). Cooperative learning in the geological sciences. In B. J. Millis (Ed.), *Cooperative learning in higher education: Across the disciplines, across the academy* (pp. 181–200). Sterling, VA: Stylus.

O'Bannon, B. W., & Britt, V. G. (2011). Creating/developing/using a wiki study guide: Effects on student achievement. *Journal of Research on Technology in Education*, 44(4), 293–312.

Oakley, B., Felder, R. M., Brent, R., & Elhajj, I. (2004). Turning student groups into effective teams. *Journal of Student Centered Learning*, 2(1), 9–34.

Obeid, R., & Hill, D. B. (2017). An intervention designed to reduce plagiarism in a research methods classroom. *Teaching of Psychology*, 44(2), 155–159.

O'Brien, J. G., Millis, B. J., & Cohen, M. W. (2008). *The course syllabus: A learning-centered approach*. New York, NY: John Wiley and Sons.

O'Brien, K. (2010). The test has been canceled. *Boston Globe*. October 3. Retrieved from http://archive.boston.com/bostonglobe/ideas/articles/2010/10/03/the_test_has_been_canceled/.

Oettingen, G., Kappes, H. B., Guttenberg, K. B., & Gollwitzer, P. M. (2015). Self-regulation of time management: Mental contrasting with implementation intentions. *European Journal of Social Psychology*, 45(2), 218–229.

O'Flaherty, J., & Phillips, C. (2015). The use of flipped classrooms in higher education: A scoping review. *The Internet and Higher Education*, 25, 85–95.

Oh, S., & Jonassen, D. H. (2007). Scaffolding online argumentation during problem solving. *Journal of Computer Assisted Learning*, 23(2), 95–110.

Oldenburg, C. M. (2005). Use of primary source readings in psychology courses at liberal arts colleges. *Teaching of Psychology*, 32(1), 25–29.

Oliver, J., & Kowalczyk, C. (2013). Improving student group marketing presentations: A modified Pecha Kucha approach. *Marketing Education Review*, 23(1), 55–58.

O'Neal, C., Meizlish, D., & Kaplan, M. (2007). Writing a statement of teaching philosophy for the academic job search. University of Michigan Center for Research on Learning and Teaching. Retrieved from http://www.crlt.umich.edu/publinks/CRLT_no23.pdf.

Onwuegbuzie, A. J., & Seaman, M. A. (1995). The effect of time constraints and statistics test anxiety on test performance in a statistics course. *Journal of Experimental Education*, 63(2), 115–124.

Onwuegbuzie, A. J., & Wilson, V. A. (2003). Statistics anxiety: Nature, etiology, antecedents, effects, and treatments—A comprehensive review of the literature. *Teaching in Higher Education*, 8(2), 195–209.

Oppermann, M. (2008). Digital storytelling and American studies: Critical trajectories from the emotional to the epistemological. *Arts and Humanities in Higher Education*, 7(2), 171–187.

Oravec, J. A. (2002). Bookmarking the world: Weblog applications in education. *Journal of Adolescent and Adult Literacy*, 45(7), 616–621.

Orr, J. C. (2005). Instant assessment: Using one-minute papers in lower-level classes. *Pedagogy*, 5(1), 108–111.

Ouellett, M. L. (2007). Your teaching portfolio: Strategies for initiating and documenting growth and development. *Journal of Management Education*, 31(3), 421–433.

Paddock, J. R., Terranova, S., & Giles, L. (2001). SASB goes Hollywood: Teaching personality theories through movies. *Teaching of Psychology*, 28(2), 117–121.

Padgett, V. R., & Reid, J. F. (2002). Five year evaluation of the student diversity program: A retrospective quasi-experiment. *Journal of College Student Retention: Research, Theory and Practice*, 4(2), 135–145.

Padrón, Y. N., Waxman, H. C., & Rivera, H. H. (2002). Issues in educating Hispanic students. *Yearbook of the National Society for the Study of Education*, 101(2), 66–88.

Page, D., & Donelan, J. G. (2003). Team-building tools for students. *Journal of Education for Business*, 78(3), 125–128.

Paglia, A., & Donahue, A. (2003). Collaboration works: Integrating information competencies into the psychology curricula. *Reference Services Review*, 31(4), 320–328.

Pai, H.-H., Sears, D. A., & Maeda, Y. (2014). Effects of small-group learning on transfer: A meta-analysis. *Educational Psychology Review*, 27(1), 79–102.

Paivio, A. (1991). Dual coding theory: Retrospect and current status. *Canadian Journal of Psychology*, 45(3), 255–287.

Palmer, S., Holt, D., & Bray, S. (2008). Does the discussion help? The impact of a formally assessed online discussion on final student results. *British Journal of Educational Technology*, 39(5), 847–858.

Pan, D. (2009). What scholarship of teaching? Why bother? *International Journal for the Scholarship of Teaching and Learning*, 3(1), 2.

Panitz, T. (2010). Cooperative learning structures help college students reduce math anxiety and succeed in developmental courses. In B. Millis (Ed.), *Cooperative learning in higher education* (pp. 57–68). Sterling, VA: Styíus Publishing.

Papastergiou, M. (2006). Course management systems as tools for the creation of online learning environments: Evaluation from a social constructivist perspective and implications for their design. *International Journal on E-Learning*, 5(4), 593–622.

Park, D., Ramirez, G., & Beilock, S. L. (2014). The role of expressive writing in math anxiety. *Journal of Experimental Psychology: Applied*, 20(2), 103–111.

Parker, K. R., & Chao, J. T. (2007). Wiki as a teaching tool. *Interdisciplinary Journal of Knowledge and Learning Objects*, 3(1), 57–72.

Parkes, J., Fix, T. K., & Harris, M. B. (2003). What syllabi communicate about assessment in college classrooms. *Journal on Excellence in College Teaching*, 14(1), 61–83.

Parkes, J., & Harris, M. B. (2002). The purposes of a syllabus. *College Teaching*, 50(2), 55–61.

Parlow, J., & Berlyne, D. E. (1971). The effect of prior guessing on incidental learning of verbal associations. *Journal of Structural Learning*, 2, 55–65.

Partridge, L., & Sandover, S. (2010). Beyond "listening" to the student voice: The undergraduate researcher's contribution to the enhancement of teaching and learning. *Journal of University Teaching and Learning Practice*, 7(2), 4. Retrieved from http://files.eric.ed.gov/fulltext/EJ910074.pdf.

Pashler, H., & Harris, C. R. (2012). Is the replicability crisis overblown? Three arguments examined. *Perspectives on Psychological Science*, 7(6), 531–536.

Pashler, H., McDaniel, M., Rohrer, D., & Bjork, R. (2008). Learning styles: Concepts and evidence. *Psychological Science in the Public Interest*, 9(3), 105–119.

Pathways to College Success Network. (2004). A shared agenda: A leadership challenge to improve college access and success. Retrieved from http://files.eric.ed.gov/fulltext/ED514440.pdf.

Paulus, T., Evans, K., Halic, O., Lester, J., Taylor, J., & Spence, M. (2009). Knowledge and learning claims in blog conversations: A discourse analysis in social psychology (DASP) perspective. In Proceedings of the 9th International Conference on Computer-supported Collaborative Learning (Vol. 1, pp. 93–97), Rhodes, Greece. Retrieved from https://www.researchgate.net/profile/Olivia_Halic/publication/269031812_Knowledge_and_learning_claims_in_blog_conversations/links/5.

Penningroth, S. L., Despain, L. H., & Gray, M. J. (2007). A course designed to improve psychological critical thinking. *Teaching of Psychology*, 34(3), 153–157.

Perkins, D. V., & Saris, R. N. (2001). A "jigsaw classroom" technique for undergraduate statistics courses. *Teaching of Psychology*, 28(2), 111–113.

Perlman, B., & McCann, L. I. (2001). Student perspectives on the first day of class. In R. A. Griggs (Ed.), *Handbook for teaching introductory psychology with an emphasis on assessment* (Vol. 3) (pp. 12). Mahwah, NJ: Lawrence Erlbauam Associates.

Perrine, R. M., Lisle, J., & Tucker, D. L. (1995). Effects of a syllabus offer of help, student age, and class size on college students' willingness to seek support from faculty. *Journal of Experimental Education*, 64(1), 41–52.

Perry, R. P. (2003). Perceived (academic) control and causal thinking in achievement settings. *Canadian Psychology/Psychologie Canadienne*, 44(4), 312–331.

Perry, R. P., & Hamm, J. (2017). An attribution perspective on competence and motivation: Theory and treatment interventions. In A. Elliot, C. Dweck, & D. Yeager (Eds.), *Handbook of competence and motivation: Theory and application* (2nd ed., Vol. 2006) (pp. 61–84). New York, NY: Guilford Publications.

Perry, W. G. (1970). *Forms of intellectual and ethical development in the college years: A scheme*. New York, NY: Holt, Rinehart and Winston.

Peterson, D. J. (2016). The flipped classroom improves student achievement and course satisfaction in a statistics course: A quasi-experimental study. *Teaching of Psychology*, 43(1), 10–15.

Petress, K. (2006). An operational definition of class participation. *College Student Journal*, 40(4), 821–824.

Pettijohn, T., & Perelli, E. G. (2005). Using group web page and video clip creation exercises in introductory psychology courses. *Teaching of Psychology*, 32, 54–56.

The Pew Research Center. (2015). The smart phone difference. Retrieved from the Pew Research Center website: http://assets.pewresearch.org/wp-content/uploads/sites/14/2015/03/PI_Smartphones_0401151.pdf.

Pfaff, E., & Huddleston, P. (2003). Does it matter if I hate teamwork? What impacts student attitudes toward teamwork. *Journal of Marketing Education*, 25(1), 37–45.

Picciano, A. G. (2002). Beyond student perceptions: Issues of interaction, presence, and performance in an online course. *Journal of Asynchronous Learning Networks*, 6(1), 21–40.

Pierce, R., & Fox, J. (2012). Vodcasts and active-learning exercises in a "flipped classroom" model of a renal pharmacotherapy module. *American Journal of Pharmaceutical Education*, 76(10), 196.

Pintrich, P., & Schunk, D. (1996). *The role of expectancy and self-efficacy beliefs: Motivation in education: Theory, research and applications*. Englewood Cliffs, NJ: Prentice-Hall.

Podlucká, D. (2017). Collaborative inquiry project in the first-year seminar in psychology: Students' agentive authorship of learning and development. In R. Obeid, A. M. Schwartz, C. Shane-Simpson, & P. J. Brooks (Eds.), *How we teach now: The GSTA guide to student-centered teaching* (pp. 269–281). Retrieved from the Society for the Teaching of Psychology website: http://teachpsych.org/ebooks/howweteachnow.

Poe, R. E. (1990). A strategy for improving literature reviews in psychology courses. *Teaching of Psychology*, 17(1), 54–55.

Poirier, C. R., & Feldman, R. S. (2007). Promoting active learning using individual response technology in large introductory psychology classes. *Teaching of Psychology*, 34(3), 194–196.

Poling, D. A., & Hupp, J. M. (2009). Active learning through role playing: Virtual babies in a child development course. *College Teaching*, 57(4), 221–228.

Pontes, M. C., Hasit, C., Pontes, N., Lewis, P. A., & Siefring, K. T. (2010). Variables related to undergraduate students preference for distance education classes. *Online Journal of Distance Learning Administration*, 13(2), 8.

Powers, K. L., Brooks, P. J., Galazyn, M., & Donnelly, S. (2016). Testing the efficacy of MyPsychLab to replace traditional instruction in a hybrid course. *Psychology Learning and Teaching*, 15(1), 6–30.

Powers, K. L., Brooks, P. J., McCloskey, D., Sekerina, I. A., & Cohen, F. (2013). Hybrid teaching of psychology. In M. Hamada (Ed.), *E-learning: New technology, applications and future trends* (pp. 147–166). Hauppauge, NY: NOVA Science Publishers.

Prensky, M. (2001). Digital natives, digital immigrants part 1. *On the Horizon*, 9(5), 1–6.

Pressley, M., Wood, E., Woloshyn, V. E., Martin, V., King, A., & Menke, D. (1992). Encouraging mindful use of prior knowledge: Attempting to construct explanatory answers facilitates learning. *Educational Psychologist*, 27(1), 91–109.

Price, M., & O'Donovan, B. (2006). Improving performance through enhancing student understanding of criteria and feedback. In C. Bryan, & K. Clegg (Eds.), *Innovative assessment in higher education* (pp. 100–109). London, U.K.: Routledge.

Price, P. C. (2006). Are you as good a teacher as you think? *Thought and Action*, 7. Retrieved from www.nea.org/assets/img/PubThoughtAndAction/TAA_06_02.pdf.

Pusateri, T., Halonen, J. S., Hill, B., & McCarthy, M. (2009). The assessment cyberguide for learning goals and outcomes. American Psychological Association. Retrieved from https://www.apa.org/ed/governance/bea/assessment-cyberguide-v2.pdf.

Pychyl, T. A. (2008). Education is not the filling of a pail, but the lighting of a fire: Motivation, procrastination, and Yeats. Psychology Today blogpost, 2016. Retrieved from https://www.psychologytoday.com/blog/dont-delay/200805/education-is-not-the-filling-pail-the-lighting-fire.

Radford, A. W., Cominole, M., & Skomsvold, P. (2015). Demographic and enrollment characteristics of nontraditional undergraduates: 2011–12. National Center for Education Statistics. Retrieved from https://nces.ed.gov/pubs2015/2015025.pdf.

Radhakrishnan, P., Lam, D., & Tamura, E. K. (2010). Guided experimentation with databases improves argumentative writing. *Teaching of Psychology*, 37(3), 210–215.

Rainie, L., & Tancer, B. (2007). Wikipedia users: Pew Internet and American Life Project. Retrieved from http://www.pewresearch.org/daily-number/wikipedia-users/.

Rankin, S. R., & Reason, R. D. (2005). Differing perceptions: How students of color and white students perceive campus climate for underrepresented groups. *Journal of College Student Development*, 46(1), 43–61.

Rankin, S. R., Weber, G. N., Blumenfeld, W. J., & Frazer, S. (2010). 2010 state of higher education for lesbian, gay, bisexual and transgender people. Retrieved from the Campus Pride website: https://www.campuspride.org/wp-content/uploads/campuspride2010 lgbtreportssummary.pdf

Rattan, A., Good, C., & Dweck, C. S. (2012). "It's ok—Not everyone can be good at math": Instructors with an entity theory comfort (and demotivate) students. *Journal of Experimental Social Psychology*, 48(3), 731–737.

Raue, K., & Lewis, L. (2011). Students with disabilities at degree-granting postsecondary institutions. Report from the National Center of Educational Statistics. Retrieved from http://nces.ed.gov/pubs2011/2011018.pdf.

Rawson, K. A., & Dunlosky, J. (2011). Optimizing schedules of retrieval practice for durable and efficient learning: How much is enough? *Journal of Experimental Psychology: General*, 140(3), 283–302.

Rawson, K. A., Dunlosky, J., & Sciartelli, S. M. (2013). The power of successive relearning: Improving performance on course exams and long-term retention. *Educational Psychology Review*, 25(4), 523–548.

Read, J. P., Ouimette, P., White, J., Colder, C., & Farrow, S. (2011). Rates of DSM-IV-TR trauma exposure and posttraumatic stress disorder among newly matriculated college students. *Psychological Trauma: Theory, Research, Practice, and Policy*, 3(2), 148–156.

Reardon, K. M. (1998). Participatory action research as service learning. *New Directions for Teaching and Learning*, 1998(73), 57–64.

Reddy, Y. M., & Andrade, H. (2010). A review of rubric use in higher education. *Assessment and Evaluation in Higher Education*, 35(4), 435–448.

Reid, M. J., & Moore, J. L. (2008). College readiness and academic preparation for postsecondary education: Oral histories of first-generation urban college students. *Urban Education*, 43(2), 240–261.

Rendon, L. I. (1992). From the barrio to the academy: Revelations of a Mexican American "scholarship girl." *New Directions for Community Colleges*, 1992(80), 55–64.

Renner, M. J. (2004). Learning the Rescorla–Wagner model of Pavlovian conditioning: An interactive simulation. *Teaching of Psychology*, 31(2), 146–148.

Reverby, S. M. (2000). Introduction: More than a metaphor, an overview of the scholarship of the study. In S. M. Reverby (Ed.), *Tuskegee's truths: Rethinking the Tuskegee syphilis study* (pp. 1–11). Chapel Hill, NC: The University of North Carolina Press.

Revere, L. (2004). Classroom jeopardy: A winning approach for improving student assessment, performance, and satisfaction. *Decision Line*, 23(3), 4–6.

Richardson, M., Abraham, C., & Bond, R. (2012). Psychological correlates of university students' academic performance: A systematic review and meta-analysis. *Psychological Bulletin*, 138(2), 353–387.

Richland, L. E., Kornell, N., & Kao, L. S. (2009). The pretesting effect: Do unsuccessful retrieval attempts enhance learning? *Journal of Experimental Psychology: Applied*, 15(3), 243–255.

Richmond, A. S., Berglund, M. B., Epelbaum, V. B., & Klein, E. M. (2015). A+(b1) professor–student rapport+(b2) humor+(b3) student engagement=(Ŷ) student ratings of instructors. *Teaching of Psychology*, 42(2), 119–125.

Richmond, A. S., Boysen, G. A., & Gurung, R. A. (2016). *An evidence-based guide to college and university teaching: Developing the model teacher*. New York, NY: Routledge.

Richmond, A. S., Boysen, G. A., Gurung, R. A., Tazeau, Y. N., Meyers, S. A., & Sciutto, M. J. (2014). Aspirational model teaching criteria for psychology. *Teaching of Psychology*, 41, 281–295.

Richmond, A. S., & Hagan, L. K. (2011). Promoting higher level thinking in psychology: Is active learning the answer? *Teaching of Psychology*, 38(2), 102–105.

Risko, E. F., Anderson, N., Sarwal, A., Engelhardt, M., & Kingstone, A. (2012). Everyday attention: Variation in mind wandering and memory in a lecture. *Applied Cognitive Psychology*, 26(2), 234–242.

Ritzko, J. M., & Robinson, S. (2011). Using games to increase active learning. *Journal of College Teaching and Learning (TLC)*, 3(6). Retrieved from https://www.cluteinstitute.com/ojs/index.php/TLC/article/view/1709.

Robbins, S. B., Lauver, K., Le, H., Davis, D., Langley, R., & Carlstrom, A. (2004). Do psychosocial and study skill factors predict college outcomes? A meta-analysis. *Psychological Bulletin*, 130(2), 261–288.

Roberts, J., & Styron, R. Jr. (2010). Student satisfaction and persistence: Factors vital to student retention. *Research in Higher Education Journal*, 6, 1–18.

Robertson, J. (2011). The educational affordances of blogs for self-directed learning. *Computers and Education*, 57(2), 1628–1644.

Robin, B. R. (2008). Digital storytelling: A powerful technology tool for the 21st century classroom. *Theory into Practice*, 47(3), 220–228.

Robinson, D. H., & Kiewra, K. A. (1995). Visual argument: Graphic organizers are superior to outlines in improving learning from text. *Journal of Educational Psychology*, 87(3), 455–467.

Robinson-Keilig, R. A., Hamill, C., Gwin-Vinsant, A., & Dashner, M. (2014). Feminist pedagogy in action: Photovoice as an experiential class project. *Psychology of Women Quarterly*, 38(2), 292–297.

Robison, F. F. (2014). It's a game! Evaluation of a classroom game to enhance learning in an introductory counseling course. *Comprehensive Psychology*, 3(1), 10.

Rocca, K. A. (2008). Participation in the college classroom: The impact of instructor immediacy and verbal aggression. *Journal of Classroom Interaction*, 22–33.

Rocca, K. A. (2010). Student participation in the college classroom: An extended multidisciplinary literature review. *Communication Education*, 59(2), 185–213.

Rodriguez, M. C. (2005). Three options are optimal for multiple-choice items: A meta-analysis of 80 years of research. *Educational Measurement: Issues and Practice*, 24(2), 3–13.

Roediger, H. L. III, Agarwal, P. K., McDaniel, M. A., & McDermott, K. B. (2011). Test-enhanced learning in the classroom: Long-term improvements from quizzing. *Journal of Experimental Psychology: Applied*, 17(4), 382–395.

Roediger, H. L. III, & Karpicke, J. D. (2006). Test-enhanced learning taking memory tests improves long-term retention. *Psychological Science*, 17(3), 249–255.

Roediger, H. L. III, & Marsh, E. J. (2005). The positive and negative consequences of multiple-choice testing. *Journal of Experimental Psychology: Learning, Memory, and Cognition*, 31(5), 1155–1159.

Roediger, H. L. III, & McDermott, K. B. (1995). Creating false memories: Remembering words not presented in lists. *Journal of Experimental Psychology: Learning, Memory, and Cognition*, 21(4), 803–814.

Roediger, H. L. III, Putnam, A. L., & Smith, M. A. (2011). Ten benefits of testing and their applications to educational practice. *Psychology of Learning and Motivation*, 55, 1–36.

Roediger, H. L. III, & Pyc, M. A. (2012). Inexpensive techniques to improve education: Applying cognitive psychology to enhance educational practice. *Journal of Applied Research in Memory and Cognition*, 1(4), 242–248.

Roig, M., & DeTommaso, L. (1995). Are college cheating and plagiarism related to academic procrastination? *Psychological Reports*, 77(2), 691–698.

Romero, C., López, M.-I., Luna, J.-M., & Ventura, S. (2013). Predicting students' final performance from participation in on-line discussion forums. *Computers and Education*, 68, 458–472.

Rose, D. H., Harbour, W. S., Johnston, C. S., Daley, S. G., & Abarbanell, L. (2006). Universal Design for Learning in postsecondary education: Reflections on principles and their application. *Journal of Postsecondary Education and Disability*, 19(2), 135–151.

Rose, D. H., & Meyer, A. (2002). *Teaching every student in the digital age: Universal design for learning*. Alexandria, VA: Association for Supervision and Curriculum Development.

Roskos-Ewoldsen, D. R., & Roskos-Ewoldsen, B. (2001). Using video clips to teach social psychology. *Teaching of Psychology*, 28(3), 212–215.

Rosman, T., Mayer, A.-K., & Krampen, G. (2016). A longitudinal study on information-seeking knowledge in psychology undergraduates: Exploring the role of information literacy instruction and working memory capacity. *Computers and Education*, 96, 94–108.

Rosnow, R. L. (1990). Teaching research ethics through role-play and discussion. *Teaching of Psychology*, 17(3), 179–181.

Rossiter, M., & Garcia, P. A. (2010). Digital storytelling: A new player on the narrative field. *New Directions for Adult and Continuing Education*, 2010(126), 37–48.

Rotter, K. (2004). Modifying "Jeopardy!" games to benefit all students. *Teaching Exceptional Children*, 36(3), 58–63.

Rounding, K., & Adelheid, A. M. N. (2015). The effects of temperature on perceptions of loneliness. Retrieved from http://www.teachpsychscience.org/pdf/65201515726PM_1.PDF.

Rovai, A. P. (2003). Strategies for grading online discussions: Effects on discussions and classroom community in Internet-based university courses. *Journal of Computing in Higher Education*, 15(1), 89–107.

Rovai, A. P. (2007). Facilitating online discussions effectively. *The Internet and Higher Education*, 10(1), 77–88.

Rowinsky-Geurts, M. (2013). Digital stories in L2 classes: High-impact practices and affective learning. In J. W. Schwieter (Ed.), *Studies and global perspectives of second language teaching and learning* (pp. 91–112). Charlotte, NC: IAP Information Age Publishing.

Rowland, C. A. (2014). The effect of testing versus restudy on retention: A meta-analytic review of the testing effect. *Psychological Bulletin*, 140(6), 1432–1463.

Ruchensky, J. R., & Huss, M. T. (2015). Making it count: How SoTL can aid in the tenure/ promotion process. In R. Smith, & B. Schwartz (Eds.), *Using SoTL to enhance your academic position*. Retrieved from the Society for the Teaching of Psychology website: http://teachpsych.org/ebooks/.

Ruscio, J. (2001). Administering quizzes at random to increase students' reading. *Teaching of Psychology*, 28(3), 204–205.

Sagendorf, K., Noyd, R. K., & Morris, D. B. (2009). The learning-focused transformation of biology and physics core courses at the U.S. Air Force Academy. *Journal of College Science Teaching*, 38(3), 45–50.

Sallie Mae. (2014). How America pays for college. Retrieved from http://news.salliemae. com/files/doc_library/file/HowAmericaPaysforCollege2014FNL.pdf.

Sandars, J., & Murray, C. (2009). Digital storytelling for reflection in undergraduate medical education: A pilot study. *Education for Primary Care*, 20(6), 441–444.

Saville, B. K., Lawrence, N. K., & Jakobsen, K. V. (2012). Creating learning communities in the classroom. *New Directions for Teaching and Learning*, 2012(132), 57–69.

Saville, B. K., Zinn, T. E., Neef, N. A., Norman, R. V., & Ferreri, S. J. (2006). A comparison of interteaching and lecture in the college classroom. *Journal of Applied Behavior Analysis*, 39(1), 49–61.

Sawyer, J. E., Obeid, R., Bublitz, D., Schwartz, A. M., Brooks, P. J., & Richmond, A. S. (2017). Which forms of active learning are most effective: Cooperative learning, writing-to-learn, multimedia instruction, or some combination? *Scholarship of Teaching and Learning in Psychology*, 3(4), 257–271.

Sayer, P. (2009). Using the linguistic landscape as a pedagogical resource. *English Language Teachers Journal*, 64(2), 143–154.

Scanlon, J. (1993). Keeping our activist selves alive in the classroom: Feminist pedagogy and political activism. *Feminist Teacher*, 7, 8–14.

Schafer, P., Hammer, E., & Berntsen, J. (2012). Using course portfolios to assess and improve teaching. In M. Kite (Ed.), *Effective evaluation of teaching: A guide for faculty and administrators* (pp. 71–78). Retrieved from the Society for the Teaching of Psychology website: http://teachpsych.org/Resources/Documents/ebooks/evals2012.pdf.

Schelly, C. L., Davies, P. L., & Spooner, C. L. (2011). Student perceptions of faculty implementation of universal Design for Learning. *Journal of Postsecondary Education and Disability*, 24(1), 17–30.

Schmidt, R. A., & Bjork, R. A. (1992). New conceptualizations of practice: Common principles in three paradigms suggest new concepts for training. *Psychological Science*, 3(4), 207–218.

Schnell, C. A., & Doetkott, C. D. (2003). First year seminars produce long-term impact. *Journal of College Student Retention: Research, Theory and Practice*, 4(4), 377–391.

Schommer, M. (1990). Effects of beliefs about the nature of knowledge on comprehension. *Journal of Educational Psychology*, 82(3), 498–504.

Schommer-Aikins, M., & Easter, M. (2006). Ways of knowing and epistemological beliefs: Combined effect on academic performance. *Educational Psychology*, 26(3), 411–423.

Schraw, G., Bendixen, L. D., & Dunkle, M. E. (2002). Development and validation of the epistemic belief inventory (EBI). In B. K. Hofer, & P. R. Pintrich (Eds.), *Personal epistemology: The psychology of beliefs about knowledge and knowing* (pp. 261–276). Mahwah, NJ: Erlbaum.

Schraw, G., & Moshman, D. (1995). Metacognitive theories. *Educational Psychology Review*, 7(4), 351–371.

Schuetze, P. (2004). Evaluation of a brief homework assignment designed to reduce citation problems. *Teaching of Psychology*, 31(4), 257–262.

Schwartz, A. M., Powers, K. L., Galazyn, M., & Brooks, P. J. (2017). Crowdsourcing course preparation strengthens teaching through collaboration. In R. Obeid, A. M. Schwartz, C. Shane-Simpson, & P. J. Brooks (Eds.), *How we teach now: The GSTA guide to student-centered teaching* (pp. 69–82). Retrieved from the Society for the Teaching of Psychology website: http://teachpsych.org/ebooks/howweteachnow.

Schweitzer, N. J. (2008). Wikipedia and psychology: Coverage of concepts and its use by undergraduate students. *Teaching of Psychology*, 35(2), 81–85.

Scott, S. S., & Edwards, W. (2012). Project LINC: Supporting lecturers and adjunct instructors in foreign language classrooms. *Journal of Postsecondary Education and Disability*, 25(3), 253–258.

Scott, S. S., Mcguire, J. M., & Shaw, S. F. (2003). Universal design for instruction a new paradigm for adult instruction in postsecondary education. *Remedial and Special Education*, 24(6), 369–379.

Seabrook, R., Brown, G. D., & Solity, J. E. (2005). Distributed and massed practice: From laboratory to classroom. *Applied Cognitive Psychology*, 19(1), 107–122.

Seely, S. R., Fry, S. W., & Ruppel, M. (2011). Information literacy follow-through: Enhancing preservice teachers' information evaluation skills through formative assessment. *Behavioral and Social Sciences Librarian*, 30(2), 72–84.

Segool, N. K., Carlson, J. S., Goforth, A. N., von der Embse, N., & Barterian, J. A. (2013). Heightened test anxiety among young children: Elementary school students' anxious responses to high-stakes testing. *Psychology in the Schools*, 50(5), 489–499.

Seipp, B. (1991). Anxiety and academic performance: A meta-analysis of findings. *Anxiety Research*, 4(1), 27–41.

Seldin, P., Miller, J. E., & Seldin, C. A. (2010). *The teaching portfolio: A practical guide to improved performance and promotion/tenure decisions* (4th ed.). San Francisco, CA: Jossey Bass.

Seligman, M. E. (2012). *Flourish: A visionary new understanding of happiness and well-being*. New York, NY: Simon and Schuster.

Senzaki, S., Hackathorn, J., Appleby, D. C., & Gurung, R. A. (2017). Reinventing flashcards to increase student learning. *Psychology Learning and Teaching*, 16(3), 353–368.

Serafin, A. G. (1990). Course syllabi and their effects on students' final grade performance. Paper submitted to the Faculty of the Instituto Pedagocico of the De Caracas, Caracas, Venezeula. Retrieved from http://files.eric.ed.gov/fulltext/ED328202.pdf.

Shadle, S. E. (2010). Cooperative learning in general chemistry through process-oriented guided inquiry. In B. J. Millis (Ed.), *Cooperative learning in higher education: Across the disciplines, across the academy* (pp. 35–55). Sterling, VA: Stylus.

Shah, P., & Hoeffner, J. (2002). Review of graph comprehension research: Implications for instruction. *Educational Psychology Review*, 14(1), 47–69.

Shane-Simpson, C., & Brooks, P. J. (2016). The dos and don'ts of Wikipedia editing in the undergraduate psychology classroom. *APS Observer*, 29(2). Retrieved from http://www.psychologicalscience.org/index.php/publications/observer/2016/february-16/the-dos-and-donts-of-wikipedia-editing-in-the-undergraduate-psychology-classroom.html.

Shane-Simpson, C., Che, E., & Brooks, P. J. (2016). Giving psychology away: Implementation of Wikipedia editing in an introductory human development course. *Psychology Learning and Teaching*, 15(3), 268–293.

Sharan, Y. (2010). Cooperative learning for academic and social gains: Valued pedagogy, problematic practice. *European Journal of Education*, 45(2), 300–313.

Shaughnessy, J. J. (1979). Confidence-judgment accuracy as a predictor of test performance. *Journal of Research in Personality*, 13(4), 505–514.

Shearer, E., & Gottfried, J. (2017). News use across social media platforms 2017. Pew Research Center. Retrieved from http://www.journalism.org/2017/09/07/news-use-across-social-media-platforms-2017/.

Sheff, N. (2008). *Tweak: Growing up on methamphetamines*. New York, NY: Atheneum Books for Young Readers.

Shertzer, J. E., & Schuh, J. H. (2004). College student perceptions of leadership: Empowering and constraining beliefs. *Journal of Student Affairs Research and Practice*, 42(1), 111–131.

Sidelinger, R. J., & Booth-Butterfield, M. (2010). Co-constructing student involvement: An examination of teacher confirmation and student-to-student connectedness in the college classroom. *Communication Education*, 59(2), 165–184.

Sikorski, J. F., Rich, K., Saville, B. K., Buskist, W., Drogan, O., & Davis, S. F. (2002). Student use of introductory texts: Comparative survey findings from two universities. *Teaching of Psychology*, 29(4), 312–313.

Silva, K. M., Silva, F. J., Quinn, M. A., Draper, J. N., Cover, K. R., & Munoff, A. A. (2008). Rate my professor: Online evaluations of psychology instructors. *Teaching of Psychology*, 35(2), 71–80.

Silver, P., Bourke, A., & Strehorn, K. (1998). Universal instructional design in higher education: An approach for inclusion. *Equity and Excellence*, 31(2), 47–51.

Sim, J. W. S., & Hew, K. F. (2010). The use of weblogs in higher education settings: A review of empirical research. *Educational Research Review*, 5(2), 151–163.

Simkins, S., & Maier, M. (Eds.) (2010). *Just-in-time teaching: Across the disciplines, across the academy*. Sterling, VA: Stylus Publishing.

Simon, A. F., Galazyn, M., & Nolan, S. A. (2012). Internationalizing research methods in the western psychology curriculum. *Psychology Learning and Teaching*, 11(3), 439–444.

Simon, A. F., & Nolan, S. A. (2017). Internationalizing your teaching: Bringing the world to your classroom. In R. Obeid, A. Schwartz, C. Shane-Simpson, & P. J. Brooks (Eds.), *How we teach now: The GSTA guide to student-centered teaching* (pp. 238–251). Retrieved from the Society for the Teaching of Psychology website: http://teachpsych.org/ebooks/howweteachnow.

Simons, D. J. (2014). The value of direct replication. *Perspectives on Psychological Science*, 9(1), 76–80.

Simons, L. (2015). Measuring service-learning and civic engagement. In R. S. Jhangiani, J. D. Troisi, B. Fleck, A. Legg, & H. Hussey (Eds.), *A compendium of scales for use in the scholarship of teaching and learning* (pp. 102–122). Retrieved from the Society for the Teaching of Psychology website: http://teachpsych.org/ebooks/compscalessotp.

Simpson, K. E. (2008). Classic and modern propaganda in documentary film: Teaching the psychology of persuasion. *Teaching of Psychology*, 35(2), 103–108.

Simpson, K. E. (2012). Hitler's genocide: Teaching the psychology of the Holocaust. *Teaching of Psychology*, 39(2), 113–120.

Sinkavich, F. J. (1995). Performance and metamemory: Do students know what they don't know? *Journal of Instructional Psychology*, 22(1), 77–87.

Sinski, J. B. (2012). Classroom strategies for teaching veterans with post-traumatic stress disorder and traumatic brain injury. *Journal of Postsecondary Education and Disability*, 25(1), 87–95.

Slamecka, N. J., & Graf, P. (1978). The generation effect: Delineation of a phenomenon. *Journal of Experimental Psychology: Human Learning and Memory*, 4(6), 592–604.

Slavin, R. E. (1980). Cooperative learning. *Review of Educational Research*, 50(2), 315–342.

Slavin, R. E. (1995). *Cooperative learning: Theory, research, and practice* (2nd ed.). Boston, MA: Allyn and Bacon.

Slavin, R. E. (2011). Cooperative learning. In E. G. Aukrust (Ed.), *Learning and cognition in education* (pp. 160–166). Boston, MA: Academic Press.

Slotter, E. B. (2010). Using wiki contributions to induce collaborative learning in a psychology course. *International Journal of Technology in Teaching and Learning*, 6(1), 33–42.

Smith, B. L., Holliday, W. G., & Austin, H. W. (2010). Students' comprehension of science textbooks using a question-based reading strategy. *Journal of Research in Science Teaching*, 47(4), 363–379.

Smith, K., & Tillema, H. (2001). Long-term influences of portfolios on professional development. *Scandinavian Journal of Educational Research*, 45(2), 183–203.

Smith, K. A. (2000). Going deeper: Formal small-group learning in large classes. *New Directions for Teaching and Learning*, 2000(81), 25–46.

Smith, M. K., Wood, W. B., Adams, W. K., Wieman, C., Knight, J. K., Guild, N., & Su, T. T. (2009). Why peer discussion improves student performance on in-class concept questions. *Science*, 323(5910), 122–124.

Smith, P. C. (2007). Assessing students' research ideas. In D. S. Dunn, R. A. Smith, & B. C. Beins (Eds.), *Best practices in teaching statistics and research methods in the behavioral sciences*. Mahwah, NJ: Lawrence Erlbaum.

Smith, R. A. (2008). Moving toward the scholarship of teaching and learning: The classroom can be a lab, too! *Teaching of Psychology*, 35(4), 262–266.

Smith, R. A. (2010). A tasty sample(r): Teaching about sampling using M&Ms. In L. T. Benjamin (Ed.), *Favorite activities for the teaching of psychology* (pp. 8–10). Washington, DC: American Psychological Association.

Smith, R. A., & Schwartz, B. M. (2015). Using SoTL to enhance your academic position. Retrieved from the Society for the Teaching of Psychology website: http://teachpsych.org/ebooks/.

Smyth, J. M., Hockemeyer, J. R., Heron, K. E., Wonderlich, S. A., & Pennebaker, J. W. (2008). Prevalence, type, disclosure, and severity of adverse life events in college students. *Journal of American College Health*, 57(1), 69–76.

Snow, W. H., Lamar, M. R., Hinkle, J. S., & Speciale, M. (2018). Current practices in online counselor education: A preliminary exploration. Manuscript submitted for publication.

Society for Teaching and Learning in Higher Education. (1996). Ethical principles in university teaching. Retrieved from https://www.stlhe.ca/awards/3m-national-teaching-fellowships/initiatives/ethical-principles-in-university-teaching/.

Sorcinelli, M. D. (2003). Encouraging civil behavior in large classes. *Essays on Teaching Excellence. Toward the Best in the Academy*, 15(8), 2003–2004. Retrieved from https://www.mtholyoke.edu/sites/default/files/teachinglearninginitiatives/docs/Encouraging%20Civil%20Behavior%20in%20Large%20Classes_MDS-1.pdf.

Soysa, C. K., Dunn, D. S., Dottolo, A. L., Burns-Glover, A. L., & Gurung, R. A. R. (2013). Orchestrating authorship: Teaching writing across the psychology curriculum. *Teaching of Psychology*, 40(2), 88–97.

Sparks, D., & Malkus, N. (2013). First-year undergraduate remedial coursetaking: 1999–2000, 2003–04, 2007–08. Statistics in Brief. NCES 2013-013. National Center for Education Statistics. Retrieved from http://files.eric.ed.gov/fulltext/ED538339.pdf.

Sparks, J. R., Katz, I. R., & Beile, P. M. (2016). Assessing digital information literacy in higher education: A review of existing frameworks and assessments with recommendations for next-generation assessment. *ETS Research Report Series*, 2016(2), 1–33.

Spicer, S., & Miller, C. (2014). An exploration of digital storytelling creation and media production skill sets in first year college students. *International Journal of Cyber Behavior, Psychology and Learning*, 4(1), 46–58.

Spivey, N. N. (1991). The shaping of meaning: Options in writing the comparison. *Research in the Teaching of English*, 25(4), 390–418.

Spooren, P., Brockx, B., & Mortelmans, D. (2013). On the validity of student evaluation of teaching: The state of the art. *Review of Educational Research*, 83(4), 598–642.

Springer, L., Stanne, M. E., & Donovan, S. S. (1999). Effects of small-group learning on undergraduates in science, mathematics, engineering, and technology: A meta-analysis. *Review of Educational Research*, 69(1), 21–51.

Stacey, E., & Rice, M. (2002). Evaluating an online learning environment. *Australian Journal of Educational Technology*, 18(3), 323–340.

Stacey, G., & Hardy, P. (2011). Challenging the shock of reality through digital storytelling. *Nurse Education in Practice*, 11(2), 159–164.

Staib, S. (2003). Teaching and measuring critical thinking. *Journal of Nursing Education*, 42(11), 498–508.

Stalder, D. R. (2005). Learning and motivational benefits of acronym use in introductory psychology. *Teaching of Psychology*, 32(4), 222–228.

Standing, L. G., & Huber, H. (2003). Do psychology courses reduce belief in psychological myths? *Social Behavior and Personality*, 31(6), 585–592.

Stanovich, K. E., & West, R. F. (2000). Individual differences in reasoning: Implications for the rationality debate? *Behavioral and Brain Sciences*, 23(5), 645–665.

Stansbury, J. A., & Munro, G. D. (2013). Gaming in the classroom an innovative way to teach factorial designs. *Teaching of Psychology*, 40(2), 148–152.

Stark, E. (2012). Enhancing and assessing critical thinking in a psychological research methods course. *Teaching of Psychology*, 39(2), 107–112.

Stebleton, M., & Soria, K. (2013). Breaking down barriers: Academic obstacles of first-generation students at research universities. University of Minnesota Digital Conservancy. Retrieved from http://hdl.handle.net/11299/150031.

Steele, C. M. (1988). The psychology of self-affirmation: Sustaining the integrity of the self. In L. Berkowitz (Ed.), *Advances in experimental social psychology* (Vol. 21) (pp. 261–302). San Diego, CA: Academic Press.

Steele, C. M. (1997). A threat in the air: How stereotypes shape intellectual identity and performance. *American Psychologist*, 52(6), 613–629.

Steele, C. M., & Aronson, J. (1995). Stereotype threat and the intellectual test performance of African Americans. *Journal of Personality and Social Psychology*, 69(5), 797–811.

Stellmack, M. A., Keenan, N. K., Sandidge, R. R., Sippl, A. L., & Konheim-Kalkstein, Y. L. (2012). Review, revise, and resubmit: The effects of self-critique, peer review, and instructor feedback on student writing. *Teaching of Psychology*, 39(4), 235–244.

Stephens, N. M., Fryberg, S. A., Markus, H. R., Johnson, C. S., & Covarrubias, R. (2012). Unseen disadvantage: How American universities' focus on independence undermines the academic performance of first-generation college students. *Journal of Personality and Social Psychology*, 102(6), 1178–1197.

Stephens, N. M., Hamedani, M. G., & Destin, M. (2014). Closing the social-class achievement gap: A difference-education intervention improves first-generation students' academic performance and all students' college transition. *Psychological Science*, 25(4), 943–953.

Stephens, N. M., Townsend, S. S., Hamedani, M. G., Destin, M., & Manzo, V. (2015). A difference-education intervention equips first-generation college students to thrive in the face of stressful college situations. *Psychological Science*, 26(10), 1556–1566.

Stetsenko, A. (2017). *The transformative mind: Expanding Vygotsky's approach to development and education*. New York, NY: Cambridge University Press.

Stewart, T. L., Myers, A. C., & Culley, M. R. (2010). Enhanced learning and retention through "writing to learn" in the psychology classroom. *Teaching of Psychology*, 37(1), 46–49.

Stocking, V. B., & Cutforth, N. (2006). Managing the challenges of teaching community-based research courses: Insights from two instructors. *Michigan Journal of Community Service Learning*, 13(1), 56–65.

Stoecker, R., Tryon, E. A., & Hilgendorf, A. (2009). *The unheard voices: Community organizations and service learning*. Philadelphia, PA: Temple University Press.

Stowell, J. R., Addison, W. E., & Smith, J. L. (2012). Comparison of online and classroom-based student evaluations of instruction. *Assessment and Evaluation in Higher Education*, 37(4), 465–473.

Stowell, J. R., & Nelson, J. M. (2007). Benefits of electronic audience response systems on student participation, learning, and emotion. *Teaching of Psychology*, 34(4), 253–258.

Strand, K. (2000). Community-based research as pedagogy. *Michigan Journal of Community Service Learning*, 7(1), 85–96.

Strasser, N. (2014). Using Prezi in higher education. *Journal of College Teaching and Learning (TLC)*, 11(2), 95–98.

Strijbos, J.-W., Narciss, S., & Dünnebier, K. (2010). Peer feedback content and sender's competence level in academic writing revision tasks: Are they critical for feedback perceptions and efficiency? *Learning and Instruction*, 20(4), 291–303.

Strobel, J., & van Barneveld, A. (2009). When is PBL more effective? A meta-synthesis of meta-analyses comparing PBL to conventional classrooms. *Interdisciplinary Journal of Problem-based Learning*, 3(1), 44–58.

Stroebe, W. (2016). Why good teaching evaluations may reward bad teaching: On grade inflation and other unintended consequences of student evaluations. *Perspectives on Psychological Science*, 11(6), 800–816.

Stroessner, S. J., Beckerman, L. S., & Whittaker, A. (2009). All the world's a stage? Consequences of a role-playing pedagogy on psychological factors and writing and rhetorical skill in college undergraduates. *Journal of Educational Psychology*, 101(3), 605–620.

Strohmetz, D. B. (1992). The use of role-play in teaching research ethics: A validation study. *Teaching of Psychology*, 19(2), 106–108.

Stuart, R. B. (2004). Twelve practical suggestions for achieving multicultural competence. *Professional Psychology: Research and Practice*, 35(1), 3–9.

Suárez-Orozco, C., Casanova, S., Martin, M., Katsiaficas, D., Cuellar, V., Smith, N. A., & Dias, S. I. (2015). Toxic rain in class: Classroom interpersonal microaggressions. *Educational Researcher*, 44(3), 151–160.

Suárez-Orozco, C., Katsiaficas, D., Birchall, O., Alcantar, C. M., Hernandez, E., Garcia, Y., … Teranishi, R. T. (2015). Undocumented undergraduates on college campuses: Understanding their challenges and assets and what it takes to make an undocufriendly campus. *Harvard Educational Review*, 85(3), 427–463.

Sue, D. W. (2010). *Microaggressions in everyday life: Race, gender, and sexual orientation.* Hoboken, NJ: John Wiley and Sons.

Sue, D. W., Capodilupo, C. M., Torino, G. C., Bucceri, J. M., Holder, A., Nadal, K. L., & Esquilin, M. (2007). Racial microaggressions in everyday life: Implications for clinical practice. *American Psychologist*, 62(4), 271–286.

Sue, D. W., Lin, A. I., Torino, G. C., Capodilupo, C. M., & Rivera, D. P. (2009). Racial microaggressions and difficult dialogues on race in the classroom. *Cultural Diversity and Ethnic Minority Psychology*, 15(2), 183–190.

Sue, D. W., & Sue, D. (2016). *Counseling the culturally diverse: Theory and practice* (7th ed.). Hoboken, NJ: John Wiley and Sons.

Sun, Y. C. (2010). Extensive writing in foreign-language classrooms: A blogging approach. *Innovations in Education and Teaching International*, 47(3), 327–339.

Susser, J. A., & McCabe, J. (2013). From the lab to the dorm room: Metacognitive awareness and use of spaced study. *Instructional Science*, 41(2), 345–363.

Sweet, M., & Michaelsen, L. K. (2007). How group dynamics research can inform the theory and practice of postsecondary small group learning. *Educational Psychology Review*, 19(1), 31–47.

Sweet, M., & Michaelsen, L. K. (2012). Creating cognitive apprenticeships with team-based learning. In M. Sweet, & L. K. Michaelsen (Eds.), *Team-based learning in the social sciences and humanities: Group work that works to generate critical thinking and engagement* (pp. 5–32). Sterling, VA: Stylus Publishing.

Sweller, J. (1988). Cognitive load during problem solving: Effects on learning. *Cognitive Science*, 12(2), 257–285.

Sweller, J. (1994). Cognitive load theory, learning difficulty, and instructional design. *Learning and Instruction*, 4(4), 295–312.

Szpunar, K., Moulton, S., & Schacter, D. (2013). Mind wandering and education: From the classroom to online learning. *Frontiers in Psychology*, 4(495).

Talley, C. P., & Scherer, S. (2013). The enhanced flipped classroom: Increasing academic performance with student-recorded lectures and practice testing in a "flipped" STEM course. *Journal of Negro Education*, 82(3), 339–347.

Tanner, K. D. (2013). Structure matters: Twenty-one teaching strategies to promote student engagement and cultivate classroom equity. *CBE-Life Sciences Education*, 12(3), 322–331.

Taraban, R., Maki, W. S., & Rynearson, K. (1999). Measuring study time distributions: Implications for designing computer-based courses. *Behavior Research Methods, Instruments, and Computers*, 31(2), 263–269.

Taradi, S. K., Taradi, M., Radić, K., & Pokrajac, N. (2005). Blending problem-based learning with Web technology positively impacts student learning outcomes in acid-base physiology. *Advances in Physiology Education*, 29(1), 35–39.

Tarrant, M., Knierim, A., Hayes, S. K., & Ware, J. (2006). The frequency of item writing flaws in multiple-choice questions used in high stakes nursing assessments. *Nurse Education in Practice*, 6(6), 354–363.

Tarrant, M., & Ware, J. (2008). Impact of item-writing flaws in multiple-choice questions on student achievement in high-stakes nursing assessments. *Medical Education*, 42(2), 198–206.

Tatum, B. D. (1992). Talking about race, learning about racism: The application of racial identity development theory in the classroom. *Harvard Educational Review*, 62(1), 1–25.

Taylor, S. (2011). Documentary films for teaching psychology. Retrieved from the Society for the Teaching of Psychology website: https://teachpsych.org/resources/Documents/otrp/resources/taylor11.pdf.

Tejeda, M. J. (2008). A resource review for diversity film media. *Academy of Management Learning and Education*, 7(3), 434–440.

Terenzini, P. T., Springer, L., Yaeger, P. M., Pascarella, E. T., & Nora, A. (1996). First-generation college students: Characteristics, experiences, and cognitive development. *Research in Higher Education*, 37(1), 1–22.

Thaxton, L., Faccioli, M. B., & Mosby, A. P. (2004). Leveraging collaboration for information literacy in psychology. *Reference Services Review*, 32(2), 185–189.

Theophilides, C., & Koutselini, M. (2000). Study behavior in the closed-book and the open-book examination: A comparative analysis. *Educational Research and Evaluation*, 6(4), 379–393.

Thiry, H., & Laursen, S. L. (2011). The role of student-advisor interactions in apprenticing undergraduate researchers into a scientific community of practice. *Journal of Science Education and Technology*, 20(6), 771–784.

Thiry, H., Weston, T. J., Laursen, S. L., & Hunter, A.-B. (2012). The benefits of multi-year research experiences: Differences in novice and experienced students' reported gains from undergraduate research. *CBE-Life Sciences Education*, 11(3), 260–272.

Thomas, S. B., & Quinn, S. C. (1991). The Tuskegee syphilis study, 1932 to 1972: Implications for HIV education and AIDS risk education programs in the black community. *American Journal of Public Health*, 81(11), 1498–1505.

Thompson, B. M., Schneider, V. F., Haidet, P., Levine, R. E., McMahon, K. K., Perkowski, L. C., & Richards, B. F. (2007). Team-based learning at ten medical schools: Two years later. *Medical Education*, 41(3), 250–257.

Thompson, W. B., & Fisher-Thompson, D. (2013). Analyzing data from studies depicted on video: An activity for statistics and research courses. *Teaching of Psychology*, 40(2), 139–142.

Tibbetts, Y., Harackiewicz, J. M., Canning, E. A., Boston, J. S., Priniski, S. J., & Hyde, J. S. (2016). Affirming independence: Exploring mechanisms underlying a values affirmation intervention for first-generation students. *Journal of Personality and Social Psychology*, 110(5), 635–659.

Timmerman, T. A. (2000). Survey design and multiple regression: Frequently encountered, but infrequently covered. *Teaching of Psychology*, 27(3), 201–203.

Tinto, V. (2000). Learning better together: The impact of learning communities on student success in higher education. *Journal of Institutional Research*, 9, 48–53.

Tomcho, T. J., & Foels, R. (2012). Meta-analysis of group learning activities: Empirically based teaching recommendations. *Teaching of Psychology*, 39(3), 159–169.

Topping, K. (1998). Peer assessment between students in colleges and universities. *Review of Educational Research*, 68(3), 249–276.

Tran, R., Rohrer, D., & Pashler, H. (2014). Retrieval practice: The lack of transfer to deductive inferences. *Psychonomic Bulletin and Review*, 22(1), 135–140.

Traphagan, T., Traphagan, J., Neavel Dickens, L., & Resta, P. (2014). Changes in college students' perceptions of use of web-based resources for academic tasks with Wikipedia projects: A preliminary exploration. *Interactive Learning Environments*, 22(3), 253–270.

Trueman, M., & Hartley, J. (1996). A comparison between the time-management skills and academic performance of mature and traditional-entry university students. *Higher Education*, 32(2), 199–215.

Tsui, L. (2002). Fostering critical thinking through effective pedagogy: Evidence from four institutional case studies. *Journal of Higher Education*, 73(6), 740–763.

Tuckman, B. W., & Jensen, M. A. C. (1977). Stages of small-group development revisited. *Group and Organization Management*, 2(4), 419–427.

Tufte, E. R. (2006). *The cognitive style of PowerPoint* (2nd ed.). Cheshire, CT: Graphics Press.

Twigg, C. A. (2003). Improving quality and reducing cost: Designs for effective learning. *Change: The Magazine of Higher Learning*, 35(4), 22–29.

Tyler-Smith, K. (2006). Early attrition among first time eLearners: A review of factors that contribute to drop-out, withdrawal and non-completion rates of adult learners undertaking eLearning programmes. *Journal of Online Learning and Teaching*, 2(2), 73–85.

U.S. Census. (2014). Young adults: Then and now. Retrieved from http://census. socialexplorer.com/young-adults/#/report/full/nation/US.

U.S. Department of Health & Human Services, Office for Human Research Protections (OHRP). (n.d.). Code of federal regulations. Title 45. Public welfare. Department of Health and Human Services. Part 46. Protection of human subjects. §46.101 To what does this policy apply? Retrieved from https://www.hhs.gov/ohrp/regulations-and-policy/regulations/45-cfr-46/index.html#46.101.

Umbach, P. D., & Wawrzynski, M. R. (2005). Faculty do matter: The role of college faculty in student learning and engagement. *Research in Higher Education*, 46(2), 153–184.

University of Minnesota Center for Educational Innovation. (n.d.). Writing your teaching philosophy. Retrieved from http://www.umn.edu/ohr/teachlearn/tutorials/philosophy.

Uttl, B., White, C. A., & Gonzalez, D. W. (2017). Meta-analysis of faculty's teaching effectiveness: Student evaluation of teaching ratings and student learning are not related. *Studies in Educational Evaluation*, 54, 22–42.

Valentine, J. C., DuBois, D. L., & Cooper, H. (2004). The relation between self-beliefs and academic achievement: A meta-analytic review. *Educational Psychologist*, 39(2), 111–133.

Van Merrienboer, J. J., & Sweller, J. (2005). Cognitive load theory and complex learning: Recent developments and future directions. *Educational Psychology Review*, 17(2), 147–177.

Vanags, T., George, A. M., Grace, D. M., & Brown, P. M. (2012). Bingo! An engaging activity for learning physiological terms in psychology. *Teaching of Psychology*, 39(1), 29–33.

VanderStoep, S. W., Fagerlin, A., & Feenstra, J. S. (2000). What do students remember from introductory psychology? *Teaching of Psychology*, 27(2), 89–92.

Vaughan, E. D. (1977). Misconceptions about psychology among introductory psychology students. *Teaching of Psychology*, 4(3), 138–141.

Vernon, J. (2008). Involuntary free riding—How status affects performance in a group project. In M. v. D. Heuvel-Panhuizen, & O. Köller (Eds.), *Challenging assessment—Book of abstracts of the 4th Biennial EARLI/Northumbria Assessment Conference 2008*. Berlin, Germany: Breitfeld Vervielfältigungsservice.

Vess, D. L. (2005). Asynchronous discussion and communication patterns in online and hybrid history courses. *Communication Education*, 54(4), 355–364.

Vianna, E., Hougaard, N., & Stetsenko, A. (2014). The dialectics of collective and individual transformation: Transformative activist research in a collaborative learning community project. In A. Blunden (Ed.), *Collaborative projects: An interdisciplinary study* (pp. 59–88). Leiden, The Netherlands: Brill.

Vianna, E., & Stetsenko, A. (2017). Expanding student agency in the introductory psychology course: Transformative activist stance and critical-theoretical pedagogy. In R. Obeid, A. M. Schwartz, C. Shane-Simpson, & P. J. Brooks (Eds.), *How we teach now: The GSTA guide to student-centered teaching* (pp. 252–266). Retrieved from the Society for the Teaching of Psychology website: http://teachpsych.org/ebooks/howweteachnow.

Vipond, D. (1993). Social motives for writing psychology: Writing for and with younger readers. *Teaching of Psychology*, 20(2), 89–93.

Virtanen, P., Myllärniemi, J., & Wallander, H. (2012). Diversifying higher education: Innovative tools to facilitate different ways of learning. In Proceedings of the 12th International Conference on Information Communication Technologies in Education (pp. 105–116), Rhodes, Greece. Retrieved from http://www.icicte.org/Proceedings2012/Papers/03-2-Virtanen.pdf.

von der Embse, N. P., & Hasson, R. (2012). Test anxiety and high-stakes test performance between school settings: Implications for educators. *Preventing School Failure: Alternative Education for Children and Youth*, 56(3), 180–187.

von der Embse, N. P., & Witmer, S. E. (2014). High-stakes accountability: Student anxiety and large-scale testing. *Journal of Applied School Psychology*, 30(2), 132–156.

Vygotsky, L. S. (1978). In M. Cole, V. John-Steiner, S. Scribner, & E. Souberman (Eds.), *Mind in society*. Cambridge, MA: Harvard University Press.

Wade, D. T. (2009). Goal setting in rehabilitation: An overview of what, why and how. *Clinical Rehabilitation*, 23(4), 291–295.

Wagner, M., Newman, L., Cameto, R., Garza, N., & Levine, P. (2005). After high school: A first look at the postschool experiences of youth with disabilities. A report from the National Longitudinal Transition Study-2 (NLTS2) Retrieved from http://files.eric.ed.gov/fulltext/ED494935.pdf.

Wallace, M. L., Walker, J. D., Braseby, A. M., & Sweet, M. S. (2014). "Now, what happens during class?" Using team-based learning to optimize the role of expertise within the flipped classroom. *Journal on Excellence in College Teaching*, 25, 253–273.

Waller, J. E. (1994). Philosophies of psychology: A discovery process for undergraduates. *Teaching of Psychology*, 21(1), 33–35.

Walton, G. M., & Cohen, G. L. (2011). A brief social-belonging intervention improves academic and health outcomes of minority students. *Science*, 331(6023), 1447–1451.

Walton, G. M., Logel, C., Peach, J. M., Spencer, S. J., & Zanna, M. P. (2015). Two brief interventions to mitigate a "chilly climate" transform women's experience, relationships, and achievement in engineering. *Journal of Educational Psychology*, 107(2), 468–485.

Wang, S.-K., & Hsu, H. (2008). Reflections on using blogs to expand in-class. *TechTrends*, 52(3), 81–85.

Wang, X., Yang, D., Wen, M., Koedinger, K., & Rosé, C. P. (2015). Investigating how student's cognitive behavior in MOOC discussion forums affect learning gains. In Proceedings of 8th International Educational Data Mining Society, Madrid, Spain.

Wang, Y.-m., & Chen, V. D.-T. (2008). Essential elements in designing online discussions to promote cognitive presence—A practical experience. *Journal of Asynchronous Learning Networks*, 12, 157–177.

Warner, C. B., & Meehan, A. M. (2001). Microsoft Excel™ as a tool for teaching basic statistics. *Teaching of Psychology*, 28(4), 295–298.

Watson, W. E., Kumar, K., & Michaelsen, L. K. (1993). Cultural diversity's impact on interaction process and performance: Comparing homogeneous and diverse task groups. *Academy of Management Journal*, 36(3), 590–602.

Weaver, M. (2006). Do students value feedback? Student perceptions of tutors' written responses. *Assessment & Evaluation in Higher Education*, 31(3), 379–394.

Webb, E., Jones, A., Barker, P., & van Schaik, P. (2004). Using e-learning dialogues in higher education. *Innovations in Education and Teaching International*, 41(1), 93–103.

Weber, L. J., McBee, J. K., & Krebs, J. E. (1983). Take home tests: An experimental study. *Research in Higher Education*, 18(4), 473–483.

Weimer, M. (2003). Focus on learning, transform teaching. *Change*, 35(5), 48–54.

Weiner, B. (1985). An attributional theory of achievement motivation and emotion. *Psychological Review*, 92(4), 548–573.

Weiss, R., & Seplowitz, P. (2017). Student-directed research collaborations between higher education and K–12 classrooms. In R. Obeid, A. M. Schwartz, C. Shane-Simpson, & P. J. Brooks (Eds.), *How we teach now: The GSTA guide to student-centered teaching* (pp. 380–391). Retrieved from the Society for the Teaching of Psychology website: http://teachpsych.org/ebooks/howweteachnow.

Weisskirch, R. S. (2009). Playing bingo to review fundamental concepts in advanced courses. *International Journal for the Scholarship of Teaching and Learning*, 3(1), 14.

Weller, S., Domarkaite, G. K., Lam, J. L. C., & Metta, L. U. (2013). Student-faculty co-inquiry into student reading: Recognising SoTL as pedagogic practice. *International Journal for the Scholarship of Teaching and Learning*, 7(2), 1–16.

Wells, J. (2016). Why we resist "leading the horse": Required tutoring, RAD research, and our writing center ideals. *Writing Center Journal*, 35(2), 87–114.

Werder, C., & Otis, M. M. (2010). *Engaging student voices in the study of teaching and learning*. Sterling, VA: Stylus.

Werder, C., Thibou, S., & Kaufer, B. (2012). Students as co-inquirers: A requisite threshold concept in educational development? *Journal of Faculty Development*, 26(3), 34–38.

Wesp, R., & Montgomery, K. (1998). Developing critical thinking through the study of paranormal phenomena. *Teaching of Psychology*, 25(4), 275–278.

Wheeler, S., Yeomans, P., & Wheeler, D. (2008). The good, the bad and the wiki: Evaluating student-generated content for collaborative learning. *British Journal of Educational Technology*, 39(6), 987–995.

Whetten, D. A. (2007). Principles of effective course design: What I wish I had known about learning-centered teaching 30 years ago. *Journal of Management Education*, 31(3), 339–357.

White House Council of Economic Advisors. (2014). 15 economic facts about millenials. Retrieved from https://www.whitehouse.gov/sites/default/files/docs/millennials_report.pdf.

White, T. L., & Kirby, B. J. (2005). Tis better to give than to receive: An undergraduate peer review project. *Teaching of Psychology*, 32(5), 259–261.

Wichowski, D. E., & Kohl, L. E. (2012). Establishing credibility in the information jungle: Blogs, microblogs, and the CRAAP test. In M. Folk, & S. Apostel (Eds.), *Online credibility and digital ethos: Evaluating computer-mediated communication* (pp. 229–251). Hershey, PA: IGI Global.

Wichowski, D. E., & Kohl, L. E. (2013). Establishing credibility in the information jungle: Blogs, microblogs, and the CRAAP test. In M. Folk, & S. Apostel (Eds.), *Online credibility and digital ethos: Evaluating computer-mediated communication* (pp. 229–251). Hershey, PA: IGI Global.

Wieman, C. E. (2007). APS News—The back page. The "curse of knowledge" or why intuition about teaching often fails. *American Physical Society News*, 16(10).

Wieman, C. E. (2014). Large-scale comparison of science teaching methods sends clear message. *Proceedings of the National Academy of Sciences*, 111(23), 8319–8320.

Wieman, C. E., Perkins, K., Gilbert, S., Benay, F., Kennedy, S., Semsar, K., Knight, J., … Simon, B. (2009). Clicker resource guide: An instructor's guide to the effective use of personal response systems (clickers) in teaching. Vancouver, BC: University of British Columbia. Retrieved from http://www.cwsei.ubc.ca/resources/files/Clicker_guide_CWSEI_CU-SEI.pdf.

Wiggins, G. (2011). A true test: Toward more authentic and equitable assessment. *Phi Delta Kappan*, 92(7), 81–93.

Wiggins, G., & McTighe, J. (2005). *Understanding by design* (2nd ed.). Alexandria, VA: ASCD.

Williams, J. B., & Wong, A. (2009). The efficacy of final examinations: A comparative study of closed-book, invigilated exams and open-book, open-web exams. *British Journal of Educational Technology*, 40(2), 227–236.

Williams, J. D., & Takaku, S. (2011). Help seeking, self-efficacy, and writing performance among college students. *Journal of Writing Research*, 3(1), 1–18.

Williams, R. L., Oliver, R., Allin, J. L., Winn, B., & Booher, C. S. (2003). Psychological critical thinking as a course predictor and outcome variable. *Teaching of Psychology*, 30(3), 220–223.

Willingham, D. B. (1990). Effective feedback on written assignments. *Teaching of Psychology*, 17(1), 10–13.

Willingham, D. T. (2009). *Why don't students like school? A cognitive scientist answers questions about how the mind works and what it means for your classroom*. San Francisco, CA: Jossey-Bass.

Willingham, D. T., Hughes, E. M., & Dobolyi, D. G. (2015). The scientific status of learning styles theories. *Teaching of Psychology*, 42(3), 266–271.

Willis, A. S. (2002). Problem-based learning in a general psychology course. *Journal of General Education*, 51(4), 282–292.

Wilson, J. H. (2017). Teaching challenging courses: Focus on research methods and statistics. In R. Obeid, A. M. Schwartz, C. Shane-Simpson, & P. J. Brooks (Eds.), *How we teach now: The GSTA guide to student-centered teaching* (pp. 339–350). Retrieved from the Society for the Teaching of Psychology website: http://teachpsych.org/ebooks/howweteachnow.

Wilson, J. H., & Ryan, R. G. (2013). Professor–student rapport scale: Six items predict student outcomes. *Teaching of Psychology*, 40(2), 130–133.

Wilson, S. G. (2013). The flipped class: A method to address the challenges of an undergraduate statistics course. *Teaching of Psychology*, 40(3), 193–199.

Wilson, T. D., & Linville, P. W. (1982). Improving the academic performance of college freshmen: Attribution therapy revisited. *Journal of Personality and Social Psychology*, 42(2), 367–376.

Wilson, T. D., & Linville, P. W. (1985). Improving the performance of college freshmen with attributional techniques. *Journal of Personality and Social Psychology*, 49(1), 287–293.

Wilson-Doenges, G., & Gurung, R. A. R. (2013). Benchmarks for scholarly investigations of teaching and learning. *Australian Journal of Psychology*, 65(1), 63–70.

Wineburg, S., McGrew, S., Breakstone, J., & Ortega, T. (2016). Evaluating information: The cornerstone of civic online reasoning. Stanford Digital Repository. Retrieved from https://stacks.stanford.edu/file/druid:fv751yt5934/SHEG%20Evaluating%20Information%20Online.pdf.

Wise, A. F., Saghafian, M., & Padmanabhan, P. (2012). Towards more precise design guidance: Specifying and testing the functions of assigned student roles in online discussions. *Educational Technology Research and Development*, 60(1), 55–82.

Wissman, K. T., Rawson, K. A., & Pyc, M. A. (2012). How and when do students use flashcards? *Memory*, 20(6), 568–579.

Wolfe, M. B. (2005). Memory for narrative and expository text: Independent influences of semantic associations and text organization. *Journal of Experimental Psychology: Learning, Memory, and Cognition*, 31(2), 359–364.

Wong, S. H. R., & Cmor, D. (2011). Measuring association between library instruction and graduation GPA. *College and Research Libraries*, 72(5), 464–473.

Wong, T. H., Ip, E. J., Lopes, I., & Rajagopalan, V. (2014). Pharmacy students' performance and perceptions in a flipped teaching pilot on cardiac arrhythmias. *American Journal of Pharmaceutical Education*, 78(10), 185.

Woods, R., Baker, J. D., & Hopper, D. (2004). Hybrid structures: Faculty use and perception of web-based courseware as a supplement to face-to-face instruction. *The Internet and Higher Education*, 7(4), 281–297.

Wooldridge, C. L., Bugg, J. M., McDaniel, M. A., & Liu, Y. (2014). The testing effect with authentic educational materials: A cautionary note. *Journal of Applied Research in Memory and Cognition*, 3(3), 214–221.

Worrall, L. (2007). Asking the community: A case study of community partner perspectives. *Michigan Journal of Community Service Learning*, 14(1), 5–17.

Worthington, D. L., & Levasseur, D. G. (2015). To provide or not to provide course PowerPoint slides? The impact of instructor-provided slides upon student attendance and performance. *Computers and Education*, 85, 14–22.

Yandell, L. R., & Giordano, P. J. (2008). Exploring the use of problem-based learning in psychology courses. In S. Meyers, & J. Stowell (Eds.), *Essays from e-xcellence in teaching* (Vol. 8) (pp. 8–12). Retrieved from the Society for the Teaching of Psychology website: http://teachpsych.org/resources/e-books/eit2008/eit2008.php.

Yang, C., & Chang, Y. S. (2012). Assessing the effects of interactive blogging on student attitudes towards peer interaction, learning motivation, and academic achievements. *Journal of Computer Assisted Learning*, 28(2), 126–135.

Yang, Y., & Cornelious, L. F. (2005). Preparing instructors for quality online instruction. *Online Journal of Distance Learning Administration*, 8(1), 1–16.

Yeager, D. S., & Dweck, C. S. (2012). Mindsets that promote resilience: When students believe that personal characteristics can be developed. *Educational Psychologist*, 47(4), 302–314.

Yeager, D. S., & Walton, G. M. (2011). Social-psychological interventions in education: They're not magic. *Review of Educational Research*, 81(2), 267–301.

Yeager, D. S., Walton, G. M., Brady, S. T., Akcinar, E. N., Paunesku, D., Keane, L., ... Urstein, R. (2016). Teaching a lay theory before college narrows achievement gaps at scale. *Proceedings of the National Academy of Sciences*, 113(24), E3341–E3348.

Yorio, P. L., & Ye, F. (2012). A meta-analysis on the effects of service-learning on the social, personal, and cognitive outcomes of learning. *Academy of Management Learning and Education*, 11(1), 9–27.

Young, A., & Fry, J. (2012). Metacognitive awareness and academic achievement in college students. *Journal of the Scholarship of Teaching and Learning*, 8(2), 1–10.

Yue, C. L., Storm, B. C., Kornell, N., & Bjork, E. L. (2015). Highlighting and its relation to distributed study and students' metacognitive beliefs. *Educational psychology review*, 27(1), 69–78.

Yuksel, P. (2017). Ten TED talk thinking tasks: Engaging college students in structured self-reflection to foster critical thinking. In R. Obeid, A. M. Schwartz, C. Shane-Simpson, & P. J. Brooks (Eds.), *How we teach now: The GSTA guide to student-centered teaching* (pp. 224–237). Retrieved from the Society for the Teaching of Psychology website: http://teachpsych.org/ebooks/howweteachnow.

Zacchilli, T. (2014). Using video creation to engage students in research methods and statistics. *Journal of Scientific Psychology*. Retrieved from http://www.psyencelab.com/uploads/5/4/6/5/54658091/videocreationinresearch.pdf.

Zappe, S., Leicht, R., Messner, J., Litzinger, T., & Lee, H. W. (2009). "Flipping" the classroom to explore active learning in a large undergraduate course. Paper presented at the American Society for Engineering Education, Austin, TX. Retrieved from https://peer.asee.org/flipping-the-classroom-to-explore-active-learning-in-a-large-undergraduate-course.

Zaromb, F. M., & Roediger, H. L. III (2010). The testing effect in free recall is associated with enhanced organizational processes. *Memory and Cognition*, 38(8), 995–1008.

Zawacki, T. M., & Rogers, P. M. (Eds.) (2012). *Writing across the curriculum: A critical sourcebook*. Boston, MA: Bedford/St. Martin's.

Zehr, D. (1998). Writing in psychology courses. *Writing Across the Curriculum*, 9, 7–13.

Zehr, D. (2004). Two active learning exercises for a history of psychology class. *Teaching of Psychology*, 31(1), 54–56.

Zeidner, M. (1991). Statistics and mathematics anxiety in social science students: Some interesting parallels. *British Journal of Educational Psychology*, 61(3), 319–328.

Zell, E., & Krizan, Z. (2014). Do people have insight into their abilities? A metasynthesis. *Perspectives on Psychological Science*, 9(2), 111–125.

Zhang, D., Zhou, L., Briggs, R. O., & Nunamaker, J. F. (2006). Instructional video in e-learning: Assessing the impact of interactive video on learning effectiveness. *Information and Management*, 43(1), 15–27.

Zhao, N., Wardeska, J. G., McGuire, S. Y., & Cook, E. (2014). Metacognition: An effective tool to promote success in college science learning. *Journal of College Science Teaching*, 43(4), 48–54.

Zhu, E. (2007). Teaching with clickers. *CRLT Occasional Paper*, 22, 1–8. Retrieved from http://crlt.umich.edu/sites/default/files/resource_files/CRLT_no22.pdf.

Zimmerman, B. J., & Kitsantas, A. (2002). Acquiring writing revision and self-regulatory skill through observation and emulation. *Journal of Educational Psychology*, 94(4), 660–668.

Zinn, T. E., & Saville, B. K. (2008). Leading discussions and asking questions. In W. Buskist, & S. F. Davis (Eds.), *Handbook of the teaching of psychology* (pp. 85–89). Malden, MA: Blackwell.

Zipp, J. F. (2007). Learning by exams: The impact of two-stage cooperative tests. *Teaching Sociology*, 35(1), 62–76.

Zuckweiler, K. M., Schniederjans, M. J., & Ball, D. A. (2004). Methodologies to determine class sizes for fair faculty work load in web courses. *International Journal of Distance Education Technologies (IJDET)*, 2(2), 46–59.

Index

Teaching Psychology: An Evidence-Based Approach, First Edition. Jillian Grose-Fifer, Patricia J. Brooks, and Maureen O'Connor.
© 2019 John Wiley & Sons, Inc. Published 2019 by John Wiley & Sons, Inc.
Companion website: www.wiley.com/go/Grose-Fifer/teaching-psychology